Tight Knit

# Tight Knit

## Global Families and the
## Social Life of Fast Fashion

ELIZABETH L. KRAUSE

The University of Chicago Press
Chicago and London

The University of Chicago Press, Chicago 60637
The University of Chicago Press, Ltd., London
© 2018 by The University of Chicago

Published 2018
Printed in the United States of America

27  26  25  24  23  22  21  20  19  18          1  2  3  4  5

ISBN-13: 978-0-226-55791-5 (cloth)
ISBN-13: 978-0-226-55807-3 (paper)
ISBN-13: 978-0-226-55810-3 (e-book)
DOI: https://doi.org/10.7208/chicago/9780226558103.001.0001

Library of Congress Cataloging-in-Publication Data

Names: Krause, Elizabeth L., author. | Bressan, Massimo.
Title: Tight knit : global families and the social life of fast fashion / Elizabeth L.
    Krause.
Description: Chicago ; London : The University of Chicago Press, 2018. | Includes
    bibliographical references and index.
Identifiers: LCCN 2017051765 | ISBN 9780226557915 (cloth : alk. paper) |
    ISBN 9780226558073 (pbk : alk. paper) | ISBN 9780226558103 (e-book)
Subjects: LCSH: Foreign workers, Chinese—Italy—Prato—Social conditions. |
    Clothing workers—Italy—Prato—Social conditions. | Immigrant families—
    Italy—Prato—Social conditions. | Immigrants—Italy—Social conditions. |
    Clothing trade—Social aspects—Italy. | Globalization—Social aspects—Italy. |
    Italy—Emigration and immigration—Social aspects. | Italy—Emigration and
    immigration—Economic aspects. | Prato (Italy)—Ethnic relations.
Classification: LCC HD8488.C5 K73 2018 | DDC 331.6/2510945519—dc23
LC record available at https://lccn.loc.gov/2017051765

*In loving memory of Opal Schweiss (1902–1997)*

# Contents

# Introduction

## Tight Knit

Antonio offered to take me on a car tour of Macrolotto to show me what the crisis looked like up close. He knew Prato's industrial district well. He used to come to these parts regularly to secure subcontracting orders, pick up yarn, take it back to his workshop, knit the yarn into sweater lengths on computerized looms, then deliver the pieces back to the factory owner. On the day of the tour, in February 2011, Antonio and I drove along the wide boulevards lined with flat-roofed, big-box structures. Chinese ideograms popped up between Italian or English names: Cherry Fashion, Christina Moda, OnlyGo Pronto Moda. Gigantic red ribbons draped across iron gates in preparation for Chinese New Year. We stopped so I could take a photo of a group of young people decorating the premises. Some buildings housed garment workers, making the trendy, readymade women's fashions, whereas others served as warehouses. Still others displayed racks of clothes for buyers to purchase in bulk. Clients included European retailers specializing in "bargain chic."[1] Meanwhile, Antonio told me, police raids targeting immigrants had become frequent. Sometimes, helicopters swarmed overhead in search of clandestine workers. My guide wondered aloud what Macrolotto would be now if the Chinese weren't there. He imagined vacant buildings—an entire industrial zone turned ghost town.

I could not get over how dramatically things had changed since I had lived in Prato in 1995–97, when every household seemed to be engaged in a phase of sweater production. Workshops extended from the city center along tributaries of the Bisenzio River, across the expansive industrialized plain that defines Prato, and into the craggy, fog-covered Tuscan hills where computerized looms might be tucked away in former sharecroppers' stone barns. I spent six months in a small sweater factory and then in a family finishing firm

FIGURE 0.1. Chinese immigrants operate cut-and-sew machines in Prato, Italy, and its surrounding municipalities to churn out fast fashion for a global market.
Photo by Agnese Morganti, 2013

in a neighborhood built during the boom years as a way to immerse myself in the cultural-historical dynamics between making a life and making a living. I was stationed at the third machine in a production line in a room the size of a home office, and my job was to attach buttons to sweaters. Each piece passed through the hands of the household head, a retired railroad worker who drove a machine with a foot pedal to mark chalk dots for buttons and buttonholes, and then the matriarch–turned–politician–cum–park curator who forged buttonholes with a growling motorized machine. We broke for lunch each day, and it was there, facing a portrait of her mother weaving straw, that I received my daily history lesson. The two years culminated in a dissertation and a book about Italian experiences of what were then the world's lowest national fertility rates (Krause 2005a). Experts sounded alarms about an aging population, gender relations, and family norms. The research exposed a rising tide of demographic nationalism.

Those days, Chinese immigrants were rare. When I returned in 2004 for a semester, pretty much everybody I knew had gotten out of the sweater business. The work culture had changed. Each time I came and went, another friend or acquaintance had sold their machines and repurposed their workshop. I was moved by the dull heartbreak and deep uncertainties that afflicted so many people as the industry as they knew it fell to pieces and another niche industry flourished, albeit with a very different workforce from distant places.

As global supply chains became the new normal, and as well-demarcated fashion seasons changed into fluid and fickle trends, the Made in Italy sector witnessed a surprising turn of events: thousands of Chinese immigrants settled into the industrial zones of Tuscany to make clothes. Warehouses blared *pronto moda*, fashion that is fast and ready.[2] Billboards increasingly displayed messages in Chinese characters. This manufacturing scene countered overseas outsourcing trends. Motivating ambitions and crushing defeats surged through an intensely globalized age. Individuals, families, institutions, and a city have become entangled in the hegemony of global supply chains.

### Fast Fashion, Free Fantasy

My own journey to this book about globalization, fast fashion, and far-flung families in many ways began some decades ago, when my grandmother and I wrote letters to each other. We had each moved from the middle of the country to what might well have been opposite ends of the earth. She had made a home next to her sister in Florida with a sun-bleached yard of grapefruit and orange trees, and I had made a home with my husband and young daughter in Oregon with a mist-saturated yard of pear trees and raspberry bushes. We were far away in distance yet close in sentiment. The letters kept us connected.

I don't know what became of most of those letters, but somehow, they inspired my grandmother to type out twenty-six pages detailing recollections of her childhood. The memoir spans the years 1907–21, ending well before she married my grandfather. As I read her account, what amazed me was that I had very little memory of my grandmother or mother or any of my aunts or uncles talking about the profound stories of her childhood. Her childhood history barely found its way into the stories that our family told about itself. The legacies in her memoir, coincidentally or not, seem to have resurfaced in my research trajectory.

Perhaps everyone has these sorts of stories in their families. Perhaps it is not that unusual for your grandmother to have her father abandon his wife and children, be left behind with a mother and two siblings, and then be sent off to live with kinfolk on a farm and various families in boarding homes before lying about her age to work in a munitions factory. Her moves were so frequent that they are hard to keep track of. The experience speaks against nostalgic ideas of the "traditional" nuclear family as an unchanging, natural, and stable institution.

In my research, I came to understand the quiet revolution from large to small families as a modern journey. I documented through archives and memories the history of straw weavers networked across the Tuscan country-side surrounding Prato in the late nineteenth and early twentieth century who worked long hours for low pay producing straw hats for a nascent global economy. Many of these weavers were certified as lacking milk and received state subsidies to pay wet nurses to care for their infants. Submersed beneath all of that "dry" mercantile activity of straw, I argued, was a wet and hidden traffic in milk. Circulating infants meant that human substances lubricated the economy and kept it "flexible" (Krause 2009). It seemed almost uncanny to me when I learned that many Chinese immigrants living and working in Prato engaged in a similar circulation of children. The world was transform-ing at a fast pace, but global histories repeated themselves and in no small part due to economies that are similar in structure though different in particulars.

Fast fashion is a recent phenomenon. It refers to a business model in which design, production, and sales phases are "so tight" as to overlap, in the words of Italian economists Dei Ottati and Cologna (2015, 41). Fast fashion falls within the category of readymade clothing produced to a standard rather than custom tailored. The difference is that fast fashion has a "just-in-time" rhythm. Retailers respond to what is trending on and off runways. Firms re-quire ultimate flexibility in terms of the flow of clothes from shop floor to store shelf. Consumers can change style on a whim.

Apparel industry analysts trace the intensification of the low end of ready-made wear to the 1960s. A radical transformation was in full swing by the early 1990s. Fashion cycles became faster, consumers expected greater variety, and retailers struggled for competitive advantage. As Jane Collins (2003, 55) notes in *Threads*, "Whereas in the past stores changed their stock twice a year, the number of fashion 'seasons' has now expanded to six to eight, and many fashion-oriented retailers change their lines monthly." Even firms that plan collections a year in advance may arrive at a given season, notice a particular item trending, and decide to launch some "flashes," in other words, some ar-ticles that are produced at the last minute. Contemporary supply chains have thrown temporal distinctions into a precarious state. Despite production chains that have gone global and sourcing that extends across vast distances spanning national borders, designs and inventories change constantly. Fast fashion is thus known for inexpensive fashion-forward clothing.

As a generic term, fast fashion covers various types of products—from the cheapest apparel sold in open markets to actual brands such as H&M or Zara—known for capturing and responding to current fashion trends and providing consumers with immediate gratification (Reinach 2005). For retailers, fast fashion has become the primary production and distribution strategy for getting wearable goods into the hands and onto the bodies of consumers. Inventories tend to be limited to keep stock moving. Notes apparel organizational sociologist Ian Taplin (2014, 248), "Firms such as Inditex (Zara), Topshop, H&M, Uniqlo and Forever 21 built their brands by targeting young people who were fashion conscious but income scarce." Such retailers are known for spotting trends, copying designs, and churning them out to meet demand.

If readymade wear represented the democratization of fashion, fast fashion is the fantasy of democracy and equality. Consider how the global supply chain manifests in the lives of consumers, retailers, producers, and investors. For consumers, fast fashion enables and promotes flexible identities through its economy of constant choice. For retailers, fast fashion offers a winning formula to push costs down and profits up. For producers, fast fashion requires flexible work regimes. For investors, the model promises potent returns.

These are very different links in the chain. They generate very different meanings. The flexible consumer conveys a positive image. Consumers supposedly like change. And they like those changes to be economical. H&M has the recipe—the trendiest of clothes, and as anthropologist and fashion consultant Simona Segre Reinach (2005, 47) notes, the super-retailer is "the fastest of them all." No wonder the quick and handsome soccer player David Beckham became H&M's model of choice for ad campaigns. He is an icon of speed and helps to reinforce the notion that fast fashion is good fashion.

Investors may feel energized by the common sense that fast-fashion firms make for a good investment. A *Forbes* columnist describes Zara as a "fast-fashion stalwart that is giving fits to traditional retailers the world over" and offered this advice to deep-pocket readers: "As an investor, if you're not paying attention to this company, you could be missing out, big time. Thanks to its innovative supply chain structure and merchandising strategy, Zara keeps its markdowns low and profit margins high, and the payoffs could be sizable for the discerning retail investor" (Petro 2015). This kind of logic reveals the hegemony of the global supply chain in action in that profit is taken for granted as the most important measure of value.[3] The case of fast fashion, like most cases of hegemony, involves consent plus the threat of coercion.

Another link in the chain reveals a less shimmery meaning of innovation and flexibility. The model requires that workers work when there is work. They have to be available. They have to work long shifts, up to sixteen or eighteen hours, when there are orders to fill—to keep inventory on hand so the trendy items can fill up and fly off store shelves. They have to work nights and squeeze in sleep during the day. They have to sew in workshops without temperature controls, making for a dank and cold environment in the winter and a blistering hot one in the summer. And they are often pressured to send their babies thousands of miles away to have others care for them. Making apparel has been a labor-intensive industry as long as there have been owners in search of a profit and workers in search of wages. It has long been an "imperfect industry," in the words of fashion scholar Joanne Entwistle (2000, 212), based on exploitation, inequality, struggle, and even tragedy.

But is imperfection the end of the story? Or is the world being remade?

Prato has become a hotbed of transnational entrepreneurial activity. As of the end of 2014, there were a total of 5,230 Chinese-managed active firms, according to Chamber of Commerce Prato data. These firms registered a dynamic 36.5 percent turnover rate. Aspiring Chinese entrepreneurs preferred manufacturing and occupied 55 percent of total firms in that sector. The vast majority, some 3,424 firms managed or owned by residents of Chinese nationality, fell into the category of *confezioni*, literally sewing or garment-production work (Caserta 2016). Fast-fashion firms in Prato tend to be small—that is, fewer than ten employees—and many immigrant workers shift in a couple of years from wage earners to firm owners. Almost 82 percent of all active firms in the garment-making sector in 2012 were Chinese-run enterprises (Caserta and Marsden 2013). As of June 2015, 30 percent of all businesses in Prato were foreign owned. Nearly 50 percent of manufacturing firms had Chinese owners (Caserta 2016). Foreign entrepreneurs constitute an increasingly influential part of the world economy (Kulchina 2016). Chinese firms based in Italy also enter into subcontracting relationships with Italian-owned artisan firms that have contracts directly with luxury brands as exposed in the investigative Italian public television *Report* (Giannini 2014). Gucci is an excellent case, as the company proudly asserts that 100 percent of its goods are produced in Italy, where it claims that worker rights are upheld. Yet Gucci reportedly has subcontracting deals with more than 3,000 suppliers. As the Clean Clothes Campaign (2014a, 51) notes, "It is unclear to us what its policy is for upholding rights in these workplaces." Exploitation appears widespread. Workers live on the edge. The system generates profits for a few, hard work and insecurity for many.

Several profound paradoxes rest behind this dizzying numerical portrait: first, that Chinese leave China, one of the world's greatest garment producers, to make clothes in Italy; second, behind the fast-fashion Made in Italy labeled clothes are primarily small family-run firms mostly owned by Chinese immigrants employing or subcontracting to other Chinese workers; and third, just as one of the world's most famous industrial districts was free falling into severe crisis under the forces of global capitalism, an immigrant niche economy took off like a winged crane.[4] These three factors alone challenge dominant assumptions about globalization. The assumptions point to a tendency toward increasingly large scales of production and increasingly homogenized cultural forms. Enormous factories come to mind such as Foxconn, where workers in white coats meticulously assemble iPhones. Globalization processes—just like fast-fashion clothes flying off factory floors, onto retail shelves, and into consumer closets—create a puzzling and overwhelming array of difference.

These differences suggest the persistence of heterogeneity within global capitalism. They matter, I argue, because even in a fast-fashion production zone, a quintessential symbol and material manifestation of globalization, diverse practices and actions oriented toward creating value reveal a crooked character of global capitalism. I use the term *crooked* as a play on words in several respects. First, it plays on the reputation of illegality that pervades Prato's fast-fashion economy, one that includes stories of enslaved and trafficked immigrant workers and tax-evading immigrant owners. Second, it points to the crooked and uneven forms and degrees of inequality that global capitalism creates and perpetuates, whether comparing workers and entrepreneurs at various levels of the fast-fashion production chain in Prato or public school teachers invested in retirement funds with top-dog hedge fund managers of Wall Street. Third, "crooked" offers an intervention directed against one of globalization's central tenets: that it represents the natural course of the free market, that the pathway to globalization is unilinear, and that the result is progress and human flourishing. Rather, my argument disassembles these assumptions. The phrase *crooked capitalism*, rather than intending dishonest as in a crooked deal, points to a form of capitalism that is not straight, not uniform, or not expected. The bends and curves, kinks and twists, open new ways to grasp how people and society live globalization.

### Putting Made in Italy in Its Place

The Made in Italy mark has continued to carry value even if it has been susceptible to variation in the quality of products. Before the rise of the low-cost fast-fashion niche, local Italian markets had become flooded with low-quality fabrics and goods. Many Italian firms have not been able to cope with globalization. By the 1990s, firms at the low end of the clothing market had "virtually disappeared from the Italian scene" (Dunford et al. 2016, 130). To stay competitive, textile and clothing establishments had to either be large enough to take advantage of trade agreements that eliminated quotas and encouraged global outsourcing in the quest for "efficiency wages" or be lucky enough to have specialized in high-end fashion, the most resilient of the Made in Italy sector.

Even as the label signified quality, it was also vulnerable to the vagaries of market forces. Italians lamented damage done to the label's reputation through low-cost products. This lament echoed through public commentary following a deadly factory fire in a Chinese fast-fashion firm in Prato. A cartoon circulated on the Internet depicting singed shirts and dresses hanging on a clothesline with a Made in Italy tag (Wilkinson 2008). The image played on the idiom of hanging dirty laundry out to dry as it referenced damage to the label's reputation. Meanwhile, television and print media reported on the complex layers of subcontracting and the hidden immigrant labor practices behind even luxury name brands.

The distinctive trajectory of Italian textile and clothing in the end has a great deal to do with the symbolic value of the Made in Italy brand.[5] Italian exports have relatively high unit values, as calculated in euros per kilogram. Consider that a boxful of Gucci women's dresses will have a higher unit value than a boxful of H&M dresses. A scan of Gucci's spring 2017 offerings featured casual dresses priced at $2,800 and above whereas seasonal H&M dresses could be readily purchased for $29.95. If there were forty dresses in a box, the Gucci-to-H&M difference would be $112,000 to $1,198. It is not surprising that wealthy countries are the most common destination of Italian exports. The global financial crisis, however, rocked the resilience of high fashion as the demand for designer clothes and accessories declined—for example, in Japan, the United States, and the United Kingdom (Dunford et al. 2016). The lower one travels on the Italian fashion ladder, the less significant is the value for the industry.

Meanwhile, economists who have long studied Prato's industrial district have characterized the growth in the fast-fashion sector as "extraordinary." They describe an integrated labor system that features strong economic and social links between small firms as well as transnational ties with China. Their explanation of this integrated system points to its heterogeneity: "efficiency is obtained thanks to relations of reciprocity rather than of authority . . . a form of integration which allows for overcoming the limitations of small firms, whose boundaries blur into the dense web of relations that unite them." They describe an environment in which "information, finished and semi-finished products, work and money move with great fluidity among firms and persons," and they offer a remarkable insight: "Consequently, the production scale upon which the efficiency depends became that of the whole system, instead of that of the individual firms. Since this scale is large, the small businesses belonging to that system are able to compete with larger firms" (Dei Ottati and Cotogna 2015, 44).[6] It is precisely that whole system that, as an anthropologist who has worked in Prato for nearly a quarter century, I dare to understand.

## Extending Metaphors, Organizing Ideas

*Tight Knit* investigates the conditions and social life behind the making of fast fashion. The tight approach to the cycle of making clothes has a ripple effect of repercussions. What family arrangements does such an economy require, repel, or generate? How do individuals and families cope with überflexible lives? What cultural logics and values emerge from encounters between fast-fashion workers and state institutions? Finally, what social worlds emerge?

The title *Tight Knit* extends a metaphor in two relevant senses: one social, the other material. First, regarding social relations, tight-knit connotes people who have close affinities as well as affections. The term can have positive implications as when closeness leads to sentiments of loyalty or love. It can also have a negative valence as when members of a family, group, or community are so tight that outsiders feel excluded. In the case of Prato, the term points to an economic landscape constructed of entrepreneurial migrants and constellations of small firms, which overcome their smallness due to dense webs of relations that unite them locally and extend them transnationally. The production scale thus is not merely what meets the eye but what stretches well beyond, in no small part due to a multitextured social weave involving hierarchies of exploitation, relations of reciprocity, and the formation of global households. In this sense, I play on dominant assumptions that globalization only has an unraveling force. In another sense, via a locally grounded approach that makes use of ethnographic methods, I trouble notions that migrants and citizens have little in common. Tight-knit as a metaphor draws attention to the ways in which disruptive and dehumanizing global forces draw people from vastly distant places of origin into a shared urban and social orbit with often clashing symbolic and material meanings.

Regardless of whether individuals or entire families migrate, workers tend to form bonds of love, relations of marriage, and have children fairly rapidly. Some experts in the host society assume circulating children to China verges on pathological parenting. I argue that the families actually are tight knit despite being far flung. They establish global households. I acknowledge that while there may be economic, cultural, and intergenerational gain in sustaining these global households, there is also pain, hardship, and personal sacrifice, and that in no small degree, when we buy and then wear our clothes, we are enveloping our very skin with those supply-chain strategies and structures.

A final significance connects cosmopolitan social relations and the materiality of fashion: tight-knit also refers to "a close group of people that all have some kind of ridiculous steeze," wherein "steeze" is a hybrid between style and ease, defined as "plain old style with eaaaaze" (*Urban Dictionary*). I take this as a reference to urbanites who look stylish but don't appear to work too hard at it. This, perhaps not coincidentally, is one of the most enduring characteristics of the Made in Italy brand, known for its reputation of relaxed elegance.

To render legible the contradictions of fast fashion, chapter 1 grounds the study in context and methods. Thereafter, the book's organization pivots on three different parts with chapters that depart from field-based encounters. Part I, "Chinese Immigration and the Made in Italy Brand," focuses on different sorts of encounters related to culture and the economy. Chapter 2, "Value," tells the story of the resilience of the Made in Italy brand. It argues that its relatively stable value in the face of a globalized textile industry stems from other-than-capitalist symbols, values, and histories. I examine how an event, the Florence flood of 1966, strengthened a popular myth, the continuity between the Renaissance and Italian fashion. Chapter 3, "Money," problematizes the explanation that Chinese migrate to Italy simply to make money. The chapter juxtaposes the disparaging version that many Italians tell about the Chinese with a nuanced version that Chinese tell about themselves. I situate Chinese immigrants' desire to make money in three structural encounters, each at a different level of scale: a Chinese regional model of economic development, a local Italian environment of small firms connected to the Made in Italy brand, and a global restructuring of the clothing industry. These encounters shape migrant experiences and reveal the complex meanings and practices behind what would appear a universal quest for money. The story challenges bargain-price assumptions about global capitalism as a homogeneous economic force. Chapter 4, "Crisis," draws on biographies of protagonists who represent three different migratory trajectories and revives the concept of *crisis of presence* to illuminate senses of existential despair and possibilities of transcendence born out of economic crisis.

Part II, "Global Circuits of Care," shifts to encounters of an embodied kind. Chapter 5, "Checkup," uses medical anthropological sensibilities to expose jarring and uncertain moments that emerge as public health institutions safeguard and discipline Chinese parents. The intimate space of an examining room allows observation of interactions between health-care professionals and parents who bring in their infants for three-month checkups. Chinese migrants negotiate expert views in ways that show how they cope with transnational lives. The encounters reveal how globalization writes itself on bodies in unexpected ways. Chapter 6, "Circulation," homes in on a paradox: more than half of the births in Prato were registered to foreign women, yet many of these babies were being sent to China. This circulation of children has given rise to a host of new discourses and interventions on parenting, from various institutions and experts, as children move in and out of Italian health-care systems and schools. The chapter juxtaposes perspectives and vocabularies of Chinese parents with the know-how of professional Italian health-care workers and educators. It brings into sharp relief the existence of global households. Parents find value in circulating children in its power to activate systems of reciprocity across kin, to create networked bodies across territories, to secure affective bonds across generations, and to free up time so as to enhance their ability to work and make money.

Part III, "The New Politics of Urban Racism," shifts to encounters connected to a globally diverse Europe that play out in the city. Chapter 7, "Integration," documents how a segregated city grapples with the globalization of fashion and garment work. This chapter places local dynamics in the context of national as well as European immigration politics. Struggles over the terms of belonging are front and center. Rich urban encounter ethnography draws on key events and public discourse. Chapter 8, "Action," exposes dueling "wars of position." On the one hand, a right-wing mayor sustained a hostile and coercive approach to dealing with the immigrant presence. On the other hand, residents along with engaged urban planners and anthropologists launched a countereffort in a working-class neighborhood that has transitioned from Little Italy to Little Wenzhou. The book concludes with "Futures," which reminds of the uncertainty facing families as well as policy implications for urban centers undergoing transformation. I synthesize the thematic threads of the book and suggest the emancipatory potential of an approach that writes to stimulate imagination and forge new worlds. *Tight Knit* brings to the fore the tensions over value, money, beauty, global families, diverse economies, well-being, becoming, belonging, and integration. At its core, this project aims to grasp the essence of economic subjects, to capture the driving ambitions and disappointing defeats of an intensely globalized age.

# 1

# Ethnography

Fangli and I walked along a worn stretch of Via Roma: empty storefronts, trash-strewn curbs, dingy bars with sticky tabletops and washed-up-looking clientele. We had just finished our second interview of the day. The first had been with a physical therapist at a public health clinic, where we had sensed the frustration of a health-care professional whose pediatric patient's care had been thrown into limbo when his parents sent him to China. The second appointment had taken us to the city's Social Services Immigration Office, where we had learned about the procedures for family reunification. The details had left my head spinning.

Our guard was down that midsummer's day. We were both famished. We took a right on Via Lazzerini, where Fangli had parked her car and earlier had happened into Pasticceria Mannori for a croissant and coins. She raved about the pastry and how the cashier had been gracious in making change for her parking meter. We were hoping to return for a scrumptious lunch. When we arrived, the shades were drawn and the door locked. The shop was closed for lunch. As we stood on the corner deciding which direction to head, a diminutive Chinese man on a bicycle approached. As Fangli and the man spoke in Chinese, I inventoried the stranger's load: four hefty steaks packaged in plastic wrap piled into a basket on the front of the bike and two cases of diapers strapped onto a rear rack.

Fangli turned to me. "He's asking me what I'm doing with an Italian," she said and repeated herself *almost* verbatim: "He's wanting to know what I'm doing with an *occidentale*, a Westerner."

I caught sight of drivers in cars gazing in our direction.

"He wants to know if you know of any way to have a boy baby."

"No! Boy and girl babies are equal," I asserted in Italian.

FIGURE 1.1. The quotidian life of local people inspired Quinto Martini (1908–90) and appeared in his sculptures and paintings, such as *Woman Who Sews* (*Donna che cuce*).
Photo by Giorgio Commini, courtesy of the Comune di Carmignano and the Associazione Parco Museo Quinto Martini

"What about in France or Germany?" he said through Fangli's translations. I shook my head. "Sex-selective abortion isn't allowed."

He asked Fangli for her cell number, and she turned to me and laughed in disbelief. I suggested she get his number and pulled out my notebook. He explained himself: given how well Fangli spoke Italian and given his knack for work, the two of them could join forces, start a business, and make a lot of money.

"Money, money, money," Fangli joked, as we walked in the other direction. She voiced one of the stereotypical refrains that Prato residents say about Chinese migrants. On a serious note, she then told me she didn't think he was "normal," that he most likely had some disturbance. She may well have been right. His chastising her for keeping the company of a non-Chinese person brought to mind the wise fool, the figure who blurts out what polite people keep to themselves.

### Local Encounters, Global Economies

A noisy part of the population in Prato was not behaving in a very polite manner when it came to issues of immigration. The very impolite book *L'Assedio Cinese*, or *The Chinese Siege* (Pieraccini 2010), was already in its second edition within two years of its original printing. Its author was none other than Silvia Pieraccini, a popular yet controversial journalist who was writing for the financial daily *Sole 24 Ore*. The book's cover shows a throng of Chinese people. There is no explanation as to where the people, primarily young women, are standing or why they are crowded in that space; it simply conveys visually the sensational subtitle, which could well be translated as *Prato's Lawless Low-Cost Fashion District*. The book speaks of women's fashion that is ready to wear at any hour of the day or night. It describes workers without unions or rights who toil sixteen to eighteen hours per day. It portrays a production zone with an overwhelming record of "births" and "deaths" of firms in a constellation of turnover. It depicts deplorable health and hygienic conditions as workers sew, eat, and sleep in workshops. It asserts how illegality has become the norm. And it outlines Italian government attempts to crack down on the underground economy and address Prato's record as the number one tax evader in Tuscany. All said, the tone is angry—a tone that echoed dominant sentiments in the city and its province.

Evidence of anti-immigrant sentiment was not difficult to find in private or in public. During ethnographic research for this project, I encountered hostility on a regular basis from Italian friends and acquaintances, old and new, because of my research topic. On more than one occasion, I was verbally attacked. Once, I came to tears and left. I had reached my human limit. Frequently, I listened as people ranted against the Chinese residents in their midst—people whom they had decided they could not trust, whether as neighbors, employers, or clients. The exception tended to be property owners who rented to Chinese tenants or real estate agents whose customers were the new-moneyed immigrant class in search of luxury villas. Health-care professionals and educators were recognized as being on the front lines of support vis-à-vis immigrants. Occasionally, displaced sweater artisans were also empathetic, saying that Prato would now be a ghost town if it weren't for the new garment niche economy and the influx of Chinese workers. By contrast, the angriest Italians told me that the Chinese were not immigrants but rather occupiers. The implication was that I should have absolutely no sympathy for such people. They were ruining the social fabric of this old Tuscan textile hub. They were to blame for the economic crisis.

Angry sentiments and behaviors—at times uncivil and racist—abounded, whether in old-fashioned or virtual public spaces. They reflected the tensions brewing not only in this historic textile city but also in many places the world over (Fassin 2011; Holmes and Castañeda 2016; Vertovec 2011). This story is one that many cities have lived in the recent past as pressures to enhance profit and shareholder value have witnessed shifts in production overseas and lured cheaper labor forces to destinations across the globe (Ho 2009). *Tight Knit* is the story of an old-world region and its difficult transition to twenty-first-century globalization. It is the story of a city known literally for its rags-to-riches history, one that has shifted from having a robust textile industry to being a flourishing international fashion center (Johanson, Smyth, and French 2009). The trials and tribulations of this passage animate this story. How individuals, families, and institutions transform, cope, and create value in the context of transnational capitalism and immigration rests at its heart.

## Getting at Globalization, Transforming a Method

The conditions of globalization create innumerable challenges for the people who move around as well as for the ones who stay put. The tool kit for understanding and addressing these conditions and the challenges they present requires refining, revising, and even revolutionizing current approaches to gathering information, making sense of it, and acting upon it. If illuminating the human condition in all its glorious and unequal diversity is ethnography's core mission, as João Biehl (2005) has suggested, then an ethnographic accounting has much to offer in terms of grasping dynamics and particu lars as global pressures rip apart a place and as people from diverse walks of life struggle to remake it. Ethnography, known for its thick description and nuanced analyses, offers a powerful albeit provincial way to interpret lived experience. Ethnographic inquiry involves sustained participation in social life. I listen for stories that fester beneath commonsense assumptions, expert tropes, and aggregate portraits. I turn to the ordinary to find the extraordinary. The aim is to confront large-scale tyrannies with oft-hidden truths, to challenge modern modes of power with up-to-the-minute modes of life. I am ever on the lookout for subjugated forms of knowledge—in other words, forms that may seem naive, quaint, or quirky. These knowledge forms are likely discounted yet hold potential for challenging taken-for-granted outlooks, practices, and forces.

I came of age as an anthropologist when Rayna Rapp's (1999) materialist-feminist incitement seemed perfect for anthropologists: to see themselves as historians of the present. Foucault's call for a "genealogical method" was all the rage. It invited a historical perspective and mode of investigation that entailed "a painstaking rediscovery of struggles together with the rude memory of their conflicts" (Foucault 1980, 83). Granted, Foucault was not much for ethnography, but the prized anthropological method of participation and observation in its sundry forms surely qualifies as a "painstaking" approach for accessing struggles that the commonsense narratives about globalization elide. It promised upending knowledge-power constellations. Like the man on the bicycle loaded with steaks and diapers, the act of asking may appear rude because the question does not traffic in the niceties of the day (see Gramsci 1971, Williams 1989). Ethnographic excavations collude with those whose "rude" memories perhaps have more to say than their provincial content might initially suggest.

Examples abound. Combining ethnography and forensic science, Jason De León's (2015) *Land of the Open Graves* illuminates the ways in which global economic inequality and transnational migration become embodied in life histories of US border crossers. Focusing on the uneven ways that immigrants in France get categorized and treated, Miriam Ticktin (2011) in her *Casualties of Care* uses ethnography to forge a field of critical humanitarianism.[1] Showing suffering among US migrant farmworkers, medical anthropologist and physician Seth Holmes (2013, 185) notes in *Fresh Fruit, Broken Bodies* that ethnography represents "an especially important methodology for understanding the multilayered meanings and vertical slices of power that make up social and cultural life, including its inequalities and justifications." I position myself as an ethnographer who straddles humanistic and social science orientations, maintaining that even in an Internet age of virtual information, there remains something incredibly potent about "being there." I envision "copresence" as a multisensory sharing of social life as it unfolds, which transforms how and what we know, including "the anthropologist's own self-understandings" (Borneman and Hammoudi 2009, 14). In other words, ethnographic copresence stimulates transformative insights.

Toward this end, I have conceptualized *encounter ethnography* to guide the investigation. In the legacy of anthropological scholarship, much has been written about encounters. The term is useful because it emphasizes experiences or processes that are at odds with one another, as in the phrases "colonial encounter" (Asad 1973), "development encounter" (Escobar 1991), "intercultural encounter" (Sahlins 2000), "clinical encounter" (Ferzacca 2000), "activist encounters" (Razsa 2015), and even "fieldwork encounters" (Borneman and Hammoudi 2009). Rather than leave encounters to the realm of theory or common sense, however, I nurture *encounter ethnography* as a theoretically informed methodological framework. I propose an orientation that places encounters, as points of interpenetration and mediation, at the center of the investigation, one that is mindful of realizing a locality analysis.

Specifically, this case study has allowed an up-close look at Prato as a "litmus test" of globalization and its triumphal assumptions (Baldassar et al. 2015, 3). Ethnographic research revolved around several sites of encounter: (1) encounters concerning child health, migration, and return; (2) encounters related to local production sites and global forces; and (3) encounters involving public places, meetings, and events. When I first developed encounter ethnography as a method, I had only a vague sense of the eventual project sites, but I imagined contexts that would expose jarring epistemological moments as when expert and lay forms of knowledge collide. Exposure is what the method is designed to do. The project reveals how such instances play out on the ground between institutions and migrants as well as between ethnographers and their "subjects."[2] This strategy allows for a focus on power-laden clashes between dominant and subordinate economies, epistemologies, social practices, ways of being, and moral orientations.

To be clear, I am not merely conceptualizing this project as a sort of global ethnography of capitalism in which the anthropologist considers the responses, or "economic 'impacts' and cultural 'reactions,'" of those legendary "people without history" to the world capitalist system (Sahlins 2000; Wolf 1982). To cultivate something beyond such a two-dimensional perspective, encounter ethnography proposes a three-pronged conceptual scheme. For starters, there are *structural encounters*—namely, economic—that shape possibilities for human action and meaning making. Next, there are *genealogical encounters*, which open space to consider contrasting intellectual genealogies and the cultural logics that collide or emerge when erudite and subjugated forms of knowledge interpenetrate. Emancipatory potential resides in consciously bringing into dialogue such authorized and disqualified forms (Foucault 1980, 78–81). Finally, *fieldwork encounters* refer to those that occur when the ethnographer embraces what I call "structured spontaneity" (Krause 2005b). Such an orientation brings the researcher into confrontations with social life as it unfolds on terms mostly of its own making. Some of the most incomprehensible yet profound things happen through unexpected encounters, often resulting from systematic perseverance and careful attention to social life. The orientation is designed to address the trap of projecting one's own understandings of the world onto those of others. Fieldwork at its core is constantly a humbling experience. When the experience of fieldwork itself is viewed as an object of inquiry, the interpersonal encounters between anthropologists and their subjects can lead to exploring crucial conundrums and producing valuable knowledge, thus making possible the co-construction of new narratives (Hartog 1988; Palevsky 2000; Raikhel 2009; Senders 2009; Stevenson 2009).

On the ground, natives and newcomers have struggled to grasp the meaning of encounters in terms of "their own system of the world," as Sahlins (2000, 417) puts it. Yet is it conceivable that what "their own" meant in the 1790s could possibly be relevant in an era of globalist identity politics? Or might "their own" have become unrecognizably fragmented due to diasporic interpenetrations and mediations? My use of encounter ethnography allows me to engage these questions. It represents a slight shift in perspective from the purpose to discover "the culture mystified in the capitalism" as when, for example, in 1793, a British ambassador to China viewed his goods as presents whereas the Chinese emperor took them for tribute (Sahlins 2000, 421). Gifts or tribute? Sahlins's reading of an envoy's musings interprets the Brit's view of presents to be "*samples* of their wares; even beyond that they were *examples* of industrial ingenuity, designed to signify the 'superiority' of British civilization and the majesty of George III." But underscoring the clash of civilizations, he reasons, "from the mandarins' perspective, if the 'presents' were indeed 'tributes' expressing the barbarians' sincere desire to turn to civilization, manifestly they could not be superior to things Chinese" (Sahlins 2000, 429). The encounter revealed profoundly different logics at work in terms of who was doing what for whom and who had the upper hand— eventually exposed in the trade imbalance between silver and tea. The Chinese view of the gifts as tribute was possible because of a noncapitalist orientation to the world. Other cosmologies were clearly at work. Transnational encounters generate possibilities for misunderstanding and misconception yet also integration and differentiation. Novel regimes of value and forms of citizen-ship or stubborn forms of disparity are likely (Appadurai 1986; Rofel 2007). In short, encounters expose the contours of future possible worlds: utopias, dystopias, or admixtures.

As the name *encounter ethnography* suggests, the approach embraces the use of empirical evidence while also maintaining a healthy skepticism toward the scientific gold standard of reproducibility. We live in an age when, even in the most prestigious scientific fields, a crisis of confidence casts a shadow of doubt over knowledge claims. "Alt facts" aside, George Johnson reports in the Science section of the *New York Times* the finding that most scientific labs have a hard time repeating experiments and reproducing the same results as the original. Johnson notes, "It has been jarring to learn in recent years that a reproducible result may actually be the rarest of birds" (G. Johnson 2014; Ioannidis 2005).

Does ethnography as a method have a chance in navigating widespread skepticism about scientific knowledge? Skepticism about the truth of science has created unlikely bedfellows: the moderate scientists who say that repro-ducibility of scientific results is rare, the far-left skeptics of funded research, the far-right climate-change naysayers, and apolitical info-philes who bask in information at their fingertips and take the production of knowledge for granted.

If reproducing the same results is a problem in a controlled lab environ-ment, it is particularly improbable in a field setting. Humans are not predict-able, nor are conditions replicable from day to day, let alone from year to year. And so it may seem like a contradiction to situate my work as empirical yet also skeptical of erudite knowledge. The challenges are many for repre-senting social life as it is encountered in an intensely globalized world. In a world that is in many ways ironically more ethnocentric than ever,[3] I would like to suggest that there is still good reason to get out of our chairs, pull ourselves away from our computer screens and devices, and get into the field. There is also good reason that Willis and Trondman (2000) wrote a manifesto for ethnography, and that aha moments have the potential to inspire. Not everything we find in the field will be inspiring, to be sure. Much is troubling. And much is messy.[4]

Claiming to offer total perspective with sweeping vision can flatten differ-ences and create a false sense of coherence, an illusion as clever and old as the trompe l'oeil.[5] I take seriously the notion that knowledge is always situated and partial, as influential feminists have convincingly argued (Haraway 1988). Everyone has partial perspective. Realities are assembled and lived. Such rec-ognition can just as easily enliven as paralyze our efforts to engage with the world.[6] It can inspire us to care about not just what we write but how we write. As a discipline, anthropology lies somewhere between literary and scientific genres. Clifford Geertz (1988, 20) argued that its leanings were toward language as praxis more than language as means, with a stronger leaning toward romances than lab reports: "anthropological discourse certainly remains poised, mule-like, between the two." And despite being labeled a second-fiddle genre (Behar 1999), this long-standing trait may be precisely what gives ethnography its hybrid vigor. The backstory of why anthropologists continue to write ethnographies, why they struggle to find a voice, tell a story, and, in the process, generate countless "paper babies" (Fordham 2011, 79), reveals a dogged commitment to creating counternarratives.

## Collaborative Processes, Enriched Ethnography

As I began fieldwork, this project felt daunting. I still remember the first night in my monastic hostel room, imagining myself at the base of a huge mountain and questioning whether I had the skills and stamina to climb it. I did not plan a solo trek. I had reached out to a longtime Italian colleague in the spirit of assembling a transnational research team. We planned to confront the frictions of an intensely globalized world together, a departure from two conventions: that of the lone ethnographer and that of the detached scientist. With maturity, I have followed a desire to join a collaborative strand of ethnographic work and foster intellectual engagement across geopolitical and socioeconomic spaces (Gubrium, Krause, and Jernigan 2014; Hemment 2015). What I gained from collaboration was far more than what I would have gained from doing it alone. The cultural closeness with Chinese and Italian individuals became spread across members of our team. On the one hand, I have misgivings about dispersing those relationships, as an ethnographer who has cultivated a host of long-lasting friendships and enduring networks over the years with residents of the Prato zone. I could not abandon the relationships I already had in the field, and in fact, it was those relationships that enabled me access to such a sensitive topic, sensitive spaces, and talented assistants. On the other hand, sharing relationships through collaboration also meant strengthening networks, widening perspectives, and enriching interpretations.

Would a perfect world be one in which I would be so gifted with abilities, time, and resources that I could do everything by myself? The reality is that ethnographic work is by nature very collaborative, but only some projects formalize collaboration. In my case, I believed deeply that a transnational team in terms of citizenship and languages made excellent sense to study a transnational phenomenon. I wish I were more gifted linguistically, but I realized my limitations and thus assembled a team of assistants in both Prato and Amherst. Collaboration enhanced the integrity of the research, and it took place at multiple levels. I had the help of my collaborator, Massimo Bressan, an urban and economic anthropologist whom I have known for more than twenty years and who also served as president of the Prato-based research institute IRIS—Strumenti e Risorse per lo Sviluppo Locale (Instruments and Resources for Local Development). He facilitated access to institutions, which required layers of permission, and the hiring of two Prato-area research assistants, Fangli Xu and Xiaoyun Liao, bilingual in Chinese and Italian. Fangli was a native speaker of the Wenzhou dialect, who at age ten migrated from Wenzhou with her family to Cremona, where the absence of fellow school-age compatriots set forth conditions that led her to acquire Italian language and habits. We joined forces to refine research design as well as ethics training and certification; identify key ethnographic sites; cultivate relationships and permissions with institutions; devise interview protocol; and recruit migrant subjects, which was slow initially due to fear and mistrust given their often precarious and also often undocumented status.

A transcultural team meant doing our due diligence to ensure research participants understood the purpose of the project when they consented to talk to us. Without the team, the endeavor would have felt compromised. For example, at least one interviewee specifically requested that a "Westerner" not be present yet gave consent for his interview to be included in the study as long as he and his factory location remained anonymous. Accusations of illegality, undocumented workers, mafia ties, criminality, and health and safety violations were widespread during the fieldwork. Suspicions ran rampant. It was a very tense time and place.

For data collection, team members conducted interviews in pairs as well as individually. Fangli conducted a number of the interviews alone, in some cases out of respect for the individuals. In all cases, researchers obtained informed consent to digitally audio record each interview. Disagreement exists among anthropologists regarding the use of semistructured data such as interviews. I believe that a complicated, transnational project calls for different kinds of data: some unstructured, such as participant observation and field notes, and some semistructured, such as interviews. Doing this kind of project requires open-mindedness and untethering ourselves from disciplinary comfort zones. As a team, our aim was to establish rapport and to solicit stories. A good interview can have a great deal of integrity. It can serve as a form of oral history (Passerini 1987). It can keep the ethnographer honest especially when translating between languages and cultural contexts and logics. Even if people do not always tell the truth, at least we know that we recorded their words and got what they said to the best of our abilities, that we were not just conveniently putting words in their mouths. The careful work of developing interview questions, of transcribing and translating interviews, of coding the interviews in data analysis software to identify themes (Bernard and Ryan 2010; Ryan and Bernard 2003)—these steps all brought a certain systematic quality to the work and allowed the researchers a big-picture perspective on people's experiences as a whole, as well as on an emergent social world.

All told, I spent 220 days between June 2012 and May 2015 conducting ethnographic research as the principal investigator in the province of Prato. I also made two trips, each of about ten days, during spring 2011 to lay the groundwork and do exploratory fieldwork. During the official course of the project, I made seven trips of varying lengths from twelve to seventy-five days: June–July 2012, January 2013, March–April 2013, May–August 2013, October–November 2013, June–July 2014, and May 2015. The team-based project was designed to elicit three different types of data: (1) unstructured, in the form of socially occurring speech and practices at rich, ethnographic encounter sites; (2) semistructured, in the form of interviews; and (3) structured, in the form of free lists. As an ethnographer, I gathered unstructured data during hospital-based participant observation in a pediatric unit as well as attendance at public meetings, conferences, health-care workshops, exhibits, and inaugurations—events related to immigrants, crisis, or local development. I listened to and participated in informal conversations during visits to immigration offices, outdoor markets, factories, and wholesale settings, and I volunteered for several weeks at a Democratic Party festival in a municipality whose firms have transitioned from mostly Italian to mostly Chinese.

The result was countless hours of ethnographic work, hundreds of pages of field notes, and dozens of interviews. We assembled an inventory of seventy-one audio recordings: forty-one with Chinese immigrants involving forty-four individuals; twenty-one with Italian health-care workers as well as Italians with connections to the Made in Italy sector; and eight of exam room visits. Two-thirds of the Chinese parents or grandparents were women. Interviews were conducted to respect the speakers' preference: Wenzhouese, Mandarin, or Italian. Audio recordings were then transcribed in the interview language. Those in Mandarin and Wenzhouese were translated into English. (Some were also translated into Italian.) We connected with the Chinese participants through a social service office, a hospital pediatric unit, and various social networks. Most of the Chinese men and women were parents in the fast-fashion niche who had experience sending their children to China.

Indeed, this turned out to be a very easy inclusion criterion to meet. In addition, our interviews included nearly an equal number of firm owners and nonowners and revealed that both entrepreneurs and workers made use of transnational care networks. Even in the few cases where parents had not sent their children away, they were considering doing so.

As a team, we collectively cast a suspicious eye toward facile ways of knowing. We were ever mindful of our aim to humanize global processes, to get beneath aggregate numbers, and to get beyond sensational statistics. Furthermore, collaboration enhanced our ability to disseminate the research findings. We conducted a substantive training with health-care professionals and a methods workshop on qualitative data analysis with local researchers. An additional major gain was a collective sense of purpose that emerged and energized the project and its possibilities for intervention. We hatched and organized an urban action project, Neighborhood Plots. The collaborative experience transformed me as a researcher, teacher, adviser, and person. It made for a richer project—one that is not simply a migrant community study but is rather a study of encounters and assemblages that result from the hegemony of global supply chains.

## Field Openings, People Plasticity

I began most days reading the newspaper at a local Casa del Popolo, a social center where people as diverse as young mothers, school-age children, Chinese teenagers, African vendors, working women, and retired Italian men came and went. At the start of my project, I was a stranger in the neighborhood and mostly got treated as such, but within the first nine months of coming and going, I had become visible and even the subject of gossip and the target of desire. Without advance planning, I often enjoyed my morning coffee and pastry with a small group of people, all of whom were parents with deep connections to the local economy. Giuseppe was a retired textile worker, Marco was a shoe wholesaler, and Daniela was a real estate agent. Marco and Daniela both conducted business with Chinese migrants, she as a real estate agent, at times selling high-end villas in the hill towns, and he as a buyer and a renter.

One March morning, Marco invited me to see his warehouse along with old photos from his radical days in the 1960s. He bought the space in the early 1990s. It was cavernous. Shoeboxes stacked atop flattened cardboard covered the floor. Marco apologized for the smell and opened the high-up windows with a pole. "They work here, sleep here, and cook here," he said of his tenants. He gestured toward a space in the very back of the room that served as their kitchen. On the other side of a plaster wall was their work-space and, up a set of stairs, sleeping quarters. Marco insisted on giving me a pair of shoes, and I tried my best to refuse. He offered to introduce me to his tenants. Against many who called them delinquents, he viewed them as hard workers.

"*A cottimo—si guadagna al pezzo*," he said, explaining their arrangement as piecework based on a system of co-responsibility and interdependence. The *capo*, or head, gets half of what the workers earn and is responsible for housing them and feeding them. They split the other half among the dependents. The more the firm earns, the more they get. So there's an incentive.

"They're plastic," Marco continued. "When there's work, they work. When there's not, they sleep." For example, at the time they were sleeping. They'd probably get up around noon. Working during the night they saved on electricity costs.

At a later date, I returned with a young research assistant, Xiaoyun, who grew up in Prato to Chinese parents. Marco accompanied us next door. We rang the bell, and a man of Chinese nationality around forty years old answered. We walked through a dark hallway and entered the workshop—a room created from plasterboard out of a larger space. Odors of fabric and laundry detergent saturated the air. Stacks of solid green and gray sleeves and bodies lay on the floor, pieces of suits to be sewn.

The *capa*, or boss, welcomed us. The workers turned, casting surprised expressions at seeing us. Meanwhile, Marco headed straight to a toddler and picked him up, then walked around holding him like a proud uncle. The *lao ban niang*, known in Italian as the giver of work (*datrice di lavoro*) came toward us. We explained we were curious to know Chinese who lived in Prato. We requested five minutes to chat. The woman invited us to sit down at a table nearby and brought us some chairs. The two of us sat, the woman remained standing for several minutes to speak to us, until we invited her to sit down as well. We asked about the child: it's her son, born in 2010, so about two and a half. She has another one in China. Both were born in Italy. The child looked at us with immense curiosity, but as soon as the mother told him to come closer, he ran off and hid. The other son was a year older, living with his paternal grandparents in China. Even the younger son had lived in China. They brought him back to Italy just recently. When we asked why she left the older one in China, she replied that he is a restless type of child and she doesn't manage to keep up with him. Besides, the baby really likes the employees and often plays with them.

The woman had been in Italy for ten years. She came in 2003 as a *clandestina*, or undocumented person, and put in a lot of time to get where she is. She had been in Prato around six years. Before coming to live in Prato she lived in a city in northern Italy. She worked in a firm in which she had the possibility to learn some Italian: a Chinese woman who knew Italian used to come every day into the workshop, when work was slow, and provide two hours of language lessons to all of the employees. To pay her, they would make a collection of €100 a head each month. Working in strict contact with Chinese speakers, she hadn't had much chance to speak Italian. In fact, she has forgotten most of the Italian words she learned. In Prato, she liked being surrounded by fellow overseas Chinese and didn't have to endure much of a language problem.

Seven employees worked in the firm. Three were women, and four were men. All were sewing except for one. He appeared to be the one whom the Chinese call *shougong*, the person who folds clothes, organizes them, and loads and unloads the truck or van. This particular guy was seated on a chair and folded jackets that were already sewn.

The employees were relatives of the owner. We asked if it was better to work with relatives than nonrelatives with whom you have only a work relationship, and she said that relatives were better because if there were problems, they could be discussed quietly. The dependents earned around €700–€800 per month, depending on the quantity of work that they churned out. They were paid *a cottimo*, based on the quantity that they produced.

Inside the firm, there was a pair of beds. In general, they slept in a house a few minutes' walk away. In the winter, given the cold, the employees were accompanied by car. Now that it was not cold, they walked. It was less hot in the house and they slept better than in the factory.

They paid rent around €1,350 per month for this room of 200 square meters. She complained it was too expensive. Just then, she answered a call on her cell phone, saying that she had to get back to work. We thanked her and said good-bye.

Fieldwork revealed several conditions of the lives of Chinese migrants living and working in Prato: that the garment enterprises were primarily small family firms, that gendered divisions of labor were relatively unimportant, that work relationships were built on relations of interdependent kin, that the circulation of children was widespread, and that Italians became deeply involved in the fast-fashion economy through rents, subcontracting, and other relationships. Marco later indicated how attached he had become to the children, and how he missed them when they were sent away. "My mother sent me away at fourteen years old," he quipped in a tone that mocked self-pity. Uncertain of Marco's intentions with his hints for sympathy, my assistant and I harmonized twin violins. Playfulness aside, he then explained how his mother had kicked him out of the house, how he had moved from the south, and how he had become involved in radical Communist Party politics in Florence of the 1960s. Later, it struck me that temporally and geographically distant experiences might be more similar than different. In any case, it seemed to account for his connection with the children.

## Tracing Migrations, Contextualizing the Local

Several vital influences shape this work. Many contemporary anthropologists study migration, both in ways that reproduce the naturalness of the nation-state and in ways that challenge its taken-for-granted authority. This was not always the case. Migration as an object of study did not emerge until the 1950s or 1960s (Brettell 2014), and even then, anthropologists tended to depict cultures as bounded, untouched, outside of time or history, and rooted in place.[7]

Tending to outside influences and power differentials entered the scope of anthropological study as fieldworkers could ignore neither the penetration of capitalist markets, the influences of colonial regimes, nor the movement of people from villages, whether to cities of their own newly independent nation-states or those of former colonial rulers. Working and living with local people often meant forging deep bonds and affections with them, as well as appreciating their accomplishments, frustrations, constraints, and struggles. Many anthropologists were compelled to study precisely the violence that colonial policies or regimes wrought on local ways of living, believing, being, and becoming. They were compelled to pay attention to the anticolonial movements themselves against ongoing empire-building atrocities. Some anthropologists continued to assist governments in their "civilizing" or "modernizing" missions, while others adhered to a do-no-harm ethics. Still others sought strategies to be change agents or activists in their own right. An anthropological perspective on culture and power emerged, particularly from critical engagements with community studies on peasants. Among the most influential was Eric Wolf's (1982) *Europe and the People without History*, an ironically titled text that upended the status quo of American anthropology with its arguments about the historical trajectory of modern globalization and capitalism's subsequent emergence as the dominant modern ideology.

Something of this influence resonates in the "global power perspective" that Nina Glick Schiller advocates. The longtime scholar of transnationalism has recently asserted that scholars must highlight the common struggle, or in some cases common dehumanizing forces, that migrants and citizens face as they try to achieve social and economic justice as the cities in which they live are subjected to the forces of capital restructuring (Glick Schiller 2012). In opposition to what has nearly become a gold standard of ethnography—that of the anthropologist going to multiple locations and pursuing a multisited research project (Marcus 1995)—Glick Schiller has refreshingly called for a "locality analysis." In some ways, this may seem like a return to the olden and golden days of anthropological study when ethnographers focused on one people bounded in one culture and one place. It is nothing of the sort.

A locality approach aims to work against reproducing separation and to rescale a given analysis; it forwards an agenda of placing "migrants and natives in the same conceptual framework" (Glick Schiller 2012, 46). The strategy can help to avoid and even subvert so-called methodological nationalism, a common side effect of migration research that feeds nationalism with its unit of analysis of the ethnic group itself. Glick Schiller identifies such a framing as problematic in that it "obscures the effects of the global restructuring of capital on the population, both migrant and non-migrant, in a specific locality" (43). Thus, rescaling based on a locality underscores the ways migrants, too, are agents in "reshaping localities" and therefore "turns our attention to the relationships that develop between the residents of a place and institutions situated locally, regionally, nationally, and globally, without making prior assumptions about how these relationships are shaped" (46). Combining relational and structural dimensions holds promise for realizing a global power analysis. As will become clear, the agency of migrants restructures a given locality as do global supply chains.

The most common question people ask me is why Chinese migrate to Italy generally and why to Prato specifically. The simple answer is to make money in Europe. The complicated answer points to value and history. Goods that carry the Made in Italy brand carry added value (Lees-Maffei and Fallan 2014). The resilience and prestige of Made in Italy clothing has drawn thousands of transnational migrants to Tuscany's prime historic industrial district to produce low-cost items for the fast-fashion industry, even to work as subcontractors for luxury brands (Clean Clothes Campaign 2014a). They come presumably to find their golden apple ripened under the sun of European modernity.[8]

The history of Prato is in large part a microcosm of the history of industry and migration. Newcomers were drawn to Prato as a new-moneyed city for decades. People in search of new possibilities migrated to the factory city initially from the nearby countryside and later from more distant points of origin, suggesting three migratory phases: regional, national, and transnational (Bressan and Tosi Cambini 2009). In the 2011 census, the province of Prato marked almost twenty years since splitting off from the province of Florence (in 1992) and boasted a total population of 248,477, of which 36,834, or 14.8 percent, were classified as *stranieri*, or foreign residents. The city of Prato's total resident population reached 185,456 in the same census, of which the total foreign population was 28,518, or 15.4 percent of the city's residents. (This compared with the rate of 6.8 percent of foreign residents nationwide.) These numbers have won the city various popular designations, such as Europe's number one multicultural city (Brandi and Sabatini 2012; Office of Statistics 2013; Istat 2011).

The first phase of migration occurred after the devastation of world war as Tuscan peasants abandoned the countryside for the city. Many peasants from the rural hinterland had been politicized as partisans in the resistance during the German occupation. During the two decades of greatest growth, 1951–71, Prato witnessed a doubling of its population from 77,631 to 143,232 residents. They brought with them a desire for autonomy. In Tuscany, migrants traded the *mezzadria* system of sharecropping with its hierarchical family organization for an urban lifestyle of factory work or industrial artisanship and the relative autonomy it promised. Work in an informal economy spread as the temperature of labor struggles became excessively hot and in turn as small family firms proliferated. A peasant ethos persisted—visceral yet mixed memories of the soil, of patron-client relations, of generational conflict, and of reciprocity. Residents with this history constitute about 30 percent of the current population.[9]

A second phase of migration, in the 1960s, witnessed the arrival of people from the deep south leaving behind diverse peasant agriculture but bringing regional habits and dialects. People of southern Italian heritage suffered experiences of quasi Jim Crow–style discrimination as they sought housing and employment. Southern Italians were long stigmatized in the Italian imagination as inferior—a status and a trope that Italian state formation reinforced, Cesare Lombroso's criminal anthropology underwrote, and Edward Banfield's "amoral familism" reinscribed. These residents now make up about 12 percent of Prato's population.

In a third phase, especially since the 1990s, transnational migrants have come onto the scene. By far the most numerous immigrant group has its origins in China, with most born in Wenzhou of the southeastern coastal province of Zhejiang (83.4 percent) or Fujian (13.2 percent). These migrants view southern Europe as a "frontier of highly developed economies," a place "where they . . . face little competition from established Chinese communities" (Pieke et al. 2004). Including only registered Chinese immigrants yields numbers around 40 percent of resident foreigners. When Chinese without residency permits are included, estimates often double the fifteen thousand on record to thirty thousand or more. There exists a great deal of uncertainty about the actual numbers because of those who live under the radar, often in the factories where they work or, following the deadly factory fire in 2013 that stimulated a new inspection regime, in apartments often provided by firm owners. And then there is the constant coming and going of Chinese workers and their children, including the noteworthy practice of sending children back to China (Sambo 2013a, 106−8). Indeed, these newest immigrants bring networking and labor strategies also moored in a family model and are renowned for their flexibility (see also Ceccagno 2003, 2009; Denison et al. 2007).

Prato offers unique features as a laboratory of globalization.[10] It ranks as the number one province in Italy in terms of the ratio of Italian to registered foreign residents. Another sign of Prato's diversity is the fact that non-Italian residents have migrated from 118 different countries. Furthermore, foreign women accounted for more than half of births each year in the hospital of Prato. It was no mere coincidence that the Chinese man who stopped us had diapers strapped to his bicycle.

Suffice to say that not all acts of reproduction are perceived equally. Births and babies may be valued according to age, race, class, gender, religion, or citizenship.[11] Certain bodies behave in threatening ways, according to prevailing logics of stratified societies: some babies are desired and others are feared. Babies come into the world always already bearing a bundle of signifiers. The reproductive practices of immigrants become one of the key tropes through which threat becomes cast. This representation qualifies as a form of what Jane Hill has called "covert racist discourse": a form of racist discourse that is relatively invisible compared to blatant slurs. Yet, as Hill (2008, 41) cogently argues, these covert forms "may be just as important in reproducing the culturally shared ideas that underpin racism." In Italy, alarmism anchors itself in the body as it points to a supposedly impending demographic demise in the context of low birthrates and an aging society (Krause and Marchesi 2007).

In a global world, making families and producing goods continue to be bedfellows. Historically, the success of the Made in Italy brand was attributed to small family firms adept at meeting work demands and deadlines. Economists lauded these firms for their flexibility. Often forgotten were the heated labor struggles of the late 1960s that led to the dynamic small-firm landscape. Even less celebrated is what made firm flexibility possible: an informal economy characterized by family arrangements tied to unwritten contracts, clandestine work day and night, and networks grounded in old-world sensibilities of secrecy, trust, and reciprocity. Much of the textile spinoff work was outsourced to small- or medium-sized family firms, often completing single stages in production cycles as wares moved from one workshop to another. Many of these long-standing practices persist, yet the status quo has changed in the context of economic crisis. Workers have intensified their ways of being flexible, and the state has deepened its mechanisms of surveillance and control. Primary targets are transnational family firms and workers.

In part, the economic downturn in Europe generally and Prato specifically translate into many Italians having lost their jobs or businesses and unemployment rates among young adults reaching 40 percent, among the highest in Europe after Spain and Greece.[12] For Pratesi to see foreign nationals succeeding when they are going bankrupt creates resentment, heartbreak, and despair. The future looks bleak. The fact that Chinese firms commonly do not follow standard working hours, and that they tend to be lackadaisical toward Italian labor laws, also fuels the flames of resentment—not to mention the ashes of forgetting. Easily and commonly forgotten are Prato's own rags-to-riches story made possible by an off-the-books economy.

Native son Edoardo Nesi recounts the city's decline in *Story of My People*, an award-winning memoir from the perspective of a reluctant third-generation textile mill owner. The book opens with Nesi recollecting the day in 2004 when he sold the family firm, T.O. Nesi & Figli. Selling the firm meant selling its history. By all means, it had a history. The narrator, born in 1964, tells a riveting family story about how at the end of World War II retreating German soldiers blew up nearly all of the textile factories, including a *capannone*, or industrial shed, that housed his grandfather's and great-uncle's production facilities. Soldiers then rounded up the townspeople at gunpoint. Nesi refers to them as "Nazi dickheads." They eventually cleared out. The hardworking Pratesi rebuilt from the rubble. At first, the family mill made blankets. With time, the firm's number one customers became none other than Germans themselves. Eventually, the old guard passed, and Nesi's father and uncle took over and shifted to making coat fabrics, one of which was made from regenerated wool, meaning recycled old clothes shredded into rags, then made into yarns and woven into fabrics—Prato's version of the Rumpelstiltskin straw-into-gold story. The fabrics, dyed in charcoal gray, black, and navy blue, were "classic men's colors," and the product was timeless: it did not change for thirty years (Nesi 2012, 18–19). What a contrast, those fabrics and coats that lasted three decades, with fast fashion, whose styles are as perishable as sun-ripened peaches.

The textile city's precrisis economic landscape had hundreds of intertwined microfirms working in different phases of the supply or production chain—"perfect little working models of the most exciting dream of capitalism, that exceedingly rare phenomenon that makes capitalism something verging on *morality*." For Nesi, the morality found its source in the fact that workers who went into business for themselves "had a good chance of succeeding, and thus taking the first step onto a society-wide escalator that never seem[ed] to stop climbing upward, creating wealth and distributing that wealth in a way that, while it may not be fair (it's never fair), is at least fine-grained and extensive." And the most fantastic quality was that "even dimwits made money, as long as they were willing to work" (Nesi 2012, 20).

Boom-era Prato may represent the dream of capitalism but hardly the reality if "even dimwits" could make money. Capitalism was never about equality—lest we confuse dreams with ideology, arrogance with fraternity. Such a small-firm-dominated economy reflected a heterodox form of capitalism, full of noncapitalist elements with all of its worker-owned firms, revolutionary labor struggles, and left-dominated political culture. The so-called Third Italy model became famous among labor scholars and economic sociologists, among others, for its diverse landscapes of unconventional capitalist strategies. Indeed, the very crookedness of capitalism comes into sharp relief when juxtaposed against the expectations for straight-ahead global capitalism. This straightness appears in the guise of mainstream economists who sing the praises of globalization for its infinite goodness and chastise Italian firms for their infinite incompetence to rise to global competitiveness; such economists time and again place blame on the small-firm business ethos that holds on to old workers and clings to quaint ideas of quality (see Nesi 2012, 47–54; Thomas 2007). Globalization's cadre of die-hard economists has sought to eradicate precisely such dreams. Their tools were the language and policies of free trade. Neoliberalism, if it was about nothing else, was about trickle-up economics and deregulation. Witness the new gilded age and unrivaled inequality (Piketty and Goldhammer 2014). Even in light of tremendous skepticism following the worldwide financial crisis, including alterglobalization movements that searched to create alternative political imaginations and economic subjectivities, neoliberalism soldiers on (Razsa 2015). And it is the irony of ironies that so-called free trade creates multitudes of people defined categorically as unfree—that is, "illegal," without ever having had a trial, fair or otherwise.

The morality of Prato's golden textile age, in Nesi's account, contrasts with the immorality of the variety of capitalism that has overtaken the city. Here, his nostalgia eerily resonates with the xenophobic *Chinese Siege*, as the journalist depicts Chinese family firms as suspect, referring to a cunning use of family networks that enable tricks of triangulation in a hidden economy (Pieraccini 2010, 43). After all, Chinese work distributes wealth in an unconventional way, across transnational borders, often outside the purview of the state and its neoliberal rules of the day.

In my role as ethnographer, I attended, co-organized, and even participated in various creative productions, screenings, exhibits, and initiatives that offered a humanizing antidote to rising xenophobia. During a visit in April 2011, as I was still wrapping my mind around the project's contours, my psychologist friend Anna Ascolti invited me to attend an avant-garde theater performance in Florence. Billed as an installation, choreographer Virgilio Sieni's *L'Ultima Cena_noi* (The Last Supper_Us) was performed in fifteen-minute actions in the intimate Cenacolo di Ognissanti museum. Domenico Ghirlandaio's Renaissance fresco, the *Last Supper* (completed in 1480), provided the backdrop for what followed: An unlikely group of thirteen male inhabitants of Florence gather to explore the margins of common breath as a passage toward recognizing oneself in the other, per the program notes. A long table is covered with gold flecks that appear to be pieces of a crown. The actors are all immigrants. The program provides their names and countries of origin (Albania, Angola, Cameroon, China, Colombia, Ecuador, Peru, Serbia, Sri Lanka). The barefoot men, clad in solid-colored shirts, stand still as statues on either side of the room, six on one side, seven on the other, lined up against the wall. The audience settles in—some sit on a mat on the floor, others on chairs, still others stand. The men begin to walk in slow motion. Music plays. They pose. They seem to fall. They make their way around to the backside of the table. Eventually, they sit. The performance is powerful. Yet the sensory message of universal human suffering is lost on some in our group. To the question, "What was it about?" someone interjects, "It's really about feeling it. You either feel it or you don't." I jotted in my field notes:

> Just before we got back into Prato Remo asked me if I liked Prato. I was half asleep in the back seat, but I perked up and said "Sì." "Really?" he asked. "You don't have to lie." Then I made my case. Florence is stuck in the past. (Obviously, there were exceptions.) It's stuck in the shadow of the Renaissance. Prato is a modern city. It has all the problems of a modern city even if it's small. It's fascinating.
>
> Remo: That's true. Right now, people from Prato put up with the situation, but they are oppressed by it. They need to figure out how to take advantage of it. Just like during the *dopoguerra*, the postwar period, how Prato took advantage when all the *meridionali* migrated here. (He also migrated when he was about two.) Prato has to figure out how to turn things around.

Individual and collective accounts suggest that Italians knew how to confront the trauma after the war. Globalization's challenges seem somehow insurmountable, as Remo's comment suggested. The action-choreography's surreal quality resonated. Men and women muscled up after the Nazi destruction of the factory city, and a majority of Prato's citizens embraced and nurtured a reputation as staunch leftists of the Italian Communist Party variety. It took more than fifty years to forget their deep hatred for fascism. It came as a surprise when that sentiment vanished into the annals of forgotten history and Prato lurched to the political right on the heels of the global economic crisis.

The integration of immigrants was a sensitive topic that extended from arts, politics, and health care to business, education, and tourism. One Saturday in July 2012, I spent the day with an old friend and her colleagues. All out-of-town Italians, they were eager to see what the city had to offer in the way of art and food. We had gone to the Museo dell'Opera del Duomo to see the cathedral's collection, including the Renaissance fresco gem *St. John the Baptist* by Fra Filippo Lippi. Afterward, part of the group gathered outside the cathedral's bricolage green-and-white marble facade and decided to go to another museum at the Church of San Domenico. At a certain point, they asked a man for directions. His reaction surprised them for several reasons: for assuming they were non-Italians, for being told they would have to go a long way (they were accustomed to the expansive city of Turin), and especially for being warned:

> But you are Italian!! I was already prepared to speak in another language. However, for the museum take the first street on your right, then at the first left continue for several hundred meters and on your left you'll find the museum. *Mi raccomando, non spingetevi oltre perché . . . da lì iniziano i cinesi!* I'm telling you, don't go beyond because . . . from there begin the Chinese!!

The local man's warning to his fellow countrymen was recounted over and over again that afternoon among friends. *Don't go beyond.* If they were to cross the walled city center's doorway onto Via Pistoiese, it was as though they would find themselves in another world. Little Wenzhou, as it was known, was hardly viewed as a friendly tourist destination as were older Chinatowns in the world, such as London, New York, or San Francisco. Instead, it was seen as a dangerous ethnic enclave. It was a place where Chinese, including the newest arrivals, subsisted and survived. Walls covered with hand-scrawled phone numbers advertising services of pretty women and massages attested to the precarious existence of many immigrants.

## Global Bodies, Local Value

At times in the course of human history, certain values dominate. The 1980s and 1990s, as David Graeber (2001, 89) suggests, will be remembered "as the era of the triumph of the World Market—one in which the most gigantic, totalizing, and all-encompassing universal system of evaluation known to human history came to be imposed on almost everything." Despite the global financial crisis of 2008 and its lingering effects, the free-market faithful, whether globalist or nationalist, continue to push neoliberal capitalism as the solution to human flourishing.

A major consequence of this supposedly universal system of evaluation is that commentators so often can see the globalized world only through a narrow lens of capitalism. This manifests itself in discourse—in how people talk about the world, in how the media represent the world, in what individuals and collectivities dream and desire. Anthropologists have long called for seeing and valuing diverse ways of being in the world. This applies to interpretations of global systems as well. New research on transnational mobility suggests the ongoing importance of grappling with the messiness of cultural exchanges and making sense of them. Julie Chu highlights the continuing relevance of Sahlins's observations, particularly concerning how the world system could just as well be put in the service of non-Western cultural logics as its own. Broadening cost-benefit approaches to studies of mobility and migration, Chu throws into question fundamental assumptions about globalization and its dispersed subjects interconnected across migratory poles (Chu 2006; Ma Mung 2004).

Such approaches enrich ways of applying anthropological thought. Anthropologists have long advocated against ethnocentrism: the belief that one's own group or culture is superior to others and the tendency for that belief to lead to judgments of another group according to one's own cultural values, standards, and practices. The concept reaches back to pioneers such as Franz Boas, Margaret Mead, Zora Neale Hurston, and Elsie Clews Parsons in the United States; Bronislaw Malinowski in Britain; Marcel Mauss in France; and Ernesto de Martino in Italy. In different ways, they and their protégés all advocated against ethnocentric interpretations and elite racial conceit. In other words, they sought to understand cultures on their own terms but with a healthy dose of criticism of dominant categories of interpretation. There exist numerous pushbacks against the assumption that a capitalist logic of value has taken over the world. Graeber's writings on anthropological theories of value have been inspirational for his understanding of value not just as price or symbols but also as action, so that value becomes "the way that actors see their own activity as a meaningful part of [society]" (Graeber 2001, 76). Tsing's work on the matsutake trade demonstrates through careful ethnographic work how these mushrooms begin and end their lives as gifts and thus convincingly shows how capitalist commodity value gets "created through tapping and transforming non-capitalist social relations" (Tsing 2013, 21). Such an approach counters much critical scholarship and popular analyses that are quick to embrace global capitalism and foreclose other interpretations.

The stakes are high. Discursive change stimulates the imagination and can manifest in new possible worlds. Critical geographers Katherine Gibson and Julie Graham draw our attention to another variety of "centrism" that has materialized. To describe it, they coined the term *capitalocentrism*. They do not situate this term in relation to ethnocentrism, in large part because of their radical feminist intellectual orientation. I see important connections. Their poststructural definition exposes superiority: "capitalocentric discourse has now colonized the entire economic landscape and its universalizing claims seem to have been realized" (Gibson-Graham 2006, 55). As evidence, they point to the most up-to-date hegemonic expression of contemporary economic activity: neoliberal global capitalism, which pedals in "freedom, individual wealth, unfettered consumption, and well-being trickled down to all" (ibid.). This makes possible a particular worldview; the subjects of this worldview tend to internalize what is considered to be normal and plain common sense. The converts, even in light of the most recent global financial crisis, remain positive about the promise of capitalism to the world. Why the coauthors find this upbeat attitude so problematic is that people broadly come to accept that a certain kind of economy calls the shots for action. People thus become blind to other possibilities. To intervene against capitalocentrism, their project focuses on language as a strategy to shake things up. They aim to make visible the heterogeneity in economic activity. To "destabilize capitalist dominance," they mindfully identify diverse economic activities and believe that much of this economic activity can be classified as noncapitalist—economic activity that is not simply wage labor produced for a market in a capitalist firm such as gifts, barter, self-employment, cooperatives, volunteering, informal economy—and that, taken together, all of this matters for understanding the world as it is and what it might be in the future.

The globalization narrative suggests a different triumph, one that stars globalization's protagonist: a species known as *Homo economicus*. This species is known for its defining characteristic as a utility maximizer. Such a trait is worthy of celebration, according to economic human's long list of famous and faithful adherents, from John Stuart Mill to Margaret Thatcher and Silvio Berlusconi to, of course, Donald Trump. The underlying story is that if everyone everywhere follows this "rational" model for human behavior, humans will flourish. Happiness will spread. Violence will decline. This is the basic tenet of utilitarianism. This basic tenet has nurtured neoliberalism. No matter the violence of globalization. No matter the ways that global capitalism warps society in unpredictable ways. According to the editors of *The Global Economic Crisis*, "humanity is at the crossroads of the most serious economic and social crisis in modern history" (Chossudovsky and Marshall 2010, xv). Or as Aurora, one of my unemployed, pension-in-waiting Italian friends in Prato called the current global moment, "the most inhumane of crises."

*Homo economicus* is a contested species with a contested history. His or her speciation is up for grabs. A number of founding economic thinkers used the term to describe what they cherished about modern humans: that they were self-interested, cold, and calculating rational actors. Utilitarian thinkers such as John Stuart Mill and Adam Smith embraced the idea of "economic man." They used it to justify the naturalness of the "free market." Perhaps it is no coincidence that sociology's founding father, Émile Durkheim, in light of his studies on suicide, paved the way for his own nephew, Mauss, to give birth to the nascent field of anthropology. Mauss posed a profound challenge to the free-market naturalists with his book-length essay *The Gift: The Form and Reason for Exchange in Archaic Societies*, first published in French in 1923–24 in the *Année sociologique*. The book continues to find an audience nearly a century later, as Bill Maurer (2016) remarks in a foreword to a new edition, because of its future orientation and reflections on how people might avoid repeating the horrors of world war as well as how economies based on sharing and solidarity might always already be within reach.

Forging an intellectual trail from sociology to anthropology, Mauss argued that there was nothing particularly natural about cold, calculating *Homo economicus*. He took the argument further. Not only was "economic man" not natural, but the arguments that had been marshaled in his favor were also based on faulty presuppositions. He drew on all sorts of evidence from ancient and non-Western societies to demonstrate the archaic character of human exchange, which he referred to as a gift economy—obligations to give, to receive, and to reciprocate. He argued that these principles were alive and well in modern humans. He sought to validate and reinvigorate these principles both in his intellectual writings and in his political engagement to revitalize France's cooperative economy.

As a scholar-educator working in a research university, I often point out that much of what characterizes my work is actually part of a gift economy: when a journal editor asks me to review a submitted article and, as a peer, to provide a written evaluation, I do so neither for pay nor for "free" but as a form of reciprocity. I know that others have done the same for me, when I submitted a manuscript to a peer-review journal, with the hope that my article would eventually get accepted for publication. Whether I offer extensive comments on a student's paper, grant proposal, or thesis, or when a student comes to my office hours, I do not charge a fee, nor are these offerings entirely free. The powerful framings and discourses of the market continue to obscure the existence of these principles and practices even though, then as now, they constitute a system—a "total social fact," or principles that structure the flow of human social relations. Similarly, Chinese workers and entrepreneurs who find their way to urban centers such as Prato may turn out to be spoilers of globalization's straightforward plot.

It would not be the first time that Mauss's insights have been prescient. Pierre Bourdieu, heavily influenced by Mauss's (1979) cross-cultural writings about body techniques, conducted his early fieldwork in late-colonial Algeria among the Kabyle, in the midst of the Algerian War (1958–62), and in a much later essay reflected on how shocked he was to learn what happened when peasants, individually and collectively, came into contact with the newly imported logics of the so-called rational economy. He recalls that he went to his field site thinking that the transplanted French economy was what it was— more or less a given. Precisely because certain ways of being come to be seen as inevitable and rational, he had not initially questioned them. He writes that nothing had prepared him to understand the economy as something entirely different, as he puts it, "*as a system of embodied beliefs*" (Bourdieu 2000, 24). He discusses effects on peasants in the process of becoming wage earners as nothing short of violence. He reveals a passionate commitment to expose what he had taken as a given—a utilitarian underpinning—was as "exotic" as anything local. He characterizes the "illusion" that buttresses "the ahistorical universality of the categories" that economists use rather than framing such a rational actor as the "product of a long collective history, and it has to be acquired in the course of individual history, in and through a labor of conversion which can only succeed in certain conditions." He notes how economic behaviors that were assumed to be elementary and universal (things such as working for a wage, saving, credit, birth control) had to be learned. It turns out that what we consider "rational" economic behavior was the product of quite particular historical conditions. As he quoted the French philosopher Henri Bergson as having observed, "It takes centuries of culture to produce a John Stuart Mill" (Bourdieu 2000, 25).

Moving beyond Mauss and Bourdieu, I draw inspiration from critical development scholars (Comaroff 2011; Escobar 2010; Ferguson 2009; Tsing 2013) to interrogate the Eurocentric foundations of development itself. In

Prato, the machinations of globalized development reflect a dramatic shift in the character of postwar industrialization. Throughout the book, I argue for an understanding of development from the "diaspora" through an intentional mooring in hybrid economic practices, such as reciprocity through networks of care, to disrupt the tyranny of hegemonic capitalism.

Asking the questions and parsing the methods that I have laid out has allowed me to open up aspects of globalization that the free-market discourse elides. Even in one of the most intense urban laboratories of globalization, people do not primarily behave in such a narrow, self-maximizing way. Characteristics of a human species other than *Homo economicus* animate life. My argument upends the stories that are possible to tell about globalization and its homogenizing effects. People who benefit most from the conventional story of utilitarianism, which has long since morphed into neoliberal capitalism, are invested in its perpetuation. The more people buy into it, the more its cogs are lubricated. I argue that even in an intensely globalized city, the economic system is far from homogeneous. It is, rather, a heterogeneous assemblage created from a tangle of human affects, discourses, practices, and encounters.

# PART ONE

# Chinese Immigration and the Made in Italy Brand

# Value

I had no idea what to expect when I was invited to an after-party for Pitti Uomo. The party was slated for a clothing store where my friend and collaborator Massimo Bressan was invited to make a rare DJ appearance after a ten-year hiatus. His adrenaline was palpable. The event was hard for me to picture—a party in a men's store? His girlfriend, Kate, was as bemused as I was. Being a hapless consumer of high fashion, I had to check the trade show's significance and, with *GQ* as my guide, found confirmation: "This unique, worldly mix is what makes Pitti Uomo so special and, in practical terms for *GQ* readers, where so many of next season's trends are first found among the rows and rows of show booths."[1] The fair is held biannually in Florence's Fortezza da Basso along with other industry events for women (Pitti W), for children (Pitti Bimbo), and for fabrics (Pitti Filati).

The idea of the after-party all started to click when we walked into Extreme, a hip men's boutique in Florence's alternative district, near Piazza dell'Indipendenza, whose owner combined ultracool rugged American wear with fashionable but down-to-earth Italian styles. Nudie Jeans and Vans were sold at European prices. Red Wing work boots mingled with locally branded sweaters woven from cottons and wools so fine that you could hardly help but fondle them. I've since seen a similar look at Banana Republic in a "heritage" section.

Bressan and another bearded DJ took turns spinning vinyl and filling the store with soul and swamp grooves. Big aluminum bins of ice were soon brimming with bottles of Budweiser. Being a native of St. Louis, with childhood memories of the smell of sweet malt that wafted from the Anheuser-Busch brewery, I felt right in my element. For the food, we had to walk outside into the cold January drizzle and around the corner into an empty art

FIGURE 2.1. Soul and swamp grooves added to the atmosphere of an after-party of Pitti Uomo, the men's fashion trade show, in a boutique clothing store in an alternative district of Florence.
Photo by Betsy Krause, 2013

gallery. It was simple Tuscan fare: panini of either freshly sliced roast pork or specially prepared tripe. I tried to follow Kate's ever-understated lead as she graciously and assuredly made her way to the chef serving the pork. The crowd offered plenty of eye candy. Not a tie in the place. No baseball caps. Not a man in a business suit. Just very stylish people. One after another. Beards appeared to be very in.

By the time we meandered back to the store, it had become a bit of a wet, frothy mess. Staff had brought out the Bud before they brought out the bottle openers. Guys were opening the bottles in all sorts of crazy ways. Some Germans used a lighter on several of our beer caps. Mine pretty much exploded and made a foamy puddle on the ground before I could drink it. It wasn't the only one. The floor was thoroughly doused—even in the window display. Miraculously, no beer soiled any of the garments, beautifully hung like objects of art.

Kate and I were amazed at how many women were wearing fur jackets or fur vests. One really stank—recent roadkill. It seemed as though a woodland cadaver enveloped her body. Crazy obnoxious. A couple of women wore ponchos with alpaca fleece cascading like furry waterfalls. I wouldn't have been caught dead in something like that. I struck up a conversation with one such fashionista and couldn't resist sharing a recollection from the 1970s, back when I was a Girl Scout. To get my sewing badge, I made a plaid felt poncho with blue fringe. The woman was quick to validate me: "Yes, ponchos have made a comeback, and they're so convenient. This season, with all the oversized shirts and sweaters, you really need a poncho instead of a jacket." I nodded politely. In the New England college town that I called home, with one boutique and its nearby line of big-box retail stores, I was far removed from such logics of convenience.

Kate and I shared a laugh afterward. We were hardly fashionistas. Especially not me. She was a natural beauty, at ease in her elegance, in a way that conveyed nonchalance and concealed effort to make style look easy and unaffected. Together, in an angle of the boutique away from the real guests, we recalled the story a friend had told us, of young Italian women who go out and strip or otherwise work as prostitutes just to have enough money to buy high-fashion clothes, shoes, purses, or whatnot. Oh, the possibilities for fashion fetishism!

The night wore on and the crowd thinned. I struck up a conversation with a middle-aged man standing alone, coolly taking in the scene in every detail, grooving on every beat. Johnny, it turned out, happened to be Extreme's owner. I complimented him on the party. He told me that the Bud rep had suggested he serve hotdogs, but he decided that would have been over the top. That's where he drew the line. The result was a compromise, he said: the Italian sandwiches with the artisan meats along with the American beer. The guy serving the *porchetta* was a famous local Florentine who made the best, he told me. Johnny and I got to talking about his inventory. He owned the company that made the sweaters sold in the store. The factory was located in Poggio A Caiano, the same southeast part of the province of Prato where I was living at the time. I told him about my project on families, immigration, and globalization. His firm made use of Chinese labor for only one phase of production, he said, *solo un passaggio*. He emphasized this point, that it was literally only one phase, to sew on collars. He stressed that it was because there simply weren't any Italians who did this phase anymore.

"What would happen," he mused, "if all the Chinese people in the world went to the moon?"

## Value and Made in Italy

I didn't know what to make of the moon comment. His tone was matter-of-fact. There seemed to be a pragmatic spirit underlying it. What was he getting at? In retrospect, the comment struck me as a remark about the centrality of Chinese workers in the global production chain and what consequences their sudden disappearance would have for the flow of goods, for the very mechanisms of the market. But why the moon? Why off the earth? In private and in public, Italians frequently commented about the migration of the Chinese into Italy. As with much popular discourse about immigrants, flood metaphors abound. In Prato, another common framing pointed to profound feelings of alienation. The moon comment seemed less outlandish when considered alongside these kinds of sentiments—sentiments of disorientation evoked alien entities or outer space. It brought to mind the comment by the local man from Prato, who had told our lost out-of-town friends *non spingetevi oltre*, don't go beyond this point, as a warning to not cross the threshold of the doorway in the city's intact medieval wall that led to the Chinese district.

Italy has held a unique position among high-income countries when it comes to making the things we wear. The *Economist* describes exports in "high-value sectors, such as fashion," as "particularly robust" (London 2013). But resilience has its limits. Michael Dunford and colleagues note that exports in Italy's clothing and textiles category witnessed a decline between 1995 and 2008, a phenomenon largely associated with trade liberalization. New rules all but eliminated quotas and shifted a good deal of outsourcing to low-wage countries. Within that category in Italy, however, textiles recorded a loss of jobs, whereas the clothing sector reported a gain—mostly due to Chinese entrepreneurs and laborers in Prato. The bottom-line value of the textile and apparel industry to the Italian economy has remained strong despite new rules of and players in the game.

In this chapter, I argue that Italy's ability to retain its position for so long and so well can only be understood if we look beyond aspects of value recorded on double-entry bookkeeping logs. Typically, people do not look to anthropologists to understand value. As Anna Tsing (2015, 439) has observed, "The most powerful theories of value in the economy these days hold that value is created by competition in markets." The most fundamental definition of value, thus, reduces it to price, which results from the link between sellers and buyers. In asking how supply chains that cut across continents create value, anthropologists such as Tsing offer some startling, yet convincing, findings about the very nature of commodities. Observations upend the reigning capitalist logic of value. Along with others concerned with how value making creates and organizes "meaningful difference" (Ferry 2013; Graeber 2001), Tsing's (2014) work demonstrates how capitalist commodity value taps and transforms social relations that are remarkably noncapitalist. I draw on such insights from the anthropology of value to examine the perseverance of the Made in Italy brand and its relative resilience in the face of globalized economies and global supply chains. In tracing its history, I show how the Italian "brand" rose from fascism like a field of red poppies sprouting from flotsam.

The flotsam-to-poppies analogy is no accident. The story I am about to tell involves a famous flood, massive rescue efforts, and beauty; it also involves humanitarian aid, antiwar student volunteers, art, and gifts. The Made in Italy brand's success would not have been possible without widespread postwar popularity in the United States and Europe. Exposing that history uncovers what lends the Made in Italy brand its symbolic capital as well as the historical sentiment that underwrites it, a sort of enduring added value, as it were, that sets the brand apart as different yet meaningful.

## Rejuvenating the Made in Italy Mark

The moon comment triggered me to think about the boutique and firm owner's professional challenge of staying one step ahead. In these parts, not many Italian sweater-firm owners or even subcontractors had stayed in the game. Just about everyone I knew and almost everyone they knew had gotten out some years ago. The small firms found themselves at the mercy of trade policies that opened the floodgates to cheap labor. How had Johnny managed?

Johnny enjoyed a reputation as a person who had a way of staying ahead of the trends, of having an eye for the understated.[2] Excited to be doing fieldwork, Bressan and I drove out of Prato center where we met with Johnny in his small firm nestled at the edge of the provincial town, beneath a steep hill where olive trees clung. The factory had distinctive paned windows and curved terra-cotta roof, a style that harked back to another era. Indeed, he confirmed that the structure was located in one of the town's original industrial-artisan districts. As he shared his life story with us, he revealed the popular culture sources of his inspiration: alternative music, cultural scenes, retro styles, and progressive politics. He was early to enter the modern globalizing apparel industry. Born in 1955 in Florence, he opened a used clothing store after graduating from high school and then another in 1975. In 1979, he opened the new clothing boutique, and after some years, in the early 1990s, he joined forces with an Italian distributor and started a brand, World Tribe. Johnny focused on the production and creation of the brand, helping to develop slogans such as "One World, One Love." He found himself traveling to China, Indonesia, and Bangladesh. He went to Thailand in search of a particular schoolboy bag—a shoulder-slung briefcase, the sort that students used. He was looking to import it. In Bangkok, he started asking around and "found out that the producers were Chinese—but Chinese in Bangkok, understand? Chinese in Bangkok." And so he asked his contact why this was the case, and the man told him, "'Look, in Bangkok the economy is completely monopolized by the Chinese because they are more, let's say, they work more than the Thai. The Thai are more relaxed, they think about other things, and the Chinese work and they are totally in charge of the economy.'" And then, reflecting a widespread sentiment, Johnny remarked, "Because the way of, let's just say, the way that the Chinese develop is really at the level of metastasis, in the sense that they grow and grow and destroy everything because at the level of price nobody can then compete, right?"[3] As a result, resentments grew.[4]

The World Tribe label thrived for a while. Eventually, it hit a wall. Consistency was nonexistent. There was no way to challenge or resolve problems. With all production delocalized and overseas, quality was falling apart. The most intense travel had coincided with Johnny marrying and having two children. The inconsistency in quality and the constant travel had left him in pieces. "I'd get home at night completely *spappolato*, destroyed." Eventually the brand unraveled. In 2002, he started a new partnership, the Group, specializing in knitwear manufacturing made back in Italy and marketed through trade shows such as Pitti in Florence and Bread&Butter in Berlin. He joked that the shift was one from "globalization" to "tribalization."[5] He was moving against the grain, anticipating a new strategy for creating value, one that played on recognizable emblems of authenticity.

An earthy cardboard-brown label dangled from one of the beautifully woven men's sweaters in the boutique. The words and images on the label as well as on the Group's website invited an analysis into understanding how value was being created in a globalized market. The website featured a photograph of a man in the form of a handsome giant, a Gulliver of sorts, sprawled out over a Lilliputian landscape with delicate features that evoked the Tuscan countryside: rolling hills covered in miniature rows of grapevines and olive trees. Silhouettes of little people roped in the sleeping giant with threads. The English-language page read:

> Founded in Tuscany in 1973, the knitting factory has developed an approach toward work combining tradition and a contemporary taste for classics.
>
> Garments are designed and manufactured in Carmignano, in the Medicean hills, a region full of agricultural and food traditions, rich in history and art.
>
> Our highly skilled workforce are [*sic*] as passionate as a craftsman who declares his endless love for his land giving his work of art his own personal character.

Core to the brand identity was an idea of authenticity that Johnny later told us he felt the Made in Italy mark had lost. His brand called forth not only the tradition but also the magic of handmade goods. It called forth a place well known for its attention to detail whether in the realm of culinary traditions, visual art, or history. In naming the Medicean hills, it indexed the Renaissance. Along with that history flowed forth a bundle of values, nothing short of a whole symbolic order known for its sense of natural beauty. These "sensorial constructs" are not merely icons of beauty but, as historian Dario Gaggio (2011, 90) argues, also brands in and of themselves. The brands receive power from the icon. In other words, they point to an "authentic narrative"—in this case, one that is connected to a particular territory. Through the process of branding, symbolic value gets converted into economic value. Moreover, what consumers or travelers experience as authentic destinations or products are ultimately embedded in specific histories that shapeshift and attach to differently valued narratives. As Michael Herzfeld (2004, 2) argues, "The increasingly homogenous language of culture and ethics constitutes a *global hierarchy of value.*" In this global hierarchy, commonsense assumptions of what is remarkable and beautiful in fact reflect the distribution of power worldwide. Claims of universal and absolute commonality call for questioning. How did places or properties come to be identified as possessing great value? Permanance and absoluteness are not what they appear to be. Herzfeld (2004, 17) discerns "a classic operation of hegemony, whereby the delicate creatures that we call local worlds are caught in the spider's web of global value and struggle."

In the case of the rural Tuscan landscape and the beauty associated with it, the specific history was not so pretty. Rural Tuscany offers tourists a sense of authenticity—coherent and fertile rural intimacy as contrasted with fragmented and sterile modern sprawl. An image of Tuscan hills, Gaggio (2011, 95) notes, "is believed to be the depiction of something authentic—of a coherent civilization or of a particular relationship between an artist and his or her physical surroundings." And yet Gaggio demonstrates how that landscape has been reinvented, branded, and marketed, how it went from crisis to mass exodus. The Tuscan "landscape of ruins," in Gaggio's (2011, 98) words, conceals its scars of abandonment. Initial revitalization in the 1960s followed political struggles that resulted in protections related to branding. European Union integration led to new regulatory controls. Such source protection standards equate to designations that heighten value; producers draw on cultural values and forge links to specific territories to generate authenticity with the ultimate purpose of enhancing economic value in the context of global capitalism (Cavanaugh and Shankar 2014, 52). Historically, not only did this politics in essence manufacture scarcity, but it also resulted by the 1980s in the dominant view that landscape was patrimony. A new kind of foreign tourism was also in the making: "Upper-class foreign tourists created colonies of art connoisseurs who aimed to relive and retrieve the glories of the Renaissance in front of audiences of their peers." Gaggio (2011, 92, 102–4) concludes that there was nothing inevitable about creating new land stewards—whether foreign tourists-turned-expats or "postmaterialistic peasant farmers" from sharecroppers-turned-Communists. Perhaps that is one irony of the giant Gulliver stretched across a nostalgic landscape being tied up by little people.

The tag attached with natural brown string to a men's sweater in the boutique had three panels of text in Italian. The first panel offered washing instructions handed down from the suggestions of "*nostre madri*"—our mothers. The middle panel provided background on the region where the firm is located, in a region known for its Denominazione di Origine Controllata (DOC)–certified products and slow foods. The third panel made clear the global sources for the raw materials, such as Australian or Peruvian wools or American pima cottons. The middle paragraph of that middle column was the most evocative:

> *L'amore per la vita naturale che soddisfa il corpo e per il sacro che illumine lo spirito, ispira ogni giorno il nostro lavoro nell'atmosfera incantevole che ha guidato anche il Pontormo nella creazione della Visitazione (1528) conservata nella locale chiesa di San Michele.*
>
> *Per questi motivi nelle etichette non scriviamo 100% Made in Italy bensì . . . Realizzato ad arte in Toscana.*

Every day our work gains inspiration from the love of natural life that satisfies the body and things sacred that illuminate the spirit. This same enchanting atmosphere guided even Pontormo in his creation of the *Visitation* (1528), conserved in the local church of Saint Michael.

For these motives we don't write on the label 100% Made in Italy but rather . . . realized as art in Tuscany.

In the case of Johnny's company, a strategy reclaimed the value of things local, of things Tuscan. Pointing to the natural world and to the spiritual world created something as intangible as beauty, something almost cosmological, something deeply spiritual, located in the soil and in the very essence of a place. These goods could boast an enchanting quality, an extension of the same force that guided the hand of a Renaissance artist in his creation. Beauty itself conveyed an otherworldly quality; it opened up the space of imagination, of possibility, of rebirth.

This place-based marketing was hardly coincidental, nor was it entirely disingenuous. During the interview with Johnny, I saw a woman sewing on a button that he told us was crafted from the wood of olive trees growing on the hills right above the factory. Tensions between desires for authentic place and necessities for global sophistication shaped this approach. There was something seductive about it—the Gulliver tied up with tiny ropes by little people. The giant slept in a dreamy place, a place of fantasy. The world being created was, at its core, sensual and sexy. The sexiness derived from the tension between things far away and exotic yet place-based and familiar. There was a back-and-forth at play between the strange and the familiar, the earth and the moon.

### Sorting Out Value and the Roots of the Made in Italy Brand

In some ways, value itself is otherworldly. It is, on the surface, inexplicable. As Malinowski observed nearly a hundred years ago, value is hardly self-evident. Malinowski set out in 1915 on a voyage to Melanesia to expand understandings of value through a study of "primitive economies." He had a full agenda. He sought to demonstrate that the field of economics was not a universal science with relevance everywhere and that its theories of the history of modern economic institutions were blinded by arrogance. Alternatives to modern economic systems existed. He went to great lengths to challenge the prevailing ethnocentric European idea that non-Westerners' economies were simple and irrelevant. In a 1921 essay in *Economic Journal*, he argued with a colleague, C. Buecher, who claimed that the "savages" were in a "pre-economic stage" (Malinowski 1921, 15). Malinowski viewed this as nothing short of rubbish. His ammunition was the nitty-gritty features of economic production. This included rites, roles, ceremonial objects, relations with divine spirits, rules governing gardening and other activities, networks of reciprocal relations, and gifts and countergifts. His research ignited a body of scholarship devoted to scientific as well as political projects of finding other possibilities to the cold, calculating species of *Homo economicus* so dear to capitalism and its free-market disciples.[6]

Malinowski made famous to the Western world the kula, an elaborate form of circular gift exchange involving shells.[7] This inter- and intra-tribal movement of goods involved the ongoing circulation of necklaces and arm shells over thousands of miles in the Trobriand Islands, an archipelago to the south and east of New Guinea.[8] Necklaces moved in a clockwise direction and arm shells in a counterclockwise direction. The practice, Malinowski (1922, 2) observed, "looms paramount in the tribal life of those natives who live within its circuit, and its importance is fully realised by the tribesmen themselves, whose ideas, ambitions, desires and vanities are very much bound up with the Kula." He sought to make sense of a type of value that mystified Western observers. As they traveled from east to west and west to east, through the hands of seafaring outrigger canoe masters, so-called trinkets accumulated histories, and these histories enhanced their value as well as their spiritual force.

The kula was anything but random. Malinowski (1922, 98) identified two principles: "that the Kula is a gift repaid after an interval of time by a counter-gift, and not a bartering" and "that the equivalent rests with the giver, and cannot be enforced, nor can there be any haggling or going back on the exchange."[9] Ultimately, kula was "rooted in myth, backed by traditional law, and surrounded with magical rites" (ibid., 85). The objects in kula were not owned but in a sense lent. Apparently, many were too small or too large even to be worn. To outsiders, all the commotion seemed silly.

What can we learn about what makes commodities valuable today from what made objects valuable in non-Western societies of a century past? The markets are vastly different, to be sure. But ultimately, value cannot simply be reduced to a mathematical formula, market price, or the cost to make it. Value is not absolute (Appadurai 1986). Nor can it be said to be merely in the eyes of the beholder. Marx's (1993) insights about use value and exchange value are of limited help even if they are important to keep in mind: use value as a commodity's utility and reflection of the useful human labor embodied in it, and exchange value as a quantitative relation that changes from time to time and market to market. Dissecting these differences only goes so far to explain our puzzle. What accounts for value in a globalized economy? What is the story behind how the Made in Italy label acquired value as a generic brand? What can this history tell us about value generally speaking, for now and for the future?

As I was writing this chapter and living in Durham, North Carolina, I happened into a T.J. Maxx, the clothing chain that bills itself as selling designer brands at discount prices. A sign above a round rack of wool and blended-wool cardigans caught my eye:

be a standout gifter
Made in Italy

The top part of the sign was rendered in white lettering against a rectangular green background, with the bottom part presenting the white lettering against a larger rectangular black background. The implication of the message to "be a standout gifter" was that the shopper who chose one of these sweaters as a gift would set himself or herself apart from others; the value of a sweater crafted in Italy was somehow superior to sweaters crafted elsewhere, for example, in China. In presenting the message in lower-case lettering, the marketers were also attempting to create a subtle message. They did not need to shout out this message with all caps or exclamation points because shoppers with taste would know it to be true. For consumers who had forgotten that country of origin might make a difference in quality, the sign offered a gentle and welcome reminder.

As fashion scholars have observed, the Made in Italy label has become synonymous with good taste, elegance, style, and quality—the last referring to attention to design, fabrics, as well as craftsmanship.[10] How and when did Made in Italy gain its reputation? When did people begin to fetishize it? How did it become an object of fascination? The answer has a good deal to do with Italian fashion during fascism, the postwar Americanization of the economy, and purposeful as well as indirect linkages with the Renaissance in the buying public's social imaginary.

The birth of modern Italian fashion dates to 1951. It assumed an international profile only in the 1970s (see Belfanti n.d.; Merlo and Polese 2006; Segre 1999; Settembrini 1994; Steele 1994). Various historians contrast the exclusive, custom-fit haute couture with an emerging, democratized ready-to-wear clothing industry. Of course, tailors and designers existed in Italy before its industry's birth, but they had limited influence or recognition in the world of fashion. They could hardly compete with the dominant Parisian haute couture houses, with their prestige deriving from proximity to the court of Versailles and their reputation among elites as the go-to place for good taste. Despite a weakened fashion monopoly after the war, Parisian prices were relentlessly high, a fact that "chilled relations with the most important clients, the buyers for leading American department stores" (Settembrini 1994, 484). Furthermore, the future hub of fashion was up for grabs as the symbolic impact of an American lifestyle, especially New York, began to spread. Consumers sought comfort and affordability (see especially Merlo and Polese 2006, 420).

The significance of such a specific birth date can be traced to a fashion show that put Florence on the map as one of the main contenders to follow in the footsteps of Paris. Buyers leaving Paris were lured to Florence for a fashion presentation on February 12, 1951. The brainchild of the event was Giovanni Battista Giorgini, a descendant of a noble Florentine family whose knowledge of the American market derived from his experience as a buyer of Italian artisan products—ceramics, glass, lace, embroidery, and straw—for several US department stores (Merlo and Polese 2006, 424; Belfanti n.d., 13).

In Giorgini's words, "the aim of the evening is to enhance the value of our fashion" (Belfanti n.d., 14). It did so through displaying to its attendees a sort of genetic code of aesthetics that accounted for Italian style.

In 1952, Giorgini organized another show in Florence's opulent Palazzo Pitti, where a "myth of continuity" with the Renaissance was launched and staged for the world's most influential fashion trendsetters of the day (Belfanti n.d., 5).[11] The choice of Pitti was no coincidence. What better icon of the Renaissance than a Medici palace? As a former residence of the grand dukes of Tuscany, with its painting, sculpture, and costume collections as well as extensive Boboli Gardens, the Sala Bianca (White Ballroom) served as an elegant site for the show and an ideal place to persuade its attendees of the continuity between artistic heritage and modern taste. As fashion historian Carlo Belfanti (n.d., 4) recounts:

> The author of this happy "invention" . . . had clearly understood the con-
> cept that connecting fashion creativity to the Italian artistic heritage would,
> besides offering the interesting opportunity to attract the numerous wealthy
> foreign visitors to the artistic treasures of Italy as clients, also endow the Ital-
> ian product with an extraordinary cultural legitimization, placing it directly
> in the centre of a well-known, appreciated, not to say indisputable, tradition
> of "good taste": that of the Renaissance. Connecting Italian fashion with Re-
> naissance Italy meant in fact introducing a kind of *ante literam* guarantee
> of provenance—a "country branding"—recognized throughout the world,
> which, at the same time, evoked the splendor of a period in which Italian taste
> was a model to follow and imitate.

References to the "Renaissance effect," as Belfanti notes, have become a part of the story that Italian entrepreneurs and managers tell about themselves; such references have become conventional wisdom. News coverage of those early events, such as in *Life* and the *Los Angeles Times*, seem drunk on Renaissance genius.[12] The Palazzo Pitti itself over time "became a sort of factory seal for genuine Italian fashion,"[13] writes Settembrini (1994, 488) in the catalog for the Guggenheim exhibition *The Italian Metamorphosis, 1943–1968*. The location was eventually moved elsewhere, but the name stuck, as in the Pitti Uomo men's fashion event.

Although hardly anyone contests the magnificence of the artistic and cultural production of the Renaissance, it is the unbroken continuity between Renaissance craftsmanship and Italian fashion that critical historians challenge as being more manipulation than truth—an invention similar to other invented traditions linked to creating a sense of communal brotherhood in nation-states where community can only be imagined (Belfanti n.d., 4).[14]

Evidence of the discontinuity of great Italian artistry across the centuries can be found in a number of accounts. Consider the testimony of travelers of the Grand Tour, who chose Italy as one of their key destinations for its artistic treasures and agrarian landscape but not for its able craftsmen or refined products. The poet Shelley in 1818 offered this account in a letter: "There are two Italies, one made up of green meadows and a limpid sea, of the mighty ruins of antiquity, or airy peaks and of the warm radiant atmosphere that envelops all things. The other consists in the Italians who live in the present time, in their works and in their manners. The first is the most sublime and pleasing contemplation that may be conceived of by human imagination, the second the most degraded, repellent and disgusting" (cited in Belfanti n.d., 8). Nearly a century later, D. H. Lawrence in his *Etruscan Places* contrasted "a vivid, life accepting people who must have lived with real fullness" with the people living in the area between Tarquinia and Vulci in 1927. Such joyful characteristics of the Etruscans were lost with the Roman Empire, he asserted. "It is different now. The drab peasants, muffled in ugly clothing, straggle in across the waste bit of space, and trail home, songless and meaningless" (Lawrence 1957, 72).[15] The ugly clothing of these peasants was hardly the material to inspire Made in Italy ascendancy in the fashion world.

Images of impoverished peasants living in southern Italy were produced from books such as Carlo Levi's (2000) memoir *Christ Stopped at Eboli*, which portrays the Basilicata region during the fascist period of 1935–36 when he was exiled there, or Edward Banfield's (1958) controversial *The Moral Basis of a Backward Society*, which argued that untrusting villagers' lack of morality could explain the lack of a functional civil society. His work was both admired and reviled. Sydel Silverman (1968), who criticized his analysis, suggested that these villagers' values were not simply innate but derived from economic ills connected to overpopulation, underemployment, land hunger, and unproductive agriculture. For Silverman, values were not the basis of society but rather derived from social structure and organization.

Certain moments of continuity were handily forgotten. Seeds of an "Italian style" were sown during fascism, including tendencies toward elegance and ease. Eugenia Paulicelli (2004) traces this legacy in *Fashion under Fascism: Beyond the Black Shirt*. References to the Renaissance were countless in textile trade periodicals and fashion magazines of the era, but the Italian reputation for fashion was reserved for the fascist state. In the interwar period, the Italian economy largely closed to the world under Benito Mussolini's national project of economic self-sufficiency known as autarchy. Internally, Italian fashion houses began to compete with the French. This was largely a nationalist project. Paulicelli (2004, 41) attributes fascism's preoccupation with fashion to its envy of the French, who enjoyed a strong and unified national identity compared to Italy's fragmented national sensibility: "French couture and design were the enemy to defeat or, almost in Oedipal mode, the father to kill in order to build an autonomous identity." Paulicelli (2004, 75) demonstrates how, in fascism's ideological plan for progress, fashion was one of the main industries targeted due to its potential to contribute to "the nation's sense of self." This goal of creating a citizenry who thoroughly identified with Italy—as opposed to individuals more connected to their hometowns, as referenced in the old term *campanilismo*, a parochialism as delineated by the toll of the bell tower—was realized in no small part through propaganda, such as posters that portrayed ideal gendered subjects: Italian men were depicted as strong and athletic and contrasted with Italian women who were shown as curvy and fashionable. Newsreels during film screenings were also used to sell Italian fashion through *italianità*, a policy of exalting nationalism through regional differences also designed to counter French hegemony. Finally, a conscious strategy to expand the textile industry promoted regional handicrafts while also developing new technologies and "intelligent fibers" (Paulicelli 2004, 21).

Ultimately, according to Paulicelli, the project to nationalize the fashion industry was a failure. She highlights two reasons. First, workers and consumers did not fall into line, proving the regime to be incapable of creating a unified image of a social body. Second, the imposition of rigid models for dressing was at "loggerheads" with the characteristic of innovation so fundamental to the fashion industry (Paulicelli 2004, 143). If it seems strange that the fascist period would have inspired sartorial and industrial creativity, it is worth recollecting that fascism offered a good deal of rhetoric even as it inspired cultural production related to its version of modernity. Umberto Eco notes in an essay in the sturdy Guggenheim catalog that the creative experiments that fascism allowed were not signs of "democratic openness" but rather examples of "ideological confusion."[16]

The opening of Italy after the war created new opportunities and new vulnerabilities. The Italian economy became somewhat Americanized.[17] The Marshall Plan funneled money into industrial districts and also had a strong hand in shaping the strength of political parties particularly during the Cold War years. The province of Florence was a major beneficiary. A new industrial district named Macrolotto 1 was created in the sprawling flatlands outside the medieval wall of Prato, known as the "city of rags," for its historic textile industry that specialized in regenerating wool from secondhand clothes.[18]

Meanwhile, three cities competed to become the capital of Italian fashion: Florence, Rome, and Milan. The last would eventually prevail, according to economic historians Merlo and Polese, because of three major actors, largely rooted in Milan, who helped to exploit the American market to the benefit of Italian fashion: the Association of Clothing Industrialists (Associazione industriali dell'abigliamento), the American Chamber of Commerce for Italy, and the Milan-based department store La Rinascente. Is it not suggestive that the department store, in blatantly naming itself the Renaissance, offers an easy identification between the glorious past and the buyer's body obtainable through symbolic-consumerist rebirth? Italian industrialists found modern inspiration in the American growth model and the women's clothing sector, whose strength was "cheap, fashionable clothes whose colors and designs were continually renewed in order to stimulate constant change in women's wardrobes" (Merlo and Polese 2006, 436). The Italian clothing association followed and adopted American marketing strategies both within and beyond Italy. Fashion historian Nicola White (2000) argues that American postwar financial support, involvement in industrial organization and manufacturing methods, influence of lifestyle, and a keen market were central to the development of an internationally renowned Italian style. Merlo and Polese (2006, 446) emphasize the potency of the US market to provide the "necessary size and purchasing power to fuel the Italian fashion business." In terms of cultural aspects, strong connections with cinema, with Italian designers working in Hollywood and Rome influencing what viewers saw stars wearing on the big screen, also held sway. Salvatore Ferragamo is frequently cited as a renegade in forging a reputation for tastefully marrying craft and industrial techniques. As early as 1914, he attracted the patronage of Hollywood residents for his "hand-made, exclusive designs," returned to Italy in 1927, and set up a shop in Florence within two years (White 2000, 36). In the postwar era, industrial design products from cars and scooters to typewriters and furniture were also gaining purchase.

Even if continuity with the Renaissance was a myth, the Renaissance itself was a necessary and brilliant foil to compete with Parisian prestige. Stylistic and historical references to the Renaissance carried tremendous symbolic capital and ultimately offered an authoritative reference point for the emerging Italian fashion business. At the same time, the social revolution of the late 1960s, according to Settembrini (1994, 493), "amounted to a death sentence for the old concept of fashion" in which Paris was more deeply invested. Vehement antifashion sentiments gave way to the Made in Italy success phenomenon as the hub of Italian fashion migrated from pretty Florence to edgy Milan.[19]

The Made in Italy mark ascended to the level of national narrative without, somehow, traversing the "very thorny terrain" of national identity, which fascism had emphasized in a particularly "exasperating" way (Paulicelli 2001,

456). In part, this is a mystery. In part, the explanation may well rest in a confluence of events: postwar reconstruction aid, Cold War politics, and a disastrous turn of events that by chance strengthened the myth of continuity with the Renaissance. Cementing ties with the Renaissance had the effect of distancing a national brand from the vulgar and violent sort of nationalism that fascism had imposed on its citizens. The Renaissance was not politically threatening. As such, it allowed for a brand image far removed from labor and political struggles that became particularly poignant with the student protests of 1968 and the subsequent popularity of the Italian Communist Party, which flourished until the early 1990s.

## The Value of a Flood

To this postwar history of Made in Italy, I would like to add a watershed event (no pun intended): the devastating flood of November 4, 1966, when the Arno River surged over its banks after two days of torrential rainfall that equaled one-third of the normal amount for a year. In just forty-eight hours, nineteen inches of rain fell. Some thirty-five miles upstream from Florence, at Lévane Dam, engineers opened strained floodgates (Judge 1967, 6; Reddy 1967, 206; Taylor 1967, 126). Water, mud, and heating oil deluged 1,300 works of art and millions of books, manuscripts, and archival materials. All of this was reported widely in the press. The artistic loss overshadowed human suffering in both international and national coverage and received the bulk of the humanitarian response (Debs 2013). Ultimately, the dramatic events of the flood, and the groundswell of fund-raising and rescue efforts that followed, served as an unintentional marketing campaign for the value of things Italian. I had my own epiphany about Italy's reputation as a place of beauty as I pored over old books, articles, and archival documents. The related discourses and activities bolstered associations between the generic Italian brand and its continuity with the Renaissance, not only for elite women and men but also for average American consumers who, by the 1960s, were increasingly shopping in department stores and buying readymade clothing.

Evidence for the growing esteem of all things Italian, and later the Italian brand itself, can be found in periodicals as well as archival materials. The flood was documented within the year in numerous trade and popular publications: *ArtNews, Burlington Magazine,*[20] *National Geographic, Newsweek, Reader's Digest, Saturday Review,* among others, featured articles about the flood and its aftermath. As the author of *Dark Water* recalls, "I knew about the flood. In Minnesota, where I grew up, we'd heard about it at the time, for weeks, in issue after issue of *Life* magazine" (Clark 2008, 6). One reviewer described *A Diary of Florence in Flood*, published the next year by Simon & Schuster, as "concise, unassuming, authentic. In spirit and form it is admirably Florentine. . . . It is a tribute to man, that strange, beauty-loving animal" (Cronin 1967, 24).

In October 1967, the inside cover of *Reader's Digest* boasted a readership of "over 28 million copies bought monthly in 13 languages." That same issue featured a story about the flood, "Up from the Mud—A Second Renaissance for Florence." The article begins, "With last November's disastrous flood, this treasure house of Western civilization found itself, overnight, a morass of ruined landmarks, defaced heirlooms and battered masterworks. But, with help from all over the world, the fabled city is swiftly returning to greatness." Early on, the article quotes Elizabeth Barrett Browning who had described the Arno as "a crystal arrow in the gentle sunset." The article reports how, just hours before the river crested, the city's mayor, Piero Bargellini, was attending a dinner for industrial workers in the "fashionable" Grand Hotel, where they were shown a film about the Mississippi River. How ironic, or prescient, that the mayor quipped, "The Mississippi is a great river. But if our Arno continues to rise, it will be an even greater one." Reportedly, the crowd had chuckled appreciatively. Little did they know that a flood nearly as bad as the one of 1333 was about to gush into their city.

The damage was savage. In case subscribers of *Reader's Digest* did not know the significance of the devastation, they would soon receive an education. The article's author wrote: "'All Florence is a work of art,' Gen. Dwight D. Eisenhower had cautioned his commanders as they approached the Renaissance city in World War II. Here Leonardo da Vinci painted some of his masterpieces and Michelangelo carved his immortal David. Here Galileo improved the compound microscope and Dante wrote his first love poems to Beatrice. Now the treasures spared by war were assaulted by the flood" (Reddy 1967, 208). Even the Nazis recognized certain things of value in the city: Hitler called Florence "the jewel of Europe" and gave orders that "retreating Germans should limit their destruction to the Arno bridges, all save the Ponte Vecchio," the charming six hundred–year–old bridge lined with jewelry shops. "And so Florence was spared" (Cronin 1967, 24).

The mayor, initially marooned in the Palazzo Vecchio with about forty-five others—including a just-married couple and a convict, whose presence is never explained but seems par for the course of natural disasters (Anon. 1967a, 193; Taylor 1967, 20)—soon put out an international call for help. The world responded: German, Austrian, and American supplies, English powdered milk and vaccines, Scottish blankets, Soviet Union relief aid, Dutch water-decontamination equipment. The Florentine Relief Fund coordinated efforts of four groups: Italian-American Chamber of Commerce, America-Italy Society, Help the People of Florence, and the Clarion Music Society. Entities that raised money or donated clothing include the Catholic Relief Fund, Red Cross, Il Progresso Italo-Americano, Amalgamated Clothing Workers, the Italian Historical Society of America, and the US government.[21] Prominent art historians from Brown University and Harvard were leading the way to form the Committee to Rescue Italian Art (CRIA). By November 8, 1966, the committee sent two experts to Florence and Venice to assess the situation and officially incorporated on November 14, moved its offices to New York City, formed subcommittees, and set a goal to raise $2.5 million to restore and repair damaged works of art. Organizers moved quickly to establish local chapters across the country. Sent from the national headquarters at 717 Fifth Avenue in New York City, the *CRIA Newsletter* dated December 5, 1966, lists the following locations: Boston, Baltimore, North Carolina, Southern California, Virginia, New Jersey, Texas, Iowa, New York City, northern Illinois, Philadelphia, Wyoming, Connecticut, Providence, New York, Kansas-Nebraska-Topeka. CRIA coordinator Richard G. Carrott noted:

> It seems to me that one of the main problems facing us will be to maintain interest now that the initial enthusiasm might begin to wane. The point remains that the flood was a catastrophe: enormous damage was sustained, and, although some things have been lost forever, much can be saved. But this can only be accomplished if we raise the money that is needed. This is a grave responsibility in our time which we must all assume.[22]

Carrott's humble call to sustain interest and accept responsibility was a harbinger of CRIA's eventual far-reaching influence. The newsletter suggested fund-raising activities that had been and could be organized: advertisements, benefit concerts, benefit plays and films, exhibitions, lectures, art auctions, resale of reproductions, direct mail solicitation, social activities, press releases. Other events would eventually include fashion and coiffure shows, cocktail or champagne parties, luncheons, film screenings, and panel discussions.[23] One of the earliest events on December 20, 1967, enjoyed support from John V. Lindsay, the mayor of the City of New York, who invited New Yorkers to attend the Clarion Concert for Italian Flood Relief and donate to victims of flood disaster: "I urge you to generously support this important effort to bring aid both to the families and friends of so many New Yorkers, and to help in the restoration of a great cultural heritage."[24]

Appointed as CRIA's honorary president was none other than the American queen of style, Jacqueline Kennedy. Her reputation for style encompassed

public and private life. She had earned a reputation for spending money lav-
ishly on her and Jack's house's design—a project that biographer Sarah Bradford (2000, 116) describes as part of a desire to "give her house the touch of
class that Kennedy homes notably lacked"; this desire extended to successful attempts at transforming Jack Kennedy's life from "meat-and-potatoes
Kennedy family style" to "putting him on the level his WASP and European
friends enjoyed." Her appointment coincided with a period in her life when
she had come out of a deep depression following President Kennedy's assas-
sination and was "traveling frenetically" to visit "the Beautiful People on both
continents," which in January 1966 had included Rome, where "seamstresses
worked through the night to make Jackie a black dress for an unscheduled
visit to the Pope" (Bradford 2000, 313). Committee members must have been
extremely well connected to appoint someone as prominent as Jackie Kennedy to serve as their honorary president.

CRIA moved quickly. Initial allocations were made in December. Within
a month, fifty branches of the committee had formed across the country.[25]
Within ten months, CRIA had grown to sixty-five chapters and raised nearly
$2 million (Reddy 1967, 215). Some evidence will need to be gathered, but I
would like to suggest that the flood, together with Jackie Kennedy's appointment and the plea for aid and subsequent international awareness of the
value of Italian art, were enormously significant in terms of spreading love
for things Italian and the Renaissance.

Jackie Kennedy reportedly appeared at a gala in May 1967 for "The Italian Heritage" exhibit, which *Newsweek* described as the rescue committee's
"most interesting benefit so far." The exhibit was held at New York's Wilden-
stein gallery. The catalog's preface by Bates Lowry, chairman of CRIA's National Executive Committee, noted the "swift formation of CRIA and the
continued commitment of its members" as "encouraging testimony to the
life and strength of the humanist tradition in our country."[26] Apparently, being part of this humanist tradition was a draw for members of high society.
The guest list reads like a who's who of New York City elite, beginning with
the Honorable and Mrs. Nelson A. Rockefeller; His Excellency Mr. Piero
Vinci, Italian ambassador to the United Nations; and the Honorable Vit-
torio Cordero di Montezemolo, consul general of Italy, and the Marchesa
di Montezemolo. It continues in alphabetical order with the names of more
than sixty couples (e.g., Mr. and Mrs. Frederick B. Adams, etc.), and lists the
names of twenty-two women members of the New York Benefit Committee
giving dinner parties. The exhibition was hailed as demonstrating "the cultural debt of the western world to Italy," a prominent theme in the call for

support.[27] A CRIA press release went so far as to frame the exhibit itself as a tribute to a debt owed:

> Planned as a distinctively American tribute to the debt that Western civiliza-
> tion owes to the art and culture of Italy, the exhibition includes examples
> by more than 40 Italian painters and sculptors and by 16 who represent the
> diffusion of the Italian tradition to France, Germany, the Netherlands, Swit-
> zerland and Spain. Side by side with famous Italian artists such as Donatello,
> Verrocchio, Giovanni Bellini, Mantegna, Titian, Tintoretto and Veronese ap-
> pear such notable masters of other national schools as El Greco, Velasquez,
> Holbein, Rubens, Van Dyck, Francoise Clouet, Poussin and Claude Lorrain.[28]

CRIA's emphasis on the debt that Western civilization owed to Italy for its art and culture could not have been clearer. What is obvious, yet none-theless needs highlighting, is that this "distinctively American" debt was not incurred through a monetary loan. Rather, the source of debt burden was none other than the gift of humanism that the Renaissance gave to the world through its intellectual and artistic legacy.

The exhibition director, Charles Seymour Jr. of the Yale Art Department, in an interview with *Newsweek* similarly reminded the reading public of the significance of Italy to the Renaissance: "For four centuries all of Europe was influenced by the Italians, who had generated what may have been the most revolutionary and far-reaching intellectual and artistic movement in Western Europe" (Anon. 1967b, 89).

Playing to the sentiment of responsibility to reciprocate in essence is pre-cisely what Marcel Mauss (1990) suggested in his classic essay *The Gift* and the archaic principles to give, receive, and reciprocate. In repaying this debt through supporting the exhibit, attending a benefit, or making a donation, supporters could prove the strength of the humanist tradition in the United States. They could also gain prestige from participating in something so grand.

*National Geographic* continued the crash course on Italy's contribution to Western heritage in July 1967, featuring a forty-three-page spread on the flood and its aftermath: "It is fair to say that much of what we know today of painting and sculpture, or architecture and political science, of scientific method and economic theory, we owe to the artists, politicians, statesmen, bankers, and merchants of the Renaissance—that explosion of intellectual artistic energy in Italy between 1300 and 1600" (Judge 1967, 2).

An event that brought international attention to the cause was the auc-tioning off of a painting donated by Pablo Picasso, and a CRIA press release used the success as evidence of the widespread public desire to preserve cul-tural heritage:

$105,000 was bid for *Femme Couchée Lisant*, the painting donated by Pablo Picasso to the Committee to Rescue Italian Art, over National Broadcasting Company's trans-Atlantic spectacular, "Brave Picasso!" last night. The hour long color program celebrating the great master's works, culminated in an international auction reaching bidders in Paris, London, Dallas, Fort Worth, Los Angeles, and New York. The auction, conducted in the New York NBC studio by Sotheby's Peter Wilson, moved quickly to the winning bid of $105,000 offered by the Fort Worth Museum of Fine Arts.

On the open market, it was estimated that the painting would sell for $70,000. The combination of television excitement and of the strong desire to assist CRIA in conserving the many damaged art works, from the grandest monuments to the page manuscripts, are the causes attributed to raising the bidding over the hundred thousand dollar mark.

Bravo Picasso! and, Thank you, Picasso! for having contributed so generously to our cultural heritage, first through your work of art and now through your assistance in rescuing what remains of our cultural heritage in Florence.[29]

Shortly after the auction, CRIA reached the $1 million mark, crediting this milestone in part to Picasso's gift and announcing grants to salvage damaged paintings.[30]

While this fund-raising effort was clearly out of reach for average TV viewers, others were more accessible. The array of activities on college campuses, in communities, and even at high schools was impressive. Several campuses devoted an entire week to the cause. The University of California Medical Center at Berkeley planned a "Florence Week." The University of California, Riverside, campus held a "CRIA Week." City College in New York designated "Rescue Italian Art Week." Events included exhibits, films, lectures, raffles, and dramatic productions. By May 1967, organizers across the country had booked a total of 130 screenings of the documentary *Florence: Days of Destruction* filmed by Franco Zeffirelli during and immediately after the flood and narrated by Richard Burton;[31] one press release addressed to residents in Syracuse made reference to "the full length version, in color, which aroused widespread praise in its TV presentation."[32]

Popular appeals of CRIA organizers also occurred during college athletic events. An undated document, likely sent to members in November 1966, offered this "timely suggestion":

Football games (and other sports events) provide an ideal captive audience of students, faculty, and general spectators for a CRIA appeal. If televised the appeal can also reach a large area audience. At the Harvard-Brown and the Yale-Princeton games last weekend, the following appeal was found both attention-riveting and successful when broadcast during halftime:

AN ANNOUNCEMENT ON BEHALF OF MRS. JOHN F. KENNEDY,
THE HONORARY PRESIDENT OF THE COMMITTEE TO RESCUE ITAL-
IAN ART. IN ORDER TO PREVENT THE GRAVE DAMAGES TO ITAL-
IAN RENAISSANCE ART, ARCHITECTURE, LIBRARIES, AND ARCHIVES
CAUSED BY THE RECENT DISASTROUS FLOODS FROM BECOMING
PERMANENT LOSSES, WE NEED YOUR HELP NOW. TEAMS OF CON-
SERVATION EXPERTS AND SHIPMENTS OF RESTORATION MATERI-
ALS ARE NEEDED IMMEDIATELY AND IN LARGE QUANTITY. WON'T
YOU PLEASE GIVE AS MUCH AS YOU CAN TO HELP PRESERVE THESE
DAMAGED WORKS OF ART AND LIBRARIES—THE VERY CORNER-
STONE OF OUR CIVILIZATION.
    SEND YOUR CONTRIBUTION, WHICH IS TAX DEDUCTIBLE, TO:
CRIA, INC., P.O. BOX 1414, PROVIDENCE, RHODE ISLAND 02901

Another phenomenon that helped to spread appreciation for the value
of Italian heritage was that of student volunteers who hailed from across
Europe, the United States, and Canada. Giorgio Batini's (1967a, 1967b) *Arno
in Museo*, published simultaneously as *The River Arno in the Museums of
Florence* within the year, recounts how hitchhikers converged on Florence.
"Wonderful youth. Call them beatniks, call them long-haired pansies, call
them what you will. . . . They asked for nothing in return for their labour:
they came, as they aptly put it, 'to save culture'" (Batini 1967a, 30). Referred
to as mud angels, muddy angels, or blue angels—after the blue jeans that
became covered with mud—they were said to provide "perhaps the greatest
lift of all" (Reddy 1967, 215). Several American universities with programs in
Florence were among those whose students volunteered: Harvard, Stanford,
Smith, Syracuse, Florida State, and Gonzaga. Through their toils, they also
received an education in the value of art, manuscripts, and other cultural
resources, such as those housed in the Uffizi and Biblioteca Nazionale, and
undoubtedly returned home to spread the word (Zachert 1970).[33] The Syracuse Students for Florence Relief Committee clearly felt they owed something
back to the Florentines themselves. This spirit of reciprocity, firmly rooted in
noncapitalist gift principles, appears in a student press release:

> Just as the loss of a Cimabue crucifix has broken the hearts of millions of art
> lovers around the world, the losses of the people of Florence, Italy have bro-
> ken the hearts of the Syracuse University students who have been welcomed
> into their homes for the last seven years. The art lovers have organized and
> have begun a mass restoration of the flood-devastated city—the Syracuse stu-
> dents have also organized to form the Syracuse Students for Florence Relief
> Committee.

Since 1959, hundreds of Syracuse University students studying in the Syracuse Semester in Italy have lived with Florentine families. Today there are
roughly 60 families who welcome American students into their homes. Now
many of these families have no homes.[34]

The full extent of the damage was reported as one hundred people
drowned; hundreds of horses and farm animals killed; four thousand families left homeless; eleven thousand citizens with serious losses; six thousand
shops and seven hundred restaurants, bars, and *trattorie* destroyed; fifteen
hundred works of art; eighteen churches; and millions of priceless books
and manuscripts damaged or ruined. "Single greatest loss to art" was how
*National Geographic* described the damage done to Giovanni Cimabue's
*Crucifix*, which was painted around 1280 and hung in the Church of Santa
Croce, where invading water reached twenty feet and left "a greasy film of
nafta—thick, black furnace oil flushed from the city's fuel tanks."[35] The crucifix became CRIA's poster child of sorts, and the flood-ravaged crucifix was
pictured on a flyer that conveyed the urgency in its message: "The art of Italy
is a heritage that no generation can monopolize. Its fate is a responsibility that
we must face. . . . The glory of Italian art must be preserved."[36] Both *National
Geographic* and *Reader's Digest* made sure to mention the plans that Leonardo
da Vinci had drawn for an "intricate system of dams, lakes and locks designed
to prevent a recurrence of floods like the one of 1333" (Reddy 1967, 206), as
if to reinforce the genius of that Renaissance man and others like him and
perhaps lament the sorry lack of such intellect in the modern age.

In accounts that followed the flood's aftermath, the artwork is continuously anthropomorphized. The language choices animate the paintings,
sculptures, and frescoes in numerous ways. Health metaphors are rampant.
The cleanup is referred to as a "rescue" mission. CRIA describes its relief
funds as the "first aid aspect of the operation."[37] The huge *limonaia*, or lemon
house, in the Boboli Gardens was converted into a "hospital for paintings"
(Batini 1967a, 90), including about 340 paintings on panels treated with rice
paper and a gradual diminishing of humidity. The damaged works of art were
referred to as "*i feriti*" (Velen and Velen 1966, 56), a term typically used to
refer to injured or wounded persons. A fact-finding mission reported on the
CRIA vice-president who "watched specialists, recruited from all over the
world, work within the limited quarters in an attempt to nurse the canvases
and panels through the crucial drying stages and to repair the damage caused
by the flood waters."[38] The *Burlington Magazine* reported, "The return to
health will be slow and laborious" (Anon. 1967a, 193). A sponsor from South

Africa "adopted" Santa Maria del Fiore and other museums, and monuments and works of art later found "foster parents" (Batini 1967a, 84). The recovery itself was called a miracle. The repeated use of such metaphoric language for the art objects contributed to infusing them with a certain magical quality.

Ultimately, the flood had a humanizing effect on art. The Renaissance treasures were cast as helpless victims. They might have resided in marble palaces and churches, but they were not beyond the reach of nature's most destructive forces. Works of art were vulnerable to injury. They, too, had a certain mortality. They, too, could be the subjects of a rescue mission. And in all of this, these works of art had a spirit.

Links to the fashion world were not without mention. In the memoir *Diary of Florence in Flood*, Taylor (1967) makes frequent reference to fine clothes and accessories. She points to the "enduring virtue of Florence": "in a mechanized century they keep alive the practice of craftsmanship, of the finest handwork in gold and silver, in leather, copper, onyx and marble, enameled wood, copies of antique furniture, embroideries, fabrics, and high fashion." Her descriptions undoubtedly stimulated desire for quality goods. It is unclear, however, how readers might have reacted to her description of being "overawed, even shaken, and certainly bewildered among the thousands of elegant shops, which offer a choice of treasures of artisan make that she finds just too much for her" (Taylor 1967, 26). If all girls could have such troubles! The *Reader's Digest* article also made reference to Italian fashion. It had this to say about the "indomitable Florentines" and their work ethic: "Famed fashion designer Emilio Pucci lost more than 150,000 yards of fabric to the flood. Yet he and his 1000 employees were back at work the moment the waters receded." The article concluded with the idea that the "universal response" to the disaster "imbued the old city with a new spirit" and closed with a quote from Pucci himself: "It's a new Renaissance in which the whole world has shared" (Reddy 1967, 216, 219).

Fifteen years earlier, when Giorgini launched the Pitti fashion show, the Made in Italy mark became identified with luxury products. The devastation of the flood had the unintended consequence of popularizing art, of making it available to a broad public, through mainstream magazines, news reports, newspapers, documentaries, letters home, and other firsthand accounts. The news coverage and fund-raising communicated the significance of the value of art to much of the world.

The significance of Renaissance art, and preserving it, became uncontestable. It became common sense. Yet common sense often has an underlying class element. Take the example of *sprezzatura*, which traces its roots to court society and was used in its day to describe easy elegance, grace, or nonchalance (Castiglione 1969, 44–47). The term, no longer in common usage, conjures up the art of concealing art; it connotes "lightening" without effort (Paulicelli 2004, 6). This gets to the heart of grace as when looking good is made to appear easy and not affected. Baldassarre Castiglione's *Il Libro del Cortegiano* (*The Book of the Courtier*), published in 1528 as a sort of book of manners, became so popular in Renaissance court society that it helped create a discourse on fashion, which echoed all over Europe. The book offered the definitive guidelines for appropriate ways to dress for different occasions, drew attention to the symbolic meanings of dress, and raised awareness of how dress codes regulate social hierarchies. As Paulicelli (2004, 10) points out, it had a huge impact on the "creation and codification of cultural models and patterns of behavior, in their role in forming a canon of common sense." It eventually "trickles down" from elite court society into the city and piazza to inform what is now the widespread notion of *la bella figura*. Literally "beautiful figure," this concept and practice points to the importance of taking care of one's appearance in a way that mixes elegance and ease (Paulicelli 2004, 6, 13, 76). Although the term *sprezzatura* has fallen out of contemporary usage, making room for shorter words with negative associations, such as *sprezzare* (to despise, to scorn) or *sprezzarsi* (to neglect oneself), the form of self-presentation retains deep roots in court society and has become taken for granted in Italian style. Codified within its common sense are underlying elements that historically reproduced power and inequality.

I use common sense here in the Gramscian sense of conceptions of the world that are "lived uncritically" (Forgacs 2000, 421). Commonsense notions may, for example, make inequality seem natural and thereby serve to sustain it (Crehan 2016). I draw inspiration from Gramsci's commitment to nurture critical consciousness as a way to challenge hegemony. The *National Geographic* phrasing leaves no doubt of the value of Italian art and intellectual activity to Western culture. The categories of people mentioned, however, give pause. The list includes elites and the propertied classes. Left off are the common folk: peasants and laborers—the vast majority of sixteenth-century Italian society. Similarly, given the personalities cast in lead roles, the CRIA rescue mission had an unmistakable elite social dimension. As Bourdieu (1984, 7) notes in *Distinction*, "art and cultural consumption are predisposed, consciously and deliberately or not, to fulfill a social function of legitimating social differences." Likewise, Stuart Plattner (1996, 490) in his study of St. Louis art markets observed that raising prices often stimulated demand, a tendency he attributed to a certain class of consumers "hungry for the status that possession of high-culture goods is supposed to give."

It might seem bizarre to suggest that the Made in Italy brand rose from murky floodwaters. But as two anthropologists remind in relation to making sense of events, even natural ones: "Hurricanes and earthquakes do not make history; people's conceptions of such phenomena, and responses to them, do" (Farnetti and Stewart 2012, 432). The extensive response and concern generated from the tragic flood event created an international discourse on beauty, and as Batini (1967a, 83) reported, "In Florence, beauty is an industry." Indeed, the flood coincided with an economy that was booming with particular sonorous quality, and migrants from the south were descending on northern cities, such as the industrial district of Prato, then in the province of Florence, to partake in the so-called economic miracle. Hence the influx of art aid was happening coterminous with intense economic growth and the most stylish, jet-setting woman in America turning her attention to be the spokesperson for saving Renaissance treasures. Jackie Kennedy was nothing if not an icon of the *bella figura*. Given the strong link that had been made between the Renaissance and contemporary things Italian, it is worth suggesting that in saving Renaissance art, rescue workers were saving the spirit of good taste.

## Historical Sentiment as Value

Arrogance has prevented observers from seeing how archaic gift principles are embedded in the Made in Italy label. A humble reading of the myth of continuity with the Renaissance allows insight into how ultracapitalist fashion items tap and transform noncapitalist histories and social relations.

One day, Malinowski had an epiphany. He was determined to find a reasonable motive that accounted for individual actions. What could possibly be the value of all those shell trinkets? Western economists and missionaries couldn't figure out what all the fuss was about over shells that, in their view, traveled willy-nilly in different directions between different islanders. Malinowski (1922, 86) was set on explaining how what he half-jokingly described as "two meaningless and quite useless objects," which passed from "hand to hand," became the foundation of an extensive institution that encompassed numerous islands and their inhabitants. Why, Malinowski asked, were the kula objects valued? He drew a bold parallel as he was trying to break the kula code. He turned to something familiar: the crown jewels at Edinburgh Castle. He recounts the significance of a sightseeing trip in Europe after six years in the South Seas and Australia. In a charming and memorable moment of self-reflection, he writes:

> The keeper told many stories of how they were worn by this or that king or
> queen on such and such occasion, of how some of them had been taken over

to London, to the great and just indignation of the whole Scottish nation, how they were restored, and how now everyone can be pleased, since they are safe under lock and key and no one can touch them. As I was looking at them and thinking how ugly, useless, ungainly, even tawdry they were, I had the feeling that something similar had been told to me of late, and that I had seen other objects of this sort, which made a similar impression on me. (Malinowski 1922, 88)

The other "ugly, useless, ungainly, even tawdry" objects were those very shell trinkets of the Trobriand Islands. This comparison between Trobriand shells and Scottish crown jewels led Malinowski to propose that the two objects share something profound: *historical sentiment.* In both cases value was not intrinsic per se. Rather, "both heirlooms and *vaygu'a* are cherished because of the historical sentiment which surrounds them," he observed. Presumed "standards" of beauty or utility seemed of little relevance. Regardless of how "valueless an object may be, if it has figured in historical scenes and passed through the hands of historical persons and is therefore an unfailing vehicle of important historical associations, it cannot but be precious to us" (Malinowski 1922, 89). Associations create value. The same type of mental attitude that allowed Europeans to value their heirlooms allowed the people of New Guinea to value their *vaygu'a*, those shell valuables that circulated in the kula. In each case, the objects served as potent symbols of power and prestige.

The links between historical sentiment and value can be extended to the prestige of the Made in Italy label. The myth of continuity with the Renaissance serves as a symbolic resource in terms of satisfying certain desires at the point of consumption but also in terms of generating ideas related to conditions at the point of production. For consumers, the link to the Renaissance is partly about beauty and the potential such authenticated beauty has for self-enhancement. This is, after all, one of the primary ways in which clothing and the fashion industry work. The clothing industry invests in fashion and design innovation and then in marketing through brands and image creation. In *The Fabric of Cultures*, Jane Schneider (2009, 24) observes how the industry's "heavily promoted logos and labels, especially when mixed with seductive evocations of the sexual being beneath . . . the clothes, convey a kind of spiritual power—a resource for self-enhancement." The idea here is that consumers seek to enhance their attractiveness or mark their affiliation with certain social groups through what they wear.

The significance of the links between the myth of continuity and the value of historical sentiment extends to the conditions of production: the kinds of associations that a consuming public has between the Renaissance and artisans. In a discussion of the history of cloth across societies, Schneider describes artisans as "a fortunate lot." Compared with factory workers, they have historically garnered "the respect of elites who value their talents, they also enjoy relative equality in the workplace . . . and [they] benefit in the production sphere from the treasured condition of autonomy" (Schneider 2009, 18). The historical attachment to the figure of the artisan serves to distance consumers from thinking about actual relations and conditions of production, and the ongoing global inequalities and tragedies so prevalent in the apparel industry. As the *National Geographic* story noted, "Florence is probably the last European city where an economy rests so heavily and happily upon handcraftsmen and small manufacturers, many of them using the tools and techniques handed down through the generations" (Judge 1967, 42). Similarly, the authors of a *Saturday Review* article characterized Florence as a "city of small artisans and shopkeepers," and attributed recovery from the flood to "the remarkable spirit of the Florentines—the spirit of the Renaissance 500 years dormant" (Velen and Velen 1966, 26).

By 1966, artisans were facing tough competition from industry. The number of firms and employees in fashion-related industries that existed in the municipality of Florence was a small fraction compared with those in its province (which then included Prato), according to data from the census years before and after the flood: in the city, the numbers steadily decline from 183 firms with 2,527 employees in 1951, to 167 firms with 2,813 employees in 1961, and then 179 firms but with only 1,923 employees by 1971. Meanwhile, workers were following industry to the province as evidenced in numbers such as 1,226 firms with 24,951 employees in 1951, to 6,794 firms with 44,197 employees in 1961, and 9,525 firms with 51,229 employees by 1971. Artisans crafting their wares in the city at the time of the flood were a small portion of the employees making a living in the province and thus were more of an ideal type than a reality (Merlo and Polese 2006, 427).[39]

Just as those Trobriand shell trinkets accumulated histories, and those histories enhanced their value as well as their spirit, so too did the myth of continuity with the Renaissance enhance the spirit of things labeled Made in Italy. The international aid effort and rescue activities surrounding the disaster generated and intensified historical sentiment. Simultaneously, the strengthening of linkages with the Renaissance was safe: it distanced those objects from a more recent past—whether the violent years of fascism or the turbulent years of postwar labor, feminist, and political struggle. On a nearly worldwide scale, reportage on the flood served indirectly to boost the association that the public had between the value of Renaissance art and things crafted in Italy. In other words, the flood and the subsequent rescue effort indirectly fueled the myth of continuity, connecting Renaissance art to the idea of Italian good taste.

While the value of Italian style had been legitimated in the United States, among specialized buyers as well as middle-class consumers, these associations were meaningless in non-Western parts of the world, such as in Mao's China. The Cultural Revolution was launched in 1966 with the aim of destroying the "Four Olds": customs, culture, habits, and ideas. Fabric was rationed until 1983. The unisex Mao suit dominated the fashion scene until the 1990s.[40]

The Chinese might as well have been on the moon.

# 3

# Money

*Senza lilleri un si lallera.*
*O nini, ci voglion i dindi.*

Without money you can't do a thing.
Oh darlin', you gotta have some change.
FLORENTINE SAYING

### "Fistful of Tears"

In Prato's Little Wenzhou, with its public signs that warn "No Spitting," above a sewing workshop and a wholesale store, Peng pulled himself out of bed. His mother-in-law had woken him up. He was dragging. The night before, he worked into the wee hours. It was a typical rhythm, one he had more or less adapted to over the years.

Peng had come to Italy alone and angry as a nineteen-year-old. In Wenzhou, he was a badass. He fought at school every day. His father sent him abroad as an education of sorts to fix his adolescent troubles. It took a year to leave, waiting for the visa, working through people who made the arrangements. His father had paid 160,000 RMB for him to be "smuggled" in. The debt belonged to Peng. He finally made the trip in 2006. He didn't have to climb mountains like some of the immigrant parents our transnational research team interviewed during 2012–14. Rather, he flew into Europe under the pretense of making a business trip. Technically, he was traveling on a thirty-day tourist visa. It would take much longer than that to pay off the debt.

His initial destination was Greece, where he stayed with his hometown neighbors' relatives. There, he looked after the store for this "aunt"—she was a wholesaler and sold all sorts of things—but he stayed only a week. He felt out of sorts and so bought a ticket for Italy, where a cousin he sometimes calls a brother was living. The visa was still valid. He flew into Rome and this brother picked him up. In Prato, Peng got a job in a factory that an aunt from his hometown owned. Although he didn't have any skill in making clothes, he soon found himself sitting hours on end at an industrial sewing machine, taking cut pieces of fabric and stitching them into whole garments. In China, he had once tried the work but then ran away after a week. He had done a

FIGURE 3.1. Postwar hanger-style *capannoni* of Macrolotto Zero continue to house cut-and-sew activities. Photo by Agnese Morganti, 2016

lot of running as a youth. He was like his name, flighty as a bird. In Prato, he couldn't fly away.

"There's really no choice after you come here; you can only make clothes here. There's nothing else you can do." Plus his visa had expired, and he had nowhere else to go.

"Fistful of tears," he said, recalling his initiation into working in Prato's fast-fashion sector. "When I was learning, I felt disheartened. I lay in bed and cried at night." He was slow at his work, and people scolded him. He wasn't learning fast enough. He explained that after people scolded him, he felt wronged and uncomfortable, but he couldn't say a thing. "I can't talk about my feelings." He learned skills from his aunt. In general, she was his teacher and treated him well. But in a work context, relations are different.

"To be honest, I came here to earn money, and I am getting older," and then he added emphatically, "I used my youth as exchange for money, not my labor."[1]

## Money and Globalization

What is it to exchange youth for money? On the surface, the exchange may serve as evidence of the grinding maws of global capitalism. It might be

tempting to use Peng's story to argue for the idea that people everywhere—
locals, migrants, indigenes—are helpless in the face of such powerful forces,
that they can only react, that they are everywhere always already that self-
maximizing, free-market species *Homo economicus*, and that the market is
destiny of not only a personal order but also of a cultural magnitude. This
chapter draws inspiration from critical anthropologists who have interro-
gated the Eurocentric foundations of development and have questioned not
only the inevitability and homogeneity of those models but also their failure
to deliver on promises to improve social and economic well-being (Comaroff
2011; Escobar 2010; Ferguson 2009; Tsing 2013; Wutich and Beresford 2015).
In myriad ways and contexts, these scholars have challenged the universal-
ist claims of neoliberal capitalism and even collaborated with radical activists who seek to undo the hegemonic notions and practices of globalization
such as privatization, deregulation, and austerity (Razsa 2015). In Prato, the
machinations of development from the diaspora reflect a dramatic shift in
the character of postwar economic production.

Some years ago, Marshall Sahlins (2000, 415) joined a chorus of anthropologists in a clamorous protest "against the idea that the global expansion
of Western capitalism, or the World System so called, has made colonized
and 'peripheral' peoples the passive objects of their own history and not its
authors." His essay "Cosmologies of Capitalism" criticized the Western historiography of the world system for having intellectually carried out what it had
sought to dismantle. Blinded by its own tropes, much of this historiography
ended up denying people cultural integrity. Sahlins proceeded to construct a
scaffold for understanding intercultural encounters. Time and again in the
course of world history, as Sahlins (2000, 418) observed, "capitalist forces are
realized in other forms and finalities." Global forces are mediated. Outcomes
are not predetermined. Local peoples or migrants may be incorporated into
the world system, but they may also "exploit the new culture to their own
ends" (Sahlins 2000, 449).[2] Everywhere does not always produce the same,
flat, homogeneous inevitability.

Just when it seems the matter has been settled, that same dominant assumption once again lays itself bare: that the terms of hyperglobalization no
longer require people to share anything other than the means to exchange
money. Writing as part of a group of European scholars who seek to em-
power immigrants and take down xenophobic politics, Fabio Bracci (2012,
107) paints a portrait of Prato as a city that has been reduced to homogenized,
chrematistic logics: "The new context does not require sharing values or anything other than mere economic transactions." This perspective echoes that

of any number of social scientists who have lamented the corrosive effects of money. Georg Simmel's (1978, 259) classic work on *The Philosophy of Money*, originally published in 1907, viewed money as a colorless and indifferent object that repainted the modern world in an "evenly flat and gray tone." Vivian Zelizer's (1994, 2) *The Social Meaning of Money*, on the other hand, challenged the money-as-destroyer hypothesis—"that money is a single, interchangeable, absolutely impersonal instrument" that replaces "personal bonds with calculative instrumental ties." In Prato, such perspectives have transmogrified into a dominant stereotype that takes on a decidedly hostile refrain. It goes like this:

"Money. Money. Money."

That's what most people would say about why the Chinese had come to Prato. Some loathed them for this. They saw this particular swath of the Chinese population as vulgar, uneducated money-grubbers. They referred to the Chinese residents here as the lowest of the low. They are ugly, I heard people say. They eat cats. They don't bury their dead. They bathe in watermelons.[3] They don't have any culture. They don't appreciate beauty. They don't have a clue about Italian history. They don't care. They are culturally vapid. They are a threat. They are invaders. They are occupiers. They are clueless about all the labor struggles and the labor victories. They are bankrupt as citizens. They don't participate in political life. They don't pay taxes. They don't take authorized taxis. They don't respect the environment. They trash it. They spit. They don't respect the laws of hygiene. They don't even respect the rights of their countrymen. They are just here for the money.

The explanation that Chinese migrants have come to make money is also a story that the Chinese tell about themselves—albeit with a different tone. Indeed, they say they came to Prato to earn money. They heard it would be easy. Their version is not full of shame or embarrassment about their desire to make money. They emphasize their willingness to work hard and make sacrifices. They do not keep all the money for themselves, but as with immigrants the world over, they send a part of their earnings back. At times, they admit to misgivings that they came. They struggle with belonging. They struggle with success. There are huge differences between those who have found their pot of gold and those who have not. These gaps are immediately evident driving from the center of Prato through the factory district of Macrolotto 1. On the bypass of Viale Salvador Allende, some Chinese residents cruise in luxury SUVs while others ride secondhand bicycles, often two to a bike, legs dangling out into traffic.

Money is not simple. Making sense of money talk and action offers a route into thinking about what matters to people. It offers a way to ground value. I am not proposing to study money per se—others have done so and convincingly argued that money may sometimes flatten social relations but is just as likely to create new relations that are equally complex (Maurer 2006). I am suggesting that money is an important aspect of how society in an intensely globalized historical moment is making sense of itself. Given the predominance of the discourse on and about money, it only makes sense to pause and join in that sense making, and if not to upend it at least to turn it sideways and look inside.

Meta-economic categories can be particularly persistent. Along these lines, the anthropologist Mayfair Mei-hui Yang seeks to halt misguided representations of "monolithic global capitalism." To this end, she coins the term *economic hybridity*. Yang draws on her field-based research in the small towns and rural areas of Wenzhou to describe how people experience what is often glossed as global capitalism as they renew remnants of noncapitalism. She bears witness to "the interweaving of a centralized state socialist economy, transnational capitalism, a revitalized premodern market economy based on household production, and a ritual economy" (Yang 2000, 477). Yang draws on popular religious revival and documents the burning of paper money, paper replicas of modern luxury consumer goods, and even stories of real money at ancestor events. Such displays signal ritual excess. Her analysis challenges the trope of one-way capitalist penetration. She demonstrates how alternative logics and social formations channel global movement toward other ends than simple rational economic ones.

Quests for money undergird globalization. Money, as Graeber reminds us, as a generic object generally cannot accumulate history. That, after all, has been the point of money. Money serves as both a "measure" and a "medium" of value. It is a measure when people use it to "compare the value of different things," such as the cost of one pound of ground beef to a bag of hamburger buns. It is a medium when people use it to buy such things. In these two instances, "money is simply a tool," one that facilitates action. Graeber points to Marx for having innovated a third meaning: "money as a value in itself." This is when money is no longer simply a tool but the end. Graeber (2001, 66–67, 88, 213) reflects: "It becomes the very embodiment of value, the ultimate object of desire." Using a lens of economic heterogeneity to comprehend the immigrant quest for money deepens our grasp of how workers on the move are transforming themselves, transforming one local territory, and also transforming the global economy.

## Structural Encounters

Behind Peng's exchange of youth for money, and inside that fistful of tears, dwells a world: a world of regional structures and sentiments that collide with a globalized local context. To break from a monolithic interpretation, I situate Chinese immigrants' desire to make money in three structural encounters, each at a different level of scale: a Chinese regional model of economic development saturated with an exuberant ritual economy, a local Italian environment of small firms connected to the Made in Italy brand, and a global restructuring of the clothing industry. These encounters shape migrant experiences and reveal the complex meanings and practices behind what would appear to be a universal quest for money. Instead, I show how archaic, yet persistent, principles transform and animate new rationalities of global economic activity.

So often as scholars report on the structural adjustments of capital and shifts to flexible accumulation (Harvey 2005; Ong 1999) they fail to consider "sentiments as forces of production" (Yanagisako 2002, 7). Besides shaping the dynamics of firms such as those Sylvia Yanagisako studied in northern Italy, such sentiments are dispersed and travel from points of destination to places of arrival and back again (Coe 2014; Ma Mung 2004). Even in the context of more recent transnational joint ventures, Yanagisako noted the persistent significance of kinship sentiments among Italian family firms that enter into collaboration with Chinese entrepreneurs. The ironic twist to the story is that, as she puts it, "the agents of Western capitalism—namely the Italian capitalist families—aspire to enrich and develop a cultural logic that does not fit comfortably into evolutionary models of capitalism" (Yanagisako 2013, 82). To understand sentiments such as those clenched in a fistful of tears as forces of production, I ground sentiments in structural encounters.

Migrants become actors within larger global forces. These forces are often capitalistic, but as a close look at the case of Chinese migrants demonstrates, the forces are not limited to capitalist ones. The forces and social relations also articulate with and are in opposition to values and strategies that Massimo De Angelis refers to as "other-than-capitalism." He highlights "an abundant literature" that has developed to theorize and document what he describes as a "relational field in which not commodity and money, but commons, gifts, conviviality, affects as well as traditional forms of oppression such as patriarchy are the prime shapers, makers and breakers of norms of social relations, the prime context of value and meaning creation" (De Angelis 2007, 35). Examples of noncapitalist practices among overseas Chinese cut-and-sew workers and entrepreneurs range from housing accommodations and wage systems to food provisioning and child-rearing practices. I place structural encounters between global dynamics and local work characteristics in the service of revealing how the global marketplace, as an outgrowth of neoliberal policies and ideologies, does not merely produce a coherent or unified set of ideas, as Aihwa Ong (2006) has observed, but rather results in varied rationalities and regimes that end up being remarkably heterogeneous, particular, and unexpected. Below, I draw on structural encounters from three different levels of scale—local, regional, and global—to make sense of the lived experience of the migrants' quest. To sort out the meaning of money and the underlying force of desire, I take seriously two contrasting sentiments: bitterness as a form of social suffering and high-mindedness as a sign of social success.

## High-Minded and Dissatisfied

Peng's migratory experience began with his father's plan to straighten him out. He went from adolescent troublemaker to adult entrepreneur. After his initial difficult period, Peng described life as "smooth." He met his future wife, Lily, working side by side in the factory. The next year, in 2007, his father and her father opened their own factory; two years later, in 2009, he and Lily bought it. In September 2010, Lily gave birth to their son; eight months later, in May 2011, Peng recalled, they found themselves terribly busy and unable to take care of their son. He asked Lily to send the infant back to China and asked his parents to quit their jobs to care for the baby.

At the time of the interview, Peng hadn't sewn clothes for two years. He stocked, allocated, and sorted fashion items. He had also become responsible for trading and managing interpersonal relationships in the factory. In the production chain, he was busy getting merchandise as well as delivering materials to various dependents who sewed in other small workshops. He managed the movement of orders outside of the factory, whereas Lily tended to the inside. Compared to China, the opportunities in Prato were much greater. But there had been sacrifices. Peng was working hard to make money.

He sums up this group of migrants' relationship to work and money. "Chinese here can stand hard work." He attributes this to the character of people from Wenzhou. "People from Wenzhou think money is very important." Peng speaks from experience. "People attach great importance to money; they only want to make money. People from other parts of China are different; once they settle down, they are satisfied with whatever they can earn. People from Wenzhou are different; if they earn 1,000 this month, they want to earn 1,200 next month."

FANGLI: So is it because people from Wenzhou are insatiable? Or are they high-minded?

PENG: High-minded and dissatisfied.[4]

The adjectives *high-minded* and *dissatisfied* carry with them a world. To understand that world, I trace the roots to Wenzhou, the municipality and prefecture in Zhejiang Province. This province is located at the midpoint of China's eastern coast, south of Shanghai. Residents from here are believed to account for about 80 percent of Chinese migrants in Italy, and estimates are that as many as 90 percent in Tuscany have roots in Wenzhou (Pedone 2013).[5] Both a municipality and a prefecture, Wenzhou includes under its jurisdiction a territory with a population of nine million residents. The area has a unique history in twentieth-century China and a particular resonance in terms of overseas Chinese. A ring of mountains, a coastal port, and acute land shortages played a role in shaping particular modes of survival and innovation.

The population was largely rural. The numbers resonate as counterintuitive. Geographer Kok Chiang Tan describes an area in 1986 with a total population of about 6.3 million people, of whom only 0.37 million lived in the city and the rest were scattered across nine counties. In other words, a rural population of 5.93 million accounted for 94 percent of the prefecture's total population. Tan (1991, 221) describes a situation of "acute" land shortage, which in "old China" earned it the reputation as an area of "'three plenties': plenty of thatched huts, plenty of people being forced to sell their children, and plenty of famine-stricken beggars."

These "plenties" resulted in a good deal of suffering and a significant surplus of rural labor. The hardship also gave rise to a host of adaptations. They became known for rural handicraft industries and as traveling vendors and traders. They cultivated acumen as artisans, service providers, and entrepreneurs. The networks developed through these practices gave rise to a particular form of economic activity largely based in households. People from Wenzhou became resourceful at cultivating networks. By the time the People's Republic of China came to power in 1949, the Wenzhouese were well known as wanderers, merchants, and artisans throughout China and even overseas (Zhang 2001b).

The entrepreneurial spirit was formidable. In light of the Communist Revolution, people from Wenzhou became infamous for their defiance. They stubbornly ignored the central government's initiatives under Mao, specifically regarding economic reforms. Officials viewed them as insubordinate. The political scientist Alan Liu (1992, 698) notes that "the entire province suffered from serious political discrimination under Mao, due partly to Zhe-jiang's being the home province of Chiang Kai-shek" but also due partly to the fact that the "Maoist collectivization program, which required Wenzhouese to stay put and farm, went against the grain of craftsmen and long-distance traders." As punishment, Wenzhou residents did not typically benefit from central government investments. As the Mao era came to a close, the new leadership of Deng Xiaoping shifted to a pragmatic style. December 1978 wit-nessed a watershed event: at the Third Plenum of the Eleventh Central Com-mittee of the Chinese Communist Party the country's leaders embraced the so-called Four Modernizations—agricultural, industrial, national defense, and science and technology. This established a pathway for economic "eman-cipation" (Pedone 2013, 61). The new goals initiated a market-oriented econ-omy that would pave the way for increased participation in a global economy (Pedone 2013; Tan 1999; Zhao 2013). The plan also cast the economic activi-ties of Wenzhou in a new light. Wenzhou was no longer seen as a territory of insubordinate ne'er-do-well wanderers and petty capitalists. Instead, the official view was that Wenzhou would serve as a model for economic devel-opment (Wei 2011).

## The Wenzhou Model

The Wenzhou model refers to a prevalent way that people in Wenzhou have organized their economic activity. The model is famous among globalization scholars, particularly those interested in the role of regional economies in the rise of China in the global economic landscape. The geographer Y. H. Den-nis Wei (2011, 239) defines the model as a "distinctive pathway to industri-alization and economic development in China." The model is best known for small-scale family businesses typically clustered together, according to a principle of "one township–one product–many operations" (Tan 1991, 219; Wei 2011, 243). Specialized towns emerged with focused production on com-modities such as buttons, zippers, badges, lighters, shoes, or knitted bags, to name a few.[6] The model in Wenzhou contrasts with other areas known for different approaches. Local yet state-directed, collectively owned enterprises at the level of town and village characterize the Sunan model; by contrast, the Pearl River Delta model relies on externally driven industrialization and urbanization with frequent leveraging of foreign direct investment as a key feature (Jeong 2014; Wei 2011, 237).[7]

Recall, Wenzhou was a land of "three plenties." For many peasants whose lives were plentiful with misery, rural industrialization allowed a pathway to make a living. In the 1980s, nonagricultural production began to surpass agricultural work. As historic practices of artisanship and trade transformed, the people of Wenzhou became competent at finding and filling market niches. They became known for hard work. They were driven. In the words of Chinese migrants in Prato:

QIAO: Living expenses in China are high, if you can't earn enough money, your living conditions will be bad. People will judge you if you wear the same clothing every year. (Lived in Prato since 1999, mother of two children.)[8]

YAN: I wanted revenge. I wanted to come to Italy, because people said it was easy to earn money in Italy. That's why I came to Italy. (Lived in Prato since 2004, father of one child.)[9]

Migrants commonly referred to the social pressures they felt to leave their hometown and to show that they had the wherewithal not only to go abroad but also to demonstrate economic success. The reference to wanting revenge was mostly to the Chinese government whom Yan felt was unfair in its meting out of punishments and favors. Out-migration was not merely an individual decision but part of a social world and a moral orientation to that world. As migrants left their homes, whether their destinations were within China or abroad, they brought a variety of skills with them. They made use of their *guanxi*, their social networks and relationships, wherever they went. To varying degrees, they replicated the Wenzhou model abroad. They are infamous for spreading Chinese-style commerce across the globe. Nanlai Cao (2013, 86) points to three prominent features of this reform-era development: "private enterprise, moral contingencies, and aggressive global business outreach." They are known as global go-getters. They are also known for conversion to Christianity. Even so, whether migration is to Paris or Prato, the freedom to practice religion appears to play a small role in their motivations to migrate to the West. Cao found no connection between their faith and their decision to migrate. "Most migrate with the dream to get rich," observes Cao of Wenzhou migrants in Paris. The same has been said for Wenzhou transplants elsewhere in Europe.

The driving forces of economic development have primarily been in private enterprises centered on household production. Debates continue about the model's features and origins. Some authors write about the model as though it sprang from China's economic reforms, in the late 1970s. Others draw attention to preexisting circumstances and practices. The versions that offer a historical perspective are the most illuminating in terms of understanding Wenzhou's success both at home and abroad. These discussions parse how historic institutions adapted to modern conditions. Liu (1992,

699–700) describes the Wenzhou success formula "as a combination of 'three M's'—mass initiativeness, mobility, and markets" (see also Pomeranz 2000). In practice, these translate to driven people who run household industries or work as sales agents. This formula seems to follow the migrants wherever they go.

Leaving the homeland was not a welcome act during the first three decades of Socialist China. It was forbidden. The mechanism for policing population movement within the People's Republic was a household registration system known as *hukou*. Two major divisions distinguished between urban and rural residents. The government prohibited people with a rural status from migrating to cities. If rural dwellers left the countryside anyway, they would find themselves in a tough situation: "Their rural residential status denied them access to state-subsidized foodstuffs, housing, employment, and other essential services reserved for urbanites only" (Zhang 2001a, 182). These migrants who ignored official policies became known as the floating population. The term captured their status as floaters in the metaphoric sense that they were not connected. In practice, the consequences were concrete. This class of citizens did not enjoy typical rights. Government policies considered certain migrants as "illegal." Sanctioned discrimination stemmed from the household registration system itself. The type of residency permit that the government issued to any given household therefore played a heavy role in the household members' collective fates. The post-Mao era relaxed policies toward migration, but the label stuck. By 2000, Zhang estimates that there were some 100 million people in the category of the "floating populations." These rural transients typically left villages and moved to cities in search of work and business opportunities. Observes Zhang (2001a, 182): "The floating population consists of people with diverse socioeconomic and regional backgrounds, but their primary goals are the same: to get rich by migrating to the cities" (see also Greenhalgh 2003).

In Beijing, Wenzhou residents in the 1980s established an enclave in a marginal farming area, and eventually it evolved into a famous migrant settlement known as Zhejiangcun. At the time, Beijing's residents faced severe shortages of clothing. Wenzhou migrants jumped on the opportunity. They focused on the manufacture of low-end garments, including leather jackets, popular in Beijing at the time (Jeong 2014, 334; Zhang 2001b). A standout feature of the Zhejiang settlement in Beijing, according to labor historian Luigi Tomba (1999, 286), was a "complete economic system of production, trade and services."

As the migrants made their way to Tuscany, they initially settled in the industrial outskirts of Florence and set to work in the leather industry. Whether they migrated as families or engaged in chain migration, many eventually set up small household-based firms (Tomba 1999). As of 2009, the 3,379 small garment-sewing firms registered in Prato's chamber of commerce appear to have surpassed the 2,500 garment-sewing enterprises registered with the Wenzhou Clothing Business Association (Caserta and Monticelli 2010; Wei 2011, 243).[10]

## Made in Italy, Made in Small Firms

Chinese migrants have come to dominate the small-firm landscape of economic activity in Prato, particularly those in garment and sweater production. When Chinese migrants first arrived in the environs of Florence, they found themselves in a strikingly similar environment in terms of the small-firm household-based workshops so common to Wenzhou. "The economic and social conditions of industrial districts in Tuscany fitted the Chinese, steeped in the Wenzhou tradition, like a glove" (Tomba 1999, 285). The glove metaphor is hardly a stretch. Central Italy's mode of regional development resulted in about 90 percent of firms being small to medium sized. The transformation was so swift that observers from economists to historians to journalists came to describe it as an economic miracle.

Historically, what eventually became the success of the Made in Italy "brand" was attributed to small firms lauded for their flexibility in meeting work demands. The small-firm model evolved in stark contrast to the large-scale industrialization of the Italian north and the corrupt underdevelopment, state-assisted landscape of the Italian south (Bagnasco 1992; Bagnasco and Sabel 1995; Blim 1990; Della Sala 2004; Economist 2005; Lazzeretti 2003). This alternative earned it the moniker of Third Italy, known for decentralized production. In other words, production moved from big factories with brutal conditions, often resulting from pressures to speed up assembly line work, to microenterprise subcontracting firms with semiautonomous industrial artisans. Imagine landscapes scattered with family-run workshops nestled beneath clay tile-roofed residences in which kitchens sat tucked into adjacent rooms.

A lens on heterogeneity within capitalism brings into focus a nuanced interpretation: a network of small individually run and owned firms was founded on indigenous social formations, namely a kin mode of production involving extensive self-employed workers, recently unyoked from the rigid obligations of patron-client relations, yet a diffuse ethos of reciprocity. This story comes to light in Michael Piore and Charles Sabel's (1984) widely lauded *The Second Industrial Divide: Possibilities for Prosperity*, which docu-

ments how countries that tried to duplicate US standards of industrial efficiency could never quite succeed. As the authors compare different national
contexts—France, Germany, Japan, and Italy—their detailing of the organization of mass production reveals diverse economic arrangements.

Their explanation for the Italian case integrates cycles of collaboration and
conflict between capital and labor with local conditions. Italy came rather late
to industrialization, in the 1880s, first in heavy industries and, then at the
turn of the century, in consumer industries, such as FIAT and Olivetti. Labor
and industry made strides to collaborate but fell apart after World War I and
entered a phase of intense strikes and then violent reprisals with the rise of
fascism and the March on Rome in 1922. After World War II, a rural exodus
brought about decreasing wages, yet increasing competitiveness on the world
market. Former peasants who left agricultural life, hoping to escape its op-
pressive hierarchies and throw off the shackles of patriarchal power, wanted
to retain relations steeped in reciprocity. They sought a communitarian experience. Instead, as they migrated to industrial cities, they were shocked and
dismayed by what factory work demanded of them, and this manifested in
a sort of "militant egalitarianism." Trade union struggles peaked with the
Hot Autumn of 1969, and worker demands led to both reforms and con-
cessions. Victories included the comprehensive Workers' Statute, which improved labor conditions. Employers reacted with decentralized production.
Subcontracting exploded. By the 1970s, workshops had sprung up in houses
and garages in the towns surrounding the factories. The "factories" themselves became points of distribution for raw materials and partially finished
pieces that traveled from workshop to workshop. Economists categorize this
kind of localized outsourcing as a form of flexible specialization in terms of
its elastic labor processes. Mass subcontracting became the norm and small
firms proliferated. The small family firm where I worked a machine to sew
buttons onto sweaters during my dissertation fieldwork in 1995–97 was one
such operation (Becattini 1998; Blim 1990; Della Sala 2004; Harvey 1989, 147).

Many workers traded their positions in factories for their own small
workshops and became industrial artisans, such as Antonio, participating
in a web of local subcontracting.[11] The proliferation of small manufacturing
firms was, according to Ian Taplin (1989, 410), "one of the most remarkable
features of post–World War II economic growth in Italy." Cost advantages
were notable. Some aspects of production were informal, known as *lavoro
nero*, meaning part of an underground economy, in that certain activities
were beyond the reach of taxation and other costly controls. Small-firm outsourcing typically relied on unwritten contracts—a less-celebrated feature of
the informal economy but one that was essential to Prato's miracle.

The model became the "darling of neoliberal development theorists," according to anthropologist Michael Blim (1990, 3). Firms were adaptable and spontaneous in terms of production due to their size—small—and their form—family run.[12] In the 1970s, the neo-Gramscian, pro-labor left had a different take on decentralization: they suspected this development strategy was designed to quell labor unrest, reduce labor costs, and enhance profits. Blim's analysis offered a nuanced picture, tracing linkages between family enterprises and durable elements of an "indigenous social formation" (see also Becattini 2001, 46).

This indigenous social formation became key to the Made in Italy system. The historic sharecropping system, *mezzadria*, once a pervasive form of land tenure in north-central Italy, after the war witnessed a full-scale exodus. The organizing principles, however, did not disappear. Instead, they underwrote the new enterprises—although in surprisingly contrasting ways. The old organizing principles had both conservative and radical tendencies.

On the conservative side, as Gaggio (2011, 95) notes, "Classical *mezzadria* was imagined for centuries as a partnership between a landlord, who provided most of the capital necessary for agriculture, and the head of a peasant family, who contributed his labor and that of his relatives." The partnership, though, was hardly one of equals, and within the family its members did not have equal say. Hierarchies prevailed. Distance was structured. The landlords, who frequently held a noble title, did not manage the farms themselves. They hired a middleman, the infamous *fattore*, to oversee the peasants. Hence, rigid hierarchies prevailed both within the family and between the family patriarch and the patron.

On the progressive side, protest to these hierarchies was already brewing when the Nazi-Fascist occupation occurred in 1943–44. Tuscan sharecroppers were well positioned to support the antifascist partisans, who tended to find themselves on the opposite political side of their wealthy landlords. Peasants participated widely in the Resistance, and this had a number of far-reaching consequences, including Nazi-led retaliation in the form of several infamous massacres as well as tragic partisan deaths related to dangerous acts of resistance (Contini 1997).[13] A long-lasting consequence manifested in the bonds between peasants (as well as day laborers) and left political organizations, namely, the Communist Party. As migrants arrived from the Italian south to partake in Prato's booming economy, they also joined political movements. These were volatile years in which democratic communism was a real possibility.

This history was crucial to the small-firm character of the Made in Italy economic reality. On the one hand, these features generated the crisis and light industry along with eventual labor unrest. That same labor unrest in many ways contributed to the small-firm reality. On the other hand, features of peasant ethos and family cohesion underwrote these new enterprises. The economist Giacomo Becattini (1998, 83) describes tensions on the order of a "peasant protest, particularly by women and youth, not so much against the countryside itself as against the rigidity of the pecking-order in the family and against their close economic dependence on its older male members." The sons and daughters of former peasants objected to the rigid patriarchal family form. Their objections fueled a desire for autonomy, relatively speaking, especially vis-à-vis individuals' self-assertion in monetary matters. People rejected sharecropping and turned to industry. But the old peasant ethos was steadfast especially in terms of networks grounded in archaic habits of patron-client relations—sometimes summed up with the Italian phrase *amicizia*, or friendship.

## Fast Fashion and Global Restructuring

The textile and clothing industry is iconic in terms of globalization. The hands of Chinese people have come to play a hugely important role in making clothes that people wear the world over. As one geographer puts it, "The most significant change in the global map of production is the spectacular rise of China since the launch of reforms in the late 1970s" (Wei 2011, 237). Particularly notable are changes since the 1990s. Various measures point to China's formidable role in the apparel industry. Most impressive is its share of global apparel exports, including footwear: 10 percent in 1990, 23 percent in 1995, and 30 percent in 2007. Remarks Wei (2011, 240), "a miraculous rise in the global market."

Hardly "miraculous" but nevertheless distinctive has been Italy's trajectory. *The Economist*, drawing on the widely used Trade Performance Index, reported in 2013 that "Italy has remained the world's top ranking exporter in textiles, clothing, and leather goods" (London 2013). This makes Italy distinctive for developed economies. Characteristics of this "distinctive trajectory," dating to the 1970s, include Italian clothing and textile firms' resistance to moving offshore and instead a commitment to increase domestic output, expand exports, and stave off "import penetration" (Dunford et al. 2016, 118). Italy has been unusual compared with other economically advanced countries in that it remained competitive for a long time in the textile and clothing industry, a "traditional" industry in which emerging economies typically specialize (Dunford et al. 2016, 132).

Despite Italy's lofty ranking, other lenses suggest a different story. Italy's textile and clothing output peaked in 1995. The landscape of textile and cloth-ing production has changed radically. Imports from China have risen from just 5.7 percent in Italy's peak production year of 1995 to 30 percent in 2010. A team of economic geographers' analysis of industry data demonstrates that Italian firms, employment, and overall value have all declined. Between 1981 and 2007, the total number of establishments decreased by more than half as did the number of employees. Yet striking differences exist within the in-dustry; some sectors shrank while others grew. Those same geographers cite Prato as a case in point. In the decade between 2001 and 2011, the number of textile enterprises more than halved, from 6,372 to 3,079. Jobs declined as well, from 38,658 to 18,700. Yet the garment sector, historically smaller in Prato than textiles, witnessed an increase from 4,117 to 11,000, and the num-ber of enterprises proliferated from 2,168 to 4,504. Dunford and colleagues' (2016, 12) explanation is relevant: "The growth of the clothing sector, though, was almost entirely due to the growth of small Chinese enterprises."

Below, I turn to perspectives from migrant workers themselves to lend shape to the forms of fluidity and reciprocity that derive force through the clothing sector's dense webs of relations.

### "Everybody Else Is Doing It"

Bo's story paints a vivid picture of life in the flexible fast lane. The constant motion is like a shuttle on an expansive loom, moving to and fro, creating a textured, yet frayed, cloth. Moves have been multiple within Italy and be-tween China and Europe. Job circumstances have been in flux. Networks remain extensive. Bo left China because he had heard there were more op-portunities overseas. "I'd had a plan to immigrate since 1999, because I didn't know what I wanted to do in life when I was in China," he said. "For example, I didn't have money to do business; and then I heard some people say it was easier to earn money overseas. Everyone had that kind of mentality."[14]

For Bo, Italy made sense as a destination because he had friends there from his hometown. He could be sure to have a place to stay once over-seas. He traveled with his sister in 2000 from Wenzhou to Florence (making leather handbags), to Crotone in Calabria (working in a retail store), and then got amnesty in 2002, the year the Italian government had an amnesty program for immigrants. He went back to China in 2006 for a period, then returned to Prato in 2008, when he started a fast-fashion firm of his own. His sister started her own firm, too.

"Everybody else was doing it," said Bo, who at the time of the interview was twenty-seven years old, married with a daughter and son, ages four and one, both living in China. In Prato, the follow-the-leader phenomenon has caused problems. The world of fast fashion has become supercompetitive. "There is one problem with Chinese companies—that is, when someone is doing well in one certain industry, more people will follow the trend. . . . Therefore, if we Chinese are doing business, the life of business is usually not that long," Bo said. "It's vicious competition. It's all about price competition."

Migrants in Prato did not typically brag about get-rich-quick schemes but more commonly lamented how hard it was to make money especially after the financial crisis of 2008. They spoke of a disconnect between the promise to make a lot of money and the hardship. They also spoke of the burden as migrants related to economics, taking care of children, learning the language, and interfacing with the legal apparatus of the Italian state. There were busy times and slow times, the cost of living was high, and there were endless ways to spend money, as several women report:

CHU-HUA: I feel it is not easy to earn money now, it's like . . . I am wasting time here.[15]

QIAO: It doesn't matter if business is good in the first half of the year, in the second half of the year . . . every year, we earn money in the first half of the year, and lose money in the second half of the year.[16]

DAO-MING: They say that the life overseas is good. Earlier, they also said that it is easy to earn money and that all the other aspects of life abroad are good, too. Basically, we don't feel like this is true. Besides, the euro fell the year we went abroad. Work is boring. When it is the busy season, I am busy; when it is not the busy season, I am not busy.[17]

FEN: I didn't gain much, I didn't earn money, and there is not much money for me to earn, because I spent money.[18]

FEI-YEN: You know the economic situation. . . . I planned to earn money when I went abroad. . . . Now with the financial crisis, a lot of people have become unemployed. . . . If I cannot build a career here, I may go back. I cannot work for other people forever. It is meaningless working for other people. I can only earn a little money.[19]

Work for work's sake was meaningless. The point of working was to gain autonomy, make money, and earn respect. Migrants in Prato felt the global financial crisis. Migrants conveyed a sense of biding their time, even wasting their time, because of such an ever-more-competitive market. The point of migrating was not merely to get by. The point of it all was to show success. That's why there were so many small fast-fashion firms in Prato. Migration was meaningful for people from Wenzhou when they were able to set out on their own and realize their entrepreneurial destiny.

Dreams of getting rich were not easily realized, however. A number of migrants described the situation as a wash in terms of what they had gained and what they had lost from migrating. Hard work required sacrifices and adjustment. With success in short supply, the biggest yield might be bitterness. One woman, Niu, who had joined her husband through the family reunification process in 2009, had worked a bit on her own before the couple decided to move from Reggio Emilia to Prato and start their own fast-fashion business. In the ensuing years, they also had two children, and both were living with them. All things considered, Niu reflected, "It seems to me that what I lost and what I gained, it seems to me equal."

Her husband, Deshi, went so far as to describe his and his wife's situation as similar to a constant state of wandering. He lamented the fact that they'd never have a pension, that taxes were high, that requirements for residency permits were costly, that standing in line outside of Prato's police headquarters to obtain the permits was difficult and demeaning.

> I mean, there is no retirement in Italy, no destination. Our lives are the same as a homeless dog. Here it is not . . . like in China. No matter if we have a good or bad life in China, we would definitely have a house to live in. Even if we work so hard at another place [outside the household] and feel so tired, we can go home after work. In Italy, it's not so simple. If I work for other people, when I stop working, I would have no place to live. Where can I go if I don't have money? I have no place to live. It is hard here. . . . Just like I said before, we don't have a home here. We live here like beggars. Work here for a while, work there for a while. In the past few years, foreigners have treated us better. You know the situation of Chinese people here. Then the tax in Italy . . . we need to spend hundreds of euro in order to change our residence. Some need to change every year, some every half a year. The line in Prato is so long.[20]

Signs of inequality and desperation were also evident in public spaces. In Prato, walls scrawled with phone numbers proliferated with offers of massage and sexual services. Women strolled in city parks, such as the Piazza Mercatale, and propositioned male passersby with "*amore*." These signs of new money and new gaps between the haves and have-nots are troubling. They have been appearing back in China as well. Although the Wenzhou model is often celebrated for its economic success, it also has its critics. The specter of income gaps and socioeconomic inequality was already in evidence as early as the 1980s. In a survey of sales and purchase agents, nearly 30 percent reported that they were on the edge of business failure. The geographer Tan (1991, 225) offers a list of problems linked to spontaneous, unplanned development: ad hoc housing construction, uneven development between the more accessible coastal area and the remote and hilly interior, inadequate funds set aside for schools or health and culture facilities—"thus suggesting a lack of concern for the common good and the future needs of the town." Many of the "evils" that disappeared during Mao's Communist era have reappeared: "School children drop out early to apprentice as sales and purchasing agents under their father and/or elder brother; parents betroth their children early to families with similar economic power to cement cooperative ties. . . . [There is] conspicuous consumption in the form of elaborate house and grave construction" and the resurfacing of "nonsocialist" ills such as gambling and prostitution (Tan 1991, 228). Another set of problems historically has been child labor, which "exposed the general conditions in the Chinese countryside" (Liu 1992, 707), namely, lack of education for rural children and abundance of traditional discrimination against females.

### "They Are Not Strangers": Old Principles, New Ways

The three encounters of a structural order—the Wenzhou model, the Made in Italy model, and global restructuring—would be far from complete without consideration of what Chinese migrants do with the money they earn. They keep some, they spend some, and they send some. In the interviews with migrants, the issue of sending money back to relatives, especially their parents, in China came up frequently. The migrants in numerous ways and on numerous occasions signaled that they were not making money for only themselves. Reflecting on what she had gained and what she had lost from migrating, Ju replied, "Yes, there's an advantage. We have managed to earn a little money, we have brought it to my mother, as though one generation is finally earning a little something, right?"[21]

This nod not only to individual gains but also to generational advances was widespread. Migrants who had sent their children back to China, often to live with their parents, meaning the children's grandparents, took offense at any suggestion that they might be paying their relatives. Frequently, migrants send back money, a fact well known from the proliferation of money-wiring businesses and media reports on money transfers, some of which exceed legal amounts. As Fen noted about sending money back to her mother, "Yes, I would give her more money if I had money; they are not strangers, right?"[22]

This notion that they were not strangers, that they were family, and hence people with whom resources must be shared, exposes how traditional principles animate new economic practices. In other words, earnings and success were not cast merely in the self-maximizing individualistic language of the Western species of *Homo economicus*. Rather, making money was also cast in a collective sense of the kin group. Peng also spoke of sending money back to his father every year.

FANGLI: Oh, that's for treating them with filial respect. [laughter]

PENG: At best, that's treating them with filial respect; at worst, it's giving them money for watching my child. [laughter]

FANGLI: So what do you think? Is it treating them with filial respect, or is it worse—giving them money to watch your child?

PENG: Part of it is treating them with filial respect, and part of it is for their help. I will give them more if I want to treat them well. If I earn money, it's OK to give my elders more money.[23]

Peng cast their caregiving as help as opposed to labor and his money as a gift rather than remuneration. Migrants bring back all manner of gifts, and many are modest, such as shampoos, creams, red wine, chocolates, and baby formula. Less common are expensive brand-name clothing items. Never mentioned are the clothes the migrants made themselves. Those do not seem to qualify as appropriate gifts, or at least not ones that were mentioned. Occasionally, gifts are showy, such as a framed collection of euro coins and bills, from the smallest to the largest. This kind of gift allows the owner to display prestige. Clearly, there is more to money than bills and coins; "Money still possesses its magical power and is still linked to the clan or the individual," Mauss noted (1990, 72), maintaining it is "something other than utility that circulates in societies of all kinds." Indeed, the concepts of use value and exchange value can hardly touch on the emotional attachments that people have to money, the deeper meanings that follow money. History does not inscribe itself on individual bills quite like on kula shells that Malinowski famously documented as a corrective to economists' hubris of his day.

Behind the fast-fashion small-firm phenomenon stands Wenzhou itself, a homeplace whose residents have developed vast overseas networks and a keen awareness of opportunities. Taking advantage of those opportunities comes with pressure. Not doing so comes with stigma. Minghuan Li, who worked with Chinese migrants both in the Netherlands and Wenzhou, describes a strong "overseas consciousness" that circulates back and forth between Wenzhou and non-Wenzhou destinations. The consciousness leads many in Wenzhou to view getting rich in Europe as a sort of "special opportunity"; those without such opportunities are viewed as lacking in resourcefulness, whereas those who do not take advantage of their opportunities and do not go abroad risk being ridiculed as "lazy or strange." As Li (1999a, 194) summarizes, "They believe 'getting rich in Europe' is their common destination."

The stakes have not lowered as China's economy has grown. Migrants who send back money to relatives or who return with money are placed into "a highly visible and respectable social category"; indeed, they are considered a "rich and lucky group" (Li 1999a, 193). Conspicuous consumption has become widespread. Such displays of wealth, designed to heighten status, are evident both in Wenzhou and in Prato. In Prato, newly moneyed migrants invest in ostentatious villas, drive luxury cars, and dine at upscale restaurants. Indeed, migrant social mobility and consumption are essential to the survival of a number of local businesses, such as car dealerships (Berti, Pedone, and Valzania 2013). In Wenzhou, migrants or relatives build elaborate houses as well as ancestral tombs—a practice not evident in Prato.

Li recounts having attended a funeral rite in Wenzhou for a seventy-year-old Chinese man whose two sons had migrated to France, where they ran a restaurant and leather workshop. Li expressed disbelief at both the tomb and the ceremony. Up in the mountains, a stone structure had been constructed in the style of the Great Wall to protect the gravesite, and hundreds of villagers in attendance received cakes, cigarettes, and drinks. Back at the village, about seven hundred villagers attended an elaborate banquet—seventy tables each set for ten with sons of the deceased walking from table to table distributing 100 yuan notes to all guests, saying, "You should get wages for having dinner here." The surprised anthropologist reported, "All the guests admired the ostentatious funeral." She also noted the comment of one guest who recalled an even bigger and better funeral banquet; another guest lamented the fact that he would never be able to dream of such an honorable funeral given his lack of wealthy overseas kin.

The most obvious way to interpret this funerary practice is conspicuous consumption. Indeed, Li interpreted the event as such: consumption that heightens status. There are, however, other things going on here, considering the circulation of small gifts or larger sums of cash, and it can best be understood if we look a bit deeper into money, if we remain mindful of the three models that are encountering one another, and if we recall that archaic principles are animating rationalities of global capitalism. The description sounds reminiscent of a potlatch, which among the Northwest Kwakiutl grew increasingly spectacular with encroaching market economies and catastrophic population loss, all of which destabilized old hierarchies (Wolf 1999). Such practices appear to be a case of Western goods being "incorporated as indigenous powers," as Sahlins has said often occurs. Yang's description of Wenzhou as an exuberant ritual economy exposes the Wenzhou model as manifest in Prato as not simply a stepchild of Western capitalism but rather a vibrant hybrid system in its own right. Calling such a system global capitalism is a misnomer that becomes a flattening device, a low-cost label that is as cheap as fast fashion.

## Metamorphosis and Globalization

Peng used his youth in exchange for money. That was his analysis. If we take it seriously, we might see this as a sort of metamorphosis but of what sort? Prato became famous as a city known for a spectacular postwar economic miracle. Celebratory tones contrasted the ruins of war with the flourishing of prosperity. Becattini describes the bittersweet features of this transformation. His classic *The Caterpillar and the Butterfly* points to a profound and awe-inspiring metamorphosis rooted in the case of Prato. The first decades of the postwar "witnessed a massacre of traditional crafts (tailors, shoemakers, blacksmiths, carpenters, etc.)," and this massacre rather neatly fit the theories of the day: that the natural, desirable, inevitable course of economic development would move from "self-provisioning, putting-out, craft-based production to the factory system"—that is, from smaller to larger units of scale (Becattini 2001, 23). In reality, the metamorphosis took on a different form. Becattini points to 1954–73, when Italian craft production disappeared in some areas but was reborn in others, specifically, those of Prato's industrial district, so that he speaks of "its metamorphosis, since many of those craftsmen . . . reappeared in the guise of small craft-based industrial firms specializing in a phase product, clustering together in a defined territory and aiming from the outset at production for the domestic market . . . and then soon afterwards for the international market" (Becattini 2001, 23). Included in these figures were a category of "new small entrepreneurs," which had a mix of backgrounds including industrial-wage earners, independent shopkeepers, and those with agricultural or sharecropping roots.

The significance of metamorphosis for the human condition is captured in the writings of a Smithsonian research associate's essay. He cast the caterpillar and the butterfly in the title role for his essay because of their exemplary status of insects "in which the young differ so much from their parents that they must go through a reconstruction called a metamorphosis in order to attain their own adult form." He noted that this transformation from a crawling wormlike form into a splendid winged type struck human observers as so marvelous that "it has been taken as a symbol of human resurrection. In ancient Greek the human mind or soul was called psyche, and the same name was given to the butterfly, presumably the emancipated soul of the caterpillar" (Snodgrass 1961, 1). Metamorphosis is rebirth and loss all at once. Hormones trigger the caterpillar to metamorphose into the butterfly, and there is no turning back to the fuzzy, crawly creature. In Peng's self-account, the high-mindedness of people from Wenzhou becomes as essential and formidable as triggering hormones.

How does his figure of the metamorphosis layer over that of the Italian craftspeople who preceded him? Were their souls emancipated through industry? Was his soul emancipated? There is, of course, something deeply imperfect about these ontological questions. There is also something provocative. Consider Pulitzer Prize–winning novelist Jhumpa Lahiri's (2016) journey from linguistic exile to belonging as she embarks first on learning Italian and then writing in Italian. She comes to recognize her learning another language as sort of metamorphosis: "A new language is almost like a new life, grammar and syntax recast you, you slip into another logic, another sensibility" (Lahiri 2015, 34). She comes to realize that metamorphosis is a process both violent and regenerative. In the end, she finds herself "in Italian, a tougher, freer writer, who, taking root again, grows in a different way." The limit to her toughness was expressed in her refusal to translate her own work from Italian back into English, and thus a professional translator performs that labor. Any metamorphosis has its limits.

The metamorphosis through cutting-and-sewing labor does not feel like a resurrected soul; it feels more like a worn-out soul, a worn-out psyche, a troubled psyche, wondering what one has done. That fistful of tears, holding that world so tight, signals regret but also pride and the realization of a new person: in becoming an entrepreneur, in paying off debt, in making a family, in fulfilling what remains to be fulfilled of filial piety.

This, in essence, is the quintessential "develop-man" bargain. I borrow that figure of speech from Sahlins to stand as a counterpoint to the Western figure of *Homo economicus* rejuvenated from the alleged triumph of the so-called free market. The "develop-man" term came into being by accident when Sahlins was at the University of the South Pacific where he overheard a speaker insert the English word *development* in a pidgin sentence. Sahlins misheard it as "develop-man." The term is intended to capture a self-realization not of a "simple penetration of capitalist relations" but rather of the process wherein indigenous people may come to view the world system's exploitations as energizing and enriching for local systems, practices, and meanings. (That doesn't necessarily make them any less exploitive.) Continuities with the past abound. They may also assume new forms. Sahlins (2000, 419) emphasizes, "*the strongest continuity may consist in the logic of the cultural change.*" In other words, the driving force of change may be an underlying traditional cultural logic itself—even where "their own system of the world" may be fragmented, I would argue, due to diasporic interpenetrations and mediations. Wenzhou migrants are not complete strangers to develop-man bargains. They have expanded their business model into Europe, acquired new skills, and confronted new challenges along the way. They have also realized new horizons of high-mindedness as they have taken advantage of the demand for fast fashion and exchange rates to support families and compete with neighbors.

To be sure, quests for money undergird globalization. They create new sensibilities. Even if money itself is mostly "historyless stuff," as Graeber (2001, 213) puts it, the quest for money makes history. People bring different experiences to that quest, and from that, new histories emerge. Money can also be used to make history, to make memories. There is far more meaning to money than balances in bank accounts. Money gets transformed into history through homes built, children raised, and families extended.

Grounding sentiments such as high-mindedness in structural encounters reveals much about local work characteristics and the meaning of the migrant quest for money. It allows for avoiding just-in-time interpretations that workers are merely duped by their own self-exploitation or that they are vulgar money-grubbers. Immigrants bring their own histories as they act within larger global forces that underwrite the überflexible production of fast fashion and the transnational social relations that it requires and enables.

# 4

# Crisis

Retired farmers demonstrated haymaking to the delight of a handful of bystanders. Once again, they enlisted a bulky red farm machine for the occasion. Once again, it made lots of noise, lots of smoke, and lots of bales. Enthusiasm for the event had admittedly waned over the years. Nevertheless, a group of diehard volunteers kept at it. The drive for their devotion was not immediately obvious, and newcomers were slow to join. The uninitiated sat on park benches across the way as though an invisible barrier separated the two groups: those participating from up close and those observing from afar. There were a few exceptions of those who penetrated: a Chinese child joyfully rode her bicycle across the concrete rink area in the park's center, a Chinese man read the festival menu with curiosity, and a little boy who might have been Chinese turned pages for the accordion player and was the first to clap after each tune.

The event on July 8, 2012, marked the seventeenth annual Festa della Battitura del Grano. As always, it was held in the park that marks the heart of the hamlet of Seano, which spreads out between beloved terraced hills beneath Mount Albano and dystopic industrial plains toward Prato's city center. That evening, volunteers had prepared for the traditional dinner and placed four long tables at the edge of a grouping of bronze sculptures. The sculptures, much more so than the threshing machines, kept the volunteers loyal to the park. A big part of their mission was to generate social life in this public space: the Parco-Museo Quinto Martini. In all, thirty-six original bronze sculptures grace its grounds. Most were inspired by quotidian moments in the lives of townspeople and created between 1931 and 1988. One sculpture of a seated woman had a leg damaged from fascist soldiers who loathed the artist's work for the respect it showed for working people. Martini made art

FIGURE 4.1. *Joan of Arc* (1978), with her arms reaching toward the sky, per the artist's wishes was placed near the foot of the bridge over the Furba, looking toward the church, to welcome visitors to the Quinto Martini Museum Park.
Photo by Hollis Brashear, 2013

not only *about* the people but also *for* the people. He believed in the sovereignty of the people. The life-size statues call to mind a bygone era, when agricultural livelihoods were more common than industrial ones, when the lives of the count and the peasant were intermingled, when the relations of family were hierarchical according to age and gender. They depict moments of intimacy: a person braving the rain (*La Pioggia*), a nude crouching inward (*Natura*), a figure peering from behind a shutter (*Dietro la Persiana*), a father carrying a son (*Padre e Figlio*), a rooster puffing its feathers (*Il Gallo*).

By 9:00 p.m., the ninety-seven-degree temperature was dropping as cool air from Mount Albano settled into the valley. I bought twenty euros' worth of color-coded food tickets: *primo* (pasta), *secondo* (meat), *contorni* (vegetables), *vin ruspo* (rose wine), *acqua frizzante* (mineral water). The highlights would be the *papero e anatra*, meats prepared from gosling and duck and simmered slowly for hours to make the base of the sauce. I tried to help out but to no avail. My efforts were shot down—there were literally already too many cooks in the makeshift kitchen. I bowed out. The seats filled modestly. I counted thirty-eight guests. The host, Letizia, sat me at a table of honor with others who were volunteers. I hardly knew any of them despite my seventeen years coming and going from the area. My host did her best to make

*[margin annotation: ostracized for her work on Chinese immigrants]*

me feel welcome, but her efforts backfired when she introduced me as a researcher doing a project "on the Chinese." It was, to say the least, a conversation stopper. Complete silence. Of the kind that yearns for rescue. Letizia then said to me, cheerfully, "I hope you find something useful." It was an ambiguous remark that could be taken as a jab or as encouragement. My mood was dark. The comment made my stomach turn. I could only imagine what people were thinking. I was at a loss to say much in my own defense. I had arrived only two weeks earlier; the project was barely under way.

Conversations fell flat. I admired the winemaker's *vin ruspo*, a fresh rosé in the simple peasant tradition, but he seemed reluctant to talk to me. I mentioned a friend in common, but that didn't go over well either. I feigned interest as an older woman across from me complained incessantly about how much families today had changed, how they were nothing like families before when they had so many kids and everyone got along. I let an elderly man keep taking my bottle of wine, which I had been happy to share, but he did not realize that I had bought it, and thought it belonged to him. Everyone else at the table was a volunteer and hence was eating a free meal. He likely figured I did not have any right to the "free" wine. By then, it was too late and too embarrassing to say anything. I let it go.

Afterward, as I lingered and helped where I could, a tense scene unfolded near the snack hut. A Chinese man with long stringy hair, wearing a white shirt and white pants, and smoking a cigarette, approached the hut and ordered ten beers. The volunteer, Daniela, wanted to know how many people there were and how old they were. The customer claimed to be in his thirties. Daniela, a retired schoolteacher, was quick to make a rule and explained that this was not a regular bar and she could absolutely not sell them ten beers. However, she could sell them three beers. That was the solution. He paid, took his beers, and went to join his friends at a picnic table.

A little later, Daniela said how lovely the night had become, how she loved these summer nights when it finally cooled down. "I love coming to the park at midnight," she said. "*Si sta veramente bene tranne questi cinesi, che sono maleducati.* It's really nice except for these Chinese, who are so rude."

Another retired schoolteacher approached with her dog. She had a southern Italian accent. "Prato is a city completely invaded by Chinese, unfortunately. It's a real problem."

I looked around. The few Chinese people seemed fine, minding their own business. The segregation disturbed me, particularly the sense that people resented the immigrants' presence whether in the province generally or in the park specifically. There were a few moments of interaction, but a heavy sense of separation felt impossible to bridge.

I couldn't help but wonder what kind of sculptures Quinto Martini would make today. What would be his view of the museum park, how would he make art about the new people moving into the area, about the interactions between the Chinese and Italians?

A man sitting at a picnic table attributed only a small portion of the crisis to the Chinese. "About 30 percent. The rest is the new generation and the state. The state taxes entrepreneurs at 60 percent. Whenever the pensions of the older generation are gone, we're going to be in—How do you say it in Americano?"

"How do you say it in *Italiano*?" I asked.

"*Merde*."

"Shit."

"The crisis—we're only at the beginning."

*[handwritten margin note: parallels the past issue) of South v. North & working class vs. facism]*

## Crisis and Migration

*[handwritten margin note: highlights the ever present "good ol' days"]*

The festival scene offers a window into a historical sentiment that placed a premium on continuity with the past, yet exposed uncertainty that plagued the present. Indeed, there was a palpable "crisis of presence" in the air while conducting field research for this project. I borrow this turn of phrase from De Martino, the Italian anthropologist who dedicated his life's work to studies of culture and power. He used *crisi della presenza* to describe a sense of existential despair akin to an individual standing at the edge of the earth, precarious and disoriented. He drew from philosophers and political theorists, namely Hegel and Gramsci, to develop a way of thinking about the relationship between selves and the outside world: a dialectic of "presence in the world" and "the world which presents itself." The first speaks to experiences of internal being, whereas the second points to perceptions of an external reality. As the historian of anthropology George Saunders (1993, 883) observes, De Martino's crisis of presence describes "a situation in which one is absorbed in the world" in a way that one loses control of one's own existence." This loss of self-consciousness includes a loss of one's sense of purpose in the world. I draw on De Martino's profound work to capture the kind of melancholic mood that I frequently encountered in Prato. The world as people knew it seemed to be spinning out of control. De Martino was interested in what Saunders (1993, 882) describes as "the perennial problem of subaltern groups" and "one's ability to act on the world rather than simply be a passive object of action." Saunders' optimistic reading, that "the crisis also produces the possibility of transcendence," was also discernible, although at lower decibels.

In the remainder of this chapter, I put encounter ethnography to work. I use chance happenings that occurred through moments of both systematic and spontaneous fieldwork to capture the essence of crisis grounded in specific time and place. Conversations transpired in the course of social life as well as interviews that were tape recorded, transcribed, and translated. This chapter sheds light on economic crisis from the vantage point of four protagonists with starkly different histories. In essence, two strands of encounter comprise this chapter's cloth: public encounters that occur at festivals and the biographical encounters that I disentangle from different migration histories—local, regional, and transnational.

The first section features Letizia, a longtime Tuscan native and prominent art and public works advocate whose frustrations with the new immigrants manifested in concerns for beauty and the environment as well as occasional angry outbursts; the second section highlights Wang, an entrepreneur, believed to be the Chinese person with the oldest business activity in Prato, whose leadership in an Italian artisan association and his own firm's practices suggest a changing political landscape and a range of capitalist and other-than-capitalist underpinnings; the third section focuses on Antonio and Aurora, a couple who migrated from different parts of Italy (he from the hinterlands of Tuscany, she from rural Calabria) to become sweater artisans and whose insights bring things full circle as they draw parallels between Chinese today and Italians past. Together, these protagonists reveal nuanced social relations as well as hybrid economic practices and moral orientations that disrupt notions of globalization as a homogeneous economic force. The figures expose the heterogeneity of global capitalism and its desiring subjects. The stories allow me to trace and make tangible the diverse ways in which crisis and transformation manifest and to reveal how individuals' own life histories relate to encounters with global forces resulting from different trajectories vis-à-vis migration. They allow me to tell a story about how local practices and individuals create social life in the midst of globalization.

### "One World Ends, Another One Begins"

Letizia pulled her hair back in a tight bun. She hung a towel to cover the bathroom vanity. She had more important concerns than fussing over herself in the mirror. She defended her habit to her three adult children. She had fought tirelessly keep the common space of the Parco Museo vibrant with social life and cultural happenings since it was established in 1988. She constantly planned and organized events for the townsfolk even as she showed signs of exhaustion, even as her knee gave out. She engaged in a war of signage with town leaders who hung confusing placards immediately at the park's entrance that indicated an Etruscan archaeological park. For Letizia, life was a battle and she was a warrior, a living version of the Joan of Arc statue that graced the park's entrance near the Furba, that cunning little creek that she treasured. She fought for two causes: art and the environment.

Letizia was rooted in place, culturally and politically from the left, pushed to the right of late, angry and full of fear, adamant that she and her town had been subject to a hostile takeover. She agreed with the popular journalist who framed the Chinese migration to Prato as a siege. She asserted her local roots, saying that her ancestors had always been Tuscans, proudly noting that her paternal grandmother was from the commune of Vinci, home of Leonardo, and that her father, a contractor with communist sensibilities, had initiated a cooperative-style of financing during Prato's boom years, in the burgeoning San Paolo neighborhood, in which dwellers could pay rent and eventually own their houses without the burdens of an official mortgage. When her father was killed suddenly in a street accident, the unpleasant job of paying debts and liquidating the firm fell to her. She was only eighteen years old at the time, but she did it, because she was the one in the family who had the wherewithal to do so. That is the kind of person she was, even as a young woman. Give her a job, she would make sure it not only got done but also done well.

Letizia, born in 1941, grew up during the transformations of the *dopoguerra*, the postwar. She watched her town transition from agriculture to industry and characterized that change thus: "One world ends and another one begins," a phrase she repeated like the refrain to a song. In the days of sharecropping, there was hardly any money. Once factory work took off, things changed.

"The son of a peasant in one month in a factory, in one month, could earn as much as the entire family in a year," Letizia said. "There was no comparison."

For a while, families made ends meet with some members working in Prato's factories and others continuing to work in the fields. The economy was mixed. Capitalist modes of production intermingled with noncapitalist modes. The capitalist form manifested in the factories, which employed workers in the form of wages. A semifeudal economic form survived albeit in a scaled-back form as some peasants continued to work within the patron-client sharecropping system in which about half of their yield went to the landowner. Crops became focused on olive oil and wine, the use of farm animals fell out of favor, and stalls in the old stone farmhouses gradually emptied out. Something else began to happen. The peasants, some with permission from their landlords and others in secret, began to acquire a loom or two to put in those empty stalls. Eventually, they abandoned the countryside altogether, moved down to the flatlands, and built their own houses. During the harvest season, they might go back and work at an hourly rate for their ex-landlord. A number of Letizia's neighbors were former sharecropping peasants who had managed to buy and renovate the old farmhouses.

Then, like a newly hatched butterfly with its own Made in Italy wings, another industry took flight: *la maglieria*, knitwear. This niche, which countered Western intuitions of large-firm capitalist development, was still in evidence during my fieldwork in the mid-1990s. Big-box warehouses served as points of distribution of the production chain. Besides knitting sweater pieces, workshops specialized in singular jobs such as cutting and sewing; attaching or making buttonholes, buttons, labels, and collars; and ironing, folding, or packaging. For several years in the mid-1990s, Letizia and her retired husband, a former state railway employee who had migrated to Tuscany from Campania, in the south, operated a sweater finishing firm. They opened the activity at a time when they needed a little cash flow to finish paying off the house. A relative was in knitwear, and the activity was something easy to launch with little risk and great promise for immediate earnings. That's where I learned that not every job attaching buttons on sweaters was the same. Some sweaters made a lot of lint and made the sewing slow and miserable. Others were fast to work. Even so, subcontractors could never say no to an order. They could say lots of other things.

Unlike the current period of crisis, at that time, work was easy to find and workshops were everywhere—like parsley, or *come il prezzemolo*, an Italian colloquialism that draws an analogy with the common culinary usage of this popular herb. Letizia helped me out in all kinds of ways I will never be able to repay. She could be both critical about an American doing fieldwork in a country that was not her own and enthusiastic about the attention that same researcher was giving to her town and to the hidden histories of women as workers and mothers. At least that's what she told me. At the time, she also once asserted that she would never consent to my interviewing her. Never. I took that to heart. When I began my new project, sixteen years later, I did not dare to ask her for an interview even as she suggested people I might contact. Much to my surprise, however, she started dropping hints that she would like for me to interview her after all, even though it was a mixed invitation. Her barbed critiques of anthropology continued. "If you want to do a serious project," she told me, "you need to go follow the young people to the cinema and see how segregated they are." Right before one interview with a laid-off factory worker that she had arranged, she insisted that I justify the discipline.

I consented, framing my work as a history of the present. She interrupted, saying that researchers had an ethical commitment to objectivity. I found myself trying to explain anthropology's critique of the objective, detached observer, that knowledge is often co-constructed between the anthropologist and his/her interlocutors. I was linguistically at a disadvantage. As an adult learner of Italian, while I had decent fluency to the point that my mother-tongue interlocutors would often ask me why I spoke such good Italian (often, I felt, after I made a mistake!), when my emotions stirred up and I felt under attack, I often floundered. Inside her house, the walls adorned with her uncle's paintings, I drew a parallel with his passion to represent quotidian experiences and my efforts to produce not just an objective scientific report but rather a literary interpretation of social life. That went over like a lead balloon. For her, artists who enjoyed the stature of her uncle represented the apex of human existence. Artists were more saintly than saints. They were so valuable, she halfway joked, that they ought to be taxed like property! Unable to produce a satisfactory response, I reminded myself to be grateful that she saw enough potential value in what I was doing to engage me and to help me out on her own terms.

Several days before I was scheduled to leave in August 2012, she insisted that I interview her, and so I did, the day before my departure. The change of heart perplexed me, and I cannot explain it. I can say that she spoke freely and that it was rich, moving, and at times difficult.[1]

"Knitwear worked like this: every house was a little workshop. What the Chinese do now, *closed in the ghettos of their big workshops*, was done by the Italians, and in a certain sense we ourselves were the Chinese working in the houses with machines *al nero*," literally, black, unregistered, or off the books and thus illegal. Despite Prato being the birthplace of Francesco Datini (1335–1410), the merchant credited with adopting and spreading the practice of double-entry bookkeeping, precise accounting was rare among Italians especially between the 1970s and 1990s (Origo 1984; Padgett and Powell 2012). As Letizia spoke about the Chinese, each word was drawn out, as though to emphasize a contrast with what the Italians did, back then, to what the Chinese were doing, now, only to realize that as she described the work, it sounded pretty much the same. Workshops with heavy equipment were often registered, but women, retirees, or youth who did finishing work by hand were 90 percent unregistered. The people who delivered the work were figures with their own name, *fattorini*. People tended to despise them, she said, because they could be rude, demanding, and even demeaning.

"They would bring the work from the firm, literally throw it on the floor of people's houses, the women would take these bundles of sweaters, finish each piece, and then these guys would come and pick them up," she explained. "And on our work that they would pick up, the deliverymen would make a certain amount. Their work consisted in bringing and picking up, bringing and picking up, not to firms but to microfirms, just like we had in that period, in the household." There were any number of scenarios that contracting firms could use to get around paying some taxes. Off the books were the pensioners, teenagers, and elderly women who did finishing work by hand. "It was work totally *al nero.*"

For the microenterprises that proliferated in the environs of Prato in the 1980s and 1990s, in Letizia's eyes, there was a justification. This economic activity enriched the area. It gave women and pensioners a bit of cash so they could indulge themselves every now and then. It was a classic case of household-based economic activity entangling with a global market in which factories did their outsourcing not beyond national borders but rather within their own territory. At the end of the 1990s, immigrants were known to open enterprises with secondhand equipment, beat the Italians at their tactics of circumventing tax laws, and charge half the price per piece. "This wiped out the microeconomy," she said.

Although the Pratesi, too, were after money, Letizia asserted they were also capable of desiring something beautiful, and that is where art and the environment came into play.

"Our equilibrium is very delicate; it's been thrown into crisis by many things," she said, reflecting on her own values and highlighting democracy and art. "You can't live without beauty; otherwise, we are really just brutes."

Notions of beauty, despite seeming natural and universal, result from historical and social constructs. The cultivation of certain tastes is deeply linked to civilizing and socializing processes with profound class elements. Fine art in Italy and elsewhere is typically associated with high culture. Indeed, Lilith Mahmud (2014) in her ethnography *The Brotherhood of Freemason Sisters: Gender, Secrecy, and Fraternity in Italian Masonic Lodges* makes a brilliant case for the paradoxical place of high culture in the project of liberal humanism. In particular, she demonstrates how performances that cultivate taste for certain forms of knowledge regarded as legitimate are key in reproducing elite European society. The artistic field, like any field of cultural production, "is a *field of forces,*" but it is also a "*field of struggles* tending to transform or conserve this field of forces," as Bourdieu (1993, 30) so famously noted. The paradoxes in the Italian context are twofold. First, although Italian national education curriculum formally guarantees knowledge equality to students, depending on which type of high school they attend, Mahmud (2014, 130) reminds how curricular content is "a highly gendered, racialized and classed knowledge formation that expresses and reproduces nationalist and Occidentalist values as canonical." Second, despite this national commitment to enculturating the masses through education, in day-to-day understandings, high culture is viewed as not so easily teachable. Particularly in cosmopolitan urban contexts such as Florence or Rome, there exists an unwavering and widespread belief that high culture is a result of socialization through the family that a person happens to be born into. Hence the phrase, *La cultura si fa a casa,* high culture "is made at home" (Mahmud 2014, 131).

Letizia's passion for art came from a somewhat different place. During her guided tours of the museum park, she made sure to convey her conviction that people are sovereign and that art is for the people. Quinto Martini's work lent itself to these principles first because of its subject matter and second because of its accessibility. The subjects of both his paintings and his sculptures interpreted life from his hometown of Seano and captured extraordinary aspects of ordinary lives. Residents or passersby could take in the bronze sculptures adorning the park anytime, day or night.

A woman beggar (*Mendicante*) in the Parco Museo extends her right hand, several coins in her palm, and with her left holds a shawl closed at her neck. She wears a cardboard box on her head. Flanked at her side a separate sculpture of a man under the rain (*Uomo sotto la pioggia*) is caught in mid-stride, hands buried in his pockets, gaze cast into the distance. Surely, Letizia reasons, Martini observed this scene. The sculpture captures the moment right after the man gave the woman the money, she reasons. He avoids looking at her because the person who has the means to give money experiences a sense of embarrassment. The pope and the priest say we should look the beggar in the eye when we give money, she says, but that's hard to do. One feels empathy yet shame at the same time. It reflects a profound sentiment of the human condition. In Letizia's interpretation, the *Mendicante* wears the cardboard box like a queen wears a crown, and she knows that being poor isn't her fault. She has dignity.

It struck me as an ironic victory that the beggar was one of five works from the Parco Museo that curator Sergej Androsov of the Hermitage Museum in Saint Petersburg selected to add to the museum's permanent collection of twentieth-century European sculpture.[2] The sculptures were recast in bronze from the original molds in a studio outside of Florence, carefully treated, cleansed, packaged, and transported to Russia in anticipation of the inauguration. The Associazione Amici del Museo Ermitage, a Florence-based friends of the Hermitage Museum, organized about sixty people who made the three-day trip. I was honored to join this cultural delegation, which included Italian dignitaries, art restorers, family members, and friends. In addition, the delegation had a subgroup, including the mayor, promoting products Made in Italy in hopes of expanding the market in Russia. A buffet featured Italian wines and a combination of Tuscan appetizers with Russian delicacies.

Remarkably, world leaders in the field of art restoration from Florence's Opificio delle Pietre Dure (literally, the Laboratory of Hard Stones), known for its meticulous restorations of Quattrocento and Renaissance paintings and sculptures, the likes of Ghiberti's Golden Doors of Paradise whose replica adorns the Baptistery in Florence, had taken the park under its tutelage. As such, they offered promise of ongoing care to Martini's sculptures, subject as they were to the elements, both natural and human (Agnoletti et al. 2014). The director and staff experts made the trip and gave a presentation on the Opificio's history, technical innovations, and applications to works in the Parco Museo to about sixty attendees, including Hermitage staff.

On May 24, 2013, the day of the inauguration, several hundred people crowded into an elegant round room of the former Czar's Palace in anticipation of the Italian and Russian dignitaries' addresses to mark the opening. To think, the grandiose rooms with their marble floors had once only been open to members of an elite court society. What a profound contrast, to the art of Martini, born into a peasant family as he was, and committed to representing quotidian life.

On the other side of a ceremonial ribbon, the door to the exhibition room was slightly ajar. I set eyes on the *Mendicante*. She stood alone. I felt unsettled. A sense of awe and sadness overcame me all at once: awe for the beggar's presence in such an opulent museum, sadness for her solitary position. "She seems abandoned," several of us repeated to one another. No longer did she have the man at her side. No longer was she in the comfort of her hometown. The curator, in conversation, remarked that it was better for her and the others here, inside a museum—"*stanno meglio che al parco*"—but Letizia challenged his view. Her daughter and I joked that he would soon be pursuing bronzes from the Parco Museo itself. Letizia looked worried, if only for an instant. Although she valued the attention on her late uncle's work, she preferred the sculpture in its original context, open and dedicated to the people, as Quinto Martini wished, at home, in the context in which they were created.

The next day, when Letizia and several others returned to the room, they observed something remarkable: museum visitors placing coins in the *Mendicante*'s palm. Letizia was stunned—people had actually given her alms. The beggar's charisma touched them just as it had touched the Russian museum's curator and the Florentine restorers.

In Florence, modern art was typically on the losing end of cultural happenings. Much to my surprise, a year after the Hermitage event, upon my return in June 2014, Letizia invited me to accompany her to the inauguration of the Museo Novecento. The opening of a museum featuring twentieth-century art was noteworthy in the heart of the Renaissance city, and its location in the famous Piazza Santa Maria Novella made it all the more radical. The building literally stood opposite the basilica with its gracious inlaid black-and-white marble, Romanesque-Gothic arches, and collection of Renaissance art classics such as Masaccio's *Holy Trinity* (1427), known for its remarkable trompe l'oeil and its inscription that gestured to every human's ultimate crisis of presence: "I once was what you are, and what I am you will also be."

I was curious and welcomed the invitation. When I arrived at her house at the agreed-upon hour, at two o'clock, she had changed the plan, telling me that due to insufferable long lines, we would be better off going later that evening, after the Italy versus Uruguay soccer game. Eventually, we left at eight o'clock. An hour later, after getting lost and succumbing to a numbing anti-immigrant earful, we arrived in the center of Florence. She pulled up to a curb alongside the train station, near a 0–24 tow zone sign, and despite my protests, left the car parked there. I had to let go of my drastically different comfort zone regarding parking laws, as well as my fear that if we got towed, the responsibility would fall on me to take care of my aging companion. In the United States, I reasoned, she probably would have qualified for a handicapped permit. I followed her across the busy street in front of the station, gasping as she almost got taken out by a bus, and then across the piazza, telling myself that we would not be gone long.

Museum patrons—mostly Italians except for a few outliers such as the American anthropologist—were gathered in full force outside a huge locked iron gate. Counter to my expectations, the crowd of about fifty people was riled up. The inauguration hours had been advertised as continuing until 10:00 p.m. that evening, and it was only 9:00 p.m., so people were angry that the museum staff had closed the gates an hour prior to their expectations. One woman was trying to shove her way through. Another waved her invite in the air. There was a scuttle through the bars between the museum staff inside the gate and a woman outside the gate. A woman staffer berated them: "If you had wanted to come, you should have come earlier!" Finally, one of the museum staff decided to let the protesting patrons have their way. Where else could I witness a near revolution for admission into an art opening?

Inside, exhibited on a second-floor courtyard, was Quinto Martini's *Bombardamento*—a provocative work in cement of a female figure protecting a child beneath a piece of cement. We took photos to document the moment, and I could see that Letizia was pleased. Her struggles were paying off. We finished our tour of the museum, somewhat in haste as the museum staffer who followed us and other visitors hurled threatening comments about how little time we had.

We headed out into the piazza. Letizia made disparaging comments about its condition and the way immigrants occupied the space. The contrast between her satisfaction at having her uncle's art on display in an important modern museum and her displeasure at how immigrants were entering into the fold was palpable. She voiced the dominant and resentful sentiment that the Chinese refused to integrate into Italian society, that they isolated themselves, and that of Italians or Italian culture they could give a damn—*a loro non gliene frega un tubo degli italiani.* In fact, she would welcome integration, she told me. "We aren't against the Chinese, but we also have to defend ourselves, they *divorano tutto, divorano tutto, di-vo-ra-no let-ter-al-men-te tut-to,* they devour everything, literally everything, then what will they give us in exchange?"

In these moments, when her talk shifted to an anti-immigrant rant, I reminded myself of her conviction that without beauty humans become brutes. I reminded myself of how she had expressed her values for a democratic society in which everyone has a shot at a decent life and in which beauty is fundamental. The way Letizia consistently articulated and manifested her principles also suggested that the immigrant presence was, for her, deeply connected to a precarious and uncertain future.

> Having said that, it's also the case that you need to appreciate it, you need to defend it, you need to protect it. I don't know how in this world things will go forward, because if everything has to be based on production, if everything has to be based on consumption. Christ failed, communism failed, capitalism failed. I believe only in the environment. I have faith in the environment and in art. . . . It's necessary to grow culturally, only the environment and culture will save the world, nothing else. All this talk of economic recovery, recovery, recovery. Recovery means to consume, consume, consume. People are going to have to be more cultured, more attentive, and more informed.

As for changing dynamics, the township of Seano and the adjoining one of Poggio a Caiano, both in the province of Prato, between 2003 and 2010 witnessed an increase in the migratory presence of more than 400 percent (Sambo 2013a). Such numbers represent dramatic and quick social and demographic changes. Tensions manifest. On the bus, just beyond the site of a summer festival, I caught sight of a banner with black writing: *Morte ai cinesi e ROM.* Death to Chinese and Roma. I reported this to Letizia and her eldest son, one of the organizers, they expressed concern, and the banner disappeared.[3]

Making a link between the immigrant presence and De Martino's crisis of presence, Cristiana Giordano notes that "recognizing the other is fraught with the danger of losing one's own center, . . . of losing one's own presence." For foreigners and natives alike, lifestyles or practices that seem strange and incomparable—what Giordano labels "mutual incommensurabilities"—can be a source of conflict. In her book *Migrants in Translation,* she interprets the crisis of presence itself as referring not only to existential fears but also to the temporality of being—in other words, humanity's place in history. Ultimately, the crisis of presence is triggered in the individual "by situations that challenge his or her ability to handle external and internal realities" (Giordano 2014, 54, 85). The task of culture, or its failure, De Martino observed, is to suture inner and outer worlds together and subjects in their everyday making of meaning.

Letizia's mode of realizing her vision, in addition to the work with her uncle's legacy, had been to serve the city for eighteen years, four on the town council and fourteen as an assessor, initially as the head of public works and finally as the head of the environment. This placed her in a privileged position to see certain abuses among residents, and she pointed to the Chinese with cut-and-sew activities who in her view practiced uncivil means of disposing of garbage or dangerous ways of handling pressurized gas canisters. If an Italian firm would leave out dozens of garbage bags, she recounted, a Chinese firm would leave out hundreds of bags. She called it a "shocking" amount that suggested an abundance of production. For someone who had worked in knitwear, the quantity was mindboggling. Her mantra that one world ends and another begins was linked to another essential view: those endings and beginnings cannot simply be left to their own devices. They had to be overseen and managed with care. *One world ends, another one begins.* It had become very difficult to reconcile the changing world, and how it appeared out of control, with the one she wanted to foster.

### "Cut and Sew"

Talk of constructing new worlds was as prolific as fast fashion. On my scouting rounds, I came across a flyer announcing a public encounter: "Italy-China, opportunity of economic-cultural exchange," to be held on July 25, 2012, at the Festa Democratica Seano. The event promised a panel of important guests: the president of the province of Prato, the mayor of Carmignano,

the president of the Prato branch of Confederazione Nazionale dell'Artigia-
nato e della Piccola e Media Imprese, a small business association for artisans,
and its lauded Chinese vice-president. It was an ethnographer's dream panel.

From Prato's central station I boarded an 8:25 p.m. bus and watched as it
followed the route along Via Roma, meandered through the outskirts of the
city, traversed the industrial district of Macrolotto 1 with its fast-fashion firms
between apartments and sunflower fields, and crossed the one-lane bridge to
arrive at Seano's Zona Pista Rossa, or the Red Track Zone. The Ferris wheel's
yellow lights blinked around an orange sunburst. The fair was under way. I
arrived a little before 9:00 p.m. The session was set for 9:30 p.m. Letizia's oldest son, one of the festival organizers, warned me that it would probably start
late. A storm threatened. A poster announcing the evening's event hung from
a cordoned-off area in front of a stage. The seating area was empty except for
a pair of men. I had time to kill.

The fair took place each year in this zone, a public space known for at-
tracting people to walk its large looping track especially come late summer
evenings once cool air descended from Mount Albano. Not coincidentally,
the creation of this public walking space was one that Letizia proudly saw to
fruition when she headed up the public works department. The plot of land
sits at the intersection of the well-trafficked Strada Statale Pistoiese, which
links Florence to Pistoia, in one northwest-southeast direction from a roundabout, and in a crosswise direction, via Baccheretana connects the industrial
zone of Bocca di Stella to townships under the jurisdiction of Carmignano,
one of seven of the province's municipalities.

I walked around the track and checked out the stands and the rides. Vendors sold kitsch goods such as makeup and fingernail polish, secondhand action figures, tickets for a lottery fund raiser, and lots of food and sweets. The
wind blew. Dark clouds threatened rain. I repeated my walk, then decided
to get a bottle of water from the Young Democrats' stand. I gave a young
guy a €50 bill, and he gave me back two €20 bills, a €10, and a €2 coin. I
fumbled with the change, realizing the volunteer had given me back €2 more
in change than I had paid him. I hesitated to mention the mistake. I suspected
it would embarrass him. But in good conscience I did so anyway. Indeed, he
seemed pissed off and ignored his coworker, who told him he should thank
the *signora*.

I sat on a bench, alone. There was no sign of the Italy-China event. I felt
annoyed at being an anthropologist. I pretty much would rather have been
anyone else, anywhere else. The weather was another annoyance, being alone
in public at a fair was still another annoyance. Especially as a woman. I felt
like a freak. The freak-foreign-woman show. I wrote a field note, 9:45 p.m.:

"This is miserable. Winds. Gusts. Dust." One guy cast a leering gaze at me; a woman with a man glared suspiciously. A grating voice blared over a loudspeaker: "*Oh signori io sono pronto a giocare.*" Oh ladies and gentlemen, I am ready to play!

I abandoned my Protestant sense of time and purpose to observe what was happening around me. Over and over again, people told me the Chinese here were *brutta gente*, ugly people. I had heard this from all types of people, from all walks of life and political persuasions. On the fairgrounds, I noticed a group of four young Chinese men, then three women, wearing fashionable black-and-silver fitted tops paired with white pants, and five teenage girls donning stylish haircuts. They were hardly the dour Chinese dressed in gray Mao suits of decades past.

I looked at my watch. It read 10:00 p.m. Could the debate really be starting this late? I decided to look in the food tent. Organizers had moved the event inside, I was told, because of the threat of inclement weather. Ah, to be only partly in the loop. I felt stupid—I had been waiting at the stage outside. I brushed it off. About fifty people sat at long tables, many with empty pizza plates. I noticed most attendees were men. There were six women. Most were Italian, except for six Chinese. A panel of eight men sat up front. The mayor spoke. I didn't seem to have missed much.

Mayor Doriano Cirri pointed to what he called the big question: What can be done about the crisis? He called on his audience to stop talking about the crisis and start talking about something concrete. He called on listeners to create networks and promote the richness of the territory. He criticized Prato's leaders for putting so many resources into police raids of Chinese firms with few results. (Recall, this was the Democratic fair, and he was from the left-leaning coalition, whereas Prato's elected leaders were from the right-leaning one.) By contrast, as far as concrete things, he emphasized three: innovation, responsibility, and courage. Finally, he praised Wang, the vice-president of the artisan association, for his ten-year membership, leadership, and bridging between Italian and Chinese economic activities.

The next speaker, a former *assessore*, or council member, who had traveled at least eighty times to China since 2000, described China as an intriguing market with demand for Italian products. His message was a common one for the evening: products that deliver quality of life and hence goods related to fashion and food. He underscored his view that Made in Italy offered value-added quality. Others, too, would emphasize the value of quality products, even certified ones. Still, he acknowledged that Italian firms moving to China had not enjoyed good results. He attributed this to poor organization.

Wang brought a different perspective to the floor as he emphasized the challenges, especially for Chinese migrants, and pointed out that now children were born in Italy, that some eventually attempt to become Italian citizens. As the event wound down, the mayor took the microphone one last time to call for working through relatives in China to strengthen Italy's ties with the market there. Reiterating the potential, yet challenge, of selling in China, he ended on three points: to know oneself well, to have trust, and to work together to get out of the crisis.

A year later, in July 2013, I volunteered several nights a week at the same Festa Democratica in a pizzeria set up in the heart of the fairgrounds. I was stationed at the drink counter with volunteers from the Democratic Party's Youth Association. This struck me as funny, given the age difference, not to mention the gaffe from my well-intended correction of incorrect change the previous year. I wore one of the festival T-shirts and laughed at the jokes. We took turns filling orders: pouring beer and Coke from a spigot or filtered water from a dispenser and carrying the beverages out to the thirsty fairgoers. I was embracing my inner anthropologist again—excited, stimulated, curious, and immersed.

One evening, while reaching across the table to serve a beer to a patron, I took a double take. It was Wang! "*Siamo co-paesani!*" he pronounced, "We're co-townies!" He recognized me and explained that he lived nearby. I was touched. I had no idea we were living in the same part of Prato's environs.

Wang claims to hold the record of having the longest business activity of any Chinese individual in Prato. His tale of becoming an entrepreneur has its share of twists and turns as well as legal and precarious statuses. He recounted his story to Bressan and me during an interview at the artisan association office in Prato. It was inspiring to hear his story after having seen him publicly on stage at the fair. His account illuminates a hard journey with a remarkable ending. It sheds light on the particularities of people from Wenzhou and their "spiritual insistence," as he put it, related to the pursuit of becoming an entrepreneur.

In some ways, Wang was an unlikely candidate to end up in his role of Prato's honorary historic Chinese entrepreneur. Born in 1958 and raised in a family of teachers, he left China in the early 1980s after finishing college to continue his studies in Brussels. He had an opportunity. An aunt ran a restaurant in Brussels, and one of her clients directed a university-level school in the neighborhood. She approached her client about her nephew, and the director offered to invite him to attend his school. When Wang arrived, at twenty-four years old, he was eager to learn. Within six months, he got kicked out.

"The director said, 'You don't speak English or French, how can you study?'" he said, chuckling as he recalled that part of his migratory story.[4]

He went to Paris where he did two years as a clandestine immigrant. The way he put it, using the verb *fare*, to do, it sounds like military service. He worked as an undocumented immigrant in the clothing sector. And then, he recalled, came 1986, the year Italy was offering its first amnesty under the Martelli Law.[5] When amnesty was announced, within twenty-four hours he had to present himself at offices in Rome, where he received a *permesso di soggiorno*, a residence permit, for Rome proper.

He ended up getting a job in the fast-fashion sector in Campi Bisenzio, an unremarkable municipality between Florence and Prato. One day, the police showed up. His residence permit was for Rome, not Campi. So he had to go back to Rome's *questura*, the police headquarters that handle such affairs, and eventually found housing and work in Empoli, about an hour from Prato, once again making clothes. Through his networks, he eventually found an opportunity to start a business. He took the required classes for business owners, studying for three hours every night from 8:00 p.m. to 11:00 p.m. for about eight months, learning about laws related to commerce, taxes, import-export, and the like. In 1988, he moved to Prato with his small business certification (Registro Esercenti il Commercio, or REC) and opened his firm.[6]

"They tell me there exists only one Chinese who has a longer activity than twenty-five years in this city: it's Wang," he teased.

As we asked him about the value of working in the Made in Italy, at first there seemed to be some confusion as he pointed to the more elite strata of Chinese consumers who want the luxury brands such as Gucci, Dolce & Gabbana, and PINKO. I clarified, asking whether Made in Italy serves as a sort of magnetic force for migrants. Confusion endured. A struggle came to mind that Fangli and I had over a question related to value as we developed our interview protocol. I wanted a question that got at value, in particular, that addressed the paradoxical situation that Chinese left China and came to Italy to make products sewn with a Made in Italy label. Fangli insisted that the question did not make sense to Chinese from Wenzhou, that it would be challenging to translate and complicated to explain. I had a hard time wrapping my head around her assertion of complexity. The question seemed obvious to me. The allure of the Made in Italy brand was so powerful. Only later when I began to read about the Florence flood of 1966 and develop the argument that value was related to historical sentiment did I realize the significance of this historical process and meaning. Bressan clarified my question and asked whether it served as a *spinta*, a motivation, for people to come to Italy. "Look, no. I am a connoisseur, but I don't know many things," Wang said. I sensed there was still some confusion. And then he said something profound: "Italy is a market and like this. . . . Exports are very important if, as a brand, Italy helps exports—that is, they also help employment for the Italian economy. If it's not that, then what? Especially clothing for Prato, for the economy in Prato."

His firm specialized in sewing yarns. He provided materials to cut-and-sew firms, known as *taglia e cuci*. Most of his business was with China—to the only factory in China known to make great yarn—but customers also included Italian and American firms. He has watched his ratio change from 100 percent Italian customers to 20 percent Italians, 80 percent Chinese, in the last two decades. Some of his products were semifinished sewing threads, which were then dyed in Prato, whereas others were already finished and ready to sell and use. He became known for his quality product and managed to arrange an exclusive deal with a large firm that was acquired by Chinese owners. For this large company, he explained, "Italy is exclusive to Wang." The agreement was made on trust—for the most part, there were no written contracts. The Chinese company didn't know anything about yarn at the time they acquired machines from Savio, an Italian leader in the yarn finishing machine sector.[7] As Wang described how he worked with them, teaching them about yarn, he drew on a metaphor. In his Chinese-inflected Italian he said, "*lubrificazione con la sella*." Translated, the gist of his phrase is grease the wheels, to make things go smoothly. His lubricating efforts worked wonders.

"So at this point the factory asks me, 'Wang, you want a part of the commission or what do you want from us?' I said that I've helped them make yarn of quality, I wanted an exclusive to Italy for this yarn—until now [I've had it]."

A sort of globalized *guanxi* informed the business transaction. *Guanxi* may be described as personal connections—"a social testament at any one time to the relative depth and breadth of one's network of loyalty and reciprocity" (Chu 2010, 89).[8] Once largely kin-based, *guanxi* has become a cultural metaphor for shoring up social relationships. Scholars caution against understanding *guanxi* as a bounded and unchanging practice destined to wither away in the face of the rules of commerce in an age of global capitalism (Lem 2010; Lo and Otis 2003). Novel social arrangements in transnational zones of encounter may be easily overlooked: "The newness of these arrangements has largely gone unnoticed, for their distinctive strategies of accumulation are obscured because they take the guise of 'traditional' patterns of family and of networking based on *guanxi* particularism" (Nonini and Ong 1997, 11). While *guanxi* practices may decline in some contexts, they may be just as likely to flourish in others. Observers should treat *guanxixue* "as a multifaceted ever-changing set of practices" (Yang 2002, 459). The heterogeneity of *guanxi* is most certainly due to historical shifts—its origins in Confucian times contrast with modern influences. Mao's communist era condemned Confucianism, undermined the power of the patriarchal clan, and essentially laid the groundwork for more elastic practices: "Untethered from guanxi bases," for example, the family, "social actors could build guanxi ties with anyone, just by starting a series of favor exchanges" (Hsu 2005, 314). *Guanxi* "evolved into a flexible tool which allowed people to create trustworthy, expansive business networks in the absence of adequate legal guarantees—a type of capitalism without contracts" (Hsu 2005, 311).

Wang's firm was anchored in such heterogeneous organization and had robust activity. It would be considered small by most any standard. It had four employees, plus family members, depending on time-of-year exigencies. This type of small business mirrors the 1980s in Prato, when there was a boom in microfirms. "All our families had themselves a microenterprise," chimed in an association staff member who sat in on the interview.

"The Chinese in Prato within ten years have made a central district of fast fashion. This is a good share of the city," Wang said. He credits Chinese initiative for helping Prato become the center of clothing production in Europe. In the past, Prato was known for fabrics and threads, but not clothing. The exception was the sweater-making niche. Without Chinese workers and entrepreneurs, he added, fast fashion would not be competitive in Prato—a widespread viewpoint, one that a recent Clean Clothes Campaign echoes: "Chinese workshops have made a fundamental contribution in maintaining the competitiveness of the Italian fashion industry, providing their clients with flexibility and cost reductions" (Clean Clothes Campaign 2014b, 19).

To explain this entrepreneurial spirit, Wang points to the formative policies of Deng Xiaoping, especially during the 1970s to the early 1990s, and his policy of *duo lao duo de*, which means "if you work more, you should earn more." A good swath of Chinese people embraced this ideology during that time, he said, as did migrants who left for Europe. This is one of Deng's most significant ideologies and represents the transformation from a planned economy to a market economy in China starting in the late 1970s. This became a primary characteristic of a socialist market economy in China. For Chinese migrant workers, major social and legal problems may arise from this entrepreneur spirit. Wang has observed Chinese migrant workers who lack consciousness of the law.

Unlike in China, where factories tend to be massive, firms in Prato are small, typically fewer than ten workers. Opportunities for a person to own his or her own firm were therefore greater in Italy than in China. Wang characterized becoming an entrepreneur in the current Chinese context as very difficult. He emphasized that in Prato, the value of being an entrepreneur does not mean that you "can be just bossy and earn a lot of money." Entrepreneurship often means the opposite. Most entrepreneurs work very hard, even harder compared to ordinary workers, and don't earn that much. A common theme in our interviews with Chinese migrants was hard work, the ultracompetitive environment, and the struggle to make money. Nevertheless, the migrants desire to be entrepreneurs, Wang said. It is in large part a desire for autonomy. This means they can have their own business, no matter how small. They can have the right to decide what they do and how to do it. Instead of just working for other people, doing the same things, they can shift responsibilities from cutting and sewing to other aspects of firm management, such as deliveries or commercial interactions.

Firm organization countered models of global capitalism in at least three important ways. First, noteworthy is that there was not a significant gendered division of labor. This contrasts with scholarly observations of firms in China, where gender-based inequalities tended to be pronounced (Greenhalgh 1994). The minimal gendered division of labor in Prato's manufacturing sector was notable among the Chinese firms. Two types of data support this observation. First, official statistics from Prato's chamber of commerce offer comparisons across business ownership by country of origin. Chinese entrepreneurs showed a relatively small gap in terms of the percentage of male to female owners: 55 percent men as compared with 45 percent women. Other groups, such as Albanian, Moroccan, and Pakistani business owners, all suggested a much wider gender gap of 90 percent men versus 10 percent women owners. Romanian entrepreneurs had a split of 82 percent men as opposed to 18 percent women (Caserta and Marsden 2014). The other source of data was through our interviews and participant observation, where we discerned a low degree of a gendered division of labor in the fast-fashion sector. Men were as likely as women to be cutting and sewing the garments. As Wang put it, "It does not matter because in textiles both men and women send the machine forward equally."

Second, the family is central to Chinese firms in Prato. Many parents sent children back to China for periods of time, especially when children were young. Wang hesitated, at first, then told us that in his family, it happened with both of his children. His son was born in 1987 and then two years later was sent to China for a year, then brought back to Italy to begin preschool. Wang's mother, the child's paternal grandmother, cared for him. To this end, strategies of flexibility, reciprocity, and *guanxi* extended to the family.

Third, firm owners' relationships with their employees had tentacles that reached well beyond the shop floor, for better or worse. Part of this can be understood through a diverse economies framework in which economies, even on the global stage, are hybrid. As such, owner-employee relationships cannot simply be reduced to ones of utility or of classic capitalist ones of profit extraction, or even exploitation—although both of those also exist— but also involve complex relations of reciprocity. Wang and others spoke of trust, or *guanxi*. In a business context, this means that relationships tend to be informal and unwritten rather than formal and written. Deals based on oral agreements rather than written contracts mirror postwar Prato of the twentieth century. Conditions remain ambiguous. On a negative side, rights are far from guaranteed, and wide use of subcontracting, informal sector, and migrant labor in supply chains can be a red flag. As the Tailored Wages report notes, "we would not consider Italy to be a 'low risk' country in terms of rights" (Clean Clothes Campaign 2014a, 52). The report underscores that health and safety problems were widespread in the area. On an ambiguous side, in the millennial context of intensified immigration policy, firm owners tend to have a good deal of control over the legal status of their employees in terms of paperwork related to residence status. The Bossi-Fini immigration law of 2002 tightened the link between residence status and employment contracts. Owners reportedly sometimes pay workers not by the hour but by the piece, to motivate faster work and, on a positive side, even engage in bonuses or profit sharing with their workers.

Wang told us of one entrepreneur who struck a deal with his workers in which he paid them the same salary regardless of whether work demand was intense, requiring putting in eleven or twelve hours a day, or whether demand lagged, requiring little to no work. During slow times, the employee could take off three months. "Three months of vacation, I can go back to China for three months; however, the stipend is the same," Wang explained. Everybody was happy. In the past, this system existed in Prato among Italians, but it was technically not in line with labor laws.

Another form of reciprocity manifests in the widespread practice of firm owners providing food and housing to their employees. Until 2014, it was extremely common for workers to live in makeshift sleeping quarters within the cut-and-sew workshops and come together for meals in a separate room or an angle of the workshop dedicated to cooking and eating, as our visits to factory floors also confirmed. In our interviews, we learned that many fast-fashion workers felt compelled to save money to pay off the debts incurred as a result of the journey. In addition, we often heard that migrants had a normal house back in China but that, here in Italy, they did not want to spend all their earnings paying rent. Some of them knew it was not right to live and work in the same space, but they still took the risk; as Wang noted, "no matter if it's a white cat or a black cat, if it can catch a rat, it's good cat."

The practice of living in work spaces began to lessen in 2014 after the tragic Teresa Moda fire, which changed the tenor and purpose of factory inspections. Wang was critical of the initial government response, using force to shut down factories. "I thought the government did not think about how to make or help these factories become legal. I told the government that if you shut down all the factories . . . the economy of Prato, of the whole Italy will be affected." Wang advocates a carrot-and-stick approach. He calls for a system of controls not solely based on punishment but also on praise. To improve safety and sanitary compliance, he believes, the key is to find a way to educate firm owners.

To that end, one of Wang's missions has been to recruit Chinese firms and help them conform to the most important health, safety, and finance regulations. As of mid-2013 about one hundred firms were association members. Wang sees bringing them into the fold as a win-win situation. "To be enrolled also means to better know the rules and also to be less afraid of controls," he explained. Membership entails embarking on a journey designed to lead to legal status. Most firms, regardless of ownership, are said to be out of compliance in one way or another. Foreign-owned firms, in particular, minimize their risk of being closed due to ever-changing rules, and compliance also means providing more humane conditions for workers.

Another one of Wang's initiatives has been to provide leadership for building public housing in the industrial district of Bocca di Stella, located just across from the site of the summer festival in Seano, with the goal of moving workers' living quarters out of nearby factory spaces. He worked with the Chinese consulate to secure lending from China with the loan backed by land or housing. The Chinese, he said, have made fast fashion central to Europe, but their presence in Prato has also created challenges of image and governance for the city.

Conversation shifted to matters of illegality and then–security minister Aldo Milone, mastermind of the infamous blitzes and known for iron-fisted efforts to rid the city of lawlessness. Wang may not agree with all of the security minister's tactics. He called on the cut-and-sew sector to draw a metaphor. Good city leaders must study the situation, then keep the good and cut out the part that's not so good. Some firms work within the rules; others do not. "How do you cut with scissors?" he asked, rhetorically. The Chinese who use fake names just to escape paying any taxes, for example, they should be cut out, he said. If the city cuts out the not good, in Wang's opinion, they help out the Chinese as a whole. But the situation needs to be studied closely. Like with sharp scissors, leaders need to cut with care. "Scissors must cut well," he said. The approach arguably shows respect for the migrant spiritual insistence and carves out space to cultivate this entrepreneurial characteristic. He added, "Yes, yes, cut and sew, yes, cut and sew. In my opinion, the stick and the carrot."

### "A World Undone"

The world was pushing up against a precipice.

Aurora and Antonio invited me to come with them after we finished dinner in their garage-turned-kitchen. Around 10:00 p.m. on July 2, 2013, the destination was the park next to the Statale. A red track cuts a five hundred–meter loop through a big grassy field, once again the site for the Festa Democratica Seano. Signs of the summer festival were appearing: a tent frame, trucks, and RVs, all awaiting the assortment of rides and the opening of vendor and game stalls. Most nights, there was a lively scene as the park attracted people from all walks of life: old-timers, newcomers, citizens, and immigrants.

My thoughts turned to a curbside image from my day's fieldwork. At the hospital in Prato, parents of an infant had not come for their scheduled exam, giving the medical staff, my research assistant, and me a sense of having been stood up. To make the best of our time, my young assistant and I decided to visit the clinic that served undocumented migrants, but it was closed. Outside, a sign on the door read:

> Aperto nei giorni:
> MARTEDI—GIOVEDI—VENERDI
> Dalle ore 17.00—alle ore 19.00
> Caritas Clinic
> Open during the days:
> TUESDAY—THURSDAY—FRIDAY
> From 5:00 p.m.—7:00 p.m.

Prospective patients had begun to congregate. A Chinese woman with a long ponytail had arrived at 3:00 p.m. She wanted to make sure she got served given that the clinic was open for only two hours and could be crowded. She was suffering from pain in her lower back. She had been in Italy ten years, had children in China, and worked in *confezione* (sewing clothes). She took a napkin, spread it out on the sidewalk, and sat down.

Now, back on the red track, Antonio and Aurora enjoyed walking at this time of evening. He lumbered along solidly in his security guard physique. She struck a similarly relaxed pace, comfortable in her stocky frame, taking in the cool air on her nape, exposed by her bleach-blond hair pulled up with a claw clip. They spotted another couple, Mario and Celeste, fit and athletic, from their neighborhood. I was struck at these two couples, now both without work, women and men I had known well when they were productive sweater makers in the mid-1990s and early 2000s. I remember when my kids were little how they would play on their shop floor with cardboard spools and bits of yarn. That was during our various visits, especially the longer stays. Shortly after 2004, Antonio sold his looms, tore down his workshop, and built condominiums. Shifting from production to real estate was a common strategy for subcontractors like him. There was no longer any money to be made as a sweater artisan. Now, when I come to visit Antonio and Aurora, instead of furiously finishing sweater orders, they spend their days doing errands, making and keeping medical appointments, and smoking a lot. Aurora jokes that she is "under house arrest" although she has made peace with her caretaking role for a mentally unstable sister given that both of her parents have passed. She has found passion in cooking. Antonio keeps a steady rhythm in his trips to the bar and occasional ventures up into the hills to collect asparagus, greens, or wild mushrooms. They tend a little garden. They keep in the know, him through his male networks, her through her female circles. They eat well. They watch lots of TV and get annoyed at the state of affairs. He draws a pension. She gets furious every time the government raises the age when she will be eligible for her pension. They seem unsettled, even anxious. Many times, face to face and over the phone, she has ranted about the situation: "This is an inhumane crisis."

As they walked, in the park, the topic of the economy came up. A relative of Celeste was out of work. Being out of work wasn't unusual these days. The unusual part was that he had been working for the utility company, laying gas lines, which would seem like a secure job. He'd been working there about a year after being laid off from a textile company. Talk turned to the Chinese.

"*Ci hanno fregato*," said Mario. "They've screwed us."

"*Sanno lavorare*," countered Antonio. "They know how to work."

Mario did not have a response.

After a few more laps around the track, we passed a Chinese couple with a cute little boy. He was playing with a water bottle and stuffing it down his white T-shirt and laughing. Celeste asked how old he was: four years old. "Alessio" was his name, and the man and woman with him were attractive and well dressed. The woman wore her hair in a fashionable bob. All of us were squealing over this cute little guy as he put that water bottle down his shirt. I looked closer at his shirt—a cartoon image of a male figure with the words *Gangnam style*—and when I said, "Gangnam style!" he broke into a little dance. Celeste patted his butt and commented on how round it was, as he darted off.

We walked about an hour and a half until it was well after 11:00 p.m. Then Antonio suggested we all sit on a park bench. He sat first, then Aurora and Celeste. I hesitated, not sure if there was really room. Mario was last to give in, and we all fit. Someone made a funny quip about getting close, and Aurora, nearly always good for a laugh, joked that I was in a state of abstinence so everyone had better look out! I had been in the field and away from my husband since May. Meanwhile, in sitting down, my mind replayed the scene of the suffering Chinese woman who spread open that napkin to sit on the sidewalk, a profoundly human gesture in a world where dignity was hard fought.

Aurora and Antonio showed compassion for Chinese migrants on a regular basis despite having had their own livelihoods dislodged in recent years. They pointed to their intersecting histories as the source of their political identities.

To understand crisis means understanding its opposite. In the case of Prato, this meant the postwar boom, the economic miracle. Becattini's *Il Bruco e la Farfalla* loses a bit of its meaning translated into English as *The Caterpillar and the Butterfly*. In Italian, *bruco* is "worm." A caterpillar is not quite a worm. Or if it is a worm, it's of the cute, wooly, snuggly variety, which doesn't really make it a worm at all. In any case, Becattini's point is clear in the book's subtitle: "An Exemplary Case of Development in the Italy of the Industrial Districts." The story is a triumphal one, and the source of its triumph was the boom years.

Both Antonio and Aurora came to Prato in the years of the postwar boom and met during the hot years of labor struggles. Aurora's family migrated from Calabria in the south. Antonio's moved from Maremma in rural Tuscany. Aurora was five years old and her little sister was three. She was born in 1954. The year would have been 1959. My father had a lot of courage to move from Calabria to Tuscany," said Aurora, "because back then, it was a totally different world. It was like going to America, let's say, in those days. We were emigrants, really, they actually called us *marocchini*, but *really*, eh. They called us *marocchini* because we emigrated from the bottom of Italy—Sicily, Calabria, Naples—and came up here.[9]

The term *marocchini*—literally, Moroccans—has been used as a disparaging slur initially against southern Italian migrants and more recently against non-European immigrants. People discriminated against them, refused to rent to them initially. Her father saved up money, bought property, and eventually built a home.

*[margin note: similar to Chinese]*

Sometime around middle school, when she was fourteen or fifteen, she started working with her mother and sister in their home-based workshop sewing sweater collars. There were no fixed hours. Someone would bring the sweater pieces and say, "Finish these for tomorrow." And so you had to say to yourself, "OK, then, I have to do these because I have to do them!" There were no time sheets to sign, nothing like that. There were no contracts; it was all *a voce,* just verbal agreements. "*A quei tempi era tutto a nero, purtroppo*—back then, it was all under the table, unfortunately. Yet there was the possibility to work. Now you see that slowly, slowly everything has stopped," Aurora continued. Almost everyone in the entire town was doing this sort of work. They were paid by the piece, but it was never like, "This is yours" Her father kept it all. "We were kept in the cottonwoods—we were coddled. We didn't keep track of whose was whose. Even so, everyone knew they were contributing. Women could contribute to the household."

Now, she said, people were desperate. Her pension had been pushed back at least seven years. She had to wait until 2022. It pushed people to the edge and over it. And it changed people. It made them greedy. Everyone seemed to have only their own interests at heart. Too much "progress" had taken people back. "*Io vedo un mondo tutto disfatto, molto aggressivo, molto violento*—I see a world completely undone, very aggressive, very violent," Aurora said. To illustrate her point, she offered a story:

> The world now is based on swindling. I mean, I screw you, you screw me. And that's how things go forward. I see it in so many families. I'll give you an example. Those folks where we go get the wine. They're people who have millions. They really have money. . . . So there were these vases that they had planted with strawberries. When was the period of strawberries? Two months ago? Two months. So when I go there I like to talk, to make eh—I was, so to speak: how much self-interest and how much—I mean. I wouldn't have been capable of doing this. There was this vase, these vases that were full of strawberries. But, I say, "Y' know, we like sweets." Today I made a bowl of strawberries with lemon and sugar. I say, "Do you also have strawberries?" She says, "Y' know, yes, go see them down there, go see how many there are." So I went ahead to go see them. And they had a row of vases full of those strawberries. Politely, I did not take a single strawberry. . . . If that person doesn't tell you, "Take one," right? I mean, I would have been like, "Take one. Look how many of them there are." I mean, that's like, what ten cents? If you go to buy oil and wine, whatever, if for example, you give up ten cents, those ten cents you exchange [eventually] ten euro for ten cents. I wouldn't be able to do that. . . . *Penso che non sia la fine del mondo, eh?* I don't think that it's the end of the world, right? But instead, now it's all based on money, I mean, fear of, they are afraid of taking a loss, they don't offer you a coffee. There's just a completely

*Italians lost their sense of guanxi*

different character because if I offer him a coffee, if I have something—Betsy, but now there's crazy self-centeredness. But are you kidding? The world today is all about swindle, swindle even among relatives. Even between relatives, there's no longer the sincerity, I mean, now it's all, all diffferent. There's egoism, their own [financial] interests before everything else, interests before everything else. For me, I think that the value of life is respect, sincerity, and love. All these things here.[10]

Aurora's recollection of the woman who had an abundance of strawberries yet refused to offer her a single berry—a sample as a small gift—stands as a parable for broader changes in social relations. With the economic crisis, people have become more individualized and selfish. Aurora observes the withering away of relationships based on reciprocity, a poignant echoing of Mauss, and it troubles her. At a certain point in her story, Aurora voices the idea that for such a person to give up one strawberry, even if it did not result in a sale, would not be "the end of the world," meaning that it would not be a great loss. Ironically, Aurora's story itself speaks profoundly to a different sort of "end of the world," which she characterized as a world undone.

Her sentiments are reflected in scholarship of the reconfigurations of work and social life in light of an austerity-squeezed neoliberal welfare state (Molé 2012; Muehlebach 2012). Related to the crisis, everyone seemed to have a tragic story: a suicide, femicide, or homicide. As evidence of the state of affairs, Aurora pointed to a grizzly double murder-suicide in the next town over, Poggio A Caiano, believed to be the planned outcome of an economically distressed couple whose bodies were discovered after being dead for two months in their house. The case made national headlines and stimulated conversations of people pushed to the brink in times of economic hardship and institutional abandonment.[11]

## "We Are the Chinese"

Antonio migrated when he was a boy from a rural area of Maremma. His family had left their homestead outside of Bologna during the war as they found themselves living in the hellish environs of the Gothic Line of World War II. They migrated to southern Tuscany and assumed a life as sharecroppers. As the war gave way to the postwar, the parents wanted their two children to study. Schools were hard to come by in Maremma, so, with the lure of some kin and a booming economy in Prato, they moved. Antonio studied through middle school and then at fifteen quit to go to work. There was a lot of it back then.

"I wanted freedom," he said. He got that and more.

He'd leave home on his bicycle at 5:20 a.m. to be at the factory by 6:00 a.m. sharp. Back then, the shifts were twelve hours a day with no overtime pay. Labor struggles ensued. Things heated up, and there was even a violent confrontation with the owner.

He told me the story originally in 2004, as we sat in his sweater workshop, the size of a two-car garage. His three automated knitting machines were turned off; the fluorescent lights flickered. Little did I know that would be the last time I saw the shop.

"Eh," he laughed, "*sono cose passate ormai*—these things are past by now."

"*Dai,*" I said, sharing the laugh. "Come on." At the time of this interview, we had known each other for nearly ten years. During 1995–96, I lived two floors below him and his wife in the basement apartment, which my husband and I rented from his mother-in-law. My daughter became like a niece to the couple, like a granddaughter to my landlady. She didn't have any grandchildren of her own.

Antonio seemed hesitant at first to speak to me about this period, but soon he told the story, and it revealed how he came to occupy not only a factory but also a flexible niche in the textile sector of the Made in Italy brand.

It was 1967–68. The factory where he worked was not unionized. Some organizing began, and he describes himself as having some connections to far-left labor organizations. He was recruited to join the struggle. He said he was a bit uncomfortable that the confrontation became violent. There was one really old woman who hardly got paid anything. In that period, for the young men, it was really easy to find work, which likely empowered the workers to make demands.

"We blocked it. We were there at the gate by five in the morning. We kept the factory closed, honestly," Antonio said.

"The next day they called me into the office, they read me the riot act. I remember Piero, he told me, 'Me and you, the next time we'll get out the guns.' To scare me, underst—he really said that, this I'll swear it to you on whatever you like. And he told me, 'Now, stay three days at home without coming to work.' I told him, 'I don't think so. Tomorrow morning I'll be here at work.' And in fact I went to work, and nobody said a thing to me. Then, nothing, I quit working there in '75–'76 because I bought the machines."

Like many others, he set out on his own and became a sweater artisan. Eventually, the factory had 180 artisans working outside its walls. Subcontracting exploded as employers used decentralized production as a strategy to contain labor costs and keep production flexible. For years, Antonio cranked out reams of knitwear in his small family firm. Over the years, he had a lot of contact with foreigners initially as he bought equipment from the Germans, later, as he worked with machine technicians to learn the tricks of the trade and, more recently, as he found himself alongside new Chinese immigrants entering the subcontracting scene.

The idea of an eight-hour workday became a distant notion as the phases of sweater production moved outside of the factories. For subcontracting artisans, a fixed workday didn't exist.

"You've seen how it is in Prato?"—referring to how firms cut costs— "I mean, if Prato in this period had not been flexible like this, we would have already closed everything. *Cioè i flessibili siamo noi i terzisti più che altro*— thus, we subcontractors are the flexible ones more than anything." Antonio continued to explain that a regular worker cannot compare in terms of flexibility. "In the moments when there's a lot of work, we manage to do it; we work Saturday and Sunday, twenty hours, eighteen hours, sixteen hours. *I cinesi siamo noi*, We are the Chinese."

His self-representation with the words, "We are the Chinese," gave me pause. The metaphor illustrates the similar structural positions that Italian internal migrants shared with contemporary Chinese immigrants.

Visiting old friends, I picked up on a sense of a lost world and a profoundly uncertain future. Connections once woven through relations of work seemed difficult to weave now with new neighbors who had moved into the apartments that occupied the spaces where workshops once stood. Meanwhile, many Pratesi were now making their living off rental income— including those who rented to Chinese tenants. In areas that used to profit from strategic textile spinoff niche activities such as sweater production, now many people were at a loss. Among Italians, a sense of uncertainty teetering on despair hung as thick as winter fog.

### The End of the World?

I can't shake a scene from De Martino's *La fine del mondo*—*The End of the World*. Trying to forge a new humanism in his studies of down-and-out southern Italians, De Martino and his research team got lost at sunset driving along a solitary road in Calabria. Unsure of their itinerary, they were relieved to happen upon an old shepherd. The local's directions, however, were so convoluted that they pleaded with the old man to show them the way. They offered to compensate him for his time. The idea was for him to ride in the car until the fork in the road, just a few kilometers away. At that point, the researchers would take him back to the location where they had first encountered him. Somewhat reluctantly, the shepherd agreed. De Martino describes the key moment thus: "He got in the car with some suspicion, as though fearful of a trap, and his suspicion transformed into a reference point of his extremely circumscribed domestic space. Due to that disappeared bell tower, the poor old man felt completely disoriented." Only with great effort were they able to take him to the fork in the road and get what they needed to know. Afterward, they took him back quickly, according to the agreement, and described him as "remaining with his head out the window, scrutinizing the horizon, to watch for the bell tower of Marcellinara to reappear: until when finally he saw it, his face relaxed and his old head calmed." Once the car stopped, De Martino notes, "he disappeared wildly without saying goodbye, by now outside of the tragic adventure that had ripped him from his existential space from the bell tower of Marcellinara" (De Martino and Gallini 1977, n271).

The old shepherd, thrown into a state of disorientation, grounds the crisis of presence. For De Martino, the bell tower stood for place and signified recognition—a symbol of the relations between the subject and his social and cultural world, as Clara Gallini has observed in a posthumous volume (De Martino and Gallini 1977). Losing sight of the bell tower triggered in the shepherd a profound sense of disorientation. It was as though he had arrived at the end of the earth and fallen into an existential abyss. This story captures the misplaced sense of being within the subject who, displaced from his social and cultural center, experiences a crisis of presence. Nothing short of anguish accompanies the loss of presence (Farnetti and Stewart 2012). As De Martino makes clear, the presence is put at risk when it touches the limits of its existential homeland, when it loses the bell tower of Marcellinara.

Economic crisis can lead people to become economic exiles in what once felt like a familiar homeland. As economic horizons contract and morph, subjects activate the past and seek a dignified place in it in different ways (Narotzky 2016). In other words, economic turmoil shifts how people think about the past, present, and future. Crisis stimulates temporal thought (Knight 2015). "Crises turn ordinary daily routine inside out," as Daniel Knight and Charles Stewart (2016, 3) observe in their introductory essay to a special issue on ethnographies of austerity. Predictable time can become strangely suspended—as when Aurora's pension keeps getting delayed, throwing her sense of future security into a state of purgatory in which precarity is experienced as unending. Or when Antonio, a once-productive sweater maker, wrestles day in and day out with idleness, not having intended to retire so early.

Encounters with Letizia, Wang, Antonio, and Aurora illuminate different orders of tension and nuance vis-à-vis the crisis of presence. Each of these protagonists is profoundly aware of the changing world around them. Each has composed a dramatically different script in terms of how to confront the crisis of presence. Each is a participant in making sense of and producing cultural worlds through their talk and actions. The projects of Letizia and Wang are far more public than those of Antonio and Aurora, but each contributes to worlds that are not, obviously, entirely of their own making.

More than anyone else, Antonio and Aurora suffer from a sort of melancholy that defines the crisis of presence. They are like so many. They have withdrawn from public association life. Their involvement in politics has become more of a memory, one cautious of easy nostalgia, for the time when the left had substance and labor struggles fostered solidarity. Yet Antonio is the first to admit that industrial sweater artisans like him were as Chinese as the Chinese in terms of work rhythms and self-exploitation. This relationship to the past has a potent force for forging a future as Antonio and Aurora recognize the structural similarities between their historic positions and those of the newer global laborers. Their grasp of the undulating landscapes of oppression and the ways in which the system has unmade a world that seemed graspable in those hot seasons of the 1960s reveals a sharpened historical consciousness. They bear witness. They call out the very hegemonic forces that for Gramsci named the problem: "how the power relations underpinning various forms of inequality are produced and reproduced" (Crehan 2002, 104).

Letizia also recognizes the parallels between the days of the thriving local microeconomy and today's informal migrant economy. Even so, her vitriol erupts with the force of water breaking through a cement dam. It is of such violent tenor that I feel paralyzed, sensing I should challenge her perspectives as they become laden with "occupier" finger-pointing, but knowing full well that if I do, I will take the brunt of her outburst. Out of self-preservation I proceed with caution, ever aware of my partial perspective. I know full well that her stories are full of life experiences. I deeply appreciate her view about the delicacy of the world's equilibrium. I get her insight that this equilibrium has been thrown into crisis. Democracy, art, environment—these are just a few of the things she values and works to enhance with dedication. Her boundless energy serves to fend off the crisis of presence on a daily basis. What might she see when she catches a glimpse of herself in the mirror? The image would surely contain triple-strength threads for suturing together directions for a new world. Rights, beauty, and the environment all for the common good would be central strands.

Wang undoubtedly suffered as he struggled to gain a foothold in Europe as a full-fledged immigrant-resident, *sans papiers* at one point, always already in a state of exception, being the laughing stock of the school director in

Belgium for his inferior linguistic abilities, toiling in the shadows of a cut-and-sew workshop in France, finally persevering as an entrepreneur and an association activist on behalf of his *co-paesani* in Italy, his fellow country-men writ large. He sees tremendous potential in global networks. He seeks to cultivate the "spiritual insistence" that animates the fast-fashion world. Although he has lived the double-bind of the immigrant and has known all too well a crisis of presence, his script aims to transcend a decentered self. His metaphor of cut and sew suggests a measured and careful craftsman dedicated to an approach for moving beyond mutual incommensurability toward mutual commensurability. The proportions will be right. The pieces will all fit together. The assembly will be gentle and measured. Energies will tend not only to monetary aspects but also to aspects of cultivating networks and relations of reciprocity for the long term. Wang's cut-and-sew metaphor reveals a politics of possibility, a place where crisis also contains the seeds of transcendence.

As each protagonist comes face to face with a changing world, each simul-taneously encounters alterity, and each confronts it differently. Letizia's "one world ends and another begins," Aurora's "world completely undone," Anto-nio's "We are the Chinese," and Wang's "cut and sew" together reveal worlds that are changing, being remade, with endings and beginnings. They have thought deeply about the changes. In varying degrees, they each continue to make the world anew through their actions.

If we agree with De Martino that the challenge of culture is to suture inner and outer worlds together, then its purpose is also to provide subjects with tools for their everyday making of meaning. With each stitch, mutual incom-mensurabilities may become less incommensurable. But nothing is guaran-teed. The subject may or may not be capable of handling or resolving internal and external realities that go hand in hand with economic, social, and cul-tural change and feelings about their place in the world. The bell tower may slip out of view as quickly as it may come back into view.

# PART TWO

# Global Circuits of Care

# Checkup

I set out for the hospital in a cold January rain. Puddles covered the grounds of the sculpture park, and I searched to avoid them. Looking up, I saw a hunched figure in bas-relief. The bronze woman in *Rain* also seemed to be battling nature's wet, windy, and fickle forces. She grasped a piece of fluttering cloth over her head. Etched lines created the illusion of a downpour. A dog at her side, its head lowered, was barely visible. That sculpture commemorated a different storm. The sculptor, Quinto Martini, had suffered loss in the great Florentine flood of 1966, when waters surged the banks of the Arno River, deluging works in his studio. In the days following the flood, the writer and antifascist activist Carlo Levi went to check on his friend. Levi described walking the streets with mud up to his knees. The mud was strange. It leeched color from all things, Levi noted, like faces rendered listless from flu or plague. Inside the sculptor's studio, he discovered his friend had already begun a series on rain. Even though those works were marinating in mud, he detected powerful messages being transmitted, based in a language he described as a "mysterious hieroglyphics of water." Martini himself attributed his fondness for rain to having been born in a rainstorm. The devastating flood seemed only to harden his conviction to the theme itself and techniques to represent it.[1]

I took shelter under a bus stop in the parking lot, the end of the line. The bus pulled up, I stepped into its warm interior and validated my ticket in the time-stamp machine. The route circled the rotunda and passed the *casa rossa*, a landmark red house of bygone patron-peasant days, the color used purposefully to mark property that belonged to Count Alessandro Contini-Bonacossi (1878–1955). The shrewd man settled in the area in 1920 after making his fortune dealing in international art. His success enabled him to

FIGURE 5.1. Discarded boxes from a fast-fashion workshop include a makeshift rocking horse.
Photo by Agnese Morganti, 2017

purchase his title and, according to local lore, the land and farmhouses he could see from the Capezzana estate atop a grand hill above the expansive valley.[2] The patron-client relations sputtered to an end, as many peasants abandoned the land for the city, some eventually setting up their own small firms and a handful purchasing the old estates (see also Holmes 1989). From here, the bus lurched across the Ombrone River, legendary for its history of flushing downstream all shades of dye from the factory city. The bus then began its excursion across the plain, winding its way along the roads lined with metal fences that secured the fast-fashion warehouses and workshops that drew so many Chinese from Wenzhou to Prato.

My destination was the Ospedale Misericordia e Dolce. I had an appointment with Fangli, who had built on our team's initial efforts in July 2012 and during the fall secured necessary permissions to observe follow-up medical exams. We were interested specifically in visits with Chinese parents and their infants. A nurse gave us appointment times. I was excited but also uncertain. The project had continued as planned in my absence, while I fulfilled teaching duties back home. I regretted having been away. I did not, however, regret our team's collective decision of a focus: rather than observe visits with specialists involving parents whose children had severe diagnoses, we chose to concentrate on the hospital checkups, which often involved babies born prematurely but not necessarily with serious conditions.

The delivery of health care to immigrants in Prato, as with elsewhere across Italy and Europe, faced intense politics and scrutiny. Demographic trends and reporting related to births contributed to debates (Krause 2012b). Cultural differences became inscribed on bodies. In 2011, Prato was ranked as Italy's most diverse province—and this bore out in terms of the portion of immigrants to total residents. Beginning in 2009, Prato's public health agency recorded that births to foreign women exceeded births to Italian women. By 2011, some 3,270 babies were born in Prato's hospital, and babies born to non-Italian citizens represented 53 percent of those births. This shift occurred in large part due to increases in births to women of Chinese nationality, whose percentage of the total grew from 15.5 percent in 2006 to 36.1 percent in 2011 (Bracci 2013, 45; Istat n.d.; Sambo 2013a, 106; 2013b). For those who track numbers and those who work in the hospital, these changes were noteworthy and dramatic. The trend fueled both political alarmism and innovative outreach. Headlines were racialized, announcing babies with "*gli occhi a mandorla*," or almond-shaped eyes, and the article that followed sounded alarms over the "new record" yet went on to report on the context in which the birth data were disseminated: a conference with Prato's health agency (l'azienda sanitaria locale [ASL]) organized by the region of Tuscany, called "*Di razza ce ne una sola: quella umana*," or "There's only one race: the human one." The event featured a decidedly antiracist program during which a video was screened regarding the birthing experiences of new mothers in Prato's hospital (La Nazione 2008).

The contrast between the hyper-racializing headline and the super-humanizing text was a common feature of the city's social dynamics. Healthcare workers encountered and managed diversity on a daily basis. Certain illnesses and conditions showed up at a higher rate among Chinese babies, whose mothers tended to adhere at a lower rate to prenatal-care protocols. The hospital staff saw a higher incidence of Chinese babies born with hearing impairment or deafness, likely due to cytomegalovirus, a prenatal infection, which could also affect the liver, kidneys, and eyes. Autism was also fairly frequent.[3] Health-care workers were sensitive to the fact that suffering did not have any particular citizenship. When the Bossi-Fini law was passed in 2002 and set up barriers to prevent immigrants without residency permits from accessing health care, three different entities joined together to form a special clinic where immigrants without the proper paperwork could be served. These included a branch of the national health-care system, ASL, the Catholic Caritas, and the Hospital of Prato. Leaders in the public health sector had taken the lead in defending the rights of all to access health care. Such practitioners took pride in their progressive stance and creative actions. But challenges were ongoing and real. In a city such as Prato, where the population was dense and concentrated, residents made frequent use of the public health services.

✳

The bus stopped across from the hospital entrance. Passengers spilled out onto a sidewalk. I crossed the street, passed a newsstand, and headed down a long walkway. People filed nonstop into the hospital—it seemed like the entrance to a major league sporting event. Once inside, there was no sign of Fangli. Had I gone in the wrong entrance? I became worried about making my appointment on time when I realized that the information directory did not exactly correspond to the word I was looking for, *maternity*. Two different wards had the word *Obstetrics*. Other options included Gynecology or Pediatrics. I asked the information officer on duty for directions. "Just follow the main corridor and keep going." The unit was on the first floor. The corridor I took brought me to a café bustling with medical staff and hospital visitors downing espressos and cappuccinos. I asked someone in a white coat and badge for directions, and she gestured with a flip of her wrist in a different direction. A long hallway with an orange sign "Percorso D" gave me a feeling of being trapped in an airline terminal in a bad dream. Different directions got me to a closed pharmacy desk with no exit. I asked for directions again. I was lost in a labyrinth. I believed my doctor friend's history lesson: powerful heads of units had manipulated the public health system, secured resources, and haphazardly built onto their wings, resulting in a shamefully chaotic layout. I felt sorry for sick people who had to figure it out, whether immigrants or Italians, let alone unsettled and homesick anthropologists.

At one point, someone told me to take the elevator or the stairs up to the first floor. This I understood. Here I was, silly American, thinking I was already on the first floor! One floor up, I spotted a sign that read "Ostetrica 1" with a waiting room in the middle. There was not a check-in or information desk in sight. There were, however, two doors on either side. Again, this presented an interesting puzzle as staff seemed to be hidden on the other side of locked doors rather than on the public side. Suddenly, I spotted a pair of passing medical personnel in white coats and badges, signs of official status that had by now become false signs of reassurance. I approached them and asked which door I should go into. They suggested I go to the door on the left. Entering this door required permission. A Chinese man pushing a pregnant woman in a wheelchair asked me to ring the buzzer and answer the receptionist's question. I cautiously complied. They entered and I followed.

On my trusty old flip phone, the one I activated each time I returned to Prato, I got hold of Fangli, who was close but not in sight. Our conversation became ridiculous as we tried to figure out each other's location. Beside myself, I approached a young woman in scrubs and a badge, holding out my phone and asking her to take charge. She was not convinced. Searching in the core of my being for the most gentle and patient voice I could muster in hopes that she would take pity on me, I desperately tried to explain in my distraught Italian that the two of us were trying to find each other, that I was lost, and that I didn't know how to explain my location. Everything looked the same to me: bare white walls, swinging doors, people in scrubs. The strategy worked. The staff person gestured for me to follow her through a door on the right, into a corridor with visiting rooms. She explained that indeed Fangli was right outside the door by the elevators. I opened the door and *voilà!* What a sight for sore eyes. I had made it to my destination: a site of medical encounters. I had imagined such a site for months, and now here I was, here we were.

The journey had been wet and convoluted.

Drenched clothes will inevitably dry if they are spread out and hung up well. Floodwaters will eventually recede. With perseverance, patience, and time, confusion may also give way to clarity. Hieroglyphics may be deciphered. It is not as probable as clothes drying or floodwaters receding, but it is possible. This is an essential part of the method of *encounter ethnography.* The ethnographer sticks with it. She cultivates patience and social relations. She observes social life in a systematic and sustained way, improving memory skills and recording field notes. She allows things to happen, balancing spontaneity with discipline. Sometimes she gets lost. Other times she finds her way. Waiting for floodwaters to recede can be scary. It can test a person's patience and sense of control over things, to be sure. Commiseration may come from unexpected places, such as a sculpture, or from unexpected persons, such as medical staff.

I do not often start a journey as a lost traveler, but the experience of travel, confusion, and translation is more or less what I study. When I conceived of the idea of encounter ethnography as a method, I drew on a good deal of previous work by anthropologists about the sort of knowledge that is produced from "encounters."[4] Encounters involve dissonance between forms of knowledge that are not only different from one another but also differently valued. The idea of encounter ethnography was to understand what was happening in such jarring moments; various people's interpretations were based on starkly different presuppositions. This happens commonly when erudite forms of knowledge collide with subjugated forms, as with doctors established as experts and patients positioned as non-specialists.

The fieldwork process itself generates certain kinds of knowledge and surprises. The anthropologist may unintentionally, even unknowingly, shift roles as mediator, meddler, interpreter, and traitor. Pirandello long ago observed "*traduttore, traditore*," a turn of phrase that loses its poetic luster as soon as it is translated into English: "translator, traitor." For the social scientist with a desire to linger in the details, to revere the gods of small things, in hopes of ultimately grasping the proverbial world in a grain of sand, the problem becomes one of reducing lots of tidbits of information to graspable categories. We need categories for sense making. Yet categories also have origins.

This leads to a profound paradox. De Martino grappled with precisely this paradox, as he struggled to engage with poor southern Italians in the 1940s–60s, when he encountered ways of thinking, acting, healing, and practicing religion that seemed strange to educated city folk. His work represented a profound ongoing dialogue with the lessons of the antifascist Gramsci, and he was particularly drawn to illuminate how these subaltern practices occurred in relation to hegemonic systems. De Martino coined the phrase *ethnographic encounters* as a sort of sketch of what Gallini described as an epistemology of ethnographic practice (De Martino and Gallini 1977). At the heart of the practice of doing ethnography was a problem deeply rooted in more than two thousand years of Western thought: the whole of the West manifested itself in ethnographic categories. Ultimately, ethnographic encounters themselves were shot through with unresolvable contradictions.

De Martino put it like this: "The fundamental paradox of ethnographic observation and of ethnological research is the following: To observe the culturally 'alien' necessarily involves making use of determined categories of observation." His list of categories was not exhaustive but rather descriptive: "religion, magic, technique; myth, ritual; art; economy, society; rights; politics; soul, spirit, strength; normal and abnormal; healthy and psychically ill; history, culture." If the ethnographer sees the world through predetermined categories, then he or she ends up attributing things to the other culture that are ultimately his or her own—history, arguments, choices, distinctions. Our deeply ingrained categories run the risk of blocking insight. If observers see the world through predetermined categories, then they end up attributing things to the other culture that are ultimately their own. The possibilities for distortion are endless. "The paradox," De Martino continued, "then is this: either do not use our categories of observation, and then nothing can be observed, or use them, and then we will see only a projection of ourselves in the other, never the other."[5]

The paradox can never be completely resolved. For De Martino, there was a path to minimizing the negative effects of the paradox. The way forward involves becoming aware of the limitations of the categories of observation and the heightening of one's consciousness with regard to inbuilt ethnocentrism. We must read the signs, hear the directions, then recognize where our categories fail. Sometimes the first floor is one story up. This calls for keen and critical attention to the lens of observation, permission to allow the "alien" sense of things to linger, and a sort of contextualization of categories, according to different epochs, so as to move toward, even if incrementally, a rethinking of the Western categories and improve observation itself. It may also illuminate configurations of power, who and what dominate, how these relationships play out, and why it matters. This orientation enlivens encounter ethnography.

During periods extending from January to July 2013, we conducted our hospital-based ethnography. We sat in on follow-up visits in a pediatric ward. We observed uneasy encounters between patients and doctors. We received permission from staff and parents to record some encounters and took notes on others. Several parents agreed to sit for interviews, some involving both parents or a parent and a grandparent. We also interviewed more than a dozen health-care professionals together. A series of encounters described below bring into focus what unfolds in such moments when power is unevenly distributed. The collection of minute, quotidian details offers a starting point for meaningful, if partial, analysis.

### 1. Ju and Jian: From Head to Toe

Relieved I had arrived, I followed my competent assistant into a large examining room and recognized the pediatric neuropsychiatrist who was evaluating an infant. The exam room offered a space in which medical staff performed checkups typically at three months for infants who were born with a medical problem. These problems could range from mild, such as a baby being born premature yet healthy, to serious, such as a baby being born with neurological abnormalities. Parents were expected to bring their own paperwork from previous exams. Some brought bulky binders whereas others arrived empty-handed and overwhelmed.

As I entered the room, a baby was lying on a table and the doctor was waving various toys in front of the infant. She monitored his responses. The Chinese parents were in the room. There were two others in medical attire: an Italian woman (perhaps a nurse) and a young Italian woman (perhaps an intern). The staff was friendly and even seemed appreciative of our presence and efforts. Fangli offered to help with translation when needed. The hospital was able to offer only minimal translation services, insufficient for routine visits, so her skills were welcome. Fangli spoke Italian like a native, could get by in English and French, and was perfectly fluent not only in standard Mandarin but also in the dialect of Wenzhou. The dialect is so unique that it was used as a code language during the Sino-Japanese War just as Navajo was used in the United States during World War II. Learning this fact made me especially grateful to have a native Wenzhou speaker on our team.[6]

Neither of the parents spoke Italian, so Fangli got to work interpreting between them and the Italian doctors. The in-take questions revealed that the father, Jian, had an elementary education, and the mother, Ju, had studied through middle school. Such education levels were fairly common among Chinese migrants from Wenzhou. The couple was vague about their occupations.

As the neuropsychiatrist continued to examine the baby, the young mother asked her about weaning, and the doctor said to ask the pediatrician. When the pediatrician entered the room, she was quick to ask the parents about their intentions.

"This baby isn't going to be sent to live with his grandparents in China, is he?" the pediatrician asked.

Through translation, the mother replied that in fact she was planning to send her son in July, so in about six months. The pediatrician urged her to wait until the following New Year if possible, when the baby would be more than a year old, because if the doctors were going to help the baby, they needed some time. Being born premature, the baby was vulnerable.

The neuropsychiatrist and I looked at each other. I teared up. Maybe we were both thinking the same thing. *How can the mother send her baby so far away?* My own children, at the time twenty-two and thirteen, were back in the United States with their father, my husband. The oldest had just graduated from college and was working in a restaurant job, and the youngest had finished the school year and then headed off to his beloved sleep-away camp in the mountains of New Hampshire. We were apart for seventy-five days, and that brought me both independence and loneliness. The Chinese parents' situation pulled at my heartstrings. I don't know if it was more for the mother or father or for that little creature. Many of us in the room had ideas about family, reinforced in Italy through enduring notions about "normal" families (Saraceno 2017) and idealizations of the mother-child bond as depicted in ever-present Renaissance art.

The pediatrician continued her efforts to convince the mother to keep the baby in Prato. She said, jokingly, "*È nato a Prato. Ormai è pratese*," or "He was born in Prato. By now, he's a Prato boy." She then referenced the new laws on citizenship.[7] They were still in the making, but there was some hope that the future would open up new possibilities. At this point, a child of non-Italian citizens could choose citizenship at age eighteen, but the process could be onerous especially if children had lived outside of the country for a period, which triggered other restrictive rules.

The topic of infant feeding came up. "She was thinking of weaning in February," Fangli translated. She offered two reasons: first, the mother wanted to start working again, and second, she was worried that her milk was not nutritious. The doctor said there was no way to give her a pill to dry up her milk at this point, that she'd have to wean gradually. She emphasized that mother's milk is best. She explained that she could not in good conscience tell her that artificial milk is best. A person can look in any book, she said. With the winter months and the cold/flu season, the ideal thing would be to continue nursing through the spring at the very least. This would help boost the baby's immunities.

There was a tense moment. Fangli spoke to the mother and then turned to say, "The message has been transmitted." The doctor weighed the infant. The doctor measured him. She then showed the mother the growth chart and where he was, that he was growing well. "You see, your milk is fine," the pediatrician said cheerfully.

The health report was positive. The baby's heart and respiratory problems that had presented at birth had improved. But there was still a little "problem" with the head. "It's a little *schiacciata* on the back, a little flattened." The pediatrician suggested that the mother take the infant to a physiotherapist to correct it.

After the exam, the mother started to dress the baby. She added layer after layer. Finally, the pediatrician counted up the layers. She pointed out that the mother wore two or three layers as compared with the infant, who had seven.

There was a bit of laughter among the staff, but it wasn't clear whether this idea of potential overheating really was transmitted. The mother was very worried that her baby might get cold. The staff asked whether they were in a car. "*Ma siete in macchina, no?*" The Chinese parents nodded. They seemed to have no other way to answer.

The pediatrician asked about the paperwork from their visit at Meyer, the children's hospital in Florence. The doctor appeared mortified that the couple had not brought a file with all of the baby's medical documents. She explained to the woman the importance of having with her all of the documentation regarding the profile of the newborn, per the Italian medical system's expectations. Thus, Fangli communicated the importance of this fact, and they agreed that the mother would bring this paperwork to the hospital staff the following week. The mother expressed deep gratitude to the doctors and staff. Fangli and the parents spoke in Chinese, the doctors and staff offered to leave the room and let Fangli do an interview there. The next thing I knew, Fangli was whipping out consent forms like a pro. The couple consented to be interviewed and recorded. She placed the tape recorder confidently on the table. For about a half hour, the mother spoke with Fangli. She seemed at ease. Afterward, Fangli told me she suspected that the mother was grateful for her help, including an offer to call the clinic office for another visit.[8]

## 2. Shu: From Culture to Work

The next week, on January 24, 2014, hospital staff invited us to participate in two visits with Chinese parents and their infants. The first would be twins scheduled at 2:00 p.m. By 2:40 p.m., the exam room was still without patients. The infant neuropsychiatrist, the nurse, Fangli, and I began to doubt whether the parents were coming. The neuropsychiatrist explained that from time to time, patients don't show up for their appointments, regardless of nationality. I couldn't help but wonder whether the babies had been sent to China, and Fangli agreed, saying that caring for twins was particularly difficult. Our chitchat stopped with the arrival of the mother and grandmother of a three-month-old baby girl. It turned out there was not one appointment with twins but two appointments with parents who had the same common last name.

The mother spoke Italian well, so we hung back and listened. At a certain point, the pediatrician entered the room, and another doctor asked whether the mother slept together with her baby, having gathered that the baby did not sleep alone in a crib. A somewhat tense moment occurred when it became evident to the pediatrician that it was the grandmother rather than the mother who was the baby's principal caretaker. The grandmother had undressed the baby for the exam, she had redressed it, and she had been the one to calm the baby when it cried. At a certain point, the pediatrician asked why it was the grandmother rather than the mother who was caring for the child. The mother explained that for forty days postpartum she had rested, then she had started working again; therefore, it was the grandmother who watched the baby. At this point, the pediatrician attempted to show empathy.

"It's just their culture," the pediatrician said, smiling while nodding at us. "It's a cultural fact."

"It's not cultural," the mother shot back. "I work."

In the pause between family visits, the doctors reflected on the Chinese mother's reference to forty days of postpartum rest, saying that this was a practice that Italian women used to follow because they were viewed as fragile after birth. With the improved conditions of today's lifestyle, there was no medical basis for such an extended period of rest.

✶

The worse thing was when the parents didn't show up. When they didn't come back. When they just disappeared. "*Ci dispiace*," the nurse, Romana, told us while we were waiting for another appointment. "We're sorry. It mortifies us a bit." Everybody knew that the Chinese parents did not end up taking their children to another unit somewhere else in the region or even the country because that unit would contact the Prato hospital staff. Everybody knew the reason the Chinese parents didn't come back: They had sent their baby away.

Back in the pediatric follow-up examination room, on a sultry July day when three appointments were scheduled with Chinese babies, the first family was a no-show. We sat and waited, and when it became obvious there was no hope, the doctor offered to sit for an interview.[9] We had requested to schedule with her several times, and she had been too busy, but now seemed to be the right moment. Dr. Torre emphasized two difficulties in particular: language and time. The first had to do with being able to communicate with parents directly to establish trust. The second had to do with parents who often did not have a lot of time to devote to their children's health issues because they worked so much, and that is what was required of them. Dr. Torre recounted a difficult story of an infant whose parents had entrusted him to a caretaker, who gave him a pill, which got lodged in his throat. The babysitter shook the baby. The baby was diagnosed with shaken baby syndrome. It resulted in a long series of treatments for the baby. She described its parents as *dolcissimi*, very sweet. But the baby's situation was severe, and after about eight months, they had to entrust the child to another family. It was really a very difficult situation, Dr. Torre emphasized. She noted that she has seen a wide range of families, from stable to unstable economic and personal situations. She also noted the problems that arise from children who come and go between Italy and China.

### 3. Lian: From Translation to Ambiguity

On that sweltering July day, we wrapped up the interview with the doctor quickly when the second appointment arrived, an infant accompanied by its mother and a Chinese woman who spoke Italian. The mother had long black hair and wore a fuchsia tunic with ruffled short sleeves and denim shorts detailed with white lace along the bottom seam. She wore two gold necklaces, one with a rectangular pendant. She carried a Chanel-type clutch with a gold chain. Her shoes were flats, a leopard pattern with bursts of turquoise. The woman accompanying her wore a business-style navy-and-white-striped dress with heels. Her relationship with the family was unclear. She told the nurse that she was an aunt, but she told Fangli that she was not a relative and described her work as a salesperson of nutritional supplements. We suspected some translation services on the side. Fangli asked in her field note from the day, "Who had the privilege of truth?" This question brought to mind a statement by the main character in the film *Il Migliore Offerta* or *The Best Offer* (which I had seen in Italy back in January): "*In ogni falso c'è sempre qualcosa autentica,*" or "In every fake there's always something authentic."

The ambiguity of the aunt/translator's identity contributed to the dynamics of several interactions. The first question was about the infant's date of birth. The translator posed the question to the mother and rather than respond immediately, there ensued some back-and-forth between them. The nurse prodded, asking whether it was the end of March or sometime in May. The translator offered a few dates and finally explained, "She doesn't know because she already forgot the date." Everyone laughed. It was a strange moment, though, not your typical laughter. Not infrequently, there might be confusion about the age of a child because of the way some Chinese parents calculated age, which included the time in utero, but this was the first time we had encountered a mother who could not recollect her child's birth date.

The strange quality of this encounter continued as the nurse asked the mother for her paperwork and explained that she qualified for a copayment waiver because her baby was born premature. This benefit lasted two or three years of the baby's life under the current rules of the public health-care system. As the nurse spoke to the mother, there was a good deal of background noise from the doctor's examination, which included waiving a rattle over the newborn's face to see whether it could follow the sound and movement. She interacted with the infant, saying things like, "*Guarda com'è bella! Oh mamma, guarda come siamo messi. Come siamo noi? Grandi, grandi, grandi!*" "Oh, look how cute she is! Oh my, look how cute we are! How are we? Big, big, big!"

Back at the desk, the nurse asked whether the mother worked or was a housewife, and the translator quickly answered, "*Casalinga,*" or housewife. The baby started to cry. Everyone was trying to calm her down, cooing and whatnot. A pop song blasted digitized sounds through the room. It was the mother's cell ringtone. The baby cried some more. The mother said that the baby cried a lot, and she asked why. The doctor offered her expertise: "Usually when babies cry, they are hungry or tired. It's a reaction." She added, "*È molto brava,*" that the baby was wonderful. But the mother said that as soon as she was out of sight of the baby, it would cry.

"She's crying for attention," the doctor said.

Eventually, the nurse presented the mother with a document and explained that with it, she was exempt from the insurance co-pay. The nurse explained where the mother had to go and then asked about her residency status. The mother had a provisional permit. If she had been without a legal status, she would have had a problem getting care through the regular channels and had to go to a different clinic set up for migrants without proper documents. Eventually, the mother received a positive prognosis for her daughter other than the issue of the head being a bit flat and was instructed to put the baby on its belly.

At the end of the visit, the ambiguity of the aunt/translator figure lent an unusual tone to another conversation when the nurse was scheduling a follow-up visit for December. The mother said in a loud voice in Chinese, "December . . . but—" and the aunt/translator quickly shut her up with, "But nothing . . . don't say anything." Fangli deduced that in December the baby girl would probably no longer be around and so explicitly asked, "Is the baby going to China, or will she stay here?" The mother responded that it was probable that the baby would be sent away but not yet certain.

## 4. Xue: From Healthy to Overfed

There was lots of uncertainty. We might say that uncertainty was a constant theme, as constant as wreckage after a flood. Notions of normality were also constant. On the afternoon of July 4, we had come for another series of follow-up visits. There were, as usual, a lot of people in the room: father, grandmother, baby, doctor, nurse, another staff person, two interns, my second research assistant, Xiaoyun, and me. We were ten people in all. The father was hip looking. He wore a sporty white shirt and sporty cargo shorts; the grandmother wore a fashion-forward, black-and-white dress finished in turquoise shoes with sparkly studs.

Dr. Torre asked about the baby's well-being. The baby seemed very responsive and alert. "Brava!" she said. "She's developing well. The measures are perfect!" She gave the father and grandmother a good prognosis. She encouraged them to exercise the head, to adjust the position, and to avoid allowing the infant to stay on its feet because it would risk developing bad habits, such as standing on its tiptoes. She warned absolutely against a walker.

The next parent came in at 3:15 p.m. Xue was a spitting image of a fast-fashion wardrobe, clad in a blousy blue-and-white dress, gold earrings, gold necklace, purple hair clips with sparkly studs, and femme-wedge sandals with orange blingy straps. Some confusion arose over the baby's original due date. Once that was straightened out, the doctor asked about the doses of the formula that the baby was being given. A main concern was that the mother was overfeeding the infant. As the doctor continued to examine the baby, the nurse asked some questions and learned that Xue had a middle school education and that this was her third child. The nurse also explained that Xue needed to go to the clinic near her house because she was out of the regular district. The mother looked confused. Xiaoyun explained; she had a good grip on the public health system as she has worked in the hospital as a cultural mediator/translator and was studying to be a nurse.

The doctor weighed the baby. Its numbers were in the 70th and 90th percentile for height and weight, respectively.

"*È cresciuto parecchio*," the doctor said. "The baby has grown a lot, really quite a lot." The medical staff proceeded to give oral instructions for how much the baby should be eating. The mother did not seem entirely convinced.

"Isn't this a good thing?" Xue asked, defensively.

The doctor explained that it was commonplace for mothers who have babies born premature and small to overfeed them.

"But isn't it good because then she'll be bigger when she's grown up?" Xue asked.

"When she's grown up, it could cause problems, such as obesity," the doctor said. "Give her 100 to 200 grams, five times per day. *Però complimenti! È una bellissima bambina!*—But congratulations! She's a beautiful baby."

At the end of the checkup, the doctor expressed concern over the flattened back of the head because of the sleep position and recommended the best feeding position to hold the baby.

## 5. Ming: From Caretaking to Dressing

A young man and an older woman carrying a baby entered the exam room. Ming, the twenty-seven-year-old, wore a casual, yet stylish, white shirt; the grandmother was dressed to the nines, in an elegant black-and-white dress with a jacket. Ming spoke decent Italian and thus interacted on his own with the medical staff. The doctor asked him where the baby's mother was, and Ming explained that she had stayed at home because she was still in pain from having suffered a major laceration during delivery; she had required stitches and could not yet walk well. Furthermore, she was observing the traditional forty-day postpartum rest and thus not leaving the house.

The baby was born prematurely and had a problem with its heart, but now that the baby was a month old, the condition appeared to have all but disappeared. The neuropsychotherapist and the nurse asked their round of questions about eating, sleeping, and care. There was some silence. The father deferred to the grandmother to answer how much the baby was sleeping. Some confusion followed about where the baby slept at home. Fangli mediated. The neuropsychotherapist then clarified, "In the car, in your arms, absolutely no." She explained the danger and the need for a car seat. The nurse followed up with a few questions about the father's residence and age. At this point, the baby was propped up on a C-shaped, Boppy-style pillow.[10] "This is a good position for him," Nurse Romana said. "The bed is dangerous. He's wonderful like this. He likes it." She suggested that even a towel under the feet would be good.

In terms of food, Ming clarified that the baby was drinking formula because his wife, the mother, did not have any milk. "The baby sucked and sucked, but nothing came." Dr. Chiavetta, the pediatrician on duty, entered the room and asked about the baby's dermatitis, for which another pediatrician had prescribed a remedy. Ming could not recall the name of the product but managed to describe the container and the first letter of its name. The pediatrician clarified that a product that contained cortisone should be given for only four or five days. She asked about the shampoo they used and emphasized the importance of using products for newborns that do not have too much perfume, that don't create too much lather. "Marseille soap is ideal," the pediatrician emphasized, because it doesn't make too much suds. The grandmother seemed to be listening, although she did not say anything in Italian.

"Never leave your baby alone," Dr. Chiavetta warned. Talk about vaccinations and follow-up visits ensued, with the advice to the father to take the baby sooner rather than later because his current documents were in good standing.

As the visit wrapped up, the pediatrician asked, "Does the baby have other clothes? Something other than the onesie? *Ora basta in questo caldo!*"— implying that, given this heat, enough of this overdressing, adding, "The grandmother could also go without the elegant jacket."

## Global Bodies

The checkups highlight the complexity of local interactions saturated with global forces. As with a flood, when objects or structures, precious or trivial, have marinated in mud, things and their conditions are murky. Not only my journey but also the babies' and the parents' journeys were often wet and convoluted. Water breaks. Babies are born. People become parents. They, like me, eventually would find their way into the obstetric and pediatric wards. They, like me, would eventually find their way out of the hospital and make their own sense of remarks, instructions, or diagnoses. Encounter ethnography calls for its practitioners to proceed with patience, to wait for floodwaters to ebb, so to speak. It draws attention to key moments. Such moments are fleeting in real time. In the case of the health-care professionals, the jarring moments reveal dissonance. They reveal that formulations are rarely universal. These encounter moments, themselves objects of analysis, bring into relief tensions that arise in the course of clinical interactions. Cultures are produced through "friction" (Tsing 2005, 4): "the awkward, unequal, unstable, and creative qualities of interconnections across difference."

Friction comes about because of the sort of work inherent in such medical encounters. Medical personnel are taxed and do their best to deliver care, to draw on their wealth of expertise to determine which patients are well and which are in need. They tune into suffering and seek to intervene, to reduce it. They do more than that, too. As medical anthropologists from Emily Martin to Byron Good to Seth Holmes have suggested, medicine has culturally distinctive ways of formulating the human body and disease. Health-care workers, especially doctors, have been trained to see differently and to interact in intimate ways with the body and its particular characteristics. As doctors and medical staff practice medicine, they sustain attention on bodies and on signs of suffering; they also construct bodies as objects. The body itself becomes a source of experience and understanding. Indeed, the "medical gaze" reconstitutes the person (Good 1994, 73).[11] This observation is both insightful and overstated. The medical gaze attempts to remake subjects in its own vision, but whether and to what degree it succeeds is quite another matter. In these cases, in Prato, the infant patient, being prelinguistic, does not hear the messages; the guardians, often only partially fluent in the doctor's language or not fluent at all, have their own ways of perceiving and understanding.

Not only are hospitals places where the medical body is constructed and treated, but in Good's words, they are sites of "moral drama." One side of that drama involves fear, pain, and suffering. The other side of that drama involves moral messages. My observations of routine procedures in the exam room pulled back the curtain on such moral dramas. Routinized procedures aim to shape the contours of people's experiences. So-called instrumental rationality (Good 1994, 85), in other words rationality that is put into practice through routines of professional expertise, amplifies commentary on moral behavior. Before our last hospital interview of the project, the pediatrician, sitting at the bedside of a postpartum mother whose baby had to be treated for jaundice, boasted about having forbid the mother from naming her baby girl "Grace Kelly." The way she told it, she had saved the mother from committing a major cultural gaffe, explaining that "Kelly" was a last name in English. Given that Kelly could have easily stood as a first or middle name, I found her story more painful than funny. The mother, who spoke fluent Italian, really had wanted to name her baby after the American actress and princess.[12] Later, at an ethnopsychology seminar where I presented research findings in Florence at the Institute of the Innocents, held in the former foundling home and Renaissance jewel of the Spedale degli Innocenti designed by Filippo Brunelleschi, psychologist Anna Ascolti chimed in to share the anecdote. Participants agreed that the doctor had overstepped her bounds. Was it not the "expert" who had made the blunder?

Clinical encounters become contexts in which health-care professionals make practical and moral suggestions aimed at socializing parents into norms presumably for raising healthy babies. Such moments expose other worlds. This happens across cultural and medical contexts. Both directly and indirectly, the health-care workers educate the parents and grandparents in terms of what is considered to be "normal" by Italian standards: head shape, body weight, clothing, breastfeeding, weaning, and caretaking—who, where, how. These troubled moments reveal where etiology slides into ideology. In other words, moments that necessitate a medical professional to express the causes of a disease in order to decide on a course of treatment shift into occasions to express taken-for-granted norms for living. Much of what transpired in the exam room went beyond medical expertise. Advice became focused on managing the parenting practices of these migrants. The parents, meanwhile, constantly negotiated aesthetic sensibilities and caretaking logistics. Ideas about parenting are both medical and moral. They are medical because the doctors and nurses cannot reasonably deliver a program of care to hypermobile patients. Care presumes continuity. Many things in society presume continuity. These presumptions of continuity fly in the face of the demands of globalization.

Ming, the father in case 5, received countless messages about moral parenting. At the beginning of the exam, he fielded a question about the absence of the baby's mother. In an Italian context where lowest-low fertility has meant that small families have become the norm yet parenting practices and expectations remain intense, motherhood has been elevated to the level of craft (Counihan 2004; Krause 2005a, 2005b; Livi-Bacci 2001). Here, the question concerning the mother's whereabouts was anything but neutral. Warnings about moral parenting were repeatedly conveyed. Questions about where the baby slept were followed with cautions to use a car seat and never leave the baby alone. Advice was given about proper hygiene procedures and products. The caretakers were reprimanded for how the infant was dressed, and the grandmother was all but scolded for her manner of dress. The grandmother's attempt to show respect through her Sunday best, so to speak, in the context of fast-fashion production in Prato, where newly moneyed immigrants were perceived as exaggerating Italian sensibilities of taste, had an unintended consequence: the doctor took offense. Hyperpoliteness became order out of place. Dressing up for public health doctors went against the moral grain for a doctor working in the service of public health. Health care was supposed to be blind to class. Dressing to the nines was not going to get you or your grandchild better health care in Prato's hospital.

If the doctor had known the family's story, the ups and downs, she probably would not have made the remark about the grandmother's elegant jacket. In the interview that followed, the baby's grandmother, Yue-Sai, told Fangli how she had immigrated initially in 2000 because she had heard of other migrants' success stories. As a destination, Italy made sense because she already had relatives there. Soon after arrival, she managed to secure a residency permit, albeit for a high price (100,000 RMB = US$16,000). Her only son, Ming, joined her through the family reunification process. Hopes of recuperating the money doled out for the permits turned into a false dream. She worked hard making clothes, first for other Chinese-owned small firms. Ming joined her to work in the fast-fashion sector, then opened a shop, but that didn't work out, so he went back to sewing. Yue-Sai said that the family now had its own firm. When Fangli hinted that life must surely be better, Yue-Sai let out a laugh. The irony soon became evident.[13]

"Just the same, there's no peace," Ming said.

"There's no peace; we always suffer oppression," Yue-Sai lamented.

The source of oppression was the incessant work, often all through the night. Prices kept falling. Staying afloat became more and more of a challenge. And then there were the robberies. Yue-Sai recounted how robbers had forced their way into the house in the early hours of the morning, around 6:00 a.m., when her daughter-in-law was still pregnant, and they had stolen everything: jewelry, cash, keys. On their way out, they stole the car. Chinese residents living in Via Pistoiese were said to be targets of violent break-ins in which robbers reputedly carried iron crowbars. Police were of little assistance.

"There's a bit of discrimination, discrimination toward foreigners," Ming said.

At the hospital, some Italian staff were helpful whereas others were visibly unhappy to have to deal with Chinese patients, likely because of the language barrier. Nurses, he said, tended to be the exception and were nearly always well-mannered. The ups and downs of working in Prato, working for others in trying circumstances, working in their own firm with no end in sight, lacking peace of mind, particularly as Prato's economy had worsened, and then the daily hostility they faced as Chinese in Prato, had become too much to bear. Yue-Sai was afraid. She was ready to go back to China. The baby would likely go with its grandparents. Fangli asked them to reflect on what had they had gained or lost from their migration experience.

"The positive side rests in the fact that we have opened our eyes," Ming said. "The negative side is that now we know that Chinese overseas don't have a good social status."

I could not help but reflect on how Yue-Sai's elegant jacket was a way to cover up all that hardship and the fact that she and her son had not achieved the social mobility that they had set out to gain. In the moment of the clinical encounter, her effort to fend off hostility was interpreted as a showy sign of success. As I made note of the attire of other Chinese parents, they were inevitably dressed nicely with up-to-date fashions that conveyed an urban presence. The young parents in particular tended to wear the popular styles of the moment. After all, that is what they made, that is what they had at their disposal, and that is what they had an eye for.

The mother, Xue, in case 4 was typical of this kind of adornment but revealed tenacity beneath the surface as when she challenged the doctor's professional view of her baby's weight. Afterward, my research assistant Xiaoyun shared with me, in Italian, a Chinese saying: "*Bianco, bianco e grosso grosso,*" or "White, white and fat, fat." The saying sums up the ideal baby: light-skinned and plump. The light skin pointed to an aesthetic preference that was widespread in China. The "fat" referred to parents who cherished fatter babies because they were seen as more robust and hence healthier.

Lian, the mother of case 3 who came with the ambiguous aunt figure, offers insight into how the immigrants anticipate being judged. The reaction of the aunt figure is noteworthy. She evidently anticipated that the doctors would judge her "niece" negatively if they knew she was going to send her infant away to China. This raises a complex issue related to what happens in encounters. The "aunt" anticipated the medical staff's assumptions. This affected communication. The "aunt" was likely tuned into the widespread criticism of the parenting decisions among many Chinese in Prato and perhaps was thinking that she was protecting her "niece."

Case 2 closes with the mother's comeback to the doctor's quip about her not taking care of her own child as a cultural fact. Shu responded with, "It's not cultural—I work." The moment was shot through with tension. The source of that tension is in large part that people, including medical professionals, presume cultural difference. Such situations are akin to cultural borderlands in which people see those with whom they are interacting as "Other." In such cross-cultural encounters, "people find themselves struggling to bridge cultural divides, to make themselves interpretable, readable (and readable in the right way) to those they regard as foreigners" (Mattingly 2008, 139). It becomes like detective work as they try to make sense of the meanings behind others' behaviors. Indeed, the doctors viewed the mother's adherence to postpartum rest as a sort of exotic cultural holdover with no rational basis in modern medicine.

The exchange about work serves to remind that people's practices are not simply matters of Chinese and Italian culture clashes but that practices and histories are ever interlocking even if they may be enigmatic and movable. I want to make three points about the culture-work dynamic: (1) migrants from Wenzhou bring with them a particular relationship to work, (2) similarities between residents from Prato and Wenzhou are fairly stunning, and (3) demands of globalization intensify work regimens and lead people to modify their cultural practices.

Regarding the first point, nearly 80 percent of the Chinese population in Prato trace their province of origin to Zhejiang, and most come from the birthplace of the Wenzhou model of economic development. Recall, this area is famous for its tenacious private enterprise and entrepreneurial spirit. Work was no stranger to the Chinese migrants in Prato. The doctor's attempt to be culturally sensitive in effect denied this history (Cao 2013; Pedone 2013, 71–72; see also Li 1999b).

Second, the moment erased similarities between the cultural practices and economic histories of two cities. Prato was known for its proliferation of small family firms where various members lent a hand and juggled textile or sweater work with care work. Gender ideologies of nonworking mothers in the image of the Virgin Mary did not hold up in practice.

Third, cultural practices are not static, and people actively navigate their entanglements with globalization. Transnational economic forces have played a major role in explaining why Chinese migrated to Prato to work in the fast-fashion niche. Whether a migrant owns a firm or sews clothes, the work is physically demanding. It makes sense for the younger generation to do the sewing while the older generation cares for the children. This is not a simple case of career women who are aiming for independence and choosing work over family. These are women who work to invest in family as they negotiate the demands of globalization. They may forfeit face-to-face parenting, but most are not forfeiting having children. Shu's anger was palatable. She was reacting to being stereotyped. Categories of observation had failed the doctor; her attempt at being sensitive resonated with a patronizing tone.

The couple Ju and Jian, from case 1, experienced a full range of issues. The most common misunderstandings appeared to be banal, quotidian matters: the flattened head or the practice of dressing the baby so warmly. The latter may stem from the couple being from a rural background, but it may also be related to the fact that the factory where they worked was not heated and the fact that they had to wait for a long time in the cold for a bus.

The interview between Fangli and the mother, Ju, as well as her field notes, revealed a number of important details about the couple's circumstances, specifically related to the realities of global migrants and the particular conditions that they faced and how they were coping with them. The medical staff's as well as my own assumptions clashed significantly with the cultural logics of the baby's parents. This was not simply a case of clashes between, say, Chinese culture and Italian culture. Rather, these clashes derived from a globalizing world and shaped ensuing encounters that were layered with complexity.

The couple lived in Vaiano, a municipality in the province of Prato known for its strategic location along the Bisenzio Valley and its role in the development of the modern textile industry, particularly related to recycled wool.[14] The couple's employer provided their food and housing. Jian had reentered work full time while Ju was devoting herself to caring for the infant. After delivering her baby in the hospital of Prato, she then enjoyed a postpartum repose, during which time the couple had rented a room, or part of a room, in the city for her and the baby. It was common practice for women from Wenzhou who came to Prato to respect the traditional Chinese forty-day postpartum period in which the mother did nothing but rest. New mothers were expected to stay in bed and not venture outside. Even the lowest-paid garment workers would take time off and go live in an apartment, often to-gether with other new mothers, their babies, and nannies who cared for the newborns and prepared food for the mothers.[15] Ju had since returned to live in the dormitory-style accommodations in the factory.[16]

Now Ju was planning to wean the baby because, on the one hand, she wanted to start working again and, on the other hand, she was convinced that her breast milk had lost its nutritional value. From her perspective, she had reason to believe that her milk was no good. While the doctors were examining the baby, she had told Fangli that having returned to live in the employer-furnished accommodations, and no longer having the availability of a place with its own kitchen, as she had with the rental, she could not fix nutritional food for herself. Add to that the fact that to buy the good food that she wanted she would have had to walk an hour to get to the nearest gro-cery stores in Via Pistoiese, that is, stores that sold Chinese food. Therefore, Ju reasoned, if a mother did not eat nutritional things, it would follow that her milk would not be nutritious. This was her conviction. At this point, she figured, it's better to use formula. Indeed, she was already giving the baby a supplement, Humana 1, which Fangli noted was among the most expensive around. Indeed, according to shopkeepers, infant formula is the item that Chinese migrants most commonly purchase from Italian supermarkets. Of course, none of this information came out during the exam itself. Recall, after weighing and measuring the infant, the pediatrician had noted how well he was growing and exclaimed, "Mother's milk is fine!"[17]

The issue of hyperdressing was also more nuanced than it had initially appeared. Granted, the baby was very covered for an indoor heated environ-ment. The seven layers of clothing obstructed his movement. The mother explained that where they lived there was no heating—commonplace in the vast factory spaces, which were often partitioned off into several sepa-rate workshops and makeshift living quarters. She added that the couple that morning had come by public transportation, that it was cold outside (a dank 6° Celsius/43° Fahrenheit) and that they had waited about an hour at the stop before the bus finally came. The pediatrician, faced with the mother's insis-tence on putting all the layers back on the infant, at a certain point had said, "But you're in a car, right?" The rhetorical tone of the question seemed to call for an affirmative response. The doctor's candor took the mother aback. She nodded. The assumption was that with a small child just three months old, in the bone-chilling winter weather, parents would naturally drive their baby in a car. These parents didn't have their own car, or access to a car for that mat-ter. Eventually, the pediatrician gave up and allowed the baby to leave with those seven layers of clothes.

The encounter led us to reflect on the different conditions in which people live and how quick people are to see the world through their own experiences. Often, the convenience of a car is taken for granted. Fangli recalled a period in her life when her own family, immigrants to the northern Italian city of Cremona, did not have a car. I recall my mother not having her own car when she was home with my older sisters and then finally getting one when they were teenagers and I was maybe six, sometime around 1968, and then it was a thrifty Chevy II black convertible, a symbol of American car culture. During my longer periods of fieldwork, I rented a car, but during shorter periods I opted for public transportation and the generosity of friends. Temporary stays and research budgets allowed for such privileges. Succeeding in taking an Italian driver's exam itself would be no simple feat for an immigrant who did not know the language.

Besides the dressing and the feeding, perhaps the major misunderstanding related to the question of the infant's head shape. The remark actually made Fangli smile when the doctors arranged for the Chinese mother's appointment for physical therapy consultations so that she could receive guidance on the optimal position to have the baby sleep to correct the flattened back of the head. I saw the humor once I realized what had happened and could only imagine the thoughts going through the parents' minds. As it turns out, Ju was a bit doubtful and surprised by the suggestion that there was something wrong with her son's head shape because in China—at least in the province of Zhejiang, where she was from—it was a popular aesthetic. Parents so admired a flattened posterior of the head that they purposefully tried to create it. They would specifically sew pillows for their baby to sleep on in such a way as to form this sought-after flattened shape.

Finally, there was the issue of sending the baby away. The parents intended for their son to live with a relative, probably the mother's sister, in China. In the interview, Ju explained that she would be able to start working again and that her son would have better life conditions there. In the mother's mind, the baby would certainly get better attention because the relatives could devote themselves full time to his care. Besides, the stipends in euro that they earned here, in Prato, once converted into Chinese renminbi, would have stronger purchasing power, so also from the point of view of material well-being, the baby would be better off in China than in Italy. To the question of how they saw the fact that the baby would live far from its mother and father, whether it hurt them to send the baby back, the mother expressed over and over again the pressure they felt to come out ahead. The mother repeated, "There's no other way, no other way." They had to earn money. Life in Italy was more tiring than in China. If they were going to make their migration worthwhile, they had to make sacrifices. In Prato, they were poorer than back home, and they dressed more commonly. Back home, in the evenings, they would go out dancing, and that would mean getting dressed up. In Prato, they didn't go out much. They were always closed inside the firm. Ultimately, she would like to have the baby close by although, she reasoned, having the child in China meant he would have a better chance at learning Chinese. At which point her husband interrupted and said they'd better leave to catch the bus before it started to rain again.[18]

# 6

# Circulation

Banners decorated the corridor of Mazzoni Middle School. Chinese ideo-grams scripted in black contrasted with Italian words written in red: 希望 paired with *speranza* (hope), 友谊 with *amicizia* (friendship), and 中国 with *Cina* (China).[1] The art project reminded visitors to Prato's city center of the school's diverse student body. I found my way into the lecture hall along with about thirty educators and health-care workers, mostly Italian women, who had come to listen to a three-hour afternoon seminar with Roberto Berto-lino, a psychologist from the Frantz Fanon Center in Turin. With a text-rich presentation of fifty-six slides, Bertolino spoke on "Children of Migration: Routes of Development between Paradoxes and New Forms of Citizenship," focused on helping adolescents who suffer from the dehumanizing psycho-logical effects of racism and colonial domination. What began as a fairly un-remarkable continuing education session turned heated when the speaker breached the topic of the circulation of children.

Bertolino took inspiration from the Martinique-born psychiatrist Fanon, reminding the audience of the insight from *Black Skin, White Masks*: that the black man is never simply a man but is always marked as other in relation to the unmarked white man (Fanon 1967).[2] The immigrant is marked by a similar estrangement, which French sociologist Abdelmalek Sayad referred to as a "double absence," a condition in which absence is always a flaw that renders the immigrant suspect. A status of precarious residence, sometimes prolonged indefinitely, leads to the double absence. First, even in cases of documented residence status or full-out naturalization, "the immigrant is always an emigrant—absent from the society of origin, and increasingly dis-tant from it in cultural and psychological terms" (Saada 2000, 37). Second, the immigrant's outsider status in the host society is ever subject to condi-

FIGURE 6.1. Giorgio, a Chinese immigrant, age ten: "I am lost." Psychologists diagnosed him with "severe scholastic discomfort" and as having "unstable bonds." His drawing, awash in yellow, places the child at the center of the parents' attention.

tional and revocable residency status, and full participation in civil society is typically severely limited. In numerous cultural, linguistic, economic, and political ways, the immigrant stands in relation to the born and raised citizen as society's "other."

For educators to correct this sense of absence is no simple matter. Bertolino criticized current approaches to intercultural education for what he described as "the pedagogy of couscous," i.e., addressing the complexities of cultural diversity through celebratory and trivial approaches based on superficial cross-cultural cuisines. He called for attention to the links among colonialism, migration, and education, and he underscored the problem of structural violence—violence that systematically writes itself on immigrant minds and bodies yet becomes normalized and often invisible (Giordano 2011; Scheper-Hughes 1992). His empathetic stance captivated listeners until he brought up challenges. Immigrant parents often find themselves in an uncomfortable situation of "hierarchical inversion," one in which they lose their authority. Their children may become distanced from them in part as the children grow more at ease than their parents with local ways of speaking and behaving. In such situations, he said, parenting is no longer possible.[3]

At this suggestion, one audience member—a Chinese gentleman wearing a traditional gray Mao suit—took the floor and objected passionately to the stereotype, insisting that Chinese children do listen to their parents. His intervention then turned to another issue: the consequences of paramilitary factory raids that represented a crackdown on undocumented workers and were a prominent feature of local governance. They fill Chinese people with fear. Families leave Prato. Lives are disrupted. Children suffer. "What does this serve?" the Chinese man asked. He offered answers: that the children are afraid and that they suffer, both from fear and from the fact that the families commonly leave Prato, thereby increasing disruption. As his intervention continued for more than seven minutes, other audience members began to stir in their seats, murmur loudly, speak over him, and finally insist that he give the floor back to the guest speaker.

As the psychologist resumed his presentation, he agreed that the children's pain was of the greatest concern. The Chinese audience member had offered the perfect segue. Bertolino described a practice now "fairly in vogue" among Filipino and Chinese migrants, "the dangerous practice, very dangerous" of sending children back to their own country.[4] Bertolino acknowledged that the parents sought to enculturate their children, to make them "Chinese" so to speak, but that the children ended up being "*orfani ovunque*," orphans everywhere, and cited a Parisian colleague who has used the concept of "*morte psichica*," or psychic death, to describe such children. Bertolino called on his audience members: "We need to help these parents to negotiate different strategies."[5]

This ethnographic encounter homes in on a paradox: More than half of the births in Prato since 2009 have been registered to foreign women, yet, once weaned, many of these babies were being sent to China.[6] In what follows, I make sense of the vocabularies that Chinese mothers and fathers use to portray the value gained or heartache endured from the transnational movement of children. I contrast the expert views of childhood circulation with those of immigrant parents. Placing these views in dialogue with one another is a strategy for interpreting the circulation of children that follows from the encounter ethnography framework. I argue that the circulation of children underwrites capitalism, with specific advantages supporting the global supply chains involved in fast fashion. Ultimately, the idea is to grasp how diasporic families and individuals negotiate the terms of a transnational world.

Scholars of migration have documented the circulation of children under a wide variety of contexts and circumstances. The value placed on kin ties and the desires as well as strategies to reproduce or sever them vary across time and place as do the biopolitics of fertility, abandonment, foster care, and adoption. Contingencies of care lead migrants to tap into global networks and make use of reciprocities to manage challenges of the life course as well as strengthen bonds.[7]

The circulation of Chinese children is by no means an entirely new phenomenon. In his pioneering study *Emigration and the Chinese Lineage*, James

Watson (1975) observed the rapid change to child-rearing practices during 1965–75 in connection with massive emigration from Hong Kong to London in which villagers primarily left to open or work in restaurants. Through a village census, he determined that approximately one-third of the children had overseas parents and were raised by their grandparents, another one-third of the children moved between Europe and Hong Kong and hence were "intermittently in the sole charge of their grandparents" (Watson 1975, 185), and the remaining one-third of the children were raised by mothers who had not migrated and had help of grandparents. Watson's (1975, 216) study illuminated the challenges of socializing grandparents into this role of primary caretaking as well as the effects of fending off modernizing forces, both through the child-rearing and the remittances that allowed locals to "emulate some of the highest ideals of their cultural heritage." What his well-rendered study did not explore were effects of these practices, such as when overseas parents confronted different expectations and experts where they had emigrated. One goal of encounter ethnography is to challenge assumptions that follow from drawing hard boundaries around "cultures" and to grasp complexities that arise from specific historical social formations. I seek to understand how practices that look old might have new meanings and new implications.

The transnational movement between China and Italy has given rise to a host of new discourses and interventions on parenting, from various institutions and experts, as children move in and out of Italian health-care systems, schools, and society. Absence takes on contested meanings as parents circulate their children to live with caretakers far away and thus contend with the absence of their children in terms of their own emotions and others' judgments.

What happens when kin-related values and norms become entangled in the hegemony of global supply chains? Supply chains have become intensely global, and the apparel sector is more rule than exception. Globalization has coincided with a rise in labor precarity and ongoing crisis, especially in southern Europe, as large firms have mostly abandoned their commitment to managing labor. Outsourcing has emerged as the global common sense. Resources are gathered from a dizzying array of sources, and jobs are performed through diverse and, at times, surprising as well as horrifying arrangements. The goal, especially for lead firms, is to generate profits (Tsing 2015). Mindful of global impulses toward accumulation, I argue that there is another important story to be told as families become entangled in global supply chains. I suture a crucial connection between kinship and economic activity. How do different "circuits of migration" articulate (Kofman 2012)—namely, those related to labor and the family? My purpose is to challenge the "natural he-

gemony" of capitalism and *capitalocentrism*: how capitalist discourses dominate, shape analyses, outlooks, even desires (Gibson-Graham 2006). This
throne status can no longer stand. Capitalism in ruins invites new playbooks.

The remainder of this chapter draws on perspectives of the forty-plus immigrant parents who have direct ties to fast fashion and who have experience
sending their children to China. Interviews with more than a dozen Italian
health-care workers add depth and breadth. As the team transcribed, translated, coded, and analyzed the semistructured interviews, we identified major
themes.[8] Below, the analysis focuses on three themes related to the circulation of children: the alienating tempos of fast fashion, an enduring sense of
inevitability, and a salient concern for children's well-being. These themes
highlight parents' decisions to participate in the formation of global households. All told, necessity, comfort, regret, and reciprocal relations animate
the circulation of children.

The analysis brings into sharp relief the existence of global families and the
significance of global households. By global families, I mean closely related
kin members, namely parents and their children, in which children circulate
among primary caretakers often in different countries throughout the course
of their childhood. Related, I draw on an economist-geographer team's definition of the global household as "an institution formed by family networks
dispersed across national boundaries" (Safri and Graham 2010, 100). Safri
and Graham convincingly demonstrate that the global household has evolved
into a formidable economic actor. They note a rise in international divisions
of labor because global households afford flexible workers. In referring to the
household as a site of noncapitalist production, they intend household members' services of domestic work and care, services that account for as much as
half of world economic activity. The coauthors make an essential move: they
recast remittances as a "productive investment" rather than as resources that
only finance consumption (Safri and Graham 2010, 115). As such, they hint
at the multiplier effect of remittances in terms of generating and distributing
"significant monetized value." They calculate the value of world gross household product as 80 percent of gross domestic product (GDP), so that if GDP
is $50 trillion, they estimate the world gross household product at $40 trillion
(in 2006 figures) (Safri and Graham 2010, 110).

I argue that global households are not only integral to the economic organization that fast fashion requires but also reveal its other-than-capitalism
character (De Angelis 2007). It is "other than" in that the economic organization does not adhere to the straight scripts of a globalized economy. Con-
trary to expert and popular opinion in which the circulation of children and
multiple caretakers are widely devalued (Cardarello 2015; Leinaweaver and

Fonseca 2007), parents find value in circulating children, in its power to activate systems of reciprocity across kin, to create networked bodies across
territories, to secure affective bonds across generations, and to free up time
so as to enhance their ability to work and make money. That, after all, was the
point of leaving home.

### Encountering Experts

Bertolino's call to arms was moving and resonated with the audience. The
image of children wandering around in states of psychic death was terrify-
ing. It was tempting to accept Bertolino's call, with his alarms of a dangerous
parenting strategy and its slippery slope into pathology. The psychologist's
observations carried weight. He was the expert. When he framed migration
as a vehicle for transmitting trauma—"*si trasmette la trauma*"—his words
hit a chord with the Italian professionals. The Chinese gentleman's objections
were unwelcome. His perspectives bordered on being a nuisance. The two
men's positions contrasted as dramatically as their dress: the one in a blue
pullover and khaki pants, the other in a Mao suit. They spoke right past each
other. That day, only one message got through: that of the Italian expert.

The encounter gave me pause. Was it not obvious that sending children
far away from their parents was a bad idea? The commonsense reply would be
"yes." The prevailing view in Italy among educators, politicians, and health-
care workers was that the transnational circulation of children was a negative
and harmful practice. From a doctor's, nurse's, or psychologist's position of
trying to alleviate suffering or a teacher's position of wanting to educate immigrant children, a desire for continuous presence seems reasonable.

Interviews with more than a dozen health-care professionals suggested
strong themes of difficulty in managing diverse patients generally, a situation
that became all the more challenging with the Chinese population specifically and the movement of children. They pointed to growing caseloads and
shrinking staffs due to austerity-related cuts, neoliberal restructuring, and
privatization that affected social services and health care, which amounted to
a demoralizing 90 percent reduction at the national level and 60 percent in
the region of Tuscany over a ten-year period from 2004–14. Meanwhile, as
they faced an increasingly frequent caseload with Chinese parents and their
children and confronted laws that restricted care based on residency status,
health-care workers expressed feelings of discouragement, frustration, dejec-
tion, and even apathy.

Health-care workers recounted specific instances of how much time and
effort it takes to build a little trust in parents and to convince them to pursue

treatment for children—"*all'inizio si fa fatica,*" in the beginning, it's exhausting; then it becomes impossible to treat patients if they do not return for follow-up care. Many practitioners through facial expressions, gestures, and words expressed disappointment as they shared recollections of children being sent to China midcourse during a treatment. Others told of stories of children returning to Italy to find long waiting lists and not being able to get adequate therapy or get scheduled back into the regimented cycles of care. In light of a client not presenting, one psychologist explained, "I did all the preparatory work, and then it was of absolutely no use." A neuropsychiatrist expressed the difficulty of explaining to parents what she, as a practitioner, believed would be helpful to the child but felt that her explanations were lost on the adults. A speech therapist found it a challenge to evaluate linguistic problems among non-Italian speakers and described being completely "exhausted" by the work with Chinese clients. Another psychologist described her work with Chinese parents as "extremely difficult." A specialist in neonatal care pointed to the anxieties that came with explaining protocols or assessing compliance given the extensive problems of communication: "They cannot communicate, so it is assumed that there is a higher degree of difficulty to enter into communication."

Across the board, practitioners noted the limited availability of cultural mediators or translators. Even so, another expressed frustration over the "limited investment" that the Chinese parents devoted to learning Italian. While several acknowledged their own efforts to learn Chinese, the speech therapist called for "increased integration, a greater openness, but instead, I feel a lot of closed-mindedness. . . . But maybe if they don't have time for their children, they don't have time to learn Italian." Educators expressed difficulties teaching students who move between China and Italy and do not understand lessons because of language or absenteeism. As one school director with a significant Chinese immigrant student body expressed, "I think that the big problem is in the fact of this continuous migration."

Whether in the context of providing health care or education, expectations are for stability and continuity, and such characteristics are associated with certain types of families, living together in one place, with attachment and bonding ideally between mother and child, as prefigured in Renaissance paintings and sculptures that adorn churches, museums, and even intersections. Not so very long ago, in the late nineteenth century, recall the historic province of Florence witnessed its own circulation of children as straw weavers who were certified as lacking milk received state subsidies to pay wet nurses to care for their infants, on the one hand, and as professional wet nurses abandoned their own children to serve the babies of elite women, on the other hand (Krause 2009). Perspectives such as that of Bertolino, as expressed poignantly in that singular moment, fail to consider the economic constraints and care strategies of the people who are entangled within them. Indeed, how do transnational families live this variety of globalization?

## Encountering Parents

Chinese parents attribute transnational movement of children partly to complex regulations required to keep current their children's residence in Prato and not trigger the nightmarish paperwork associated with family reunification applications: thus, they must endure long lines and present their children in person to the *questura*, or police headquarters, every two years. Absence must also be understood in the context of a "complete and utter crisis of citizenship" (Mezzadra and Neilson 2013, 43). A sense of uncertainty about the future saturates their outlook. As a result, only rarely do these migrants self-identify as either temporary sojourners or permanent residents. The global economic crisis of 2008 extended its reach into the main streets of Chinese fast-fashion work and intensified competition among fast-fashion producers. Thus, the trajectory toward a stabilizing "second generation" seemed upended (Ceccagno 2004). Although the global household strategy of family-making appeared to occur more frequently among entry-level Chinese migrants who worked for others, it is a strategy that those who owned and managed their firms also use. The assumption that owners would have more free time than nonowners did not bear out in the interviews. Our research revealed that both entrepreneurs and workers made use of transnational care networks. Circulating children equates to a strategy of keeping options open and transnational networks active, not only for themselves but also for their children.

The half-joking refrain among Chinese parents, "I went overseas and earned a child," plays on the multiple meanings of the verb *to earn.* It at once references the fact that the Chinese immigrants work hard, earn money, and in the process grow their family. Chinese immigrants often laugh when they utter this phrase because it pokes fun at their own common tendency to calculate actions in monetary terms. The phrase also references the relatively greater reproductive freedom that Chinese parents acquire in leaving China because they are more or less outside of the purview of the one-child policy. Even if the policy is much less coercive than in years past (Greenhalgh 2003), parents who have two or even three children in Italy do not face the medical costs of childbearing or possible fines that they would in China (K. Johnson 2014). The phrase also hints at the importance that Chinese immigrants place

on family and social networks, and children are one way to enhance those affective bonds. As one parent of a child in China told us about her decision to
migrate and send her children to live in China, "In terms of the advantages,
the only thing that makes you feel all right is to think that in this way they can
give some company to the old folks, Dad and Mom, so that my parents will
not feel so lonely."[9]

Young parents do not necessarily set out to create a global household. As
life unfolds and social relations become entangled with global supply chains,
strategies emerge to fit circumstances, often not foreseen. One mother's story
reveals the contours as well as the trajectories that led her and her husband to
extend their household in a global direction.

Wenling's beautiful smile and her calm disposition belied her mothering
of three-month-old twins and the mountains she has climbed. That June 2013
day, she carried an iPhone with a pink case and Disney ring tone and was
dressed in trendy youthful clothes: a yellow netlike shirt over a black cami-
sole, black leggings, and espadrille wedges with turquoise straps. She agreed
to an interview after leaving the bustle of the hospital exam room with a good
prognosis for her babies. She, Fangli, and I found comfort in seats in a waiting area nook. I looked on, trying not to be intrusive, ready and willing to
hold a baby if need be.

Wenling had two older sons living in China. This is neither a tragic nor a
triumphant story but rather one that involves unanticipated hardship, adap-
tation to work rhythms, motivations for sending children back, and flourishing networks of care and remittances. Her experiences echo those of so many
others, which we thematically tease out and amplify below.

In 2003, Wenling's mother told her to leave, and she didn't think twice
about it. She was twenty years old. She listened to her parents' friends who
said that Italy was a land of opportunity—you could earn well there—and a
friend of her father's had already migrated and was living in Italy. She had no
idea what she was in for when she boarded a plane for Moscow. Once there,
she climbed mountains, stayed in underground mountaintop cottages for
days, then spent two months traveling in a truck. Grueling travel sparked ro-
mance. "We met each other while we were coming here illegally," she says of
the man who would become her husband. "An illegal trip," she adds, laughing. She stayed for another six months in the Czech Republic. Eight months
later, at a cost of more than €10,000 euro (100,000 RMB), she finally settled in
Vicenza. "The one who organized the trip had told my mother that we would
fly as far as Moscow, then we would have walked a bit, and the trip in the car
would have been quick," she recalled. "Nobody had any idea that it was going
to be like this."[10]

Unexpected conditions also awaited her in the garment sector. She had done a little factory-line work back in China but usually for only a few hours a day. Life was low key. In Italy, she became all too familiar with an inverse work-to-sleep ratio. In China, she worked four or five hours a day; in Italy, she slept four or five hours a day. Ironically, she only adjusted to the rhythms, little by little, once she had her son in 2006. The baby slept at night for seven or eight hours while both parents worked. During the day, she and her husband took turns caring for the baby and sleeping: "He would sleep four hours and then I, too, four hours." The baby was always with them, never in anyone else's care: "He's always been with me, staying with us is better," Wenling said. The couple lived in dormitory-style housing that the employer provided in the factory. Their boss allowed them to keep the baby with them, apparently an exception to the rule, in part due to the couple having been introduced by friends who knew the owner and in part from the fact that the two of them worked quickly, she said, like the other workers: "What two people were doing, we also were doing."

They did not have the option of enrolling the infant in childcare because they did not have residency permits at the time and hence were disqualified, and it also was not logistically easy to take him to school. In 2009, her husband managed to obtain amnesty, and in 2010, when her husband went to work for an Italian-owned firm, she was able to acquire a residency permit under a family unification clause. The family's experience of moving from an illegal to a legal status reminds us how such statuses are arbitrary, unpredictable, and constraining. The legal structures prohibited the couple from being able to take advantage of childcare. By the time her second son was born, in 2011, Wenling found herself puttering around more than working, and the next year she decided to take the boys back to China. At the time of the interview, her sons had been back in China for a little less than a year. The seven-year-old son was living with his paternal grandmother; the two-year-old son was living with his aunt, her husband's sister-in-law. (Her father and father-in-law were deceased.) The couple sent money to both his mother and her mother to help with living expenses and medicine.

"At the beginning, I missed them a lot," she said. "I wasn't used to it. All of a sudden, I couldn't manage. It was like in a flash there was so much silence around me. There was nothing with me. I had always had them with me; I had been with the older one for seven years." And then she stopped herself: "There were not other alternatives."

"Why did you choose to take them back to China?" Fangli asked.

"If you are in Italy for a long time and you've earned nothing, always with the babies, always with the babies, you've earned nothing," Wenling explained.

She returned to Prato and got pregnant, thought about having an abortion but then learned she was carrying male and female twins—viewed as rather rare—and decided to go through with the pregnancy. Perhaps the twins would also be China-bound. She could not say yet. However, she was convinced that the Chinese approach to education yielded brighter children.

In the next three sections I delve into the significant ways in which the tempos of fast fashion, a sense of inevitability, and a concern for children's well-being shape families' decisions to have children participate in migratory circuits.

### Tempos

Fast fashion is, well, fast, and it requires the workers to be fast, too. Typically, both parents work. Hours are reportedly long, often twelve to sixteen across day and night, and well beyond what Italian labor laws permit. Pay is commonly by the piece, so that the faster workers cut and sew, the more they can earn. In response to describing their decision to send their young children away or leave their older children behind, parents spoke of time shortages: "There is not enough time," "We even don't have enough time to sleep," "We cannot find a way to arrange our time," or "I don't have time to talk with him, to help him, or teach him."

Immigrant accounts of labor histories reveal alienation due to the rhythms of fast-fashion work, on the one hand, and strong articulations between kin networks and capitalist markets, on the other hand. Nearly all of those we interviewed spoke of coming to Italy through some kind of kinship network—either a direct relative such as a parent, sibling, cousin, aunt, or uncle, or relative of a neighbor. Transnational kin networks strongly determined destinations. As migrants assumed debt to go abroad, they found themselves in a sort of trap in which the investment constrained them to accept certain working conditions in order to repay their debt. Some spoke of this as a burden, others spoke of it casually, as like any other debt, something that could be paid off in six months or spread out over a couple of years.

Despite kin networks that softened their experiences in theory, there were poignant memories of alienation in practice. Earlier, Peng described a "fistful of tears" related to the challenging working conditions and rhythms that he faced as a novice garment worker in training. Immigrants did not anticipate the conditions. Dao-ming said, "Who knew that once you arrived here it would be like this, that you'd work so hard? We just didn't know."[11] Inter-viewees described deep feelings of alienation linked to a life reduced to work, sitting long hours at work stations, and collective listlessness. As Mei put it, "Staying here, people tend to become more apathetic, always doing the same thing, always the same, they don't have changes. Most people have this sensa-tion, that staying here stiffens the brain."[12]

During an exploratory trip in 2011, I had first heard about heartbreak-ing cases from Anna Ascolti, the sympathetic infant and child psychologist with Prato's public health agency. As time permitted, we took walks along the Bisenzio, had dinner together with her husband, children, and friends (I was the perpetual guest), and attended exhibits, plays, movies, and politi-cal events related to immigrants. I even accompanied her to a professional psychology seminar focusing on attachment theory and practice. She was constantly alert to happenings, whether in Prato or Florence, and made sure I knew about them. Of late, her job had come to include significant work with immigrant children and families. I wrote this in my field notes:

> She has a particular view of these kids because she goes to the school for visits as a psychologist. She told me of two cases. She was very eager to speak about them.
>
> (1) Chinese family with three kids. One of the kids they left years ago in China when they came to Prato. They've since had two more kids (maybe one is seven, the other ten, something like that). The oldest had recently come back to Prato. She was fifteen years old with mental challenges. Anna inter-vened and had the girl sent to the hospital for analyses. It was determined that she had something wrong with her spine, neck, and hands. She was slow. Otherwise, she was a pretty girl with striking long hair. She never learned to read and write in China but now speaks a few words of Italian. Her parents can't afford the bus. So she walks to school every day with her heavy backpack. It's a long distance. At first, her parents wouldn't let her go on school fieldtrips because they thought they had to pay for them. Now they realize the state will help out with transport. They seem desperate. They work and work but have no money. The father doesn't have a *permesso di soggiorno* [residency permit]. He's undocumented. He's been waiting a year. So this is a huge problem and may affect what the daughter is eligible for. Such a painful tale. OMG.
>
> (2) Another case of a kid who fell out of his chair, had a huge lesion to his head, and then was sent back to China and not cared for and not given any interventions and so he probably would have been at a higher functioning level now, but he's really not very functional at all.

Ascolti had many similar stories to share. The case of Giorgio offers an elaborated perspective on time and parenting from her perspective.[13] Because of her busy schedule, I interviewed her during two separate sittings, a year later, in July 2012, at the dining room table of her well-kept fourth-story apartment with its view of the city's red-tile roofs. At seven months, Giorgio was sent to China along with his older brother and in 2006 came back to Italy to attend preschool. A year later, in first grade, his parents brought him to Prato's public health agency, where Ascolti gradually had begun to see a growing number of Chinese parents and their children among her patients. Ascolti described the boy as a "very intelligent" bilingual child who excelled in all subjects; he was exceptional in math and even had the highest possible score of ten in Italian. But Giorgio was hyperactive and cried a lot in school. He was diagnosed with "severe scholastic discomfort." His case was similar to that of an Italian child who might be referred to her. The differences came with his transnational movement, relationship with his parents, and the little time they spent with him. He was given to an Italian woman from the time he was one month old. "So right from the start, he had this separation," the psychologist said, adding that he was very attached to his brother, the only person he had been with his whole life, and he tended to listen to him more than his parents.

Once back in Italy, problems arose both at home and in school. "He breaks things, he obeys only if someone gets mad at him, he is never still," Ascolti said, voicing the father. During school lunch one day, the boy put a rope around his neck and said, "I want to die." After that, he always wanted to be close to the teacher, which Ascolti described as "*bellino*," very cute. Sometimes when the parents would arrive late at school to pick him up, he would be waiting at the gate, calling out his own name, as though at the airport: "Giorgio, Giorgio. Is there someone who will pick me up? I'm here." Ascolti added that the family was meticulous, punctual, and collaborative. Like most Chinese parents she had encountered as clients, however, they put work before all else and so at home did not pay much attention to him.

During one visit, the boy drew a nativity scene surrounded by a blue sky, a smiling moon, a shooting star, and green grass. The scene was awash in yellow. In the center, a baby lay in a manger under a ceiling light. A mother and a father kneeled on either side of him (figure 6.1). Ascolti noted that he pictured himself as an Italian citizen, and she emphasized that he had placed himself at the center. At school, he also wanted to be the center of attention. Indeed, the best day of his life, she said, was the day he ended up in the hospital. He had fallen and cut his head, and the teacher had cuddled him, keeping him on her lap until his father arrived to take him to the hospital.

"He had gone to the hospital in the car with his dad, and the boy said that this had been the most beautiful day in his life," Ascolti said. "Everybody for him, he was so happy. It didn't matter one iota that to have all that attention, he had gotten a hole in his head."

During another visit, the psychologist had instructed Giorgio to play a game. "At a certain point, he made a slip of the tongue and said—instead—he meant to say that the dad did not buy him these toys because he didn't put them back in their correct places and he lost them. And instead of saying that he lost the toys, he said, 'I am lost.' But I think that he really does feel truly lost. Indeed, he has very unstable bonds."

As problems persisted and the parents returned to meet with the psychologist, she recalled suggesting that they spend more time with their son. "And I told them, 'But don't you have even a bit of time for him, even ten minutes, to play a bit with him, to read him a book?' They tell me, 'No, not even ten minutes a day. Nothing.' That's exactly what they said."

Such encounters between Chinese parents and Italian health-care workers give the impression of a good deal of incommensurability in terms of parenting. In some ways, however, the fact that many migrant parents across our interviews also lamented the lack of time to spend with their children suggests that they do share basic assumptions but that they adopt radically different strategies to arrive at standards of care. In other words, many have embraced a global household strategy so as to realize family ideals—in ways that extend beyond Italian ideals of motherhood (Krause 2005c) and the ideal of the Madonna-bambino bond. This widespread caretaking norm is one that children sense and internalize.[14] This internalization may happen as parents deal with intense constraints on their personal time (Ceccagno 2007).

## Inevitability

Many parents spoke of feeling constrained to send their children back to China. A theme emerged connected to a deep sense of necessity and inevitability. Parents used phrases such as "There is no other way," "There is no other option," or "We don't have a choice; that's life." One father acknowledged that his wife was sad, adding, "She has to bear it; there's nothing we can do." Fen, the mother of a ten-year-old living with her grandparents, explained it like this: "The reason that we sent her back to China is not that we don't like her; it's because of our job and life. There is nothing we can do."[15] Chaoxiang, who worked his way up from producing clothes to owning a fast-fashion firm, with his wife had three children: the oldest was born in China in 1997; the other two were born in Prato in 2005 and 2006. At the time of the interview, the children were sixteen, seven, and six years old. Only the youngest was living in Prato.

CHAOXIANG: We separate ourselves from one another out of necessity. It's hard to say if it's regrettable or not, but to live together is impossible.
FANGLI: But are you sorry?
CHAOXIANG: Some regret, certainly, but being apart is also inevitable.[16]

This profound sense of inevitability came up again and again as parents emphasized the conditions of their work. More than one parent used the words *vicious competition* to characterize Prato's fast-fashion scene[17] in which the life of any given business is not long. Their own living conditions, often in dormitory-style housing, and rhythms of life as immigrants in Prato were often not conducive to raising a child. They expressed being anxious having their child stay with an expensive nanny or at their side in precarious situations. They expressed feeling more at ease having their children living with close relatives, even if they were far away, than trying to watch them directly in the factory.

## Well-Being

Long-distance arrangements were seen as in the best interest of the child and the family writ large. Several parents described sorrow at the thought of missing out on milestone moments, but they reasoned that this was a small sacrifice compared to the advantages. Ultimately, parents expressed a sincere conviction that they had the child's welfare at heart.

Peng, the young man whose father sent him to Italy to straighten him out and who eventually became a firm owner, got married, and had a family in Prato, reflected on his and his wife's decision to send their son back to China to live with his parents. When the child came back to Prato for a visit, the boy seemed unhappy. "When he was here, I had to look after him in the factory. There is no place for him to go; he has to stay in the factory all the time. Now he is in China, he is very happy," Peng reasoned. As for living far from her son, he said that his wife, Lily, was sad, "but she has to bear it. There's nothing we can do." He went on to express the value of having the child live with his grandparents in China:

> Both language and [living] conditions have their value. Here, when he [the baby] is here, it's hard time for his life. I saw some children in other people's factory, they live like a cat, they roll on the floor, and when they want to sleep, they would sleep in the cardboard.[18]

Peng's view of a child living "like a cat" is not intended to bring to mind a house cat that is treated like a member of the family. Rather, the association better translates to a stray animal that lives off back-alley scraps and could itself serve as a source of food for the family as opposed to being one of its members. Metaphorically, it conveys the sense that parents have to negotiate the best possible route of care under the circumstances and demands for work. A sense of traditional intimacy also figured into decisions about the child's welfare.

Parents often expressed a desire for their children to be raised in China so as to become Chinese. A strong desire for oral and written fluency of Chinese language played a major role. One father, Bo, described placing high value on "traditional intimacy," a quality that children gained when they grew up in China close to grandparents and other relatives. In a non-Chinese environment, words and ways threatened to erode such qualities and produce a Westernized child. Even so, he admitted to having mixed feelings about having his two children, a four-year-old daughter and one-year-old son, far away, saying, "Well, I am definitely distressed, no matter what. They are my children. But there is a good side to it and a bad side to it."[19] Bo's children lived with their paternal grandparents, he sent back money as well as infant milk powder, and his parents hired a part-time nanny to help with childcare.

A strong pattern emerged around a preference to have kin as caretakers rather than nonkin. Many parents expressed fear at the thought of placing their children in the care of a stranger. Hospital health-care professionals corroborated those fears, recounting tragic cases of shaken baby syndrome, a.k.a. abusive head trauma, that they believed had a higher rate of occurrence when infants were placed in the care of someone who was tending numerous infants. Health concerns were one kind of well-being. Another had to do with emotional ties. One mother expressed the sense of relief that came from her daughter being raised by family rather than a nonkin caretaker thus:

FEN: We felt relieved as long as she lived with family. After all, there is affection between family members, that's—
FANGLI: There is kinship.
FEN: It's very natural.[20]

Benefits of kin caretakers included providing continuity across generations, of maintaining ties, and of keeping aging grandparents company. Parents frequently expressed skepticism about placing their child in the care of a nanny in Prato. There was a widespread feeling that overseas migrants had come to make money and so could not be trusted to care for a child. Trustworthy nannies cost more than most workers could afford. Furthermore, parents expressed a sense of tranquility in having grandparents or close kin care for their children as opposed to strangers. At the same time, there were trade-offs in extending care across distant territories. Misgivings were frequently related to "firsts" having to do with a child's development. Reflecting on what she had lost or gained in sending her daughter to be raised in China for the early years, Ling noted the freedom she had gained and then added, "Lost—I would say to have lost the most important thing in having a daughter, I mean that type of contact between a mother and her child."[21]

Asked what she gained or what she lost from her immigration experience, Hui Li recounted her experience in almost poetic terms:

> Speaking of advantages, yes, the only one is that we're now familiar with life abroad, while in China, we first thought that the moon was rounder in foreign places, that . . . that whoever left the country, or whoever returned home, was very glorious, it made a big impression. Now that I've experienced it, I can say that in reality, only you know how much roughness can hide behind that happiness.[22]

## Different Children, Same Family

Clara offers insight from an adult child's perspective into the logics of parents who send their children to be raised long distance while also transitioning from workers to owners. Interestingly, she drew a stark contrast between her own childhood and that of her brother, who was never sent back to China to be raised. A change in her parents' work status resulted in two siblings with starkly different childhoods. She was convinced that hers was better, that it had made her a more open, cheerful, and mature person as compared to her more introverted brother.[23]

Clara was born in Italy, where her mother had migrated alone and, unbeknown to her, pregnant. At two months old, Clara was sent back to China to live with her grandparents. She was entrusted with friends to accompany her back because her mother's immigration status did not permit easy travel across borders. Clara stayed in China until she was almost five years old. For the first three or so years, she lived with her maternal grandparents. She remembered a constant flow of aunts and uncles. Her life was rich with figures of reference. Everyone was together. She became especially attached to her maternal grandmother. Even so, she knew who her parents were because her grandmother would always show her pictures, saying, "This is your daddy, this is your mamma," so there was always a sense of family closeness and affection.

Clara remembers being sad only once and crying when she moved from her maternal to her paternal grandparents' house, where she lived a little over a year. She remembers the day her mother and father came for her. She remembers knowing that they had come to find her as soon as they landed in China. She remembers seeing them and feeling calm, a memory she attributes to a sense of closeness and affection. She did not recall having separation problems from her grandparents.

"Right away, I felt at ease," she recalled.

Back in Italy, she remembers life was starkly different. Her parents were working for another firm, and they were living together in someone else's space. As a five-year-old, she felt constrained. "In China it was different. Let's just say it was much better, in terms of the home environment and everything. . . . Because there was a house, I mean, a normal house."

In that period, after she came back to Italy, she recalls that her parents spoiled her. Both of her parents spent a lot of time with her. They would buy her things, and when they had a little free time, they would take her to parks and on outings on the train.

"It was completely different from now," she said. "My brother, by contrast, he did not experience these—these moments that I spent with my parents."

This contrast in time that the siblings spent with their parents challenged commonsense assumptions given that her younger brother had never lived far away from his parents. The big difference was that her parents worked for someone else when she was a child whereas, shortly after her brother was born, they had ventured out on their own and opened a fast-fashion enterprise. They had the advantage of having their son close by their side but the disadvantage of being owners in a highly competitive environment and thus were constantly busy with unending worries and little time to spend with Clara's little brother.

Clara reasoned that had her parents not devoted such time to her when she came back from China, she probably would have ended up a completely different person, a closed person, like her brother. If people pitied her or were inclined to say things like "poor thing," she did not see it that way. As a young child, she had her maternal grandmother. She was everything.

Nor was Clara's transition into Italian society traumatic. By the time she returned to Italy, although she had learned Chinese in preschool and did not speak a word of Italian, once in Italian schools, she acquired the language effortlessly and has fond memories of teachers and classmates availing themselves to help her especially in the first few months. In fact, she chose to use Italian for her interview. Clara speaks of herself as having a hybrid identity—as much Italian as Chinese, with an Italian first name and a Chinese surname, a Chinese passport and Italian residency. She rejects the hardened mentality of Italians as well as Chinese and aims to forge a path somewhere in between.

## Far-Flung Families, Capitalist Entanglements

How do we interpret the entanglements of families with fast and flexible capitalism? The stories of parents and health-care professionals depict a range of perspectives, all resulting from how globalization manifests locally. With all due respect to Bertolino, his analysis is skewed through the hegemony of a global supply chain. The distortions of this hegemonic order render his clinical lens an isolated instrument, unmoored from economic structures and capital flows, and thus seduce him to pathologize behaviors linked to diaspora. I do not deny that the children of immigrants may suffer from moving around, that medical care may be interrupted, that children may long for their parents or vice versa, or that they may find transitions from one school to another to be disorienting. However, I do question a blanket approach that disregards the existence of global households. Instead, I am suggesting a lens that allows for different ways of belonging and different ways of understanding globalization.

The circulation of children is not by necessity a dangerous practice that results in orphaned children who roam the world in states of psychic death. To challenge accusations of psychically "dead" children—a characterization that brings to mind armies of zombie immigrant youth—I seek to avoid naked cultural relativism. Parents, kin, and friends navigate the circulation of children and create global households that offer possibilities for children to get lost in the shuffle or to be well loved, nurtured, and enlivened through transnational networks. Global households create value through networks in their own right. Thus, themes of temporality, inevitability, and well-being can be understood to enact and enable different kinds of value.

I build on a locality analysis through encounter ethnography to note how global households create social, symbolic, and economic value across and through (1) kinship relations, (2) social networks, and (3) reciprocity as an expression of noncapitalism. The first leg of this analysis pushes a nexus between global kinship and an economy reliant on global supply chains. The second leg extends the idea of dispersion as a resource. The third leg binds the two.

First, it is important to recognize the stability of kinship even as it appears unstable. We must locate the core of kinship not in place but in sentiment.

In a provocative book-length essay, *What Kinship Is—And What It Is Not*, Sahlins (2013, ix) reminds us that kinship has to do with "mutual relations of being" and "participation in one another's existence." "Families," he counters, "consider themselves as people who belong to one another" (ibid., 22). Families may also belong across territories. That does not make their relations of being any less mutual. Granted, relations become less quotidian. But there is still a strong aspect of mutuality and how they "know each other's doings and sufferings as their own" (ibid., 44–45). Sahlins's essay highlights the multiple ways in which being and belonging can be realized. It also offers a powerful corrective to scientific notions of kinship that reduce it to biology and also of the "egocentric anthropology of kinship" infused by Western individualism (ibid., 43).

Parents circulate their children between China and Italy, between Wenzhou and Prato, to the point that it has come to seem normal for many immigrant families. In engaging in this circulation, participants constitute kinship. That is not to say it is an easy practice—emotionally or legally. They must deal with visas and residency permits and a proliferation of rules and regulations related to crossing borders as well as staying put within them. Nor is it merely a timeworn traditional practice. Within the fast-fashion niche, the circulation of children has become a coping strategy, and one that in fact, I argue, strengthens mutual relations of being across territories and allows for close relatives to participate in the child's existence across generations.

Second, far-flung social ties may be cast in positive terms; dispersion may become a resource. Indeed, they may enhance what migration scholar Ma Mung (2004, 219) describes as "inter-polarity of relationships, that is, the existence of relationships between the various poles of the diaspora." Similarly, Chu's ethnography depicts Chinese villagers waiting, with bags packed, to migrate and emphasizes the importance of "webs of relations." Children are seen as "fundamental extensions of one's social possibilities and moral legacy as a networked body" (Chu 2010, 95). They enhance and link people across mountains, oceans, continents—and markets. Measuring the experiences of Chinese immigrants against a European/Western norm of the family risks ignoring the realities of what a flexible labor force and entanglements with global supply chains mean in the context of globalization. Chinese parents send their children to China not merely to socialize them into Chinese cultural habits and outlooks as well as educational approaches but also to create networked bodies and meanwhile negotiate the demands of being flexible workers in a fast economy.

Third, transnational families pursue a mix of economic strategies as they work in global commodity chains. Mauss's (1990) classic essay *The Gift* takes

on new meaning in an intensely globalized context. Its original political intervention exposed the free marketers of the day and their restricted, utilitarian, and individualistic view of humans as naturally and narrowly inclined to
engage in cold calculation rather than collaboration at every turn. Through
unmasking the spirit of the gift, he aimed to revalue archaic practices that
were still widely used but were often not seen as mattering to modern economic activity and life. The work inspired investigations across a range of societies (Godelier 1999; Graeber 2001; Strathern 1988; Sykes 2005) and gave way
to one of Sahlins's (1972, 193) classic insights, the notion of a "spectrum of
reciprocities": generalized, balanced, and negative. Generalized reciprocity,
giving without taking account of how much is taken with the sense that in the
future something will be given back, most closely describes what comes into
play in the context of the Chinese immigrant workers' circulation of children. This insight challenges capitalism's throne status in showing how commodities derive their value in part by drawing on and altering social relations
embedded in noncapitalist activities, as Tsing (2013) has keenly documented
in her ethnography on the highly valued matsutake mushroom, which essentially begins and ends its life as a gift. I am not suggesting that Made in Italy
garments begin and end their lives as gifts. I am, however, suggesting that
these commodities are reliant on noncapitalist social relations, from historic
sentiment that enhances their value to gifts given via generalized reciprocity
in the making and sustaining of cross-territory households.

This argument complements the placement of the global household into
a diverse economies framework in which "heterogeneous noncapitalist economic activities coexist with capitalist ones" (Safri and Graham 2010, 103).
Even in the context of Wall Street investment banking, Karen Ho (2009,
13) convincingly reminds us of the resilience of kin networks and warns
that "framing kinship and family as dichotomous with, or external to, the
very processes of capitalist formation ignores the centrality of the connections and sentiments of kinship that make capitalist production possible."
Transnational families pursue a mix of economic strategies as they engage
in activities rooted in global capitalist markets. I reincarnate the insights of
Mauss regarding the stubborn persistence of gift economies even in modern
economies. Gift economy practices and principles—the obligations to give,
to receive, and to reciprocate—establish, confirm, maintain, and even ruin
relationships (Mauss 1990). They have deep social, moral, and economic consequences and continue to operate in intensely globalized economies.

Thus, what if instead of viewing circulation as an inevitable consequence
of global capitalism, as a dubious or even pathological form of parenting, or
even as a case of cultural relativism—it is just what the Chinese do; it is their

culture—we were to view it as part of the broad variety of diverse economic activities that coexist with and even underwrite capitalism? Fast fashion could not exist, the prices could not exist, the market could not exist without the global household and practices of reciprocity. When such important aspects are left out of analysis, we have understood very little about the economy or the social relations that undergird it. Sustaining the global household is key to the fast-fashion economy—how it works and how to understand it.

Ultimately, encounter ethnography reveals two crucial dynamics. The first is the enduring centrality of families to this story and the ways in which hybrid economic forms articulate and matter for understanding sociocultural systems (Wolf 1982; Yanagisako 2002; Yang 2000). The second is the challenge of understanding how such forces manifest meanings and value besides those calculated in utilitarian terms so dear to that commodity-fetishizing, European species *Homo economicus* (Mauss 1990). The method reveals the cultural logics of individuals sandwiched between kin and capitalist regimes as well as illuminates how concepts of family formation are generated and contested in this globalized economic sphere.

Kin networks articulate with capitalist activities in significant ways. Parents seek strategies to find the best care possible for their children given structural constraints. Pursuing migrant success becomes not only an individual undertaking but also an extended-family endeavor. This chapter has highlighted how parents activate relations of reciprocity, how their strategies create in themselves and their children networked bodies, and how they distribute affective bonds across borders and generations. Material and immaterial values activate relations, beliefs, and sentiments across transnational spaces and create diasporic memories, connections, and histories between global households. Under intensified twenty-first-century globalization, so-called flexible capitalism articulates with noncapitalist activities and not only encourages but also relies on far-flung family formations.

# PART THREE

# The New Politics of Urban Racism

# Integration

A distraught Chinese mother had walked more than a kilometer along Via Pistoiese grasping her lifeless eleven-month-old infant in her arms. At the Ospedale Misericordia e Dolce, she headed straight up the ramp to the emergency room. At 9:30 p.m. on February 9, 2011, her baby was pronounced dead. Newspaper reports whirled with hypotheses: that the infant had died suddenly at home of sudden infant death syndrome, that a friend of the mother's had provided a bad translation between Italian and her dialect of Chinese, that the couple had mixed illegal Chinese substances with legal Italian ones, or that the parents had misunderstood the doctor's directions for administering a prescription. The cause was still unknown, the autopsy yet to be performed, the following evening when the tragedy entered into public discussion at an event focused on the theme of integration.

Mayor Roberto Cenni's administration sponsored the event "Come fare integrazione," or "How to Do Integration." I was in Prato for one of two trips that spring and upon arrival had walked the city center in search of flyers announcing relevant happenings. I spotted posters for the event, which took place on February 10, 2011, in Prato's gracious Teatro Metastasio. It was staged like a Berlusconi-era talk show, a spectacle of sorts for the mayor and his allies. The irony of his administration hosting an event on "integration" was not lost on the mayor's political opponents. Prato witnessed a sea change after the 2008 global economic crisis. Citizens on June 22, 2009, lurched to the political right and elected their first center-right coalition mayor since the fall of fascism. Cenni, a textile and garment entrepreneur, ran his successful bid to a five-year term on a blatant anti-immigrant campaign, specifically capitalizing on fears of a "Chinese invasion."[1] Threat narratives found fertile ground (Bracci 2012). Ironically, yet not surprisingly, the winning candidate

FIGURE 7.1. Youth run through the streets of Prato's historic center during the dragon parade of the Chinese New Year festivities.
Photo by Agnese Morganti, 2013

was former president and current shareholder of Go-Fin, which the *New York Times* described as "a holding company that is behind several midrange Italian fashion companies," at least one of which "has moved much of its production to China within the last 10 years." Cenni sought to make use abroad of China's cheap labor to enhance profits, yet at home embraced antiglobalist hostility toward immigrants. One of his first actions in public office was the passage of a segregation-style ordinance that restricted hours of business and applied only to the Macrolotto Zero neighborhood—where Chinese immigrants were concentrated.

I attended the integration event with my friend Anna, the child psychologist whose clients in the public health system included immigrants. We arrived at the theater at 9:30 p.m. to find the stage set with a band, a central microphone, and four chairs awaiting the arrival of the guests: the councilor of integration, Giorgio Silli; the councilor of public instruction, Rita Pieri; the TV news producer of Tg3 Toscana, Franco De Felice; and the theater's artistic director, Paolo Magelli.

Perhaps to counter the absence of any adult representatives from the Chinese community, a so-called multiethnic rock band kicked off the event with its second-generation Chinese teenager as the lead singer and guitar player. When the teen launched into the pop song "Gianna, Gianna," the mayor's integration councilor clapped enthusiastically, pointing to his vision of successful integration—a fully assimilated youth, any remnants of Chinese cultural origins left backstage. This approach represents the arrogance of Western culture, its categories derived from millennia of thought, and an ahistorical disregard for the forces of globalization. The assimilationist desire is not unlike the sort of arrogance that twentieth-century writers or social scientists, from D. H. Lawrence to Edward Banfield, revealed as when Lawrence mistook migrant day laborers for indigenous peasants and portrayed them as "songless and meaningless" as compared with the Etruscans, or as when Banfield (1958) described southern Italians as morally incapable of civic life. In both cases, the observers made characteristics appear innately lacking, rather than connecting them to a historical relation of domination and subordination that systematically redirected resources to the Global North while leaving the Global South impoverished and in question (Schneider 1998).

Having celebrated the middle school musicians, the emcee then embarked on the core of the evening's program with a tragic announcement: the death of an eleven-month-old Chinese baby. "A painful fact," said the mayor's spokesman, "that we have received today and that pushes us to many reflections. They say the child died from a drug overdose, perhaps due to a misunderstanding of language between the mother and the doctors. We regret having to face a fact so shocking, but today we have this." Throughout the evening, the message became unequivocally clear: that Prato's new administration was on the defensive, and that problems and even tragedies were ultimately due to the failure and refusal of the Chinese to do their part to integrate.

The councilor of integration offered his perspective: "When you are faced with news like the death of a child, every political controversy becomes sterile and useless. . . . This administration spends €175,000 for translators, and both the province and region allocated more money on this front. We spend €100,000 for teaching Italian language, but in a world like ours, where foreigners number between 30,000 and 35,000, total penetration is difficult." He expressed the absolute "need" for immigrants to speak Italian.[2]

The mayor took the stage, asked the audience to set aside their ideological inclinations, discussed his view of globalization, and offered numbers: In 1995 there were three thousand Chinese citizens in the province; in 2011 there are thirty-eight thousand. Of those, he said, twenty-eight thousand are treated like slaves. "We're confronting a problem—a problem of illegality," he said to applause. He then discussed how society is out of balance and how he wants to escape from the left-right polarization. He placed some blame on consumerism and on America. He called for crucifixes in the schools. This, I thought, would have been unheard of under the previous administration.

He and others hammered home the fact that the city already spent abundant resources on providing translation services. One of his assistants compared the situation with France and noted the different ways of defining integration. One thing was indisputable: "It's no longer a choice. It's a responsibility."

The superintendent of schools spoke next, describing the schools as "the first vehicle of integration." She continued: "Knowledge of language is fundamental, but unfortunately in our schools only a small proportion of foreign children are geographically stable: many were born in Prato and raised in their countries of origin—a practice that is used especially in China." Besides language, another example of the problems that the schools encounter on a daily basis is connected to health. Children who have been absent are required to present a medical certificate of good health to return to school. The superintendent complained that the Chinese simply do not comply with this rule. "Nobody wanted to do a certificate. We tried to translate the information, put it in their backpacks." She described it as a "*quotidiniatà*," an everyday sort of occurrence, one that spoke legions to the ways schools were challenged to manage the immigrant population.

The second half of the event was billed as a question-and-answer session, but organizers allowed time for only one question from the audience. The lack of non-Italian-looking people in the audience was also troubling given the topic. Integration was clearly a one-way street: You're in our society; you need to conform to our language and our laws.

On the way home, as Anna and I crossed the Bisenzio River, she expressed her embarrassment about the content of the evening's event. She was disgusted. We agreed, though, that it was important to know how the current administration was framing the issue. She told me that nobody used to pay attention to the medical certificate regulations. In the past, the rule was very lax. The exception was if a child had been sick for a stretch and required clearance to return to school. In 2004, when my family and I were in Prato for a semester, my son came down with chicken pox and could only return to preschool after receiving a doctor's clearance. But for normal childhood colds and flus, the health documentation in the past was not enforced. Coincidentally, that same week I had lunch with a couple whose friend had taken sick leave from work, and to return, she would require a medical certificate. No, she wasn't really sick, but yes, she would obtain one. With the presence of the Chinese, the gaze had intensified. They were called out as the lawbreakers.

Several antiracist acquaintances had warned me that the integration event would be a spectacle and not to expect much progressive thinking onstage. They reminded me that the mayor's backers had won through a visceral campaign that included posters with slogans such as "To remove the yellow, it's necessary to get rid of the red," wherein the "yellow" was a racial reference to residents of Chinese descent and the "red" was a political reference to Prato's citizens with left-leaning, communist roots.[3] Thus, I was relatively prepared for the evening's strong message: that the Chinese need to adapt to us, to our rules, our regulations, our language. What I was not prepared for was the framing—the tragedy of the dead Chinese baby.

The story that most people had already heard or read, in the newspapers the morning of February 10, was that of a Chinese mother whose infant had fallen ill—a gastrointestinal illness, by all accounts. The mother had, with the assistance of a translator, sought medical care. Once back at her home, something went terribly wrong. The following day, the newspaper reported that the mother had brought her infant to the hospital earlier in the day with an intestinal problem, that medication had been prescribed, that a translator had been present, and that a few hours later the mother had returned with the dead child in her arms, having walked the full length of the central artery of Prato's Chinatown, to arrive at the hospital. The medical officials were now suggesting that crib death might be the cause of death. An autopsy was reportedly scheduled for February 12, but results were slow to emerge. In April, preliminary toxicology results indicated the cause of death was related to an excess of salt. Was it a misunderstanding of dosage? Or was it the addition of Chinese remedies?[4] I kept an eye out for additional details over the next two years, but none was reported.

Through a respected local medical doctor in July 2013, I obtained verbal confirmation of the autopsy results. The infant had a severe case of gastroenteritis, with vomiting and diarrhea, and he became dehydrated. He was prescribed a solution of *polisalina*, a saline solution that requires mixing with water. Evidently, the parents did not sufficiently dilute it and gave the child an overly concentrated dosage. The ultimate cause of death was shock due to too much salt in the child's system, resulting in diffuse and systemic suffering. When such tragedy strikes, who can be held accountable? Parents? Doctors? The translator? The hospital? Politicians? Society? Globalization?

Despite the councilor of integration's statement that "news like the death of a child" renders "political controversy . . . sterile and useless," by raising the issue of the infant's tragic death, he immediately infused it with political urgency. Instead of the parable of the Good Samaritan—that is, a mother trying to save her child—we have its inversion, the parable of the dangerous immigrant mother. Indeed, given the context of the event, the tragedy became a synecdoche for deviance. It placed the blame of social ills on the immigrants themselves. Using the tragedy of the dead Chinese baby to frame the event sent a strong message that the commonsense answer to the Chinese "problem" was for the Chinese to assimilate and learn to live according to Italian norms, rules, and laws. To do otherwise was to risk life itself.

## Integration as Political Struggle

This chapter brings to light struggles over belonging. These struggles over belonging are also struggles about race and the nation: Who belongs? What are the terms of belonging? Who is excluded? Who decides? Whose traditions count? Whose don't? Integration as a project has a great deal to do with the expression of ideologies of difference and efforts to build a sense of sameness from difference. Certain ways of imagining the present, past, and future inform these struggles. In the European landscape, Italy is a relative newcomer to immigration issues. Its shift from a country of emigration to one of immigration has its origins only in the 1990s.[5] Stefania Crocitti (2012, 81), a critical criminologist, goes so far as to suggest that as a state, Italy "refuses to recognize its new status as a country of immigration."

As an anthropologist writing about social life related to globalization, my goal in conducting fieldwork was to find, follow, and focus on concrete moments that shed light on immediate struggles, their language, and their tactics. Stuart Hall reminds us of the importance of the "cultural factor" for understanding social forces, undercurrents, and developments. His dynamic notion of culture lends credence to quotidian happenings: "By culture, here, I mean the actual, grounded terrain of practices, representations, languages and customs of any specific historical society. I also mean the contradictory forms of 'common sense' which have taken root in and helped to shape popular life" (Hall 1996, 439). This concept of culture calls for taking into consideration the play of forces in any cultural context. Some forces will be dominant. Others will be marginal.

This chapter aims for a dynamic and thus relational analysis of what Gramsci suggested was necessary for grasping how "relations of forces" might favor certain tendencies. Social imaginaries give rise to political configurations. A particular group's or political force's unity is not a given; it always involves winning consent from others with the threat of coercion always looming. Consent and coercion always exist together but in unstable proportions. Civil society can slide into a fascist state and out again.

As Emma Bell (2012) notes in her introduction to *No Borders: Immigration and the Politics of Fear*, it is common for politicians across the political spectrum, particularly in Europe, to use the "problem" of immigration as a platform on which to run a successful campaign. Such anti-immigrant strategies often focus on criminality and illegality. Immigrants become easy scape-goats as governments cut funding to social security, health care, welfare, and public services and as job uncertainty manifests anxieties. The politics of fear are at once offensive and seductive. They hit nerves not made of steel but of common sense, vulnerable to the hegemonic orders of the day.

If historical forces constitute the terrain of political struggle, the struggles over belonging are embedded in structural changes resulting from shifts in local-to-global production as well as movements from local and regional workers to transnational ones. Political forces coincided with neoliberal regimes. David Harvey defines neoliberalism as both a utopian and a political project. It is utopian in its aim "to realize a theoretical design for the re-organization of international capitalism"; it is political in its objective "to re-establish the conditions for capital accumulation and to restore the power of economic elites" (Harvey 2005, 19). Scholars have noted how a neoliberal ethos has been put in the service of authoritarian politics that extends to the militarization of cities as well as borders. They argue that Europe has become a panopticon of surveillance and repression to such a degree that human rights become more flaunted than enacted (Carter and Merrill 2007).

I rely on the concept of common sense in the critical view that Gramsci developed. Here, common sense refers not merely to practical know-how but also to conceptions of the world that contradict one another and hence form an incoherent whole. People often passively accept commonsense views, internalize them, and live their lives accordingly in uncritical ways. An example is when commonsensical notions make situations of inequality or oppression seem natural and unchangeable and thereby contribute to keeping certain strata of people down. Gramsci's philosophy of praxis argued for entering people's commonsense worldviews and getting them to arrive at a critical understanding of their own situation. Historical reflection could open up new possibilities for future change (Forgacs 2000, 421; Gramsci 1971, 324–25).

In the course of my field research, I kept expecting that the events I scouted out and ultimately attended would have audiences made up of diverse constituents. However, the more public events I attended, the more I came to realize that was a flawed commonsense logic. The audiences were an outward manifestation of a city whose population had become deeply segregated. Tensions related to segregation were rife. Segregation was partly connected to immigrant settlement patterns, common with overseas Chinese who have strong networks, as Chinatown scholars Cindy Hing-Yuk Wong and Gary McDonogh (2013) have observed. In Prato, tensions were also heightened through official and violent tactics.

A recurring refrain among Chinese parents was the expression of alienation not only from the tempos of work but specifically from living in Prato. Although they felt comfort in having many other Chinese people around them, they also deeply felt the anger and racism directed at them. Many recounted experiences of being robbed and mugged. They expressed fear and vulnerability. An adult son and his mother who had finally managed to own their own firm balked at the suggestion that things must be better for them now:

"That's still nothing," Ming, the adult son said of firm ownership.

"Nothing, we are still bullied," echoed his mother, Yue-Sai.[6]

The man was considering sending the grandparents back to China with his child because life had become intolerable.

Interviewees frequently noted the greater level of tension and discrimination they experienced in Prato as compared with other cities. Peng, the young migrant who told the story of exchanging his youth for money, recalled a story of police brutality shortly after he became a new father.

PENG: After Lily gave birth to the baby, she was having her postnatal care, and so she had to stay at home. There is no one else who can drive but me, so the company called me to pick up the goods. Lily has a driver's license, but I don't. So she was having her postnatal care, the company asked me to pick up the goods. I was driving and I still hadn't gotten the goods, and a policeman pulled me over. He pulled me over, but I can't speak Italian, so I didn't know what the policeman was saying. I just kept shaking my head. Then the police took me to the police station and asked me for the residency permits. But I didn't have one at that time; I had just applied for the residency permits during the amnesty period.

FANGLI: What year was it? 2010, she should have had her postnatal care in 2010.

PENG: There was an amnesty in 2010. I had already filed my information with the government, but the policeman said I lied to him or something.

FANGLI: So did you show him the receipt of the residence permit?

PENG: No, the receipt was at home. Yeah, no one could have sent that to me, I had the car, Lily was having her postnatal care, and my parents can't drive. So the policeman said I lied to him, and he asked me to sit inside the car. He hit me on my chest twice and on my back once. He took off his helmet and put it in front of my chest and punched me.

FANGLI: What? I don't understand, please say again.

PENG: Don't policemen wear helmets? He took off his helmet and put it in front of my chest and punched me. That way, he won't leave any bruises.

FANGLI: Like that?

PENG: Yeah, there are many Chinese people who have been caught by the police, and there are many people who have been hit by them.

FANGLI: So he punched you for no reason?

PENG: The policeman said, "You lied to me."

FANGLI: Did he say which part was a lie?

PENG: He was angry and said I lied to him, and then he punched me. There are many cases like this.

FANGLI: Like this?

PENG: Yeah, I have heard of people who were punched by the police before. There were people who don't have residency permits and worked in other people's factories. They are illegal workers, when the police would catch them, they would punch them.

FANGLI: However, the police can't punch people. You didn't sue him?

PENG: The Chinese have to suffer through it, because there are language barriers! If you don't understand the language, it's the same as not knowing anything. I can't bear it. If I don't understand the language, how can I sue him? There are people who can speak Italian well, if the police take action against them, they would sue them. Therefore, basically, there are some Chinese people here, people from Wenzhou, who don't understand the language, and they have to bear it. Policemen like this—we can only forget about.[7]

Peng did hire a "foreign" lawyer, meaning an Italian who, the next day and at the cost of €1,000, went to the police station and guaranteed him immunity. In any case, the power hierarchies are clear in this narrative. The police violently put into action the collective anger and xenophobia. Such a collective sentiment had been legitimated through democratic politics and transformed into common sense. Given this force of common sense, Peng feels powerless. The result is profound social suffering on his part and the Chinese community writ large.

The remainder of the chapter analyzes three major encounters related to the theme of integration. Each involves different players from different points on the political spectrum: first, the local right-wing government's response to a Chinese New Year celebration; second, the national center-left integration minister's tour to promote new citizenship laws; and third, the progressive left's grappling with conservative identity politics, via a Facebook controversy and then via a candidate for national office at an annual fair. Combining participant observation at events in urban spaces with reading of daily print and social media products served as a powerful reminder of the importance of quotidian cultural practices. The ethnographic events and encounters described, therefore, are not mere vignettes or just-so stories. The resulting narrative conveys a lived sense of the discourses and actions that manifest in tendencies—lurches to the right, strides to the left, jumps to the center, leaps someplace new.

## Integration as Muse

The dragon dance ushered in the Year of the Rabbit during the weekend of February 12–13, 2011. Italians and Chinese participated together. Italians affiliated with a Buddhist organization and a contemporary art group, DryPhoto, carried the dragon, animating its red head, broad nostrils, pointy fangs, and back spikes. Men from the Chinese community played drums and carried red-and-gold banners and lanterns as well as Italian and Chinese flags. On Saturday, the procession moved through the wide streets of Macrolotto 1. On Sunday, it looped through the narrow streets of Macrolotto Zero. In the newer outskirts, the festivities went smoothly. In the older neighborhood, a less fortunate story unfolded.

On the first day of the dance, I caught a ride with my collaborator, Bressan, and his partner. We passed through San Giusto, a neighborhood where high-rises had been constructed after World War II and where southern Italian immigrants had settled. The neighborhood was known to be tough back then, said Bressan, who had roots up north in the Veneto but was raised in Prato in a neighborhood rich with rag and recycled wool workshops. The narrow, curved roads of the neighborhood gave way to wide, straight roads in the factory district. We began our search for the procession, whose route I had found on an Internet site and marked on my map: Via Piemonte, Via Veneto, Via Val d'Aosta, and so on. How odd, I thought, that they were all northern place names where industry had developed earlier and along a model of large firms. The roads on the grid all looked alike and, despite rational postwar planning, disorientation came easily. Finally, we found evidence that the dragon had passed: littered bits of red paper covered the pavement. We knew we were close. Soon, we spied a traffic policewoman in the road, her vehicle parked so as to block cars. We explained our reason for being there, and she gave us permission to enter as long as we parked near that end of the street. On foot, we passed buildings adorned with red ribbons as we headed toward the commotion at the end of the long, wide street.

We caught up to the dragon and a marching ensemble consisting of drums, tambourines, banners, and flags. In the parking areas in front of the buildings, tables were set up with abundant offerings of food and drink. We were invited to sample the items, and we gratefully took a few savory rice cakes and sweet clementines as well as cans of coconut juice. Red plastic runways led from the street to the shop doors. As the dragon approached, men or boys lit the ends of fireworks that snaked across the cement. Loud, persistent crackling penetrated the crowds, and billowing smoke filled the streets. The dragon entered each showroom, and as it left, entrepreneurs and associates dashed to scoop up the red plastic tarps and then to close the large factory doors. The ritual, we were told, was designed to scare away evil spirits and bring good luck for the New Year. We felt lucky. Several men in suits carried black briefcases and collected donations, tucked away in beautiful red-and-gold decorated envelopes. The dragon made its way to a fashion accessories showroom where a mix of Italian and Chinese sandwiches, dumplings, and desserts were offered and where procession participants mingled. The dragon-dancing youth sat in a circle beneath a wall of sample belts made from chain links. A group of well-dressed Chinese women coddled a darling and well-primmed toddler who shifted in a shopping cart. We left the event, taking note of the parking lot with its BMWs and other luxury cars, ourselves full of festive feelings and tasty food.

On Sunday, I headed out in a misting rain again with my psychologist friend, Anna. We crossed the bridge over the Bisenzio River, through the enormous portal with its medieval wooden doors still intact, and into the Piazza Mercatale. We soon spotted flashing police lights, then made our way up a portion of Via Pistoiese, the long artery of the Chinese district, into its heart. Lining the street were wedding shops with satiny-red gowns and slippers; photography boutiques featuring portraits of glamorous brides and grooms; jewelry shops prominently displaying wedding bands and diamond rings; general stores selling food, playing cards, soaps, and housewares, including an extensive section of rolled sleeping mats. Residents gathered on balconies and along the road to watch and photograph the procession.

Our timing was perfect: we encountered the dragon dance coming toward us. Here, in the narrow street, the drums and tambourines resounded with a trancelike *dong-dong-dong*. They made a loud dissonance as they echoed off walls scrawled with phone numbers and solicitations. The silk dragon flags wilted in the drizzle. We joined the procession and walked through the medieval arched Porta Pistoiese, the literal and symbolic border of Chinatown. A short distance along a narrow street and the dragon entered Piazza San Domenico, the first town square within the walls of the historic center.[8] Despite the drizzle, a crowd of photographers gathered, and the procession participants posed. A few minutes passed and a cacophony of car horns blared. All of a sudden, the situation became very tense.

The police had ceased redirecting traffic, and as a result, the procession was blocking cars and drivers were flaming with anger. The honking was getting loud. The city had evidently reneged on its parade permit. I spotted one of the organizing members from the Chinese community, who was telling people that this part of the event was finished.

"Head on out!" he yelled.

The dragon took off as quickly as it had stopped. People posing for photos got moving. We hurried along to follow the dragon and its constituents, meandering through the narrow streets back toward the Chinese neighborhood. My heart raced. The event concluded at the Buddhist Cultural Center. Inside, it was another world with its red lanterns and golden Buddha statues. Everyone was invited to find a seat at one of dozens of round tables and take part in a lavish vegetarian lunch. Although people were clearly upset at the way their celebration had been disrupted, they did not dwell on it but rather enjoyed the banquet before them and its bounty of commensality.

The irony was not lost on me that the mayor's integration event was held just days before the city contained the dragon dance. Nor was this a fleeting irony. Integration had become a muse, a source of inspiration for political discourse performed in a rationalist key of exclusion. Indeed, the mayor's politics vis-à-vis the dragon did not stop that February day. The following fall, organizers of the dragon dance event once again approached the council asking permission to enter the historic city center for the next year's procession. The council did not hesitate to return a firm no. Its position was reported in *Il Tirreno*: "Chinese New Year out of the Center: The council renews its 'no' to the community who requested access."[9] The Year of the Rabbit, the reporter noted, became remembered as the year when that cute critter ended up on the "dialectical rotisserie of the city council." In other words, the council was once again symbolically roasting the rabbit. It would hear nothing of the culminating event of the Chinese New Year celebration penetrating the city's core with its gyrations. The integration councilor Silli called it "a hazardous route." Pressures were reportedly intense from the security sector of the right-wing party, People of Liberty (Pdl), and the organization Prato Free and Secure, backed by the city councilor and head of security Aldo Milone. "As with last year, we think that our intentions are balanced not to grant the space of the historic center," continued Silli. "Closing off access to the city center to celebrate a holiday that has neither national nor local value would be a mistake."

When a political leader who bears the title of "integration councilor" takes such a position, it merits questioning the meaning of integration. Calling such a popular, not to mention important, immigrant cultural event of the year something that has "neither national nor local value" is simply hard to understand. And to describe such a position as "balanced" can only be comprehended in the context of the city's hardline anti-immigrant stance. Clearly, there was no neutral ground. With the dragon dance, the answer to the question of inclusion became exclusion: the dragon was not part of Italian traditions and hence was deemed unqualified to be allowed into the space of the historic city center, as its symbolic core.

This was not the first time that the city council put a stop to the Chinese New Year parade, and it would be unfair to present this as only a move associated with political conservatives. The first ban on the dragon dance occurred in 2007, under a center-left mayoral coalition. The language used to justify the ban highlights the contrast between two points on the current political spectrum. The then-councilor in charge of multiculturalism refused to allow the event, justifying his decision with the position that the Chinese lacked the will to improve their coexistence with Italians, emphasizing the necessity to give maximum attention to improve educational pathways for children, to adhere to laws related to garbage disposal as imposed equally on Italians and Chinese, and to adhere to public decency, that is, "to not hang dried chicken and meat together with laundry" (Ciardi 2013, 53).[10] Eventually, a compromise was made and a celebration allowed at the Pecci Museum of Contemporary Art. The councilor later stipulated that permission for the parade would be granted once the Chinese community demonstrated its commitment to improve its level of integration as well as participation in civic life (Bracci 2012; Ciardi 2013; Di Castro and Vicziany 2010).

These stipulations coincided with the formulation of a national Charter of Values on Citizenship and Integration, an official statement on the common values of integration produced by the Ministry of the Interior. The document reflects a compromise of political positions and sentiments concerning immigrants (Ministry of Interior 2007). As anthropologist Milena Marchesi notes, "The Charter is a statement of the non-negotiable values of Italian society, common values that all citizens are expected to embrace." Historical leftist concerns are reflected through an affirmation of immigrants' rights related to work, access to health care, protection from discrimination, housing, and education. "In return," Marchesi (2013, 250–51) writes, "immigrants are expected to abide by Italian laws and values." It is in this latter context that the historical expressions of the right manifest, and Marchesi observes, "The Charter defines Italy in terms of its Greek and Roman history and Judeo-Christian roots, identifying these as the sources of the country's modernity." An integrated immigrant, the Charter states, shows a good command of the Italian language, knows the essential elements of Italian history and culture and shares the principles regulating Italian society. Living in the same territory means to be full-fledged citizens of that land and acquire, with loyalty and coherence, common values and share responsibilities. (Ministry of Education 2007, 2)

This message of coherence and responsibilities gives one pause as it suggests a unified and homogeneous national territory, erasing differences and inequalities across region, religion, gender, ethnicity, language, class, sexuality, and politics. This was the language of nationalism at its most convenient. It was a textbook example of Benedict Anderson's *Imagined Community*. Anderson's point was that even though members of a nation will never know most of their fellow members, they shared a sense of "deep, horizontal comradeship" that derived from a collective ability to imagine that they all belonged to the same political community—at once inherently limited and sovereign. Anderson (1991, 6) observed, "In the minds of each lives the image of their communion." A skeptical gaze must be cast toward projects of cultural coherence. In his epic *Envisioning Power*, Wolf reminded how various state societies—from the Aztecs, to the Kwakiutl, to Nazi Socialist Germany—made symbolic and material use of the unequal relations of power that inform such projects. Thus, he called for the need to ask, who is organizing cultural coherence for and against whom? Referring to his own critical stance toward the culture concept (Wolf 1982), "conceived originally as an entity with fixed boundaries marking off insiders against outsiders," Wolf (1999, 67) asserts, "we need to ask who set those boundaries and who now guards those ramparts." The fact that the city reneged on a parade permit might appear as a banal bureaucratic act. In the context of immigration in Prato, however, the move was part of a larger pattern. This larger pattern reflects struggles over belonging.

Under the Cenni mayoral regime, Prato was becoming an intensely segregated city that placed a premium on security. In the mayor's political program, a five-year plan expressed in a fifteen-page document, integration is mentioned six times. The first reference appears in the context of a section on security and stresses respect for legality. The next two references to integration have primarily economic meanings, referring to integration within the metropolitan system of central Tuscany and to strengthening the integration of cultural patrimony. Subsequently, there is a reference to integration in the schools through equal opportunity and language, including investing in linguistic resources for immigrant children. The final reference is to the role of sports in integrating citizens into the city's social fabric.

The first reference in the five-year plan offers the clearest articulation of a right-leaning expression of integration: "Only respect for the law will allow the development of real policies and practices of integration, which can never disregard the reaffirmation and safeguard of identity and of cultural traditions as well as civic and spiritual aspects of our territory."[11] Taken at its face value, Prato's official position on integration during this era had two principal features: first, it was bound in a legal framework of security; second it expressed a static and defensive notion of cultural patrimony, one in which qualifying "identity" and "cultural traditions" were rooted in the territory. In an age of globalization and diaspora, in an age of a unified Europe, how could such a stance translate into inclusive policy? How might people who have not been raised for generations from the local soil, let alone babies born to immigrant parents, ever be included?

### Integration as Birthright

Poignant differences in orientations toward immigrants became evident when a push for integration was launched at the national level. The new pope, Francis, was rejuvenating immigration as a human rights issue, and the undulating tragedies of hundreds of women, men, and children drowned off Italy's southern shores in the Mediterranean Sea, off the island of Lampedusa, and subsequent treatment of immigrant detainees in so-called reception centers, were gaining world attention. Cécile Kyenge, Italy's minister of integration appointed in April 2013, set out on a speaking tour to promote a policy of *jus soli*, citizenship based on the soil where a person is born. Kyenge was the country's first black national official. She was named to her position by Prime Minister Enrico Letta's center-left government. Kyenge, then forty-eight, was born in the Democratic Republic of Congo, came to Italy when she was nineteen to study medicine, and became a doctor and eventually an Italian citizen. Given the global landscape of countries that embrace the birthright approach to citizenship, particularly in Europe, the push was brave and radical.

A world map reveals almost the entire New World is based on *jus soli*, unconditional citizenship for people born in a given country, whereas most of the Old World is based on *jus sanguinis*, from the Latin "right of blood," meaning citizenship inherited from one's parents.[12] Current Italian law is that children born there to noncitizen parents have the right to decide citizenship at age eighteen. Procedures are complex, including a ten-year residency requirement, and efforts vary in trying to streamline the process. Furthermore, Chinese migrants are keenly aware that China does not recognize dual citizenship. Thus, acquiring Italian citizenship would mean losing Chinese citizenship.

High security marked the minister's tour. Reception was mixed and ranged from warm embrace to hate speech. On June 3, 2013, I attended Minister Kyenge's visit to Quarrata, once a thriving epicenter of stylish furniture production but more recently suffering from unemployment and crime. The commune was located some ten kilometers west of Prato in the province of Pistoia, and I went with trustworthy Antonio. We set off from his and Aurora's house in their beat-up Fiat Punto. Our destination: the Villa Medicea La Màgia. Rather than taking the main boulevard, the Statale, that runs the length of the metropolitan valley from Pistoia to Florence, my driver followed the Fiorentina, a curvy rural road that wends its way through intimate and verdant Tuscan countryside and passes Madonna shrines, placed at intersections, a reminder of Catholic cosmologies and otherworldly protections. We found our way to a villa, but the grounds seemed suspiciously empty. We headed on. A change in mood settled in like a bank of fog as we entered the city of Quarrata. The crisis had hit hard here. We passed one abandoned storefront after another. It was eerie.

"It's a *paese morto*," Antonio said, "a dead town," remembering the furniture showrooms of a bygone era. The furniture-making economy concentrated here had succumbed to the forces of globalization, first witnessing a shift from Italians to immigrant workers, then moving production overseas. He slowly pulled over to a bar, a *circolo*, and greeted a friend who had worked for fifty years in textile manufacturing. He was talking to another man, a bit younger, who had been out of work for a while, although he continued to pay into the pension fund thinking he would soon find another job. So far no luck. Neither of them was much interested in coming to the minister's event, but they happily gave us directions to the correct Medici villa.

Antonio and I continued around a rotunda, encountering roadwork and eventually a parked police car. Across the street, we spied a driveway where cars were pulling into a muddy lot. We followed suit, and Antonio suggested I get out to avoid the mud. He parked. Under a light rain, we walked up a hill along a trafficked road. It had no sidewalks, so we took care to stay out of harm's way. Soon, we arrived at a gated entrance populated with police who forbade cars from entering. We followed a long stretch of driveway flanked by overgrown shrubs and trees to the villa's meticulous garden and expansive view of the valley below. Official-looking people donning business suits and badges clustered near the police. Beyond were men and women wearing fluorescent yellow suits, and I gathered they belonged to the municipal ambulance parked in the driveway. I remarked about the crumbling villa facade only to learn later that it had been nominated for world heritage status through UNESCO. We ducked out of the rain and into the villa, joining a flow of people into an entry hall, and turned left up a magnificent staircase. Officials lined a doorway, informally controlling the crowd. However, there seemed to be no required invitation and no counting, so I forged ahead and mumbled something about being with the people in front of me. An official stopped Antonio (I am short and petite, he is tall and stocky). I quickly turned and said, "He's with me," and they let both of us enter into a palatial room adorned with late Renaissance frescoes whose grandeur was interrupted with triumphant cracks bulging from the walls.

The room quickly filled with spectators. Seats extended about eighteen chairs across with an aisle in the middle and ten deep, and I counted another hundred people standing, shoulder to shoulder, in the back and along the sides. With nearly two hundred people crammed into the room, the summer air became heavy despite two open windows behind the speakers. A few chairs were still unoccupied toward the front, so to claim them, we politely pushed our way through. A grand table awaited the minister, and behind it stood an Italian flag splashed in sunlight. The sponsors gathered around: members of the commune of Quarrata as well as of the Rete Radié Resch–Casa della Solidarietà—a nonprofit solidarity network initially founded in 1964 to address Global North-South inequality and oppressed persons and with a rich history of helping immigrants, particularly since the 1990s.[13] Men and women laden with digital and video cameras shifted to capture sound and images. Above a table where the officials would sit was a gigantic fresco of two women with milky white skin, one bare-breasted, draped in gowns that flowed across a tree trunk and limbs.

The mayor entered with a red-green-and-white sash and spoke first, framing the event with the economic crisis and how it had hit Quarrata very hard, yet how proud they were as a city to host the minister. "The rise in social conflict," said Mayor Marco Mazzanti, "has also brought to Quarrata distrust for those who are different. Not infrequently the word *immigration* is associated with insecurity and sometimes makes more headlines if the violations are committed by a foreign person. We hope for plurality of culture: between women and men, homosexuals and heterosexuals, between Christians and Muslims."[14]

Others took turns speaking. The official mood here was a sharp contrast to Prato. It was Italians as *la brava gente*, the good people. Everyone present seemed to be supportive of helping others in need, including immigrants. The most controversial aspect, however, was to come: Minister Kyenge's stance regarding citizenship and her outspoken antiracist discourse. Without hesitation or apology, she advocated for *jus soli*, birthplace citizenship. She called for a reciprocal approach to integration: "Integration must be before all else interaction among citizens." There she was, likely the only person of African descent in the Salone Affrescata, the Frescoed Salon, in the Renaissance womb of European culture, telling a roomful of white people how things needed to be. Her clear articulation of her convictions gave me chills of admiration. In part, the art of statecraft had worked its magic. However, it was also a testament to Kyenge's dignity to speak with such confidence above and beyond her accented Italian. The moment resonated as historic.

The event concluded with officials giving the minister roses and a reproduction of Beatrice from Dante's epic *Divine Comedy*, who reads the last line of the verse from Heaven, "*L'amor che move il sole e l'altre stelle*," or "the love that moves the sun and all the stars above."[15]

The next day, at the cultural center over breakfast, I chatted with friends about the large spread in *Il Tirreno* with the headline, "From My Part a Better Italy." This would become Kyenge's summer refrain to racist attacks, to become better and struggle against racism and violence: "I don't want to be left alone," said Kyenge at the end of the event. "Who thinks that the attacks were aimed at me is mistaken. Those attacks were directed at any of you, at whoever doesn't want change."[16]

Kyenge's stance on the legal status of children born to immigrant parents was also emphasized: "Citizenship is not a favor that we do for these children but a favor that we do for ourselves." She underscored the importance of struggling against stereotypes: "The *meticciato*, the hybrid, is a word that often brings fear, but it's already inside us, at our tables, in the music that we listen to." As for the rise of social conflict and crime, such as the murder of a priest in the nearby town of Tizzano in December 2012, she said, "Security of a city doesn't have a color, it doesn't have an ethnicity, it doesn't have membership. We are all equal before the law."

Such a near-paradise reception was not universal. The minister had already encountered hostility elsewhere, and the following day, the dailies reported, "Extreme Right against Kyenge."[17] A far-right group called Forza Nuova claimed responsibility for hanging a banner from a wall along the Viale Montalbano that read: "*Servono italiani che pensano agli italiani, non congolesi che pensano agli immigrati*," or "Italians are needed who think about Italians, not Congolese who think about immigrants." The group claimed that it objected to the integration minister's position on birthright citizenship.

✳

In Prato, controversy stirred a few weeks later when Kyenge's supporters hosted her for lunch on June 29, 2013, but local officials snubbed the visit. Neofascists from the Ezra Pound and Brothers of Italy organizations protested outside the event, held at the leftist Circolo Arci of Cafaggio in a working-class neighborhood in city's south ward with underpasses beneath the highway.[18]

At a rally in the northern city of Treviso on July 13, an Italian senator's slur made international news. Roberto Calderoli, from the anti-immigration Northern League, criticized Kyenge's success, saying that she encouraged "illegal immigrants" into the country. He compared her to a nonhuman primate: "I love animals—bears and wolves, as everyone knows—but when I see the pictures of Kyenge, I cannot but think of, even if I'm not saying she is one, the features of an orangutan." He went on to say that Kyenge should be a minister "in her own country." (Kyenge is an Italian citizen.) The following day he reportedly apologized, but the comments, as the BBC reported, "ignited a storm of criticism on social media and from political leaders."[19]

Barely two weeks later, at a political rally of the Democratic Party in Cervia, in the central Italian province of Ravenna, an unidentified spectator threw bananas at her. Ever composed, she described the act as "sad" and "a waste of food." Politicians of all stripes of the political spectrum rose to the occasion in her support. The BBC reported that Veneto regional governor Luca Zaia from the Northern League criticized the incident: "Throwing bananas, personal insults . . . acts like these play no part in the civilized and democratic discussion needed between the minister and those who don't share her opinion." In the same article, the BBC reported that Calderoli, the senator who made the orangutan slur just a few weeks earlier, had faced pressure to quit but admitted that his comment was a "serious mistake" and had personally apologized to Kyenge.[20]

The incidents served as stark reminders of the hostile climate and racism in Italian society as well as the tensions surrounding immigration and integration. Furthermore, the reporting of the event in the media suggests a misunderstanding of the severity of the situation. The BBC report wrote it off as "casual racism," negating the fact that any kind of racism is hurtful. Furthermore, ongoing incidents by Italian soccer fans hurled at players of African descent would suggest that it is anything but "casual." Mario Balotelli, the A.C. Milan forward known as Super Mario, was a target of racial abuse. He is of African descent but is an Italian citizen, having been born to Ghanaian parents but then adopted by Italians.[21]

Back in Prato, on July 26, in the historic center, bold political posters plastered on a storefront pane caught my eye. I stopped to photograph the display. A male passerby looked at what I was photographing and said, "*Che vergogna*," or "How shameful." His tone suggested embarrassment for his city. On the bottom of the window was the logo of the Lega Nord, a blue knight bearing a sword and shield. Among the signs was one that particularly drew my attention not only because it was handwritten but also because of the rather obscure commentary it offered on the minister's politics:

| | |
|---|---|
| Con questo | With this |
| governo | government |
| non ci resta | there's nothing to do |
| che kyenge-re | but to Kyenge |

The slogan was initially lost on me. Only after consultation with insiders and further digging could I interpret it. The handwritten placard was a play on words, a reference to the hugely successful film *Non ci resta che piangere* (*Nothing Left to Do but Cry*). The 1984 comedy stars director-writer duo Massimo Troisi and Roberto Benigni who get lost in the Tuscan countryside only to find themselves transported to the year 1492 in a village under siege by Savonarola's reformist regime. The film is famous for its comic improvisation as the men grapple with sexuality, explain technology to Leonardo da Vinci, and attempt to prevent Columbus from sailing to America. Actors Carlo Monti and Amanda Sandrelli recollect in interviews a set without a script (Benigni, Troisi, and Cecchi Gori Home Video 2007). Perhaps the idiosyncratic humor explains why the film has never been subtitled in English. In any case, it is hardly a film that aligns with right-wing politics. If anything, Benigni has been widely known for his left affiliations as with his famous first film *Berlinguer, ti voglio bene* (*Berlinguer, I Love You*, 1977), named after Enrico Berlinguer, national secretary of the Italian Communist Party from 1972 until his death in 1984. Despite its constant silliness, *Non ci resta che piangere* offers social commentary on authoritarian forms of government as the villagers live in constant fear of Savonarola's henchmen coming to slay them. Needless to say, political movements often keep strange bedfellows, particularly as they aim for populist appeal. Here, the bucolic countryside and the fifteenth century certainly evoke things indigenous to Tuscany and its genius. Given that the window display offered other slogans linked to right-wing political priorities of identity and security—"*Prima La Toscana*" or "Tuscany First" and "*Città più sicura a tutte le ore*," or "More secure city at all hours"—if nothing else, the sign's author was critiquing the minister with a gesture toward the popular film. Because the author could be certain that native passersby would get it, the slogan served its purpose.

The racial slurs and hate speech directed at Kyenge are what should make a person cry. Disturbing incidents made transnational reverberations, as when the *New York Times* reported a city council member in Padua who called for Kyenge to be raped "so that she could 'understand' what victims felt."

The comment led to the councilor's party expelling her—as it was apparently even too much for the Northern League, the same anti-immigrant party that posted the sign in the Prato window.[22] Meanwhile, another extreme-right party, Forza Nuova, launched an even more hateful campaign, "Immigrazione uccide" or Immigration Kills, and the television news that very July day showed footage of a lawn covered with bloody mannequins.

These violent images and actions attract media attention and marginalize efforts, particularly widespread in Italy's nonprofit and cooperative sector, to embrace an intercultural approach to integration and carve a "third way" against the multiculturalism of the United States as well as Britain and the assimilationist strategies of France.[23] The vitriolic manifestation of hateful feelings toward the "other" also serves as a stark reminder of the myth of cultural racism—said to be a "new" sort of banal racism that contrasts with the vulgar racism of the past. The term *neoracism* emerged among some antiracist scholars, such as Etienne Balibar, writing in the late 1980s to distinguish between old and new forms, the latter glossed as somehow more "polite" because of supposed grounding in cultural differences and relatively less vulgar name-calling (Balibar 1991). As sociologists John Solomos and Les Beck have observed, race is frequently "coded as culture" (Goldberg and Solomos 2002). At root are "cultural idioms," in the view of Carter and Merrill (2007, 258) that deploy a distorted view of cultures as essentially different and bounded. Purveyors of this form of cultural-cum-identity politics view the values of different cultures as incommensurate. Dynamics of incommensurability create an "invidious doctrine of difference" (Holmes 2011), which serves as a discriminatory rationale for inclusion and exclusion.

The structures of racist ideology continue to operate regardless of whether the targets have shifted from innate biological traits to cultural ones. In the words of a review essayist for the *Nation*: "the structures . . . now stigmatize cultural—not specifically racial—groups as deficient and dangerous" (Reiter 2002). In the Italian context, racism continues to work on marked bodies backed by the logics of cultural incommensurability. And in the end, racism always entails violence whether buck naked or dressed in sheepskin.

## Identity as "Ungrammatical"

A surge of right-wing anti-immigrant sentiment has gone hand in hand with an assertion of local identity. Identity politics in the United States more often than not have been associated with causes of underrepresented groups, as in the case of African American rights, transgender rights, queer or gay rights, Latinx rights, women's rights, and so forth. By contrast, in the cultural milieu of central Italy, "identity" has become a loaded word, one that politically aligns with far right–leaning nationalist movements, frequently rooted in avowals of local or regional belonging.

Nothing made these dynamics more salient than a scuffle that played out on a Facebook page called "*Sei pratese se . . .*," or "You are Pratese if. . . ." The page was created as a place for locals to write about what made them feel a sense of belonging to their city. All of the contributors appeared to be Italian, in name, until one day in January 2014 a young twenty-year-old nursing student named Xiaoyun Liao decided she couldn't stand it any longer. Her Facebook post, which became the subject of several newspaper articles, was this:[24]

> You are Pratese if . . . (from a "foreign" person's point of view)
>
> You are Pratese if after 15 years spent in Prato you want to stay here for decades more. You are Pratese if every two years you have to stand in line for four hours in front of the police headquarters to renew your residency permit, but you still keep your Chinese citizenship because this is who you are: half Chinese, half Italian. I am from Prato because I went to Copernicus [high school] and I don't remember an ounce of math. I am Pratese because on the weekend I prefer to walk in the city center rather than go to Gigli or Parco Prato [shopping malls]. I am Pratese because I think Prato is beautiful and I would like that my fellow countrymen thought the same thing. Danilo, "You are racist if . . . a Chinese girl from Prato challenges [you as a] xenophobe."

Another member of the group, Sauro, responded, "However, this doesn't seem like a page fit for an individual of the Chinese race." The exchange blew up into a full-fledged discussion about race, identity, and racism. Two weeks later when the incident was reported in the daily *Il Tirreno*, on February 2, Sauro's stance was described as "racial delirium" for its "ridiculous" desire for an exclusive identity. A woman named Ivana pushed back on assumptions of Pratesi purity with her sarcastic Facebook comment: "I was born and raised in Prato but from southern parents. Do I have to leave the page?" The story offered links to Rosa Parks, Luca Cavalli Sforza, and Marco Polo. A few days later, a fuller account of the tense dialogue between Xiaoyun and Sauro, a forty-five-year-old information technician, was reported. Sauro reflected on his words, admitted that he had written quickly, from the gut, not from his brain. He apologized to her in private. The newspaper reported her critique of the concept of integration, saying it was not her term of choice: "Integration is a worn word. It doesn't encompass what it really intends to mean: exchange. Better is 'interaction.' Much better." (Note that in Italian *integrazione* is *interazione* without the *g*, she explained, hence a softer approach.) "It demonstrates that when two different people come together for an exchange, neither one lacks anything. In seeking a meeting point, neither party loses a part of him- or herself, but both gain something." Her final winning argument, in the newspaper's assessment, pointed to history:

> I never pretended that people would agree with me therefore I'm absolutely not offended if someone tells me that I'm not Pratese or Italian. But if someone has a hard time understanding how a Chinese girl can feel Italian, I ask that they think about how it happens that a son of an Italian immigrant that in the last century moved to America cannot himself feel like an American.

I was especially moved. Xiaoyun had joined our research team in summer 2013, and at the time, she seemed like a shy, hardworking young woman. To hear her stand up in this way, so publicly, was inspiring for her courage in battling dominant assumptions in which belonging and the privilege to belong were being cast. She was also becoming increasingly involved in events and organizations that promoted integration, and went on to become a founder of the youth group MeltinPo'—a play on Melting Pot. Activities during the year focused on bringing Italians into immigrants' homes, hosting them for dinner. Their slogan—"*Non è un progetto gastronomico. . . . è un progetto di relazione*"—emphasized that they were not a gastronomic project but a project of relationships. On July 5, 2014, the group held its annual fund raiser in the Piazza dell'Università in Prato featuring an eclectic menu including Asian dumplings, African couscous, and Italian red wine.

Recall, suspicion and racism toward migrant newcomers have a history in Prato connected to postwar reconstruction and the rise of the new factory city. The city was a magnet for poor migrants from rural Tuscan hinterlands and southern Italy, and it was not uncommon to encounter recollections among southerner Italians who were prohibited from entering bars as customers or entering rental agreements as tenants. Aurora recalled her family being unable to find housing due to anti-southern discrimination when her parents and sister moved to the outskirts of the city from Calabria, so they initially lived in an abandoned farmhouse.

Immigration named as such and integration as a political issue, however, are relatively new phenomena in Prato. Regarding the immigration and presence of Chinese citizens, as Eleonora Ciardi (2013, 48) outlines in a 168-page thesis, before the 2000s there were no "significant happenings" in local politics. Ciardi marks the first major event in 2002, when then-mayor Fabrizio Mattei of the Left Democrats, appointed a councilor from the Italian Communists, to a newly created position: minister for patrimony and the multiethnic city, the council's response to Prato's growing ethnic diversity. Ciardi assesses the appointment as more symbolic than significant given the poor electoral showing for the Italian Communists—2.7 percent in that year's election.

This period witnessed landmark growth in the arrival of Chinese immigrants. To the degree that official statistics can be trusted, in 1989 the city had only thirty-eight persons registered from China. Two years later, in 1991, it had 1,008. The population grew steadily. The early 2000s marked a period in which heated debates emerged over how to frame and make sense of this new class of transnational residents who were both entrepreneurs and workers. At the provincial level, in 2002, the minister for the multiethnic city succeeded in establishing a twin-city type of agreement between the province of Prato and the municipality of Wenzhou. At the national level, the so-called Bossi-Fini law promoted the regularization of immigrants, a move that also instigated polemics from various quarters. Perhaps it is no coincidence that this was also the moment when the term *Chinese siege* first appeared in media representation and popular discourse (Bracci 2012; Ciardi 2013, 51). The term took hold. Locals began to feel free to vent, to claim that they were the victims of occupiers. The refrain could be heard from a wide range of points on the political spectrum. Given the volatile context, it is no surprise that Pieraccini's (2010) book of the same title went into a second printing.

The left's response to immigration was hardly compelling. It has been described as "feeble and misleading" (Bracci 2012, 108). During my fieldwork, what became worth following was how political players on the left—a very different and distraught left from two decades earlier—confronted the issue on the ground.

✳

Each summer, local branches of the Democratic Party host the Festa de l'Unità. This popular vestige of Italian Communist culture derives its name from the official communist newspaper, *l'Unità*, founded by Gramsci in 1924, several years before the fascists imprisoned him. The fairs, meant to be fund raisers for the newspaper and the party as well as events to boost leftist culture, often last several weeks of the summer and draw crowds with carnival rides, food booths, music, dancing, and political events.

I recruited Antonio and Aurora to an event in Prato that billed a national political figure campaigning to head the Democratic Party. I offered to drive my spunky rental, a black Fiat Panda. None of us had eaten. Aurora joked that she was on domestic strike, and I commended her. We'd grab a bite at the fair. The destination was a park called the Giardini di Maliseti-Narnali. There, in the Maliseti neighborhood that grew in the postwar period and was populated by many residents with roots in southern Italy, we got turned around. I pulled into an empty parking lot where two men were deep in conversation. Their intonations were a contrast in regional dialects. One spoke with a strong Neapolitan cadence, the other with a Tuscan lilt. People joked that this area was the Little Italy of Tuscany. The men were generous with directions. We headed back to the Conad supermarket, drove around the lot only to find it full but got lucky and found a space on the street. We followed people on the sidewalk to a path through some trees and into a flat, dusty park. The stage for the event, scheduled to begin at 9:00 p.m., was still empty at 9:15 p.m., but every chair in the audience was full. Lots of people were standing in the back. They grumbled about the lack of seating. Volunteers added a few folding chairs and wooden benches. We lucked out and got a seat on one of the benches. My friends lamented the poor organization. Antonio viewed it as symbolic of the low point of the left. "*Non è più sentita,*" literally, "It's not felt anymore," as though to say it has lost its appeal.

Finally, close to 10:00 p.m., a crowd of journalists, photographers, and officials gathered off to stage left. There was excitement in the audience. Pippo Civati took the stage. It was set with a wicker loveseat and two chairs on each side, a coffee table in front—a relaxed summer patio feel. Civati fit right into the fair scene—casual dress in jeans and a handsome shirt.

The left, beaten down by declining party enrollment, was looking for a leader, a charismatic party secretary. Civati was frank and fresh. He had a good sense of humor and seemed true to his political values of equality. He conveyed smartness yet with popular appeal. He seemed to be the force they just might need after two decades of Berlusconi-ismo. *We'll see,* I thought. *People still have hope.*

At a certain point what he said caught my attention: "*A Prato si usa la parola identità in un modo sgrammatica*" or "In Prato, they use the word *identity* in an ungrammatical way." Civati was making reference to the right's use of identity, in particular the term *pratesità.* Was it any coincidence that the term echoed the notion of *romanità* so beloved of Mussolini and his followers (see Nelis 2007)? According to sociologist Fabio Bracci, *pratesità* was a strategic invention of a Pratese identity used to scapegoat the Chinese, to construct them as deviant, and to blame them for the economic crisis. Bracci (2012, 11) notes that it is evoked continuously and that this "is enough to channel widespread disorientation on the rhetoric which claims that the local way-of-life is threatened by external forces." He argues that the expression reflects myth rather than reality, and that it does not make sense, particularly because practices of under-the-table payments have their own long history in the province of Prato, one that preceded the arrival of Chinese immigrants. Italians were known for their own ways of negotiating trust, for fulfilling the obligations of work and remuneration.

As Civati invited questions, topics meandered, and we began to feel the absence of dinner in our bellies. We decided it was time to go find some food. The first stop was a grill that sold sandwiches. We expected the vendor to have sausages, and although we didn't see any, a big guy with arm muscles the size of an average man's thigh insisted they had them, just not the round kind, only the "smashed kind," because the other kind didn't work well on sandwiches. We were all perplexed. Antonio asked if they had any of the "regular" round sausages. The guy went and spoke to another man who was cleaning a grill, who then disappeared in the back and reappeared with a stainless steel bin. The big man reached in with his tongs and pulled out two sausages: one desiccated skinny variety, the other a turd-sized chunk of a wider version.

"I don't like these types of sausages," Antonio said, slowly enunciating each word to make sure he was understood.

We looked at each other, I read his serious expression, he turned around to leave, and I followed him. As we walked, he told me that he was under the impression that these were pieces taken off people's plates. "Believe me! It's not below them to do something like that."

I burst out laughing. *I don't like these types of sausages*: desiccated and recycled. Who would? As a former sweater artisan, he could smell a foul deal.

I felt a tinge of guilt, later, about finding humor in the moment—it was Antonio's calm resolve more than anything else that made me laugh. I also found it funny that he would call that a "type" of sausage. Later, it occurred to me that there was something kind of sad about the encounter. Deviance could be delivered in small servings, and you had to be on the lookout, even at a fair that used to be a site of solidarity for working folks.

Aurora had long since sized up the situation and taken off to find some pizza. Antonio and I headed into the bowels of the fair, past the *ballo liscio* dance floor, candy stands, an African jewelry vendor, a clothes rack, toward the lit-up Ferris wheel and the kiddie train to a vendor who sold roast pork sandwiches in a stand that looked like an Alpine lodge. This food looked fresh. Behind the counter was a hot grill with a selection of veggies. We both picked zucchini and onion. I ordered a Corona and water and picked up the tab. By the time we sat down, there was still no sight of Aurora, so Antonio went to find her. It wasn't hard. By that point, after 11:00 p.m. on a Monday night, the place was emptying out. Only the silhouettes of a few bodies glided across the dance floor.

# 8

# Action

WITH MASSIMO BRESSAN

Publicized as "An Idea of the City," new urban questions related to diversity were at the heart of Open Prato's hosting of Bernardo Secchi, one of Italy's most renowned urban theorists and planners. The event took place in Circolo Curiel, a grungy cultural center on Via Filzi in the core of Macrolotto Zero. This borderland of ill repute sits just beyond the medieval wall of the historic city center. Here, and in the adjoining neighborhood of San Paolo, Little Italy uncomfortably comingles with Little Wenzhou. The senior planner's visit brought into relief contrasting political views on the status and stakes of visioning the city.[1]

The event drew an admiring audience and kindled controversy. Residents, activists, and students listened as Secchi said that he considered Macrolotto Zero "one of the most fascinating places of the city because it is a place of diversity." His guiding star was *mixité*—inspired by the French principle of a vibrant mixing of different social and cultural elements. "I prefer a diversity of activity and of population to socially homogeneous neighborhoods," Secchi said. "Let's not forget that the twentieth century was the century of the autonomous individual—which is exactly why it is necessary to give space to difference." He outright rejected the city council's urban planning vision, which he described as "a disaster" (*Il Tirreno* 2014).

Despite Secchi's appreciative audience, by all accounts his visit turned out to be a political bomb. In a press release a few days later, then-mayor Cenni shot back, describing the "exaltation of Macrolotto Zero as inappropriate and morally harmful" (Comune di Prato 2014). A local headline captured the extent of the disagreement and the mayor's strategy to discredit the urban planner: "Cenni Attacks Secchi over Macrolotto Zero: 'He seems to have landed from an alien spaceship.'" For a mayor to liken an urban planner's arrival to

FIGURE 8.1. Massimo Tofanelli and Sara Iacopini of the Neighborhood Plots research team work with digital storytelling participant Federica Mungioli at an elementary school in San Paolo.
Photo by Amy Hill, www.storycenter.org, 2015

a spaceship landing was a colorful and insulting way to say his foe was out of touch with reality.

The mayor went on to mock Secchi's position on diversity. He characterized him as having a "fascination" with the "Chinese fast-fashion firms and enormous uncontrolled migratory flux present in that area," Cenni wrote. "I do not see any charm in those old sheds used previously for weaving, warping, or craft activities, transformed into absolutely uncivilized workplaces, which have taken Prato back hundreds of years instead of bringing it toward the future." Cenni then referred to "niches of promiscuity," listing features such as lawlessness, tax evasion, treatment of workers "like slaves," indiscriminate use of propane gas cylinders, unhealthy and unsafe environments, and a general disregard for human dignity. All told, he questioned how such a neighborhood could qualify as a "place of difference and diversity" (Comune di Prato 2014). Rather, Cenni called for respect toward the people who lived in those neighborhoods and who must contend with such realities on a daily basis.

Meanwhile, Secchi was hardly a newcomer to Prato. He was the author of the well-known Secchi Plan completed in the 1990s and known for coining the phrase *città fabbrica* and developing a vision of *mixité*. He was invited not only because of his past knowledge of the city and his international notoriety but also because of his experience working on the urban plan of another major European city: Antwerp. Similarities were striking between the Italian and Belgian cities. They shared tensions and challenges related to a migrant presence and rapid growth of a xenophobic political party. In the daily *Il Tirreno*, Prato-based architect and urban planner Roberto Vezzosi drew comparisons between Antwerp and Prato in terms of a status of "near desperation," stemming from an incapacity to adequately confront their problems, including economic ones but especially those related to immigration and coexistence. Antwerp's new city leaders had turned to Secchi and asked, "Give us a vision of the future." In Prato, by contrast, it was not the city's elected leaders who invited the planner to share his vision but rather a group of concerned citizens. Those citizens, in fact, accused their leaders of having completely lost any idea of the city. At stake were crucial issues such as the "right" to the city, its services, and deepening segregation between rich and poor neighborhoods.

For some local residents, Secchi's vision of *mixité* was difficult to embrace. Even before the concentrated presence of non-Europeans, the neighborhood of Macrolotto Zero blended residential dwellings and manufacturing activities. Now, older residents associated the area with Chinese newcomers, economic activities that push the limits of legality, militarized security blitzes that intensified under Cenni's mayorship, compromised hygienic conditions of roads and trash receptacles, and overcrowding of private homes (Bracci 2012). All told, the migration of citizens from China rendered the neighborhood more complex and accentuated its character as a transition zone resulting from an assemblage of local and global economic and social spaces with new hierarchical relations and internal differentiations (Bressan and Tosi Cambini 2011). It has only gradually and reluctantly assumed the moniker of Chinatown. By association, the adjoining neighborhood of San Paolo has become known as a *zona di degrado*, a rough and neglected area, a place best left to its own devices, dilapidated, beyond the possibilities of planning.

If San Paolo and Macrolotto Zero have come to be considered as places to avoid, even seen as unsafe, they have also become the site of remarkable citizen and notorious government action to bring about change. Visions for the direction of change assumed dramatically contrasting tones and interventions. Drastically different ideas circulated about how to address pressing issues such as concerns with too much segregation, too little public safety, and too few green spaces. In a word, dueling "wars of position" erupted concerning the management of the changing cityscape. Cenni brought a negative valence to what Secchi had framed as positive. Secchi's visit itself became an event, one of many in the ongoing wars of position that were underway in Prato. These wars of position represent struggles for hegemony related to urban space. In this chapter, we extend a Gramscian framework to analyze contestations over the future of the city.

As with other contexts where migrant newcomers are a prominent feature of the population profile, ideological wars erupted over symbols, policies, and resources (Holmes and Castañeda 2016). These struggles to gain and sustain hegemony lend themselves well to a Gramscian analysis, particularly his concept of "war of position." Writing between 1926–37 from his prison cell, where Mussolini's regime imprisoned him with the failed aim of stopping his brain from functioning, Gramsci in *The Prison Notebooks* turned to military metaphors to define political struggle. He contrasted wars of movement with wars of position. Gramsci predicted that weak states are "gelatinous," such as Russia at the time, and will resort to a violent and head-on war of maneuver whereas stronger states will rely on a war of position to sustain their hegemonic rule. The latter involved positioning, often of the discursive type, and were common in the West, where states were strong. Hence, this version of warfare took place on the terrain of civil society. As Gramsci (1971, 235) famously wrote: "The superstructures of civil society are like the trench-systems of modern warfare." He offered the insight that Italian fascism had violent streaks, but its duration was due to its political power, to hegemony—consent with the threat of coercion. For Gramsci, hegemony named the problem: how power relations underpinning various forms of inequality are produced and reproduced (Crehan 2002, 104). Furthermore, hegemony helped explain how dominance is lived (Williams 1977). Ultimately, consent was won through wars of position and education writ large. In other words, civil society institutions played a key role in "educating" people linked to dominant values, common sense, and economic resources. Thus, political struggle, for Gramsci, had moral stakes at its core. His dynamic theories continue to have relevance for understanding cultural struggles in globalized localities.

Debates about the future of the city were being fought out in formal government settings and informal community settings. The positions between the Open Prato group and the mayor's supporters could not have been starker. On the one hand, the city government led by Prato's right-wing mayor had sustained a five-year hostile and militaristic approach to contain and conquer the immigrant presence. The mayor's allies downplayed the forces of globalization. Through policies and police forces, the mayor sought to heighten security efforts, criminalize global workers, and use them as scapegoats for political gain.

On the other hand, residents affiliated with neighborhood associations along with engaged urban planners and anthropologists launched a counter-effort to value and build a diverse city. Initiatives such as Open Prato among others aimed to bring attention to urban exigencies and spatial injustices confronting historic residents, newcomers, immigrants, and youth.[2] Those involved sought to recast the dominant narrative of perceived threats to social cohesion, drawing on a discourse of *mixité*, as opposed to racial segregation. A major source of inspiration was Secchi, who advocated for future cities as permeable, accessible, and democratic. He and his team viewed access as a fundamental right and developed visionary plans for small and large European cities alike (Boano, Astolfo, and Pellegrini 2014). His plan for Prato was shelved, however, a decision that numerous commentators found to be misguided and disappointing. The legacy of Secchi (1934–2014) has nevertheless stimulated ideas and actions for addressing social inequality and spatial injustice in urban territories.

This chapter analyzes actions as they played out in the neighborhoods. It contrasts the mayor's hegemonic strategies with counterhegemonic ones. It offers historical context of industrial rise and decline and draws on ethnographic fieldwork to explore the contours of a grassroots initiative, the Gymnasium of Ideas, as well as a collaborative action-research project, Trame di Quartiere, or Neighborhood Plots.

In documenting and making sense of diverse political encounters, we take inspiration from the anthropology of value, particularly in the sense of value as action-oriented theory (Graeber 2001). As people try to grasp what unfolds around them, they also engage in imaginative acts, which is a fundamental human process. Imagination implies the possibility of doing things differently. Through actions people ultimately pursue value, and through these pursuits, society transforms. Whether related to minerals, food, parks, or garments, as Elizabeth Ferry (2013, 9) observes, "through attempts to create things as valuable, the social and material world is stabilized in enduring ways." Attempts at value-making can also destabilize social worlds. To examine value-making in the context of human action is thus another way to understand what people value and the ways local meanings manifest and what worlds will or will not endure in the face of global forces.

## Crossroads of Diversity

The neighborhood of San Paolo flanks the western side of the city of Prato, where silent smoke stacks soar skyward like brick beacons to twentieth-century industrial fervor. Here, a chaotic layout of streets and structures reflects a particular model of a *città fabbrica*, or factory city. Narrow roads curve into dead ends. Stucco structures squeeze into tight spaces. Cement walls rise naked with rebar. Factory windows stand shattered. On one wall graffitied words blare, "OUT SARS." A lone chicken paces in a strip of weeds behind a wire fence.

The original nucleus of San Paolo adjoins the historic district known as Macrolotto Zero (map 1). The boundaries of Macrolotto Zero consist of physical barriers, such as raised railroad tracks, which slice through the neighborhood to the north and allow crossings through only a few treacherously narrow underpasses, and a highly trafficked bypass that creates a west ring. Tucked in spaces intermixed with textile and garment production live some families of Italian origin. In other spaces live Chinese residents who own or rent, at times, just a portion of the space for sewing clothes with a quick turnaround. Up until the deadly 2013 factory fire stimulated a new inspection regime, workers commonly lived inside workshops. They slept on bulky rolled mattresses that Chinese shopkeepers stocked on top shelves with other household items that new arrivals need for a night's sleep—or a day's sleep, as may be the case, because often they rested during daytime hours when electricity was at its peak demand and price.

When referring to San Paolo, some residents include the territorial area of Macrolotto Zero itself. The name resonates: *macro* translates as large and *lotto* means parcel but also has connotations that derive from *lòtto*, which refers to something that belongs to everyone—for example, land that is held in common. The plots and parcels precede the name itself, which dates to the urban vision completed by a working group coordinated by Secchi (1999b) himself.

The factory city evokes a history of labor, of sweat, and of dreams—some realized, others broken. A colorful, yet grizzly, description of Prato could easily apply to this part of town: "*la città delle mani mozze*," the city of the chopped-off hands. That reputation is a consequence of lots of textile work involving recycled rags and used clothing that arrived from ships departing from all parts of the world, especially America. The "Little Hand," an excerpt from native son Curzio Malaparte's *Those Cursed Tuscans*, recounts the story of a severed hand lacquered with gold nail polish that the author found as a child playing in a bundle of rags (Malaparte 1998).

The weaving machines were dangerous. They made a lot of dust, and people were known to spit a lot. The looms were loud, too. People went deaf—at least partially. Some still joke about the brusque local way of speaking. They'll recount in a self-deprecating way about the generation who came of age during the 1960s. They had a habit of yelling when they talked. If all that work

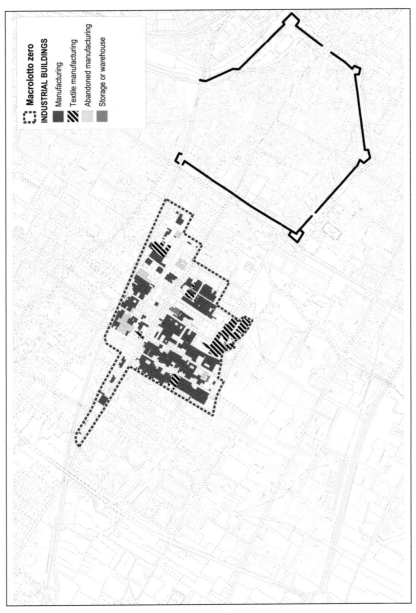

MAP 1. Macrolotto Zero and the historic city center of Prato.

around those machines didn't cost them an arm or a limb, it certainly cost them some hearing.[3]

Machines were everywhere—in side rooms of houses, in the nooks of basements, in separate workshops. Pratesi hated working for others—that's what Malaparte wrote originally in 1954 in the Italian original, *I Maledetti Toscani*, and that's what Becattini wrote in 1998.[4] So many had left the farm life, the life of sharecropping, to get out from under the rule of the *padrone*, the landlord, as well as the rigid hierarchical ordering and injustices of the patriarchal family (Becattini 1998; Malaparte 1964). In the factory city, there was work then, and a lot of it. There were also labor struggles, factory owners, returned partisans, shamed fascists, new communists, ambivalent Catholics, and new streets being named after heroic figures of the sort you'd never see lining the avenues of a US city, such as Via Marx or Via Gramsci. New communist-inspired cultural clubs were also being formed where men could drink espresso, argue, and strategize. Women eventually joined, too.[5]

A problem arose in housing the massive number of migrants arriving from the nearby rural hinterlands and the distant Italian south during the postwar decades to central and northern industrial cities. The solution was found in the familistic-private realm with its tolerance toward self-construction: agreements between small construction companies and groups of individuals and families, who purchased homes without recourse to banks but relied instead on agreements with contractors. The oldest cluster of houses and apartments along the main access routes of Via Pistoiese or Via Donizetti, roads that for some residents mark San Paolo's border, eventually became part of a dense and hectic industrial suburb resulting not from public planning processes but rather from industrialization and private initiative. The pace of construction in those years was intense. This solution proved to be viable in the short term for a large majority of Italians to the point that they were able to ignore "the obvious drawbacks that it had in terms of managing the city and its territory" (Signorelli 1996, 112–13). This version of growth offered quick responses to an urgent demand for new structures but proved detrimental to public and residential spaces.

The shape and boundaries of Macrolotto Zero came into being in a sense after the fact as a result of Secchi's (1996a) intention to carve out an exemplary physical space of urban development that revalued the factory city in all its diversity. His purpose was not, therefore, simply to identify a neighborhood—a task he preferred to leave up to the groups of people who live there—but rather to accomplish something much bigger: to recognize and represent the unique physical and social aspects and potentialities of an urban phenomenon characterized by the postwar phase of development that launched the Italian industrial districts.

## Politics of Containment

Defining the perimeters of Macrolotto Zero assumed new stakes when a policy was enacted to limit business practices operating within its boundaries. The entrepreneur-cum-mayor in September 2010 approved what proved to be a highly contested policy, "Hours for Macrolotto Zero and Adjacent Streets." Ordinance No. 2054/2010 restricted hours of operation for the "exercise of artisan, trade, administration, services, entertainment, and leisure activities that cause, because of their schedules into the late hours of the night, noise and environmental discomfort to residents." The restrictions applied only to the zone of factories, workshops, and residences of Macrolotto Zero, a targeted area that corresponded with a dense population of Chinese residents and workers. This regulation effectively marked Chinatown as a "ghetto" in the old-fashioned Italian sense of the word—a word that came to epitomize the most exclusionary way to manage Jewish populations.[6]

Cenni's supporters justified the ordinance as a necessary step for intervening in urban decay. The administration justified its action as an attempt to reconcile the exercise of economic activities in the territory with citizens' rights to quiet and rest (Comune di Prato 2010). Complaints of noise and odors motivated the policy. Residents objected to the noise from cut-and-sew surgers late into the night, as well as odors from Chinese takeout restaurants.

Critics, including members of the Chinese community, underscored the fact that the policy only applied to a limited area of the city. Its approval triggered organized legal action among shopkeepers and entrepreneurs operating within Macrolotto's boundaries. In short order, thirty Chinese business leaders filed a lawsuit and, backed by Italian lawyers' investigation, won a judgment. In March 2012, the Regional Administrative Court (TAR) deemed the ordinance to be discriminatory and thus unjustified (Bressan and Krause 2014).[7]

Despite being overturned, the policy itself illustrates the approach of local political power to manage and even incite conflict. Never before in Prato had a local administration advanced such an aggressive policy. Ironically, the city's planning office superimposed the mayor's restrictive policy over an almost identical area to what Secchi had mapped of Macrolotto Zero, originally created as a template to promote *mixité* (map 2). Thus, a redevelopment tool designed for the "factory city" became, fifteen years later, albeit briefly, a tool of segregation.

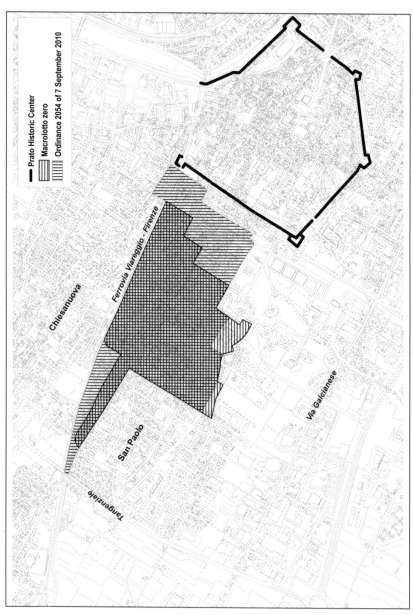

MAP 2. Macrolotto Zero per Secchi and the perimeter of the ordinance.

In Prato, as the right-wing mayor took control, the political and social climate was characterized by rampant uncertainty about the economy, xenophobic mistrust toward immigrant others, and skepticism toward the government's ability to make things better in light of accusations of widespread corruption and incompetence. Indeed, the politics of containment, on a spectrum between wars of position and movement, were toward movement and suggest a weakened state apparatus. The fact that the regional court deemed the mayor's ordinance illegal was perhaps an omen of the limited duration of the rule of the mayor and his right-leaning xenophobic-inspired politics.

In *Chinese Migration to Europe*, Loretta Baldassar and the volume editors describe the case of Prato as representing "a kind of litmus test for the possibilities and challenges of global mobility and immigrant incorporation in contemporary receiving societies" (Baldassar et al. 2015, 3). A litmus test implies a moral judgment about whether the course forward will be acceptable. The mayor's discriminatory tactics became unpalatable for too many of Prato's citizens and leaders given the city's particular postwar history and political sensibilities.

## Hong Kong, Italian Style

During the decades of rapid growth of the textile industry, between 1950 and 1970, Prato's population doubled from 77,631 to 143,232 (see Bandettini 1961; Comune di Prato n.d.; Krause 2005b, 598). The built environment followed suit. Industrial and domestic spheres intermingled: production activities were born in garages, basements, and factories. In 1953, Italy already ranked number one as the world exporter of wool fabrics—Prato's original specialization (Becattini 2001). Within this "economic miracle," a major transformation of the local production structure also took shape. In the two decades of 1951–71, small firms grew and large firms shrunk. The category of local woolen textile firms with more than 500 employees disappeared; the category with 101–500 declined from 37 percent to 12 percent of the total; the category of local firms with 11–50 workers constituted 40 percent of employment; and those with 1–10 employees accounted for one-third of the total workers. The figures are particularly noteworthy given that at the same time the total textile workers rose from about 21,600 to 50,000 (cf. Becattini, 2000, 56–60).

In this new production context, which witnessed the launch of the industrial district, a large sector of *lavoro sommerso*, or informal economy work, thrived in a realm of practices defined as a *logica dell'esenzione*, or a logic of exemption. Little attention was paid to preventing accidents and safeguarding working conditions. Meanwhile, state intervention in industry concentrated on defining incentives for the benefit of big business, while a special regime was reserved for small firms, which were exempt from costs and also "excluded from institutional advantages" (Arrighetti and Serravalli 1997, 336). The main advantage for small businesses consisted of a "silent agreement" that made them exempt from tax inspections in exchange for the creation of jobs and wealth. This form of exemption from public regulations (when they existed) extended to the environment, planning, and land use.

For its exploitive conditions, the French fashion magazine *Elle* in 1978 compared Prato to India and dubbed the city *l'inferno del tessile*, or the hell of textiles. "The city fell into turmoil, the political and economic world became involved, but it reacted almost like a cartel, and forgot about its internal conflicts" (Cammelli 2014, 28). The local textile union workers intervened, accusing the journalist of being in the city just a couple of hours and asserting that the labor situation in Prato was substantially in order. Faced with threats to local competitiveness, a homogeneous front came together and all but wiped out local debate on contractual terms as well as workplace health and safety to defend the image of the city that even then was considered a factor of competitiveness in European and global markets.

This media coverage was one of several attempts by high-profile European publications to get the scoop on the rapid success of Prato's textile industry, which had brought many European competitors to their knees. The prestigious *Le Monde* followed suit in 1980, offering a title that in retrospect seems nothing short of provocation: "Italian Hong Kong" (Maurus 1980). The journalist highlighted the city's ability to respond to any type of problem posed by production needs, whether investments for renewing machinery or provisions for supplying industrial water purification systems. With irony, the report underscored the severe effects of its development on the urban environment and the health of its citizens and workers. The article referred to "self-exploitation," a term that, the journalist asserted, had its origins in Prato.

This characterization resonates with the present: the term *self-exploitation* is commonly used to describe, often disparagingly, the disposition of migrant workers from China. In both cases, considering the Italian and Chinese migrants, discipline to incessant work rhythms occurred not on large factory floors but rather in small workshops. The types of top-down time thrift imposed on the working classes of E. P. Thompson's (1967) "Time, Work-Discipline, and Industrial Capitalism" are transmogrified in this story. Workers in Prato are known for a quest for autonomy and subsequent self-exploitation.

Contemporary use of *self-exploitation* has become disparaging. The insult, to borrow from Bourdieu, "fails to *historicize economic dispositions.*" Indeed, workers with these dispositions, or economic habitus, have a social and historical genesis. In the violent Algerian case of colonial France forcing market logics on a society with an intact precapitalist economy, Bourdieu (2000, 18) traced history in "the so-called 'rational' economic agent." His scathing critique of "rational action theory" underscored the "mismatch between economic dispositions fashioned in a precapitalist economy and the economic cosmos imported and imposed, oftentimes in the most brutal way, by colonization" (Bourdieu 2000, 18). A similar observation could be made about the collisions that ensue in globalization encounters. Considering Italian and Chinese workers, in both cases, "flexibility" has been used as a gloss for self-exploitation that serves as a "rite of passage" necessary for entry into an affluent society (Berti, Pedone, and Valzania 2013).

### The Gymnasium of Ideas

In front of the Circolo Ricreativo San Paolo on Sunday morning June 9, 2013, a neighborhood group converted a paved lot at a triangular intersection of Via Cilea into a public forum. Volunteers set up a tent, table, and chairs in front of this Gramscian-style social club. The event marked the fifth in a series of initiatives called La Palestra delle Idee, or the Gymnasium of Ideas, organized by a group based in the popular club, affiliated with the Associazione Ricreativa e Culturale Italiana (ARCI), a national solidarity association founded in 1957 in Florence to promote Italian social and cultural life.

The organizers of the Gymnasium of Ideas were desperately trying to recreate a sense of possibility. The collective sense was that city leaders had neglected their neighborhood. They were building a grassroots movement to bring attention and action to its doorsteps. On a banner, large green and red letters *PD* were printed above an image of an olive branch, the symbol of the Democratic Party. The tent provided shelter for the six panelists, three men and three women, who sat in front of about thirty-five spectators sitting in plastic armchairs. The backdrop was a three-story factory, numerous windowpanes conspicuously missing.

On the agenda was "Work and Made in Italy." This theme seemed to be on everyone's mind. How would people talk about Made in Italy in a public setting? What might be revealed about its value, its vulnerability, and its future prospects? The theme of work came up frequently across the province during our collaboration. A few months earlier, on a Sunday morning in January 2013, a different cultural club hosted an event billed as a "Democratic Breakfast." Guest speakers campaigning for parliamentary elections included one candidate for the Chamber of Deputies, Matteo Biffoni of the Democratic Party (PD), and two candidates for the Senate, Ilaria Santi also of the Democratic Party, and Francesco Paoletti of Sinistra Ecologia Libertà (SEL), or the Left Ecology Freedom Party. The local chapter had billed the theme as "Fair Italy" as a way to counter rampant disillusionment vis-à-vis national politics and kick-start a new era of trust in light of the groundswell around comedian–turned–rabble rouser Beppe Grillo and his political Five Star Movement. Candidates messaged on key challenges, particularly those related to generating work and managing immigration. Democratic Party candidate Biffoni put it clearly: "The mother of all battles will be work." The speakers were engaging and the crowd was supportive, but at the conclusion of the meet-and-greet session, widespread skepticism cast doubt on any of these candidates' ability to bring about much positive change. After twenty years of Berlusconi and his cronies, together with economic uncertainty and European-wide austerity, the problems were complex and felt insurmountable. Creative alternatives admittedly seemed absent. A half-century earlier, these clubs were known as hotbeds of possibility.

Development was on people's minds. The economic downturn had brought a sense of despair. Unemployment was rampant. Poverty was on the rise. Indicators revealed 33 percent of the population had a very low income, below €10,000 annually (IRIS 2015).Youth unemployment nationwide had reached 37 percent, a figure that appeared in the newspaper and that politicians and ordinary people threw around with regularity. Austerity measures were brutal. Local news reported incessantly on businesses that closed altogether or were under bankruptcy reorganization. Prato, with its history of industrial production, had been hit hard. In this context, the organizers of the Gymnasium of Ideas' event were taking action.

Krause attended the event as the team ethnographer. Despite the prevalent pessimistic mood toward politicians, one of the invited guests was Valeria Fedeli, vice-president of the Italian Senate, along with several local figures: an entrepreneur, an artisan serving as president of the city's industrial artisan's union (CNA), a young businesswoman, a regional representative from the national union (CGIL), and secretary of the city section of the Democratic Party. A major theme emerged around the value of the Made in Italy brand. After describing the current moment as "the worst economic crisis in the last fifty years" and pointing to serious effects on "our social cohesion," the first speaker passionately said Made in Italy should be defended because it was "one of the crown jewels of this country." Later, listening to the audio recording and hearing the metaphor "*gioielli della corona*," Malinowski's encounter with the crown jewels of Scotland and insight about "historical sentiment" came vividly to mind. Historical sentiment ran deep here, as did the desire to reclaim a sense of history gone awry.

During the event, Chinese residents walked along the street behind the speakers' tent, casting a quizzical gaze at the happenings, the flapping political party flags, and the lot filled with Italian spectators. Occasionally, an individual of Chinese descent ducked into the San Paolo bar for a coffee, a drink, a snack, or a game of video poker. None of the resident Chinese migrants joined the event. The irony couldn't have been more poignant. Their non-involvement suggested different networks, different stakes, and different realities.

The senator took the microphone and reminded, with a tone of regret, of the national incentives and bonuses that had been given to businesses willing to uproot and produce "*all'estero*," abroad. She noted the way in which Italian businesses are undercapitalized and drew negative comparisons with Germany. Finally, she discussed a new law in the works that would protect and boost the Made in Italy brand, a voluntary sort of certification designed to "*far esplodere il* Made in Italy," to make the brand explode, in a positive sense, of course. An existing law, passed in 2009, required that the label be used only on items that are exclusively made in the Italian territory, including the design, development, manufacture, and packaging.[8] The senator's proposal was framed in the language of sustainability as it emphasized a crackdown on counterfeit goods, on unfair competition, and on irregular workers. In other words, the certification would also ensure decent and fair working conditions.

The entrepreneur argued for seeing the textile and fashion sectors as deeply connected. Despite the crisis, he said, Prato remains an intensely industrial and fast-fashion district. He made a heartfelt speech about businesses that resist going bankrupt. Rhetorically, he pointed to Germany, Russia, and China and asked how Italy could possibly compete, particularly in places where democratic principles were unknown.

Speakers shared talk of teamwork and collaboration. The young woman who ran a private daycare with three associates noted how hard the crisis was hitting women and cited the statistic that one out of four firms is woman owned. She became emotional as she described her struggles for women business owners. The secretary of the union lamented the number of people in precarious work situations even when they do have work. She lamented the limits of the production chain—given that many phases are done outside of Italy—and called for the need to move beyond textiles.

At that point, rain began to fall and the group of forty or so people col-

lectively moved chairs inside the club where for the next hour members of
the public took turns participating in debate. There were criticisms of the
senator's certification proposal based on the suspicion that many big firms
oppose the idea; they don't want to be transparent because there is still a good
deal of illegality behind production—a fact that many in Prato knew well
because of the history there of *lavoro nero*, work that flew under the taxman's
radar and helped the economy thrive as subcontracting became a way of life
and small family firms flourished. Nevertheless, people expressed desires to
defend Prato and its artisans, to crack down on tax evasion (of the Italian
variety as well), to address structural problems, and to create options for the
young generation.

"Future: zero," announced one self-described twenty-eight-year-old free-
lancer who despite great effort and skill was not able to find regular work, and
if he did, rarely got paid. He described one profound desire: "*Fare la valigia e
andare all'estero*," or "To pack my bags and go abroad."

The debate concluded at 1:00 p.m. By that time, two long tables were being set for the forty guests. "You're going to stay for lunch, aren't you?" one of
the hosts asked. I (Krause) graciously accepted the hospitality. A three-hour
lunch ensued to celebrate the anniversary of the Gymnasium of Ideas initiative. The meal included several courses: a panzanella bread salad, crostini
with spreads of artichoke and liver pâté, homemade lasagna, two kinds of
meat thinly sliced (roast beef and pork) with roast potatoes. Wine and water
flowed throughout. The meal concluded with cake, champagne, coffee, and
toasts all around.

I sat next to a woman who shared with me the story of her family's hard
times, how they had gone from two incomes to one, and how it was tough
raising a child. I wondered how they managed. She recounted how they
used to have a nice car, nice things, take vacations. "We've had to cut way
back," she said. Thank goodness, she added, she had some old clothes that
she hadn't worn much because she found herself limited in buying clothes. It
occurred to me that that was a big sacrifice in an intensely fashion-conscious
place like this.

She asked me about my situation and my family, and as I told her how
my children were back in the United States with their dad, because my son
was still in school, she said, "*Ma la mamma è la mamma*—But the mom is
the mom."

After paying for the meal, truly economical at only €14, I passed through
the bar, where several people faced a wall of video poker machines. At the seat
nearest to the door, a man of Chinese origin steadied a young boy, perhaps
four years old, as the child played a virtual game. As I drove off, I listened

as an anti–slot machine campaign ad aired on the radio. Despite a GPS attached to my windshield, I got lost in Macrolotto Zero's labyrinth of streets with no exit.

## Cul-de-Sac

In Prato, a street with no exit is known as a cul-de-sac. We came to realize that we had very different associations with the category of cul-de-sac. On the afternoon of July 9, 2014, we took a field trip to the hamlet of Oste, in the commune of Montemurlo, on the outskirts of Prato with another Massimo, an architect whom Bressan would eventually enlist in the "Trame di Quartiere" action research project, aka Neighborhood Plots. *Trame* can mean "dramas," "plots," "weaves," or "wefts." We chose the translation of plots because it best captures the spirit of the initiative—full of purpose, planning, vision, and even subversive schemes to transform the previous city government's hostile approach to diversity into one that addressed social inequalities through policies that were inclusive and democratic.

The dense urban area of Montemurlo hosted multistory apartment buildings, stucco factories, and a small fenced park with little shade. The ground floor of the apartments had mailboxes in which Italian and Chinese names were interspersed. I felt like I had been transported to another part of the universe as we walked through the neighborhood, peered into factories that seemed abandoned, climbed up a wall to gaze into a canal used for textile dyes, and cautiously stepped into dead-end concrete spaces. Massimo and Massimo kept pointing out the cul-de-sacs as evidence. My field notes suggest that Robert Sheckley's (2006) *Mindswap* might offer some direction, of what sort, now, I do not know. Massimo Bressan meanwhile was using the urban outing as inspiration for colleagues who were designing an art installation at the Venice Biennale titled "Calling Home," which explored domestic spaces and change in Italy,[9] as well as for #San Paolo, the beta version of Neighborhood Plots.

The topic of cul-de-sacs kept coming up, and for some reason, I was perplexed by the association that the two Massimos were making with a cul-de-sac. They kept nodding in mutual agreement. I kept shaking my head in confusion. It was classic insider complicity. Later, over lunch at Soldano's in Prato's historic center, Massimo the architect rendered a sketch on a Tuscan-parchment-style placemat. The image on the left showed a square interspersed with little rectangular, separated, narrow entryways. The image on the right depicted a rectangle with an arched top with central artery around which was a cluster of housing plots. It was all too familiar to me. I grew up on Waverly Place, a dead-end street in Webster Groves, a historic inner-ring suburb of St. Louis established in 1896 with the merging of five communities along the adjacent Pacific Railroad line. Playing with neighborhood friends on that traffic-free street was the delight of my childhood. Massimo Bressan, by contrast, as a teenager worked in a sweater workshop located on a very different sort of cul-de-sac. It was the classic Prato factory-city variety.

In English and Italian, the word *cul-de-sac* is exactly the same but the meaning is completely different. The American cul-de-sac refers to a safe and comfortable residential neighborhood—and historically white and crime-free. In the environs of Prato, a cul-de-sac has a negative connotation. It suggests a place that is forgotten in urban plans. It is a place where toddlers can play but risk getting run over by a truck whose driver is in a hurry to make a delivery. To discover a cul-de-sac, for the two insiders, sparked intellectual satisfaction yet experiential annoyance. To realize the street led nowhere disrupted the flow of our journey and required that we turn around and retrace our steps.

Secchi himself observed the cul-de-sac feature in the built environment that reflected the district's productive system: tight integration and proximity between the fundamental activity of the textile cycle and the home, very often realized in the immediate environs of work spaces: "The residence remains at the curb of large blocks within which are located industrial workshops. These are reached by trails to 'cul-de-sacs' that often end in the domestic courtyards of factories" (Secchi 1996a, 44).

In Macrolotto and San Paolo and other similar neighborhoods with mixed industrial-residential urban features, all of these dead ends in effect block movement. Beyond the physical barriers, the cul-de-sacs become a sort of metaphor for barring connections. They prevent sociality. They prevent flow. They cause segregation. They become, in fact, a symbol of segregation and separation.

In San Paolo and Macrolotto Zero, the cul-de-sacs, lack of public spaces, as well as its confined location, partially due to impenetrable infrastructure such as the raised railway and heavily trafficked bypass, create obstacles to connectivity and diversity. Isolated streets without a way out interrupt the flow of movement inside the neighborhoods. If dead ends are an inevitable design feature, they should at least lead to a public space and a pedestrian walkway. Strategies that ensure robust and healthy neighborhood diversity include (1) mix, (2) connection, and (3) security (Talen 2008). A key inclusivity principle rests in maximum accessibility in terms of the network of roads, paths, and public spaces that residents as well as passersby use to move around a given neighborhood. Furthermore, public spaces and collective

goods—whether schools, health-care structures, sports facilities, or libraries—by virtue of their ability to provide meeting contexts, have a particular
significance in supporting the processes that favor developing and sustaining
socially and culturally diverse and vibrant neighborhoods. And yet city leaders' approach had been militaristic helicopter blitzes rather than community-
based planning efforts.

## Neighborhood Plots

Neighborhood Plots took inspiration from visions of inclusivity and *mixité*.
The action-research project sought to intervene against stubborn segregation
and in effect to awaken collective remembering that temporal distance had let
slumber. Neighborhood Plots aimed to cultivate dignified diversity. To that
end, in spring 2015, our team of organizers from the IRIS research institute
launched a series of events: a landscape architect–guided urban walking tour,
a social photography lab, documentary film screenings, and a digital storytelling workshop.[10]

The digital storytelling intervention involved a four-day workshop (May
12–15) in a classroom in the Scuola Buricchi, an elementary school in the
heart of San Paolo. Digital storytelling is a collaborative process that affords
participants the opportunity to articulate their own meanings and experiences and to gain skills in media literacy along the way. The stories are short,
first-person visual narratives that synthesize image, audio recording, music,
and text to document personal stories (Gubrium and Harper 2013). IRIS
staff assisted with outreach, recruiting, and logistics, and US graduate student Ying Li assisted with technology. Participants ranged in age, gender, and
place of origin.

As with participatory methods generally speaking, digital storytelling involves a shift in power relations in terms of the production of knowledge.
Researchers tend to be accustomed to seeing themselves as the expert. Digital
storytelling produces a set of final products that result from the interaction
between individual participants, facilitators, and the group as a whole. The
researchers and facilitators themselves have influence but not total control. It
upends the "expert" and the production of knowledge.

Our selection of the StoryCenter to facilitate the workshop assured an approach that was proven across a number of international situations. The fact
of the center's home base being in Berkeley, California, created excitement as
well as skepticism for the Italian researchers. The source of excitement was
the track record of StoryCenter's workshops; I had worked with the center's
facilitators on a Massachusetts-based project, Hear Our Stories, with young

parenting Latinas (Gubrium, Krause, and Jernigan 2014). A participatory approach that placed a premium on individual experiences stirred skepticism. The two Massimos' uncertainty was understandable given that they had a great deal of expertise invested in documenting the history of San Paolo and Macrolotto as well as a preference for a professionally produced product in which a producer captures the story of the community as a whole. Digital stories, being only two to five minutes in length, offer narrative fragments. Effective screening of individual stories relies on facilitators to provide context, and when done well in a community setting, the stories serve as a powerful resource for stimulating dialogue and building solidarity.

An intense moment came after lunch with the story circle. This exercise prompts participants to share very rough drafts of their story ideas and receive supportive feedback. The first storyteller, an active elderly woman named Federica, shared a story about driving and integration. The next storyteller, Giuseppe, among those who spearheaded the Gymnasium of Ideas initiative, recounted a story about a devastating snowstorm and a protest to protect a neighborhood park. Up next was Zen, a young professional who spoke of his experience with job precarity. Stefania, a recent transplant to Prato from southern Italy, shared thoughts about her fascination photographing abandoned industrial spaces. Davide offered a quasi-psychedelic journey through color to evoke memories from his family's south-north migration during the 1980s. Silvia, a working mother who had joined the workshop late, crafted the most sensory story about growing up in San Paolo.

As the day came to a close, another organizer from the Gymnasium of Ideas came in. I encouraged him to join the workshop, but he said he could tell a story but he couldn't write. I told him that wasn't a problem, we could write it down for him. He is a salesman of scholastic textbooks, so I found this ironic, but I know some people have a hard time putting words to paper. He shared a vivid childhood memory about riding a bicycle with one person pedaling and the other standing on the back, and they would meander through the narrow streets of San Paolo. He was very moved by the workshop—both by the individual stories and by the potential he saw in them to draw attention to San Paolo—something they'd been trying to do for so long. I wrote in my field notes:

> I can't remember a time when I felt so moved. I know how much energy he
> and Giuseppe have put into their efforts with the Gymnasium of Ideas and
> other community projects and initiatives to try to get some things going. They
> have a deep commitment to place and would like to see it transform in a posi-
> tive way. . . . The whole day was rather magical and so sensory.

In the coming days, participants worked with facilitators to write and revise scripts in the main classroom and record voice-overs in a basement archive. As a group, everyone joined together for the walking tour of the neighborhood to take photographs and video clips to be used in stories. Zen had actually worked in an employment office located just a few blocks away. The walking tour brought everyone together. We even got a tour of Giuseppe's top-floor apartment, the panoramic view of the neighborhood, and the special little garden that provided the subject matter of his story. Back at the school, as assistants, we helped the storytellers as they struggled to learn the software and assemble their stories. Frustrations with technology were released each day as participants and facilitators broke for lunch, walking across the schoolyard and through the narrow streets of San Paolo to the Circolo—the same site of the Gymnasium of Ideas project. The lunch breaks lasted about twice as long as the hour that our efficient US facilitator had scheduled. There was little to be done about it. The gracious hospitality of Circolo staff could not be denied.

At the end of the fourth day, storytellers were instructed to pull together their stories. It was a time crunch. Tensions ran high. The end of the workshop felt rushed. Participants were required to uninstall software. They had to let go of their unfinished work. There was a collective sense of loose ends. But there was also closure. Indeed, the ritual screening of rough cuts had a celebratory feel.

Over the course of the workshop, participants had produced stories on themes of their choosing: industrial abandonment, green spaces, job precarity, regional migration, diverse ways of belonging, and struggles with racism. Especially tender was the simple ritual of each storyteller remarking on their story.

Federica offered different points of view on the chaos in the changing neighborhood and the challenges of *mixité* related to the coexistence of Little Italy with Little Wenzhou. Davide sent an antiracist message. Zen told an agonizing story of a social service worker. Giuseppe offered a historic perspective on struggles over the urban environment, specifically its disappearing parks, to remind of the collective value of common green spaces. Stefania said that making the stories made her reflect on her passion for the neighborhood and her compulsion to document it—a place she is not from. Silvia gave a view of the neighborhood from the perspective of a ten-year-old girl because there is a richness of a place from the eyes of a child. For children, the place where they live is always beautiful, and even if she sees San Paolo as not so beautiful now, she wanted to convey her childhood feeling.

I live in San Paolo, not the one in Brazil, but the San Paolo of Prato. Some people say that it's an ugly place where there aren't many people that you'd care to know. They say that there are gangs, even if I've never understood what they are. I like my house—from my bedroom window you see lots of trees that make a big noise when the wind blows. In Prato the wind blows all the time. One day it was blowing so hard that it twisted the base of the streetlamp in front of the house. I always see it when I come home from school because it's there right in front. Now I cross the street alone, it's not like when I was a little girl and my mom would go with me right to the teacher's door. The schoolyard of my class borders a huge field; one time when we were playing outside we saw some syringes. It occurred to me that they were used by those gangs, but I've never seen them. I figured that they would always linger in the little field, where my nonna never took me, but at times maybe someone moves around. My street is very nice, lots of my friends live there and when there was all that snow we went in the courtyard of the abandoned factory to slide around. Now in the evening I go up on the little wall, with Natasha, while mamma takes her chair over to Lucia's. But only now that it's summer, in the winter everyone stays at their own house. Dad is the only one who always leaves and he goes out to the club, the communist club, even if he always says he's not one. When we come back home it takes me a while to get sleepy. The noise from the loom bothers me. Mamma says that work doesn't make noise, but in my view she says that because it's hers and my uncle's. Just like Sara's mom who says that the bar doesn't make noise, but in the evening when all the men go out to play cards they make noise and not just a little. They make me laugh in the summer, with those white or light blue undershirts. San Paolo isn't an elegant place, this is true.

Massimo T., who had been literally lingering on the edges of the workshop from the beginning, showing signs of allergic reaction to the ground rule to connect through emotion, suddenly dialed in. "*Delizioso*," he said, visibly taken aback. "Gorgeous."

Everyone in the room seemed moved.

"This story released a chakra," remarked staff researcher Sara Iacopini.

Federica's story was far less celebratory as she spoke to challenges of *mixité* related to the coexistence of Little Italy with Little Wenzhou. Her story captures a tense moment of traversing the city. She reflects on giving a ride to a friend and her feeling to oblige her friend's request to follow an indirect route. In one part of the digital story, viewers watch as Federica's finger traces the roundabout route on a map, giving a sense of the tensions between residents in the heart of Macrolotto Zero (figure 8.1).

Two times per week, I go to pick up my Pratese friend who lives in Via Boccherini and was born in San Paolo. I live in the historic city center and, being from Rome, I'm used to driving in chaos. When I have her get in the car,

Maria begs me to not take Via Pistoiese. I think: "She emigrated to Switzer-
land; maybe she doesn't like buses."

"Why?" I ask. "I take you in the car, you'll arrive safe and sound; you'll
see." I go as far as Via Magnolfi.

"No, no," she says. "I have enough of the Chinese. They live on my landing, and they have very different rules from ours. I hear them at three in the
night go up and down in the elevator, slamming doors, talking, going out."

"What's the matter with the traffic?"

"Oh, yes, it matters. Take the Montalese route and avoid this entire neighborhood. You'll get there sooner. The Chinese cross the street wherever they
feel like it, they don't respect anyone, even less than somebody who's from
here. Then there are many, so many. They make me afraid."

And I have to arrive to Chiesanuova and drive through the Via Montalese
until the stoplight of Via Curtatone, to turn left and then a quick right. . . . Is
it possible that Maria is so landlocked to dictate that I take such a long route
instead of letting me go where and how I want? . . .

In the neighborhood of San Paolo, there's no longer all the green. Via San
Paolo, where we used to travel by bicycle, is gone. There are no more of the
little workshops with personal handlooms. Now we move around in a world
increasingly unknown.

The desire of Federica's friend to avoid Via Pistoiese troubles our sensibilities. Via Pistoiese, after all, is a synecdoche for Prato's Chinatown. As we
watch Federica delineate her eventual route, the movements of her finger call
to mind segregation and the former mayor's infamous public ordinance. Her
story recalls the bewilderment of people in the neighborhood. It recalls the
fear underneath aggressive policies and blitzes. Our Berkeley-based facilitator expressed concern that the story is perhaps too sensitive. Even though
Federica intended it as a critique of xenophobia, the facilitator worried it may
not be a story that can be publicly screened.

The workshop closed with an invitation to each participant to offer one
hope for the neighborhood. Silvia said "pride" given that San Paolo was largely
forgotten by the administration. Stefania underscored integration. Giuseppe
said, "It can't get any worse here; it can only get better," and pointed to his
desire to make known San Paolo's history. Zen reminded that neighborhoods
are made up of people, that they construct the spirit and soul of a community, that these stories narrate memory and history, and that they democratize listening. Davide noted that every video has a link to the past that raises
awareness and consciousness about where we come from, our roots. He
spoke about different kinds of roots through the metaphor of different kinds
of trees, and noted that in the end, we are all trees. (Federica had left early to
assist an elderly woman.)

The facilitators added their hopes. I emphasized my appreciation for the different perspectives on the neighborhood and hoped for dialogue. Ying hoped for communication and integration. Sara laughed that she yearned for sleep—a commentary on her exhaustion—and then remarked on passion, which can heighten expectations, and she hoped people were not let down. Massimo T. commented that the room was full of professionals and experts and that the stories went beyond his expectations. Amy hoped the workshop would spark a desire in the neighborhood to share stories, emphasizing the value of democratization and collective storytelling. All told, the workshop ended in an emotional climax, with a sense that each story contributed to a larger whole.

From a different perspective, success came in the form of each of the participants having an authentic connection to the neighborhood. It was truly a community-based endeavor. They participated because of their own interest in the community. As such, they brought different perspectives and concerns to their stories. That meant that stories conveyed a range of messages about the neighborhood. Admittedly, one of the failures was also related to the limits of diversity. Despite the project's intentions and best efforts—including the incorporation of a Chinese research assistant into the team—we were unable to recruit members of Prato's Chinese community to participate in the workshop as storytellers.

The mixed results bring to mind Secchi's words about the twentieth century being "the century of the autonomous individual" and "exactly why it is necessary to give space to difference." In many respects, recruiting all variety of individuals to participate takes a good deal of groundwork. It is one thing to recognize the need to "give space to difference" and quite another to achieve that goal. In the case of Neighborhood Plots, through the various initiatives, strides were made toward making possible the giving of space to difference.

### Mixité 2.0

As anthropologists embarking on a collaborative project, with intertwined aims of intellectual scientific merit and broader humanistic impacts, we found ourselves initially documenting these changes and then developing engaged action-research strategies to encourage and cultivate a diverse city in line with Secchi's vision. To be sure, conflicts brought into relief contrasting ways in which the present, past, and future were perceived and valued. They also led to initiatives that stimulated people to articulate and act on what they valued.

The most recent influx of immigrants to a large extent has returned the neighborhood of San Paolo and its environs to the rhythm of the 1960s—the era of the industrial boom. Granted, the stories of the people passing in the streets, the goods that are sold in stores and circulating in vans, the languages spoken by residents, differ from those of fifty years ago. Paradoxically, the concentration of Chinese workers and families has effectively slowed down the processes of urban transformation in Macrolotto Zero. The immigrant presence has extended rather than upended the characteristic of *mixité*.

Recall, Prato drew rural Tuscan sharecroppers and southern migrants to work in its factories and family firms during the economic boom of the 1960s. Since the mid-1990s, it has been the destination for tens of thousands of migrants, primarily from the Zhejiang Province of China. Regardless of their regional or transnational origins, residents share a history of producing Made in Italy textile, knitwear, or apparel products. Despite similar tempos, their occurrence in different historical times has created social distance and dissonance. Residents grapple with bewildering transformations (Bressan and Tosi Cambini 2009) and contemporaneous contrasts in work rhythms: unemployed Italian sweater artisans and inactive household handloom workers as opposed to frenetic Chinese garment workers and entrepreneurs. Poignant was the fact that many Italians who migrated to Prato and came of age during a period of economic boom experienced their own rapid success and subsequent dizzying decline and then watched as a non-Italian population moved in, spatially concentrated, and took hold of a niche economy. Whereas spatial proximity has created tensions, temporal distance has made similarities seem strange and even unrecognizable.

Temporal distancing also figures centrally into the ongoing urban struggles among residents and city officials concerning how to live in, govern, and make sense of changing political, economic, and social dynamics. After the "Idea of the City" event, when Cenni accused the immigrant presence of taking Prato back "hundreds of years," he was drawing on temporal ideologies that effectively generated distance and dissonance between the past and the present. His appeal to moral leadership through such contrasting temporalities of past, present, and future was a clear tactic to attack the kind of vision for a diverse city that the urban planner Secchi and his supporters promoted. Temporality became a tool—a tool to win consent in the current hegemonic struggle that was playing out in the city. In retrospect, Cenni's attack was also an attempt to secure his party's foothold given the threat to his legacy and then-upcoming elections of 2014. The threat was real. Matteo Biffoni, the Democratic Party candidate, after being elected to Parliament in the winter 2013 elections, unseated Prato's mayoral incumbent in May 2014.[11]

The right-wing, antiglobalist political rhetoric emphasized the distance and separation between Italian and Chinese residents as well as businesses. Meanwhile, the interactions between workers and employers—including local Italian owners and immigrant renters—have continued as old habits adjusted to new global conditions. Public opinion reacted to transnational changes with an intensity reminiscent of the reactions to articles in the international press that portrayed the submersed side of Prato's impressive economic development of the 1970s. Parallels between those international journalists who appeared on the scene then to describe the contradictions of globalization—that is, the ways in which economic competition shaped working conditions and impacted quotidian dynamics—resonate uncannily with mainstream media descriptions of the past several years.

A clash of actions to address the future of an intensely globalized city inspired this chapter. Conflict between a famous urban planner and a controversial mayor over how to manage the city gives a sense of the distance between two ends of a political spectrum: *mixité* vs. militarization. San Paolo and Macrolotto represent a crossroads where Little Italy and Little Wenzhou uncomfortably comingle. Yet the communities share in Prato's brand of small-firm development, its history of economic distinctions, and its story of outsourcing. They share temporal rhythms. They even share in unique, if divergent, ways to bring and sustain value related to the Made in Italy brand. Finally, they share challenges of place resulting from fast and chaotic growth without planning.

The grassroots initiative, the Gymnasium of Ideas, brought together residents to foster dialogue on issues such as urban renewal and local economic possibilities. Many of the participants grappled with displacement from textile-related jobs due to forces of globalization. The organizers, who came together in a former communist—turned—moderate leftist cultural club, grappled with community members to generate ideas about the future of work, the Made in Italy brand, and the future of the city. They searched to figure out a politically viable counterdiscourse to that of the seductive xenophobic one of the right. In no small part, they were responding to hostile actions of the mayor, such as the ghetto-style ordinance, which only applied to residents and establishments in the primarily Chinese neighborhood of Macrolotto Zero. Although two years later a high court deemed this policy to be discriminatory, aggressive helicopter patrols and factory raids were ongoing as was blatant hostility toward attempts to counter segregation with diversity management and participatory planning, as evidenced in the former mayor's response to the event "An Idea of the City," which opened this chapter.

The scaffold for this chapter has been assembled through place-based ethnography and analysis, it has focused on how citizens engage in value-making actions, and it has considered how temporality is deployed—that is, how the past is conveniently forgotten to construct a certain kind of resident-citizen. Local interventions in envisioning and enacting an idea of the city revealed the challenges of bringing together Chinese and Italian residents to forge collective histories and futures.

The forces of industrial decline, financial crisis, and immigrant influx have created a "crisis of authority." Such a crisis occurs, in Gramsci's estimation, "if the ruling class has lost its consensus, i.e., is no longer 'leading,' but only 'dominant.'" Gramsci's observation applies particularly well to the crisis of presence. "The crisis consists precisely in the fact that the old is dying and the new cannot be born," yet in this whirl of crisis there exists the "possibility and necessity of creating a new culture" (Gramsci 1971, 276).

Our place-based focus on action as value making yields understanding of how urban spaces evolve over time and how grassroots action enacts value and foments the new. The presence of transnational migrant workers and their families has made San Paolo and Macrolotto Zero more complex than they were in the past, presenting new challenges and opportunities for realizing *mixité*. Historical conjunctures involve (1) transnational cultural practices and "passageways" between local/regional and global markets, (2) spheres of segregation and integration that operate on multiple levels, and (3) places where diversity is expressed in terms of an extraordinary *mixité* in the urban landscape. All told, a flow of meanings and situations require constant capacity at reading, engaging, and interpreting. The contemporary system of globalization brings people together and taxes their bodies, senses, relationships, and prospects in new ways that have inspired us to apply understanding to local conditions in which we find ourselves living, working, and collaborating.

# Conclusion

## Futures

An airplane nearly brushed treetops above me as it approached Peretola's runway. I pressed the flip phone to my ear and struggled to hear Fangli's voice on the other end. Hymns vibrated through the speaker. My GPS had led me astray. I figured I was lost when the pothole-ridden stretch of road took me into a zone of fenced-off encampments. A man rushed out toward me flailing his arms, and, feeling vulnerable, I raced off the other way. Nobody gave dwellers much notice in this forgotten patch of urban wasteland sandwiched between the airport north of Florence and the Osmannoro warehouse district.

I eventually found my way to the Chinese evangelical church, inconspicuously located in a converted *capannone*, or warehouse, inside an iron-gated courtyard. The only indication that it was a place of worship was a small cross just above the front door. Inside, on one wall towered a large bookcase stacked with Bibles and hymnals. On the facing wall hung a calendar with a listing of Chinese Christian Evangelical Churches in Italy.

The sermon was well under way. About fifty parishioners filled the fluorescent-lit room. Fangli welcomed me in, and we sat in the first pew behind the aisle. Her affectionate three-year-old daughter sat on a cousin's lap. It was a popular place for women holding young children. A few people stared at me. I was "other" in this space, the Westerner out of place.

Behind a shiny silver pulpit with a bright red cross, a preacher led the sermon. His voice shifted in charismatic waves from loud to quiet. Next to him, digitized passages from the Bible flashed Chinese characters onto a big screen. The selection was decidedly inspirational:

> John 12:35. Then Jesus told them, "You are going to have the light just a little while longer. Walk while you have the light, before darkness overtakes you. Whoever walks in the dark does not know where they are going."

FIGURE 9.1. Piazza dell'Immaginario was conceived in Macrolotto Zero as an urban experiment to cultivate interaction and possibility. The third edition, Piazza 5 marzo 2015, was created on the site of a grocery parking lot between Via Pistoiese 142/146 and Via Fabio Filzi 39, Prato.
Photo by Andrea Abati, courtesy Dryphoto arte contemporanea, 2015

The preacher directed his comments to entrepreneurs. The parishioners seemed to hang on to his every word:

> We always worry. First we worry about what merchandise to import from China. Next we worry about how long it will take to arrive, and whether the import police will stop it. Then we worry about whether it will take a long time to sell and then become stock [i.e., remaindered and thus sold below cost]. Next we worry about whether we will sell it at all. Then we worry about for how much. Then we worry about the money. Next we worry about where to put the money, whether to put it in the bank or at home. Life is always a worry.

This theme of worrying about the challenge of converting merchandise into money resonated with their situation. Concerns of a migrant entrepreneur's life were profound.

Another jet blasted overhead. Newspaper headlines of Italian protesters organizing against plans to expand the Florence airport runway came to mind. The preacher continued:

> What is the sense of life? To repeat the same thing every day? You don't know what is the meaning of life, where your life has meaning. Darkness and light.

This metaphor that moves between darkness and light. Often life is like the darkness because you do not know where you are. Lots of terrible things happen, terrible things in life.

My seasons in the field had taught me plenty of terrible things that could happen: assault, robbery, deadly fires, shaken baby syndrome, deportation, financial stress, or outright bankruptcy. Resident status and proper paperwork were a continuous source of anxiety for many migrants. Navigating the family reunification laws was an ongoing issue for many. Complying with workplace health and safety conditions created costs and fears. Another verse flashed up on the digital screen.

Matthew 24:12. Because of the increase of wickedness, the love of most will grow cold.

The preacher knew his parishioners. He knew the hard economic and emotional place in which they dwelled. He grasped how they carried the burden of those textile industry statistics, of the reports that attributed the continued success of Made in Italy to the migrant labor force. They were leading development from the diaspora. For some, faith through evangelical worship and the community itself provided an outlet for their worries. Even then, it was a faith backed by hard work. Spiritual insistence was no small part of the business model.

After the sermon, Fangli stepped up onto the stage with the kids, and they snacked on dried soybeans. Her mother offered me some, I gladly accepted, and I felt a connection. We made our way to a back room. I sensed the support of a tight-knit community, and knowing this gave me a sense of serenity. Fangli had strong social and public support for her daughter, who literally became a poster child: she was featured on a brochure celebrating October 14, the National Day of People with Down Syndrome. She introduced me to her mother's companion. He was fifty, her mom fifty-two. He was handsome and friendly. She was gracious and welcoming. He spoke English, and she spoke Wenzhouese. Fangli reintroduced me to her fifteen-month-old son who *could* have been a poster child of an Italian-Chinese union. After her three-month maternity leave, Fangli had briefly returned to the research project but then taken a job at a new bank that served migrants in the heart of Prato's industrial zone. I had attended the inauguration with Antonio, the retired sweater maker–turned–tour guide. The position paid about the same as the research work, but Fangli believed the job security was more suitable to her place in the life course: as a mother of two young children and a wife of an Italian man finishing a degree in psychology but with few job prospects, given cuts to the public health-care sector.

Three tables were set family style. I sat next to the kids and fed Fangli's daughter while she fed the baby. The girl ate like she was starving. Fangli threatened to put her on a diet. She encouraged her to eat slowly. I loved feeding her. I sensed a mutuality of being, like family. I felt useful. I missed that useful sensation of mothering that I had at home with my own children even if by June 2014 they were twenty-three and fourteen—well beyond the spoon-feeding phase. Now, before me, a child was devouring a plate of beef and rice. She refused the veggies. Fangli's mom approached me and asked if I wanted to eat. I explained that I liked Chinese food and ate it often but that I had just come from a Sunday lunch and had a dinner appointment later. She was understanding.

After the meal, a handful of people gathered in the choir room. Fangli pulled out a music book and flipped through it, showing me how the hymns did not have scores but rather numbers representing do, re, mi. The Chinese teacher, who spoke decent Italian, noted the small group and canceled the rehearsal. Ditto for the next week. It was summer mode. We headed outside. Fangli's husband took the kids. They each gave me a kiss. Fangli invited me to visit her at the beach, where she was heading for vacation, Italian style, at the end of the week.

I set out from the church and headed northwest through the municipalities of Sesto Fiorentino and then Campi Bisenzio. Back at my apartment, I freshened up only to head out into a torrential thunderstorm with an old family friend, Bonaventura, for what turned out to be a dramatic evening. A group of people met in the hill town of Poggio alla Malva at a cultural club where a mutual friend wanted to thank them for volunteer work. The eight of us sat at a long table in a tent-covered patio area, ate oven-fired pizza, and discussed the microbrewed Bottega 33 made in Poggio A Caiano. An Italian guitarist and singer duo performed, and I appreciated the way the woman belted out "Georgia." I was so moved by the song's soulful delivery that I failed to translate the words upon my friend's request. I did not get a second chance to redeem myself. The wind, rain, and lightning turned increasingly violent. Water began rushing in along the patio wall behind the electrical box. The situation turned tense. The band packed up. We regrouped inside, where Bonaventura disappeared with three twentysomething women. I chatted with the others and noticed a poster, *I Ragazzi*, from a play about the Resistance. The history of leftist struggles was on display. Bonaventura returned with the young women to tell me how in light of having lost permanent jobs at the post office, a cultural center affiliated with the town had hired them to teach a computer course. They would now be paid €400 per month—a measly stipend especially considering instructor positions were only a temporary contract. As a furniture restorer and woodworker who was heir to an artistic legacy, Bonaventura often quipped that he had little problem getting work; getting paid was another matter. On the way home, the storm produced a spectacular light show with moments of complete illumination and utter darkness. The contrasts could not have been more striking.

### Fire, Fury, and a Funeral

Uncertainty turned to tragedy on December 1, 2013, when the Teresa Moda factory fire took the lives of seven Chinese migrants. An investigation revealed that the establishment did not have emergency exits. Bars blocked windows. According to the *New York Times*, "Officials believe that a camp stove used for cooking probably caused the fire" (Povoledo 2013). The calamity fueled national outrage. Locally, then-mayor Cenni responded with a call for a day of mourning while also ramping up security measures. Few households reportedly hung the black flags traditionally used as a sign of respect for the dead.

Outside the Teresa Moda factory where the victims had sewn clothes labeled Made in Italy, located in the heart of Prato's Macrolotto One industrial district, a handwritten sign commemorated the lost lives: "Sorrow Has No Color." The sign evoked discriminatory tactics that the city had waged against a migrant workforce. The crackdown on "criminality" in the name of saving lives was a sorry cover for the hostile environment (Krause and Bressan 2014). Ultimately, the events suggested that there was a color to sorrow. Its hues were saturated by a global economic system that demands cheap and superflexible labor that makes possible trendy clothes at bargain prices.

The funeral was held on an asphalt parking lot a full 203 days after that tragic dawn. The unusually long time span between the wretched deaths and the burial ritual was incongruous with the furiously fast conditions that defined these migrant workers' lives. The contrast between the time it took for one of the oldest and most fundamental of human rites and the flexible fastness under which these workers toiled suggests something was terribly wrong: that the value of their lives was almost as inconsequential as the clothes they made.

The story of why it took so long to put the dead to rest had to do with the challenge of securing sufficient funds for those wretched souls. One reason that circulated had to do with money troubles. An association in Milan reportedly collected €20,000, but the funds had not yet arrived. Neither the Chinese consulate in Florence, the ambassador of Rome, nor the Chinese community in Prato provided help to the families of their conationals who died in the fire (Nencioni 2014).

Attending the funeral was the saddest day of my fieldwork. I was grateful that Antonio wanted to accompany me. I could not bear the thought of going alone.

The event transpired under a blazing sun on June 21, 2014. Organizers had moved it from a public assistance building to the Piazzale Ebenese to accommodate a large crowd, which was incorrectly forecast. The large piazza formerly served as the parking lot for Prato's hospital, where our team had conducted some of our ethnography before its operations were relocated to a new structure. On that hot summer afternoon, the lot was nearly empty when we arrived. In fact, it was so empty that the traffic officer, after asking us, "Who are you? Are you civilians?" (*Chi siete? Siete civili?*)—to which a bemused Antonio answered, "Yes, civilians"—allowed us to enter into the "wrong" exit. We laughed afterward. Of course we were civilians! What else would we be? Noncivilians?

I concluded that the officer's question was probably because about three hundred Chinese individuals eventually attended but very few Italians. He likely assumed we had some official role to play, otherwise why would we come? The lack of Italian presence, besides those serving in official roles, was a symbol of how segregated the city remained. I also saw the reasoning in Aurora's comment: that the first thing that comes to an Italian's mind is that these people took our jobs, so why should we go and mourn them? *Che c'è c'è*. It is what it is. By contrast, the wails and bells resounded as profoundly humanizing.

The ceremony combined evangelical, Buddhist, and secular elements. All told, it lasted about two hours. Volunteers passed out long-stemmed white gerbera daisies, water, and programs. People sat on folding chairs on either side of a red carpet, which led to a tented area under which were lined up six coffins. Dignitaries spoke. Military men in uniform laid a wreath of the state. Carriers of official flags marched through the crowd. Buddhists donning brown robes rang bells. A charismatic preacher from the evangelical church offered condolences. A choir sang hymns. The program identified the Prato church, Chiesa Cristiana Evangelica Cinese, and provided the words in Chinese and Italian to "Amazing Grace" (the title was printed in English). Antonio had not heard of the song. I, of course, had. With its message that forgiveness and redemption are possible even "for a wretch," the hymn was the most famous in the American songbook.

My little sister and I had sung "Amazing Grace" years ago, in August 1997, at my grandmother's memorial service in St. Louis. Mourning through song connected us, allowed us to participate in each other's sorrow, and kindled feelings of belonging. It provided the sort of mutuality of being that rests at the very core of kinship. I was grateful that my family had postponed the service for several weeks so that I could conclude my fieldwork in Italy and come home to take part in remembering my grandmother's life.

In Prato that day, dignitaries included the newly inaugurated mayor, the assessor of integration, a representative from the region of Tuscany, and representatives from the Chinese consulate. Collectively, they called for improved workplace safety (especially avoiding unsafe wiring and liquefied gas containers). Mayor Matteo Biffoni, the Partito Democratico candidate elected in June 2014, invoked collective mourning:

> Today we are here, representing Italian institutions, Prato citizens, and the Chinese community, to share a tremendous pain. But we are also here because we share the will to put into words the fact that the conditions of work are not acceptable to us. As mayor, I feel the need to express in the name of the entire community the pain for those who have fallen . . . and to share [a desire for] social justice, with all those who want to [realize] fundamental human rights. . . . Our children share things: they are born in the same maternity ward, they grow up in the same classrooms, they are often united in the same interests and have the same desire to grow up full of serenity. We have a moral obligation to them and to ourselves that we must push ourselves toward and guarantee in our territory respect for rights for which many people in Italy in years past have struggled, sacrificing for these same rights.

Despite the mayor's and other speakers' caring words and good intentions, everybody recognized the challenge ahead in terms of realizing workplace safety.

The final part of the ceremony was especially moving. Everyone was invited to take their white gerbera daisy up to the front and place it on a coffin. (I stupidly lost mine, but Antonio handed me what was left of his—wilted from the heat.) Survivors gathered around each of the photos of their lost loved ones. Some knelt quietly while others wailed.

I was moved to tears. As the crowd thinned, I squatted and took a photo not of the mourners but of the portraits of each of the six victims. I wanted to show my respect and remember each of them. I wanted them to know that we were with them. A tragedy of this sort was a tragedy for everyone.

Only the names of three of the seven victims were printed on the program. I surmised that only they were the members of the church. Dates of birth and death along with photos were included on the coffins, which overflowed with colorful flowers. The victims in the public funeral included two women and four men between the ages of thirty-four and fifty:

Lin Guangxing, December 29, 1962–December 1, 2013 (50)
Xue Xieqing, January 27, 1979–December 1, 2013 (34)
Zheng Xiuping, May 1, 1963–December 1, 2013 (50)
Rao Zhangjia, January 9, 1971–December 1, 2013 (42)
Su Qifu, November 1, 1970–December 1, 2013 (43)
Wang Chuntao, March 5, 1967–December 1, 2013 (46)

After perhaps twenty minutes, the time came for the coffins to be carried off and placed into the hearses. A couple of the women were so overcome with grief that others had to hold them back. They wailed and wailed. One of the mourners was treated by paramedics.

Those wailing women and quietly mourning men represented the collective grief and sadness embedded in global capitalism in all its heterogeneity. I thought about the stories of migrants whose own parents had sent them overseas and could not imagine the pain of a parent whose adult child then died in a workplace fire.

On the way home from the funeral, we drove through Macrolotto 1, with its maze of *pronto moda* fast-fashion signs, warehouses, and workshops, the majority now Chinese. I asked Antonio if he ever thought about starting up another business activity. "It's just impossible," he lamented. Besides the competition, if you calculate the taxes, Italy's infamous IVA (*Imposta sul Valore Aggiunta*, or value-added tax), forget about it. You're dead in the water before you've even started. I acknowledged how hard it must be, living on one pension, as long as that lasts, given the ever-looming threat of austerity cuts.

"Yeah, you live badly. And then you don't feel free. You feel like you're trapped," he said.

*Isn't that ironic?* I thought. That with all this globalization, these formerly flexible workers now feel like they have their hands tied. They feel unfree.

The quest for high profits and low-cost goods drives a broken system in which workers are treated as disposable commodities. Ultimately, the slow time between death and burial is a symbol of a much graver problem related to human dignity.

### Falling Ashes, Rising Security

The fallout from the fire stimulated a profound change in the politics, discourses, and policies concerning migrant workers in the historic factory city.

The region of Tuscany in spring 2014 allocated €12 million to intensify the existing crackdown on immigrant "illegality"—from housing workers in factories to ignoring safety codes and employing those who lack residency permits. Mayor Biffoni supported the measures. On the political stage, the fire brought together an assembly of members of the xenophobic right-wing party with those of the liberal center-left party. On a discursive level, the tragedy allowed both sides to position themselves as social justice supporters, accusing Chinese migrants of exploitive working conditions that mirrored slavery. On the policy front, the event gave legitimacy to regional leaders to substantially increase inspection efforts and hire seventy-five new public health "prevention inspectors," who fell under the Safe Work Project.[1]

The politicization was nothing short of ironic when some of the loudest voices in a chorus describing the Prato fire as a violation of human rights were the same ones that had supported the racist ordinance that only applied to the zone of Macrolotto Zero. This contingent was quick to call the Chinese workers "slaves" to justify an intensification of security measures—namely, factory raids and inspections. Another side used the tragedy to protect the reputation of the Italian brand. Still others sought to navigate the practical aspects of human rights. Everybody cared. Everybody had a dog in the fight.

An investigation several years prior concluded that human trafficking, smuggling, and slavery do not typically apply to the migrants in Prato (Ceccagno, Rastrelli, and Salvati 2008). The authors define trafficking as the buying and selling of people to exploit them. They define smuggling as the illegal introduction of an immigrant into a country. The Chinese in Prato do not typically see themselves as victims of smugglers or as slaves. In fact, they protested this label in newspaper articles, videos, and social media. They asserted a view of people who use networks, means, and organizations to arrive at desired destinations. The relationship between the typical migrant and snakehead often parallels that between a customer and a service provider. As we have seen, sometimes the journey does not go as planned.

Uncomfortable interdependencies continued to surface. The day before the funeral, a regional newspaper reported that seventy-nine Italians in the area had been charged with offering false paperwork to Chinese individuals seeking to immigrate. To enter and stay in the Italian territory, the non-Europeans needed local citizens willing to declare their ability to host them, rent to them, or to be ready to offer them a job. Compensation for these ghost deals ranged from a few hundred euro to €1,500 (Calamati 2014). The layers of legal violations multiplied.

Meanwhile, by early July 2014, the Safe Work policy was already having a visible impact. Chinese workers were increasingly moving out of factory dormitories and into legitimate apartments. Italian friends and acquaintances were converting empty rooms and inactive workshops into apartments and renting to Chinese tenants—something many of them would not have considered a decade earlier. Interdependencies between Italians and Chinese of Prato proliferated.

> Even if there are Italians who despise us, at the same time many Italians establish confidence with us to their benefit, they welcome us, right? Whatever you say about Prato as far as factories, there are lots of them, right? All of these are Chinese factories, Italians rent them to the Chinese, we give them money, we pay rent. There are interests [profit] behind this, right? It doesn't matter if they treat us with respect or not, they cannot address us with offensive words, their earnings depend on us, they rely on us to eat, right?[2]

Upon invitation, I visited Marco's shoe warehouse and rental space. Significant changes had already been made. His Chinese tenants had removed the makeshift sleeping quarters due to the controls. They kept the kitchen in the little back room, however, assuming that it was less of a risky violation, perhaps given the history of Italians having small kitchens adjacent to their workshops. I asked him where the workers slept now. His tenants had moved to a separate apartment.

Marco was vocal about the funds that the region of Tuscany had allocated. In his mind, hiring all these inspectors was a shameless political investment to win Tuscany's regional president votes for his future reelection. Meanwhile, the Chinese residents lived in terror. He pointed to the ones who rented from him. Their behaviors—they were always afraid. His years in local and regional politics gave him perspective. He claimed the surveillance did very little to help human rights. What about the right to work? What about the effect of turning workers into criminals?

While the Teresa Moda factory fire did not compare in numbers to the Rana Plaza factory collapse in Bangladesh that killed 1,100 garment workers in April 2013, any deaths from substandard working conditions are alarming, particularly when these kinds of incidents happen in the context of a country such as Italy where the 1948 Constitution asserts the rights of the worker-citizen. Indeed as Noelle Molé (2012, 10) notes in *Labor Disorders in Neoliberal Italy*, "It is the task of the Republic to remove all economic and social obstacles that . . . hinder the full development of the human person and the actual participation of all workers in the political, economic, and social organization of the country." The crackdown on "criminality" runs the risk of turning migrants into criminals for low wages and precarious work environments. Dignity requires more than security measures. It requires fair economic systems and political structures in which global citizens have rights and feel safe to participate.

Meanwhile, the rise of break-ins fomented widespread fear among Chinese and Italian residents. Burglars had entered Marco and his tenants' separate locked apartments on a hot summer's night while they were asleep, used ladders to climb up to second-story balconies, entered through open windows, taken money and keys, and stolen their cars. Friends offered me strategies of how to sleep safely alone in my apartment. Chinese residents felt vulnerable because their business savvy attracted negative attention. A group led by bilingual Chinese citizens organized their own patrol squads and in a show of political spectacle descended into the piazza in protest.[3]

Our conversation shifted to work. The Chinese whom Marco knew did not have much work at the moment. His situation was similarly dire. He used a phrase that he warned was vulgar: *Si cale le mutande*, that is, your underwear fall down, meaning that somebody works almost for free. He felt hopeless; it had never before been like this. All the shoes in the warehouse were already stock (i.e., they would have to be sold below price despite being high-quality Italian leather shoes). He overordered this year. He had not paid attention. He was angry with himself.

He shook it off, then insisted on giving me a pair of shoes. I was reluctant to accept, but I didn't want to offend him either. I tried on a few but shoe after shoe was too big. "*Cenerentola*," he called me, Cinderella. I had to laugh. There I was in a warehouse full of shoes and none of them fit me. The imperfect size. Reluctantly, I chose a pair of summer boots to take home to my daughter. I took inspiration from Mauss and viewed gifts as a way to create mutuality and "meaningful bonds of social solidarity" (Wilder 2015, 72). In accepting the gift, I knew I was obliging myself to our friendship.

The visit ended with a discussion of luxury brands. I had enjoyed a field trip to the Museo Salvatore Ferragamo in Florence with an old friend and her daughter, who doubled as a university student in literature and a shoe model for Ferragamo. Unlike me, she had the perfect size foot. Her foot was literally featured in a video installation in the museum about the history of Ferragamo design and shoemaking. Marco knew well the history of Ferragamo's success. He believed, however, that people were crazy to pay so much for luxury brands. "It's like a drug," he said. "It kills people." Similar desires, whether for expensive luxury brands or cheap attractive ones, fueled the fashion industry.

## Future Worlds

The future remained uncertain. This uncertainty manifested in the migrants' narratives. In the context of Italy's financial crisis, did people plan to stay put or return to China? Some were certain they would eventually return while others preferred to stay because they had become accustomed to life in Italy. Much depended on the economy. Regardless, most interviewees expressed uncertainty about the future. The consistency was profound and revealed a wait-and-see sensibility: "I don't have any plans at the moment"; "I don't know. How would I know? It's difficult to talk about things that are in the future. . . . I haven't thought that far ahead"; "It's still unknown. . . . If China becomes more developed, I can go back to China to work. . . . I am still thinking about this, but I am not sure about the future." Migrant women expressed a live-in-the-moment outlook. "About the future, I am blind. I mean, I still haven't found a goal. . . . In ten years, I definitely don't know where I will be"; "Now everybody does not know what to do. We don't know things about tomorrow now." Metaphors such as "I am blind," vis-à-vis the future, conveyed a sense that the women tended to not think far into the future. Tomorrow was an unknown.[4]

Whether fathers or mothers, refrains of uncertainty were remarkably similar. One mother said, "I wouldn't know. It's hard to say. It depends on my capability. If I have the capability to stay here, I will stay here. If I don't, then I will see." Another said, "That depends on the situation when the time comes." A third said, "I don't know about things in the future [laughs]. For now, I think wherever the conditions are better is where I will stay. . . . It depends on the economy." Another underscored the link to the local situation: "I don't know now. The situation now is not so good. We don't know how it will go. It depends on the situation of this year and next year." A father echoed the sentiment of his future being tied to the economy: "I don't have any plan. These years aren't good because of the financial crisis, but I can still earn some money here. The pay here is still better than in China." Another father also underscored the current situation: "It depends on the lives we have." Discussion of residence status was common. Several interviewees directly mentioned uncertainty about whether they would have a valid residence permit. A mother who was uncertain about her status suggested that could sway her options: "It's like, if I don't get the residence visa, we will go back to China. It's inconvenient to live here now; they are very strict about checking [undocumented migrants] now." A father who had the permit indicated the ease of travel: "I haven't thought about this. It's almost the same in Italy and in China. I have the residence [visa] anyway, so I can go back and forth between the two places."[5]

Family circumstances were a common theme as parents thought about what would be best for them as a family unit and for their children in the near and distant future. One mother had vague hopes: "Nothing [no plans], just to live better, the desires of a person become bigger, right? For example, I've been lucky, in the past year I've saved something, so I hope maybe to open a shop, or maybe start up a little business, to become an employer. One also hopes for life to be calmer, to have more time, to improve the quality of life. Everybody wants that." Many shared the view that cut-and-sew work was a temporary situation. Becoming a shopkeeper was a logical course on the life-work trajectory.

Insights came from two protagonists: Peng and Wang. Both spoke strongly about aspects related to family. Peng indicated that he would return to China because his son was there, and he did not want to bring him back to Italy. He preferred to move back to China and be with his child. "It's comforting for him to live in China, and it's better. Some people say it's better to live in Italy, some people say it's better to live in China. Lily and I think the child should stay in China, study in China, and go to boarding school." Indeed, Peng and Lily did return to China.[6]

Wang, Prato's long-standing entrepreneur, pointed to the influence on children who are primarily raised in Italy and the difficulty such young people have upon return to China. Their networks in China become relatively thin due to having grown up in Italy. He also pointed to health and the environment. Finally, in terms of simply transferring cut-and-sew shops to China, there was the problem of fashion changing so quickly that it would already be out of style when it arrived back in Italy and was unloaded from ships to be transported to markets in Europe. (Air transport was cost prohibitive.) Thus, fast fashion continued to be produced in Italy largely by migrant labor. Wang had no intention of leaving Prato. "Italian culture. And then it's serious when our children return to China: they no longer know anything, they cannot do anything. That's the truth. And then it's something serious when they return to China: the sky is always gray. No, you cannot go back to China."

Taken as a whole, prominent themes mark these responses: the economic situation, the legal status of migrants, a firm's or individual's capability, and even lifestyle issues such as air quality and social networks. Elsewhere, they spoke about their children's education and overall well-being. Many migrants talked about the bureaucratic difficulty of changing residence status because it also required a work certificate, something some employers might be reluctant to provide if, for example, they have been employing undocumented workers or if workers do not have a designated residence because they may be living in the factory or crowded into an apartment. Such situations would be a violation of Italian legal codes and thus create a strategy to dodge the eyes of authorities.

## Cosmologies of Fast Fashion

Migrants' live-in-the-present sensibility suggests a particular orientation to the world—a specific ontological presence of uncertainty. Dare I invoke the concept of cosmology? The term conjures up enchanted worldviews, as Sahlins (2000) and Chu (2010) forcefully noted. It would hardly seem the stuff of global capitalism with its proponents' assumptions of cold and rational calculation. I am not suggesting the migrants are irrational. I have moved beyond the rational-irrational binary to consider something enchanting at work in terms of the animating forces that propel certain humans to travel vast distances at such a great price only to work terribly hard, maybe acquire a firm, make a family along the way, and send their babies to be raised—at least for a time—far, far away. Some sort of cosmology is at work.

Sahlins's (2000, 419) masterful "Cosmologies of Capitalism" takes its inspiration from an eighteenth-century observation that "Western goods and even persons have been incorporated as indigenous powers." His essay can be read as a manifesto for taking seriously other societies' cultural integrity. It serves to critique approaches that take for granted Western-capitalist domination. He is not suggesting that we ignore this "modern juggernaut" of modernity, with its coercive forces, but that we view it as a generative cultural process that acquires meaning in the local scheme of things. Thus, the importance of continuing to pay attention to how people, whether indigenous or migrant or transient, "struggle to integrate their experience of the world system in something that is logically and ontologically more inclusive" (Sahlins 2000, 417). In Chu's (2010, 7) reckoning, Sahlins was interested in the "transposable and reciprocal nature of various non-Western schemas of value in both shaping and being shaped by capitalist encounters." These schemas of value could be related to money logics such as price, but they might also have symbolic or relational worth.

The inquiries into future orientations lay bare the many factors, desires, and situations that render action and value possible. A future world overrun with a wait-and-see uncertainty gets produced out of those structural encounters from the Wenzhou and Made in Italy models of economic development and the globalized fashion industry. Together, these economic structures are not immovable like rebar but flexible like rubber. It takes a flexible subject, willing to internalize and act on the desires of develop-man, to keep things moving. Returning home without success, without having become an entrepreneur and having accrued value, becomes another point of tension and another generative source that makes for an unknowable future. Generative tensions also create new social worlds. As Graeber (2001, 76) reminds, "society is not a thing at all: it is the total process through which this activity is coordinated, and value, in turn, the way that actors see their own activity as a meaningful part of it."

Extending this action-oriented theory of value, the act of becoming an entrepreneur thus reveals another angle to the cosmology of fast fashion. It is no mere coincidence that Wang's remarkable journey ends with an assessment of people from Wenzhou as having a certain "spiritual insistence," which figures prominently into their pursuit of becoming an entrepreneur. This spiritual insistence resonates with Sahlins's insight vis-à-vis cosmologies of capitalism—how local actors render capitalism meaningful in their own terms, in their own cultural context, and how such rendering may reveal capitalism as more crooked, more "other-than," more diverse than it seemed from a distance.

This study has looked at development from the diaspora as migrants move into the core of developed Europe and remake capitalism in their own vision but not necessarily under conditions of their own making. Still, they are agents in creating new worlds from encounters that they enable through their productive activities and transnational social networks. Social relations reveal a tight-knit, yet at times fraught, weave in the context of fashion made in Italy.

## Entrepreneurship and Diaspora

Entrepreneurship has become a fashionable strategy driving European economic policy in the aftermath of the 2008 financial crisis. Germany's chancellor Angela Merkel made clear during a visit to Italy in 2015 her view that entrepreneurs hold the promise out of crisis and into a golden future. As she reminded Italian prime minister Matteo Renzi, the German outlook was that entrepreneurs, not states, needed to promote jobs (Kramer 2015). On the global stage, and more specifically on the stage of development from the diaspora, a different entrepreneurial figure has emerged. This figure serves simultaneously as a transregional broker, a menace to small-firm entrepreneurial ideologies, and a paradoxical lifeboat to a crisis-ridden economy.

This book has demonstrated crucial ways in which Chinese entrepreneurs who energize Italy's fashion niche do not adhere to the straight scripts of a globalized economy. They challenge the global scripts in at least three ways: first, they have elaborated on an economy based on small firms; second, this dynamic niche has resulted from an ethos of hard work wherein contrasting sentiments of bitterness and "high-mindedness" animate intense work rhythms; and third, a systematic reliance on relations of reciprocity in the form of global households has sustained the fast-fashion industry.

The characteristics of migrant entrepreneurs parallel those with citizen entrepreneurs in terms of a commitment to hard work, a tendency to take risks, a drive to make money, and a desire for autonomy. A widespread view among the Chinese migrants is that there is little point in migrating only to spend a life working for someone else; the point is to become your own firm owner. This quest for autonomy and this dedication to hard work resonates with the Italian experience, as expressed in the accounts of Antonio and Letizia, who noted that Italians themselves were like the Chinese in terms of their hard work and self-exploitation. French fashion magazines during 1978–80 documented the conditions, describing Prato as Italian Hong Kong to characterize the hideous working conditions that Italians endured as the economy boomed and they propelled it forward with their sweat, blood, and severed hands. Today, assumptions underlying those of European leaders who call for entrepreneurial energies conjure up images of clean, law-abiding, high-tech companies. The policy makers wear blinders that render out of sight the actual necessities that global capitalism creates. The "free market" faithful thereby render invisible the hard work of migrant workers–cum–entrepreneurs and the organizational forms that manifest: upon close consideration, these forms have striking heterogeneous elements. As actors within larger global systems, migrants juggle multiple forces, which are often capitalistic but are not limited to purely capitalist ones, as they also incorporate gift economy and other noncapitalist principles.

## Absolutely Interdependent

In *Tight Knit*, I have examined how the global garment industry transforms local practices and individual lives and, conversely, how local practices and individual lives create a complex social fabric. People, families, and institutions are profoundly entangled in global supply chains. Seen up close, the extensive fabric of the global economy is woven together by individuals working sixteen-hour shifts at sewing machines, arranging to have their infants raised by grandparents, and trying to maintain tight-knit families within the cutthroat competitiveness and narrow profit margins of the fast-fashion industry. Over the arc of five years, workers, entrepreneurs, activists, health-care professionals, performers, and politicians in Prato shared their experiences in formal interviews, in informal conversations, at meetings, in public spaces, and in settings such as immigration offices and hospitals.

A final poignant irony about the fallout of the tragic fire was that the funeral was held the day after the conclusion of Pitti Uomo, a major trade show in men's fashion, just twenty kilometers away in Florence. The media celebrated the show's record attendance of buyers and visitors. Renaissance palaces and light shows served as an amnesiac elixir for the global labor behind all those handsome clothes. Such collective amnesia was strategic.

Just across the highway from the evangelical church, at the Florence airport, four years earlier I had seen a fashion billboard immediately before entering airport security. The advertisement featured a male model with long stringy dark hair, pale skin, and an emaciated frame. Next to this hipster figure were two lines of text, the designer's name—Daniele Fiesoli, Italia—followed by the tag line, ABSOLUTELY MADE IN ITALY. The ad asserted authenticity to enhance the value of the Made in Italy brand.[7] As I have argued, value is rooted in historical sentiments in which garments that don the Made in Italy label benefit from association with the Renaissance. Continuity with the Florentine Renaissance is a myth but a convenient and powerful one. Even in the context of a globalized garment industry, Italian-made or -labeled fashion has shown tremendous resilience in terms of symbolizing style and good taste. The value of Made in Italy cannot be taken for granted. The label's persistent value results from common sense, yet it is not and has not always been everyone's common sense.

In a globalized world, assertions of authenticity such as "absolutely Made in Italy" take on heightened significance and stakes. The assertion of the authentic brand taps into historic sentiment and thus enhances value. A less obvious consequence is the erasure of the conditions of labor, which include transregional flows of raw materials, commodities, labor, and children. The apparel industry has witnessed tremendous global restructuring. Indeed, the textile and clothing industry is iconic in terms of globalization.

After the global financial collapse of capitalism, new political imaginings flourished. In the Italian context, a large portion of migrant labor forces work in the "illegal" economy, rendering them largely disenfranchised from civil society political engagement. This lack of engagement related to worker struggles has been a source of consternation for many Italians. It blocks building an international movement for worker rights if those involved are unwilling or unable to join in the struggle. The migrants themselves are caught in many binds, and they know it well. Rights are not free. Costs are involved in making a small factory comply with health and safety laws. Moving workers out of factory spaces into residential dwellings costs. All of the costs cut into the small competitive margins. And yet lives are at stake.

Security issues, whether to protect or crackdown on foreign residents, will undoubtedly continue to be a major issue of policy and politics in the future given the ongoing presence of various immigrants and refugees seeking work or asylum in Europe. Imagining planetary human solidarity is essential, but realizing it remains a cosmological dream.

Before his death, Fernando Coronil published an essay about the leftward turn in Latin American politics and imaginaries. He took inspiration from these movements, likening the past to "embers" and the future to "poetry," and believing in the power of people to imagine "worlds free from the horrors of history." He recognized the uneven terrain of politics. His optimism was cautious: "But as long as people find themselves without a safe and dignified home in the world, utopian dreams will continue to proliferate, energizing struggles to build a world made of many worlds, where people can dream their futures without fear of waking up."[8]

Will Italy continue to hold its place in the global fashion world? Will Prato emerge as a crown jewel of globalization? Will the crisis of presence continue to be a disorienting force that unmakes the world? Or through political imagination and actions based on solidarity will dignified new worlds be realized? Through employing the illuminating force of ethnographic encounters in one transnational locality, my hope is that I have contributed, albeit imperfectly, to grasping how individuals, families, institutions, and communities cope with globalization and struggle to create a meaningful and dignified present and future.

# Acknowledgments

I was once scolded for thanking an Italian friend. It's a distant memory. I recall feeling a jolt of shame. Later, she explained her view that a friend should not say thank you. Rather, the better way to thank someone was through a reciprocal act. Perhaps her view was esoteric. But recently, a fortysomething Italian man expressed a similar sentiment: "Friendship is based on reciprocity." The fact that there was no time limit on when you could repay a favor, gift, or meal sometimes made me uneasy. Fieldwork taught me patience in many things, including ways to show appreciation. Having been brought up by Depression-era parents who were driven to achieve class standing through working hard and buying the good life, and then having encountered principles of an old world gift economy, I changed how I saw the world and what I wanted from my life.

In no small sense, the painstaking work I have put into writing this book over the course of five years is a form of giving back to all the people who shared their stories and interpretations for this project. I feel deeply obliged to them. This sense of obligation has driven me and made me feel that this long-term project has been the right place to focus my attention when there were numerous other places or platforms where I might have directed my energy. In many ways, my commitment to ensure that the book would find its way into the world represents a form of intellectual reciprocity. I take some solace, therefore, in the fact that I am not at liberty to name all of the Chinese and Italian individuals who participated in this project. I hope they will value my follow-through with the book itself as acknowledgment of my sincere appreciation for their countless contributions.

Deciding to commit myself to this research direction stemmed from my energizing collaboration with Mari Casteñeda and our brainchild, Mellon

Mutual Mentoring for Mid-Career Women Associate Faculty, an initiative at the University of Massachusetts (UMass) Amherst during 2009–10. The Center for Teaching and Faculty Development hosted our monthly meetings, and the center's ever-nurturing director, Mary Deane Sorcinelli, fearlessly guided our crew through stormy times at our institution. I hold on to the inspiration from colleagues: Michelle Budig, Laetitia La Follette, Lisa Saunders, Erica Scharrer, Banu Subramaniam, as well as guest Joya Misra. My mutual mentor Nancy Folbre's words of advice—to pursue an authentic research agenda—resonate to this day.

The European Field Studies Program of the UMass Department of Anthropology supported project development through my role as field supervisor during 2010–11 as part of the National Science Foundation (NSF) International Experience for Students, "Cultural Heritage in European Societies and Spaces" (Award OISE-098575), and thanks are due to my colleagues Krista Harper and Jacqueline Urla for their diligence in securing funding for our field studies program, which will celebrate its fiftieth anniversary in 2019–20. The seven years of the grant also enjoyed a partnership with the Universitat de Barcelona, and gratitude is due to Susana Narotzky for the warmth and intellect she brought to synergistic international workshops.

The research design was fostered through my participation in a Short Course on Research Methods in Cultural Anthropology funded by the NSF and held at the Duke Marine Laboratory in July 2010. My thanks to methods guru Russell Bernard as well as instructors Lance Gravlee and Amber Wutich, with whom in 2015 and 2016 I co-taught the weeklong course.

Securing funding was made possible due to crucial support from the UMass Center for Research on Families (CRF), where I was a family research scholar during 2011–12. My faculty cohort provided helpful feedback on early proposal drafts. Assistance with proposal preparation from CRF staff, especially Director Sally Powers and Associate Director Wendy Varner, was invaluable, as was their manual for newbie principal investigators, "I'm a PI, Now What?"

Funding came from the NSF, "Chinese Immigration and Family Encounters in Italy" (BCS 1157218), spanning 2012–16. I am deeply grateful to Laura Ahearn, Jeffrey Mantz, and Deborah Winslow, directors of the Cultural Anthropology Program. On behalf of UMass graduate student Ying Li, an NSF Research Experience for Graduate Students (REG) supplemented costs for the related project "Diasporic Heritage and Overseas Chinese." The Wenner-Gren Foundation funded an International Collaborative Research Grant, "Tight Knit: Familistic Encounters in a Fast-Fashion District" (ICRG-114) to me and co-applicant Massimo Bressan, president of IRIS, Strumenti e Risorse per lo Sviluppo Locale (Instruments and Resources for Local Development). Bressan and I also co-organized an Italian version of Qualitative Text Analysis with MAXQDA in July 2014, and thanks to Eugenio De Gregario, who facilitated, and to Wenner-Gren for support; Rita Romagnoli of IRIS was indispensible for logistics, and the Circolo San Paolo for provisioning us with space and food. As Bressan says, diaspora has brought us together, and for that we are grateful.

For fieldwork, vital permissions were secured from Valentina Sardi of the Servizio Immigrazione e Cittadinanza of the Comune di Prato and Marco Armellini of the Unità Funzionale Salute Mentale Infanzia e Adolescenza of USL 4, Prato's public health agency. Transnational research assistance was invaluable in fieldwork, interviews and transcription from Fangli Xu and Xioayun Liao in Prato, with additional translation and/or coding assistance from Hollis Brashear, Breanne Lamont, Melody Li, Ying Li, Chloe Morse, and John Murray, all UMass students. Andrea Malaguti's advanced Italian composition course was nothing short of transformative. Ad hoc help with translations of a sensitive or nuanced nature was possible due to the generosity of Claudia Chierichini and Luciana Fellin. Sara Iacopini tirelessly coded interviews with Italian health-care professionals. Roberta Cimenti provided careful transcription assistance of Italian interviews. Mackenzie Jackson's research assistance early in the project was enriching as was her and Mica Reel's reading of the manuscript at its tail end.

Friends from various walks of life helped keep me safe and sane, offering company, meals, humor, housing, and insight while in Italy: Adolfo Agostini, Graziano Bracciotti, Sergio Citerni, Giovanni Contini, Francesco De Ninno, Gemma De Ninno, Elisabetta Gironi, "Il Gringo," Rita Liberti, Stefania Martini, Stellina Migaldi, Aldobrando Migaldi, Federico Migaldi, Stefano Renna, and Paola Vannuccini.

For the Digital Storytelling Workshop: Iacopini and Massimo Tofanelli coordinated behind the scenes. Amy Hill of the StoryCenter facilitated, kept participants on track, and offered a sensitive hand in the final production phase to finish everyone's digital stories per their vision. Funding from the Progetto Prato of Regione Toscana was essential. Staff at the Circolo San Paolo offered gracious hospitality. I am obliged to Aline Gubrium through a separate collaboration, "Hear Our Stories: Diasporic Youth for Sexual and Reproductive Health," for exposing me to the power of digital stories to change narratives and build solidarity.

I am indebted to the National Humanities Center (NHC) for inviting me to spend a sabbatical year in North Carolina as a residential fellow. Endorsements from Lynn Morgan, Alan Swedlund, and Susan Terrio helped make it possible as did support from Tom Leatherman, then-chair of my department. The center and its staff provided a nurturing environment that forced me out of my disciplinary silo. Staff planned uplifting and fun events, including bluegrass barbecues. I wish to thank in particular Elizabeth "Cassie" Mansfeld for leadership; Lois Whittington for pretty much everything logistical; Thomas Reed for culinary reinforcements; Joel Elliott for growth in information technology; Karen Carroll Cave for valuable copyediting; Brooke Andrade, Sarah Harris, and Eliza Robertson for making the acquisition of reference materials one of life's simple pleasures; and Marsha Thomas for nurturing a group of us with Pilates.

The shaping of the manuscript benefited from dialogue with colleagues from diverse disciplines in the social sciences and humanities, ranging from anthropology, philosophy, political science, history, economics, and sociology to business, psychology, public health, classics, art history, and literature. Two of the chapters were discussed in working groups that my NHC cohort formed around shared interests. An early draft of the chapter "Integration" benefitted from feedback of members in the "History, Race & the State Group": Luis Cárcamo-Huechante, Sylvia Chong, Julie Green, Cindy Hahamovitch, Anna Krylova, Charlie McGovern, and Martin Summers. Members in the "Knowledges and Contexts Group" read a draft of "Checkup," and I am grateful to them: Lynn Festa, Andrew Jewett, Michael Lurie, Charles McGovern, Scott Nelson, Jane Sharp, Holly Smith, Noel Sugimura, Martin Summers, and Carol Symes. Their detailed readings and insightful comments gave me the gifts of intellectual stimulation and support when I particularly needed it. The chapter "Money" received careful readings from fellow fellows Lurie and Christian de Pee, whose historical depth of China was especially valuable. Simone Caron and Ian Taplin, cochairs of the Social Science Research Seminar at Wake Forest University, provided me a context to engage with seminar participants and discuss an early draft of "Value." That chapter benefited from sources from Vernon Hyde Minor as well as Andrade, who went above and beyond to secure hard-to-obtain archival materials, which arrived in the mail months after I completed my residency.

Presenting work in progress was vital, and at different phases of the project, I participated in intimate workshop, seminar, or symposium settings. As I was shifting to this new topic, I was grateful to accept an invitation from Susan Terrio, who organized "Undocumented and Unaccompanied Children: Building Bridges among Academics, Activists, and Practitioners," at Radcliffe Institute of Harvard University in June 2009. Winnie Wong asked me to present at the Shenzhen + China, Utopias + Dystopias at the Massachusetts Institute of Technology in March 2011. Narelle Mcauliffe helped organize the Sixth

Chinese in Prato and Fourth Wenzhouese Diaspora Symposia, "Chinese Migration, Entrepreneurship, and Development in the New Global Economy," October 2013, at Monash University, Prato. Giovanna Ugo arranged for Bressan and me to present preliminary findings to health-care professionals at a continuing education session, *Famiglie flessibili nell'economia globale: Il movimento dei bambini cinesi tra i poli della migrazione, le ripercussioni sulla presa in carico del bambino cinese nella Salute Mentale Infanzia e Adolescenza di Prato*, Sala delle Vele, USL 4, Prato, July 2013. Renata Sardi coordinated the *Seminario di Etnospicologia: Per una clinica contemporanea dei bambini e degli adolescent* at the Istituto degli Innocenti—Salone Brunelleschi, in Florence in May 2015. Lisa Björkman and Nellie Chu included me in "The Entrepreneur and the Broker: Mediating Transregional Flow, Scale, and Belonging," a workshop of the CETREN Transregional Research Network at Georg August University in Göttingen, Germany, in January 2016. Philip Kraeger and Kaveri Qureshi invited me to join a workshop on the Anthropological Demography of Health at the Institute of Social and Cultural Anthropology as part of the Fertility and Reproduction Studies Group at Oxford University in March 2017.

I presented papers at a variety of professional conferences, and I would like to acknowledge the organizers of those sessions for inviting me. At the Annual Meeting of the American Anthropological Association: Vanessa Fong put together "Transnational Migration and Family Decision Making" in San Francisco in November 2012; Nellie Chu and I co-organized "Along the Crossroads of Flexible Kin and Flexible Labor: Performing Gender and Envisioning Future Collectivities" in Chicago in November 2013; Cati Coe and Pamela Feldman-Savelsberg spearheaded "Governance, Transnational Migration, and Affective Circuits," in Washington, DC, in December 2014; Susana Narotzky and I co-organized "Temporalities in Ethnographic Fieldwork: Dealing with Past and Future in the European Crisis," in Denver in November 2015; Anouk de Koning invited me to serve as discussant on the panel "The Politics of Parenting and Citizenship" also in 2015. At the International Conference of Europeanists of the Council for European Studies: Carolyn Sargent organized "Immigrant Exclusion and Belonging in Europe: State Policies, Personal Politics," in Boston in March 2012. At the meeting of the Society for Applied Anthropology: Amber Wutich and Melissa Beresford organized "Rethinking Development from Below: Post, Neo, or Nothing New?" in Pittsburgh in March 2015.

These interlocutors continue to remind me of the importance of cultivating community. Thanks to Felicity Aulino and Jen Sandler for organizing the integrative faculty seminar on "Community, Economy, Health: Overcoming

Ideological Righteousness for Individual, Social, and Ecological Wellbeing," in May 2016 through the Five College Program in Culture, Health, and Science. Thank you as well to engaging conversations with graduate students and colleagues: Sonya Atalay, Emiliana Cruz, Ana del Conde, Julie Hemment, Dana Johnson, Rodrigo Lazo, Milena Marchesi, Ventura Pérez, Anurag Sharma, Boone Shear, Lynnette Sievert, Berra Topcu, and Lauren Woodard. Give-and-take rests at the heart of intellectual work.

To finish the writing, in May 2017 I attended the UMass Institute for Teaching Excellence and Faculty Development's one-day Offsite Faculty Writing Retreat, which included a workshop with Cathy Luna. Over the years, in that context, Peter Elbow's thoughts on writing have been nothing short of inspirational. Jennifer Hamilton, director of the Five College Women's Studies Research Center, arranged a four-day writing retreat, and the focused determination of two dozen participants instilled a sense of collective purpose. Thanks to Nina Scott for keeping the Beyond Reproduction writing and mentoring group going until its end.

Working with the University of Chicago Press has been a delight, and I extend gratitude to T. David Brent for his enthusiasm in the acquisition phase, Dylan Montanari for his logistical oversight, and Priya Nelson for her editorial curating. Two anonymous readers offered thoughtful reviews. Michael Herzfeld revealed his identity and thus I can thank him for his sage and detailed comments. Of course, the responsibility for shortcomings remain my own. Gratitude is due to the Publication Subvention Program at UMass Amherst, including the Office of Research and Engagement, the College of Social and Behavioral Sciences, and the Department of Anthropology. Portions of chapter 3 previously appeared in my article "The Value of Money: A Fresh Glimpse of Globalization and the Case of Prato," in *Prato Storia & Arte* 117 (June 2015): 100–10, by the Fondazione Cassa Risparmio di Prato. Other parts were published in my article "'Fistful of Tears': Encounters with Transnational Affect, Chinese Immigrants, and Italian Fast Fashion," in *Cambio* 5, no. 10 (2015): 27–40 in a special issue on Work and Difference, edited by Massimo Bressan and Sebastiano Ceschi. Portions of chapter 6 were accepted for publication from my and Bressan's coauthored article, "Circulating Children, Underwriting Capitalism: Chinese Global Households and Italian Fast Fashion," forthcoming in *Current Anthropology*. Sections of chapter 8 were accepted for publication from my and Bressan's coauthored article, "Via Gramsci: Hegemony and Wars of Position in the Streets of Prato," in the *International Gramsci Journal* 2, no. 3 (2017): 31–66.

I cannot conclude without recognizing my immediate family members: Chris Brashear, a.k.a. fiddlindoc, offered unwavering love, patience, and musical art; my daughter, Hollis, brought creativity to our conversations and was an ever-unflappable sounding board; and my son, Luca, surprised me with his curiosity about medical anthropology and, given his complaints about my computer usage, amused me with his question about when I had written the book! My mother, Marian Krause, an oil painter, sustained my spirit with her generous reading of an early version of the "Value" chapter and her report of becoming engrossed in its storyline. My father, Jack Krause, the son of an immigrant, nurtured my love of a good story with bighearted sharing of his gift of storytelling. For my three sisters, I am grateful for the memories we have made through apple pie. Thank you all for putting up with my enduring desire to honor reciprocity.

# Notes

## Introduction

1. See Rachel Donadio, "Chinese Remake the 'Made in Italy' Fashion Label," *New York Times*, September 12, 2010, http://www.nytimes.com/2010/09/13/world/europe/13prato.html?pagewanted=all&_r=0.

2. For a study of readymade in the art world, see Wong (2013).

3. Such logics are clear in efforts to democratize and demystify investment strategies (Sharma 2016).

4. The crane was known in Chinese mythology for its immortality. *Bamboo and Cranes* by Bian Jingzhao, for example, is a famous image. For more on the role of birds in Chinese mythology, see Yang and An (2005).

5. Such differences in price points contradict typical laws of supply and demand; economists refer to these as Veblen goods (Veblen and Chase 1934).

6. For another interpretation of scale, see Lan (2015).

## Chapter One

1. For a case of how human rights discourse in France came to be used against immigrants, see Ticktin (2011), chapter 5, "Armed Love: Against Modern Slavery, against Immigrants."

2. A review of literature using the term *encounter* suggests a Self and an Other across contexts, including conflicts (Bargal 2004), tourism (Khandelwal 1996), popular culture (Richards 2005), customer-shopkeeper relations (Ryoo 2005), and medical contexts (Giordano 2011; Mattingly 2008; Zhan 2009).

3. Laura Nadar made this suggestion as a discussant during the panel "Engaging Possibilities beyond the Academy: The Role of Anthropology in Community-Based and Activist Research," on which I copresented a paper, at the American Anthropological Association, November 22, 2014, Chicago. See also Nadar (2011).

4. For recent examples of edited volumes that promote the case for ethnography as a mode of knowledge production, see Borneman and Hammoudi (2009) and Waterston and Vesperi (2009) and a comparative review Krause (2012a).

5. For a discussion of practices of representation that can deceive, see Metcalf (2002).

6. Graeber (2001, 66) notes that most people are "unlikely to fully grasp the principles underlying their own most sophisticated forms of action."

7. Critical works include Clifford (1994), Fabian (1983), Malkki (1995), Wolf (1982).

8. In addition to being the name of a children's fable, a famous boutique hotel in Moscow, and a popular Korean television series (transmitted in China), the Golden Apple SRL was a Chinese fast-fashion firm that opened, liquidated, closed, and reopened numerous times between 2005 and 2007. The story of this firm begins a chapter about the district's underground economy (Pieraccini 2010, 52).

9. On social and structural change, see Barbagli (1984), Becattini (1986), Cento Bull and Corner (1993), Gaggio (2007), Marcus (2005), Silverman (1968). On the relatively recent Chinese migration, see Ceccagno (2003, 2009), Pieke et al. (2004).

10. John Hooper, "Made in Little Wenzhou, Italy: The Latest Label from Tuscany," *The Guardian*, November 17, 2010, http://www.theguardian.com/world/2010/nov/17/made-in-little-wenzhou-italy. See also Poggioli (2011).

11. For examples in different contexts, see Castañeda (2008), Chavez (2008), Folbre (2010), Ginsburg and Rapp (1995), Johnson-Hanks (2006), Sargent (2006).

12. Sam Borden, "Another Victim of Global Financial Crisis: Professional Soccer Players," *New York Times*, March 24, 2014, http://www.nytimes.com/2014/03/24/sports/soccer/pro-soccer-players-are-victims-of-global-financial-crisis.html?_r=0. For the demographic swath of the population under twenty-four, unemployment rates reached 57 percent in Greece, 56 percent in Spain, and 40 percent in Italy. Liz Alderman, "Young and Educated in Europe, but Desperate for Jobs," *New York Times*, November 15, 2013, http://www.nytimes.com/2013/11/16/world/europe/youth-unemployement-in-europe.html.

## Chapter Two

1. Matt Serba, "What Is Pitti Uomo, Anyway?" *GQ*, June 19, 2013, http://www.gq.com/fashion-shows/blogs/fashion-week/2013/06/what-is-pitti-uomo-anyway.html. See the main website for Pitti Immagine, http://www.pittimmagine.com/en/corporate/fairs.html.

2. Pseudonyms are used throughout the book for research participants.

3. Interview no. 57, April 3, 2013.

4. On our return to Prato later that afternoon, a scuffle broke out in broad daylight on the sidewalk right in front of us. We looked up just as one man ripped a gold chain off the other man's neck and took off running. The aggressor appeared to be African; the victim appeared to be Chinese. It was a story we heard over and over again.

5. Interview no. 57, April 3, 2017.

6. Graeber's (2001) insightful discussion of value devotes a great deal of attention to Mauss and the scholarship as well as activism that his work generated. Godelier (1999) offered new insights in his reading, focusing on sacred objects that are not exchanged. Feminist anthropologists applied a gendered lens to Malinowski's observations (Strathern 1988; Weiner 1976).

7. In public, Malinowski defended the Trobrianders, but in private he slipped into loathing them, and this came to light with the publication of his private diaries, which tarnished his reputation (Geertz 1988).

8. For a rereading of Malinowski's work and a discussion of its significance to the discipline of anthropology, see Sykes (2005), especially chapter 3, "Gathering Thoughts in Fieldwork," pp. 38–58.

9. References to kula goods as gifts appear frequently in Malinowski's discussion (pp. 91, 95–96).

10. Historians of fashion or economics use similar adjectives to describe qualities associated with the Made in Italy brand (Belfanti n.d.; Paris 2010; Paulicelli 2001; White 2000).

11. This event is also discussed in Settembrini (1994, 485–87).

12. Belfanti (pp. 18–19) offers detailed descriptions of the press accounts.

13. *The Italian Metamorphosis, 1943–1968*, was sponsored by Moda Made in Italy at the Guggenheim Museum in 1994–95, and as Ugo Calzoni, chairman of the Italian Trade Commission expressed in the catalog's frontispiece, these decades marked a "great period of production . . . that gave rise to the phenomenon 'Made in Italy,' in which fashion and design have been the standard bearers" (Celant et al. 1994).

14. See, for example, the scholarship generated from influential books such as *The Invention of Tradition* (Hobsbawm and Ranger 1983), *Imagined Communities* (Anderson 1991), or *The Great Arch* (Corrigan and Sayer 1985), or the landmark article "Notes on the Difficulty of Studying the State" (Abrams 1988).

15. For a discussion of the historic image of the peasant in Italy and the stigma associated with the peasant past, there is ample literature (Banfield 1958; Krause 2005a; Levi 2000; Silverman 1968).

16. Eco's essay, "You Must Remember This . . ." appears in Celant et al. (1994).

17. For the adoption of American methods of production, see Zamagni (1995).

18. There is a rich literature on Prato's economic history, especially the postwar period (Absalom et al. 1997; Becattini 1997, 2001).

19. See Merlo and Polese on the geography of fashion and how Milan became the hub.

20. *Burlington Magazine*, more than one hundred years old, bills itself as the "journal of record for all those who want to keep up with new ideas and thinking on art and art history," http://www.burlington.org.uk/.

21. CRIA, "What Measures for the Relief of Florence Have Been Taken Other Than CRIA," Syracuse University Archives.

22. CRIA Newsletter, December 5, 1966. Syracuse University Archives.

23. CRIA Newsletter, May 4, 1967. Syracuse University Archives.

24. CRIA Archive, December 20, 1967. Syracuse University Archives.

25. The papers of the Committee to Rescue Italian Art are held in several different locations. See the following: the Committee to Rescue Italian Art (CRIA) Records, 1966–68, Kentucky Digital Library, http://kdl.kyvl.org/catalog/xt7wdb7vn346/guide.

26. CRIA, Release No. 23, May 18, 1967. Syracuse University Archives.

27. CRIA, Release No. 17, May 2, 1967. Syracuse University Archives.

28. CRIA, Release No. 23, May 18, 1967. Syracuse University Archives.

29. CRIA, Release No. 8, February 6, 1967. Syracuse University Archives.

30. CRIA, Release No. 11, February 17, 1967. Syracuse University Archives.

31. CRIA Newsletter, May 4, 1967. Syracuse University Archives.

32. CRIA, April 25, 1967. Syracuse University Archives.

33. Many American students have spent a semester or more of their young adulthood in Italy learning about the Renaissance and acquiring quotidian knowledge on food and fashion. In 1984, I, too, was one of those students, having participated in the "Arts of London and Florence" program, sponsored by the Associated Colleges of the Midwest. When my parents came to visit, my mother was so taken by the beauty of Florence that she subsequently enrolled in a university art program back home and graduated at age sixty with a BFA in painting. By 2003, Italy was the second leading destination of study abroad students and remained in the number two

position in 2011–12 (Institute of International Education, "opendoors 2013 'Fast Facts,'" http://opendoors.iienetwork.org/?p=69735). The leading destination country was England, which means that Italy was the leading non-English-language destination for study abroad. See Kelly Jones's (2007) novel *The Lost Madonna*, based on how experience as a mud angel influenced a character's life and career. Footage of the flood is also available in this excerpt from the Italian series, *The Best of Youth*, https://www.youtube.com/watch?v=SRdxLWyoGRc.

34. CRIA, Syracuse Students for Florence Relief Committee, Syracuse University Archives.

35. Nearly all of the accounts mention Cimabue's *Crucifix*. This passage is from Judge (1967, 4).

36. CRIA, Syracuse University Archives.

37. CRIA Newsletter, December 5, 1966. Syracuse University Archives.

38. CRIA, Release No. 15, April 30, 1967. Syracuse University Archives.

39. Source of the data is Istat, Censimento generale dell'industria e del commercio, Rome. Even though it is well known that many small firms operated *al nero*, in other words, without being officially registered or without registering every family member who lent a hand, the numbers are a good indication. Numerous industrial artisans operating mechanized and computerized looms in small workshops registered their firms through the artisans' union.

40. Repercussions to the Cultural Revolution resonate as interest in Confucian philosophy gains official party and unofficial popular appeal as discussed in a "Letter from Beijing" in the *New Yorker* (Osnos 2014). For a comparative history of China in relation to the West, see Belfanti (2008), and for an ethnography of contemporary fashion in China, see Zhao (2013).

## Chapter Three

1. Interview no. 18, December 1, 2012.

2. Sahlins cites Codere (1950, 82) who had summarized an extensive study of official documents: "it is as though Kwakiutl were able to exploit the new culture to their own ends."

3. The director of a supermarket repeated this stereotype based on a run on watermelons that reportedly happened each summer (Brandi and Iacopini 2013).

4. Interview no. 18, December 1, 2012.

5. See also Liu (1992), who observed that Wenzhouese made up 83 percent of all Zhejiang immigrants in Europe. Tomba (1999, 281) placed the estimate at 90 percent of Chinese in Tuscany being from Wenzhou.

6. Liu (1992, 702) cites a 1984 study of merchandise that Wenzhou sales agents carried with them: hardware and appliances (28%), polyacrylic-fiber clothing (22.5%), plastic bags (18.5%), aluminum badges and placards (7.5%), fabrics (7.5%), buttons and watchbands (5.5%), and so forth.

7. By the late 1980s, there were "about a dozen major specialized towns scattered throughout Wenzhou" (Tan 1991, 212).

8. Interview no. 16, November 22, 2012.

9. Interview no. 22, December 6, 2012.

10. The data for Prato derive from 2009 annual records. The apparel industry data in Wenzhou Municipality is from 2008.

11. For a history of early outsourcing among straw weavers, see Pescarolo (1988). For a popular description of globalizing forces related to the garment industry, see Timmerman (2012).

12. For a comparison, see Dunn (2004, 60–69).

13. The Casa del Popolo in Carmignano is named 11 Giugno 1944 in honor of the day when four young partisans died after bombing a Nazi train loaded with explosives en route to Prato and its textile factories.

14. Interview no. 10, October 25, 2012.

15. Interview no. 11, October 25, 2012.

16. Interview no. 16, November 22, 2012.

17. Interview no. 17, November 22, 2012.

18. Interview no. 19, December 1, 2012.

19. Interview no. 23, December 6, 2012.

20. Interview no. 34, January 24, 2013.

21. Interview no. 31, January 16, 2013.

22. Interview no. 19, December 1, 2012.

23. Interview no. 18, December 1, 2012.

## Chapter Four

1. Interview no. 54, August 6, 2012.

2. A catalog includes images of the five sculptures donated by the artist's heir, Teresa B. Martini, together with the Commune of Carmignano, as well as images of additional sculptures and paintings from the exhibit. The four other donated sculptures were *Alcea, Natura, La Pioggia,* and *Gallo* (Martini, Androsov, and Gosudarstvennyĭ Ėrmitazh [Russia] 2013).

3. Luigi Tomba indicated in 1999 that "In Tuscany racism inspired by fear of economic competition from Wenzhou business" was not a major problem; "Chinese immigration is now generally recognized as highly valuable and is considered far less problematic in terms of social and racial tension than North African immigration" (Tomba 1999, 290). By the 2010s, fears that Florence's peripheral belt would transform into a "Chinatown" had exploded in adjacent Prato and its provincial towns. Tomba's characterization of Chinese immigrants being "associated with a positive evaluation of [their] organizational and commercial skills" seems not to have withstood the test of time.

4. Interview no. 39, July 19, 2013. A follow-up session was conducted June 3, 2015.

5. http://www.saisjournal.org/posts/italian-immigration-policies. See "Italian Immigration Laws—A Review." Legislation that regulates immigration and integration in Italy is primarily the result of two laws: the Turco-Napolitano law, which is referred to as the Single Act no. 286 of July 25, 1998, based on Law no. 40 of March 6, 1998; and Bossi-Fini law, no. 189 of July 30, 2002.

6. In Tuscany, the REC is no longer required (http://www.po.camcom.it/servizi/rec/rec .php).

7. The history of Savio's technology milestones and ownership can be seen on this time line: https://www.saviotechnologies.com/savio/en/Company-Profile/History/Pages/default.aspx.

8. Social capital theory reminds that access and use of such networks are resources with benefits to individuals (Gaggio 2007).

9. Interview no. 70, July 23, 2013.

10. Interview no. 70, July 23, 2013.

11. http://iltirreno.gelocal.it/prato/cronaca/2016/04/26/news/la-bugia-partiamo-per-la -bulgaria-1.13367037?refresh_ce.

## Chapter Five

1. A thorough description of the Parco-Museo Quinto Martini can be found in the catalog produced several years after the park's inauguration (Fagioli and Martini 1997); see p. 76 for details on *La Pioggia*, or *Rain*. The strict relationship between the observer and the work of art is discussed in relation to Martini's work in a thesis that focuses on his series of sculptures related to rain. The sculpture from the series in the museum park was completed in 1967, a year after the infamous flood in Florence. The second bronze that joined the permanent European sculpture collection at the Hermitage Museum was from the original cast. The Levi text is from an essay, "Il geroglifico dell'acqua," which appears in the introduction to an undated catalog from the exhibit, *La pioggia: sculture e disegni di Quinto Martini*, held in Florence in 1978, and cited in the thesis (Martini 2011, 10–11). The thesis author is no relation to the artist.

2. Bernard Berenson was an adviser to the Contini-Bonacossi family, which Dan Hofstadter describes as "the last Italian dealer-collectors on a grand scale" in a popular review of five of his favorite books dealing with Italian fascism (Berenson 1952; Hofstadter 2013). A short history of the count can be found on lootedart.com: The Central Registry of Information on Looted Cultural Property 1933–1945, http://www.lootedart.com/MFEU4H36531_print;Y. A brief story about the family history also appears in Krause (2005b).

3. Interview no. 69, July 10, 2013. When the doctor arrived in 2005 as Prato district's new director of infant and adolescent mental health, he was charged with reorganizing a fragmented range of services and creating a client-centered unit.

4. A robust literature in medical anthropology frames the interactions between doctors and patients as "encounters" (Mattingly 2008; O'Neil 1989). Much of this work has been concerned with compliance and noncompliance—for example, Ito's (1999) work with Vietnamese patients diagnosed with asymptomatic tuberculosis.

5. Translation is from a chapter on "Ethnographic Humanism" (1977, 409–41).

6. Li (1999a, 188) describes Wenzhouese as an "incomprehensible dialect," and even speakers label it the "devil's language." Such characterizations are evidence of widespread prejudice among Mandarin speakers against Wenzhouese.

7. The new citizenship laws were still at the level of debate at the time of this writing. See http://libcom.org/blog/new-italians-old-racists-current-italian-debate-citizenship-laws-20052013.

8. Interview no. 31, January 16, 2013.

9. Interview no. 68, July 3, 2013.

10. The pillow in the hospital had the same shape as the popular American-made Boppy nursing pillow. See http://www.boppy.com/our-story/.

11. The idea of the medical gaze has shaped numerous studies in critical medical anthropology. For an influential, in my case life-changing, example, see Martin (1987).

12. Interview no. 41, July 24, 2013.

13. Interview no. 35, January 2013.

14. Tuscany for Sustainable Tourism, see the Museum Laboratory of Terrigoli, http://www.turismo.intoscana.it/site/en/highlights/415dc302–25bc-11e3–9935–495d93063fdb/. Prato's famous regenerated wool industry traces its roots to the Bisenzio Valley (Becattini 1997).

15. Fangli had also respected this tradition when she gave birth to her son, her second child, although she stayed in her own home and relied on both her Chinese mother and Italian mother-in-law to help her. I went to visit her in her Florence apartment when I returned for additional fieldwork in March 2013.

16. Interview no. 31, January 16, 2013

17. Scholars working on breastfeeding across cultural contexts have challenged the notion of milk quality. Miriam Small (1998) has described insufficient milk syndrome as a culture-bound syndrome. For a history of pediatric advice on breastfeeding and the orientation to the clock, see Ann Millard (1990). Katherine Dettwyler (1995) has conducted biocultural research related to breastfeeding and weaning across cultures as well as nonhuman primate species. For the relationship between modernization and breastfeeding during Italy's fascist period, see Elizabeth Whitaker (2000). My work (Krause 2009) suggests that late nineteenth- and early twentieth-century straw weavers seeking wet nurse subsidies from the state was likely due more to the fact that they needed to keep working than the fact that they were lacking in milk. That research draws on archival registries and oral histories from the Commune of Carmignano and the province of Prato.

18. Interview no. 31, January 16, 2013.

## Chapter Six

1. The Chinese words were *xi wang, you yi,* and *zhong guo.*

2. This is similar to the concept of double-consciousness, which W. E. B. Du Bois (1997, 2) so powerfully described more than a century ago, that "peculiar sensation" of "always looking at one's self through the eyes of others, of measuring one's soul by the tape of a world that looks on in amused contempt and pity."

3. In Italian, Bertolino said, *"non c'è più una genitorialità possibile."* March 22, 2012, Roberto Bertolino, Psicologo, Centro Frantz Fanon, Torino, "I Figli della Migrazione, Percorsi di Crescita tra Paradossi e Nuove Forme di Cittadinanza," G. B. Mazzoni, Prato.

4. Bertolino said, *"In Italia è molto diffuso nella comunità filippina e cinese è abbastanza in vogo la pratica pericolosa, molto pericolosa, che è quella di rimandare i figli nel proprio paese."*

5. In Italian, Bertolino said, *"dobbiamo aiutare questi genitori a negoziare strategie diverse."*

6. See the polemic that arose when the first baby born in the new hospital was to a Chinese mother, http://corrierefiorentino.corriere.it/firenze/notizie/cronaca/2013/16-ottobre-2013/cinese-prima-nata-nuovo-ospedale-arrivano-offese-polemiche-rete-22234881.

7. A rich body of literature across cultural contexts speaks to issues of family-making with illuminating political economic analyses (see, e.g., Chu 2010; Coe 2014, 2016; Feldman-Savelsberg 2016; Fong 2011; Greenhalgh 2008; Hochschild, 2000; Kertzer 1993; Krause and De Zordo 2012; Leinaweaver 2008, 2013; Ni Laoire et al. 2012; Schneider and Schneider 1996; Suárez-Orozco and Todorova 2002; Watson 1975; Zhang 2001b).

8. We coded using the qualitative data analysis software MAXQDA. This chapter draws mostly from one primary code, Value of Living in Prato, and a secondary code, Circulation of Children. Subsequently, I used in vivo coding to identify nine subthemes.

9. Interview no. 5, October 11, 2012.

10. Interview no. 36, June 20, 2013.

11. Interview no. 6, October 18, 2012.

12. Interview no. 3, October 11, 2012.

13. Interview no. 50, July 26, 2012.

14. Ceccagno (2007) discusses time compression. On the craft of motherhood in the context of lowest-low Italian fertility, see Krause (2005a).

15. Interview no. 19, December 1, 2012.

16. Interview no. 1, October 6, 2012.

17. Interview no. 10, October 25, 2012.

18. Interview no. 18, December 1, 2012.

19. Interview no. 10, October 25, 2012.

20. Interview no. 19, December 1, 2012.

21. Interview no. 2, October 11, 2012.

22. Interview no. 5, October 11, 2012.

23. Interview no. 29, January 4, 2013.


## Chapter Seven

1. Biografia del Sindaco Roberto Cenni (http://www.comune.prato.it/sindaco/?act=i&fid =637&id=20090519125603982). His mayoral candidacy was backed by the following parties of a right and center coalition: Pdl, Udc, Lega, Destra, Movimento Giovani Pratesi, Liste Civiche. These acronyms stand for Il Popolo della Libertà (The People of Liberty), Unione di Centro (Union of Center), Lega Nord (Northern League), La Destra (The Right), Movimento Giovani Pratesi (Movement of Young Pratesi). See also La Pietra Dialogues of NYU, Short List of Political Parties, 2013, http://www.lapietradialogues.org/publications_det.php?id=62.

2. http://www.pratoincontra.it/resoconti/serata7/home.htm. The document was no longer accessible online as of November 12, 2013.

3. "PER LEVARE IL GIALLO BISOGNA TOGLIERE IL ROSSO," Lega Nord, Toscano. Prato's 2009 electoral campaign appears in chapter 2, "L'immigrazione cinese a Prato" (Ciardi 2013).

4. Il Tirreno, Prato, "Lunedì l'autopsia sul bimbo morto," February 12, 2011; Paolo Nencioni, Il Tirreno, Prato, "Bimbo morto, mistero sui farmaci," February 11, 2011, http://iltirreno.gelocal .it/prato/cronaca/2011/02/11/news/bimbo-morto-mistero-sui-farmaci-1.2320249; Il Tirreno, Prato, "Muore bambino cinese di 11 mesi: dubbio di un errore nei farmaci usati," February 10, 2011, http://iltirreno.gelocal.it/prato/cronaca/2011/02/10/news/muore-bambino-cinese-di-11 -mesi-dubbio-di-un-errore-nei-farmaci-usati-1.2318640; Blitz Quotidiano, "Prato, bimbo ci- nese morto: trovato un eccesso di sale nel corpo," April 3, 2011, http://www.blitzquotidiano .it/cronaca-italia/prato-bambino-cinese-morto-sale-corpo-autopsia-808169/; Il Tirreno, Prato, April 4, 2011.

5. Ethnographic case studies include Angel-Ajani (2000), Carter (1997), Cole (2009).

6. Interview no. 35, January 2013.

7. Interview no. 18, December 1, 2012.

8. This video of the dragon dance ends just before the tense moment. "Danza del dragone a Prato per capodanno cinese 2011," http://www.youtube.com/watch?v=pRbqec9nwkQ.

9. Carlandrea Poli, "Il Capodanno cinese fuori dal centro," Il Tirreno, November 13, 2011, http://iltirreno.gelocal.it/prato/cronaca/2011/11/23/news/il-capodanno-cinese-fuori-dal -centro-1.2815069.

10. The quote was from F. Federighi, "Il Capodanno cinese si farà. Niente sfilate, festa al Pecci," La Nazione, February 2, 2007.

11. "Comune di Prato, Linee Programmatiche del Sindaco Roberto Cenni, Legislatura 2009–2014," Prato, July 9, 2009: 4.

12. A report by the Center for Immigration Studies notes that only 30 of the world's 194 countries practice a form of jus soli in which they grant citizenship to children born in a coun- try regardless of the parents' legal status. See John Feere, "Birthright Citizenship in the United

States: A Global Comparison," Washington, DC: Center for Immigration Studies, 2010 (http://www.cis.org/birthright-citizenship).

13. See Rete Radié Resche di Quarrata, http://www.rrrquarrata.it/www/.

14. See "Cécile Kyenge, Ministro per l'Integrazione, in visita a Quarrata," Città di Quarrata, http://www.comunequarrata.it/flex/cm/pages/ServeBLOB.php/L/IT/IDPagina/4052.

15. The English is from Clive James's new translation (Dante Alighieri 2013).

16. Beatrice Faragli, "'Dalla mi parte l'Italia migliore,'" *Il Tirreno*, June 4, 2013. Quoted material is translated from the newspaper report as well as from my audio recording and notes.

17. Beatrice Faragli and Corrado Benzio, "Estrema destra contro la Kyenge," *Il Tirreno*, June 5, 2013, http://iltirreno.gelocal.it/pistoia/cronaca/2013/06/05/news/estrema-destra-contro-la-kyenge-1.7203607.

18. "Ius soli, arriva Kyenge la destra scende in piazza," *Il Tirreno*, June 30, 2013.

19. "Italy Racism Row: Cécile Kyenge Compared to an Orangutan," BBC News, July 14, 2013, http://www.bbc.co.uk/news/world-europe-23310837.

20. "Black Italian Minister Kyenge Suffers Banana Insult," BBC News, July 27, 2013, http://www.bbc.co.uk/news/world-europe-23480489.

21. "Racism Still Rife in Italian Football," BBC News, February 13, 2010, http://news.bbc.co.uk/2/hi/europe/8511106.stm.

22. Elisabetta Povoledo, "Slurs against Italy's First Black National Official Spur Debate on Racism," *New York Times*, June 22, 2013, http://www.nytimes.com/2013/06/23/world/europe/slurs-against-italys-first-black-national-official-spur-debate-on-racism.html.

23. For an ethnographic account based in Milan that gives attention to issues of gender, especially in relation to Muslim women, see Marchesi (2013).

24. *Il Tirreno*, February 2, 2014, http://iltirreno.gelocal.it/prato/cronaca/2014/02/06/news/sei-razzista-se-una-ragazza-cinese-di-prato-sfida-lo-xenofobo-1.8615323.

## Chapter Eight

1. http://iltirreno.gelocal.it/prato/cronaca/2014/02/20/news/ritorna-a-prato-bernardo-secchi-il-padre-della-mixite-1.8705472.

2. For a perspective on a previous initiative involving social relations and urban space, see Raffaetà and Baldassar (2015).

3. Il Museo del Tessuto is an excellent resource for the history of the textile industry in Prato, famous for the regeneration of used fibers, a niche that is receiving new attention in the context of green economy innovation. See http://www.museodeltessuto.it/.

4. Malaparte (1968, 59–60) wrote, "*poiché [I pratesi] stimano una grossa coglioneria il lavorare per gli altri . . . ognuno si adopra a lavorare per sé,*" because the Pratesi detest working for others . . . everybody strives to work for him-/herself.

5. The theater group Compagnia per l'Acquisto dell'Ottone performed a play in the piazza of Carmignano on June 11, 2013, that told the story of one of the first cultural clubs established in Prato, "Racconta da una casa del popolo," written and directed by Viviano Vannucci.

6. "Comune di Prato, Proponente: 4° Attività Economiche, 4°2 Sportello unico per attività commerciali e produttive, Ordinanza N. 2054, 07 settembre 2010, Oggetto: Ordinanza orari Macrolotto zero e vie limitrofe."

7. The court is known by its acronym Tar, Tribunale amministrativo regionale.

8. See Article 16 of Law No. 135 (http://www.camera.it/parlam/leggi/decreti/09135d.htm).

9. XIV International Architecture Exhibition, Venice Biennale, June–November 2014, Filippo De Pieri and Federico Zanfi. "Calling Home: Explorations on Domestic Change in Italy" explored houses in Italy and how Italian society was adapting to new spaces, http://www.callinghome.it/Project/; http://www.callinghome.it/Archive/Montemurlo/; https://www.youtube.com/watch?v=kWwjDm4kFxU&feature=youtu.be.

10. Trame di Quartiere: Ricucire la Memoria di San Paolo e Macrolotto 0 (http://www.pratosfera.com/2015/01/10/trame-di-quartiere-ricostruire-la-memoria-del-macrolotto-0/).

11. http://www.notiziediprato.it/news/cenni-boccia-secchi-sul-macrolotto-zero-sembra-sbarcato-da-un-astronave-aliena.

## Conclusion

1. Progetto Lavoro Sicuro (http://www.regione.toscana.it/en/progetto-lavoro-sicuro).

2. Interview no. 41, July 24, 2013.

3. La 7 Attualità 2016 Feb 2. A Prato per i cinesi la sicurezza è fai da te (https://www.youtube.com/watch?v=wFAN0SkrlPw).

4. In order of quoted text: Interview no. 6, October 18, 2012; Interview no. 12, October 25, 2012; Interview no 14, November 15, 2012, Interview no. 21, December 6, 2012; Interview no. 27, January 3, 2013.

5. In order of quoted text: Interview no. 3, October 11, 2012; Interview no. 13, October 25, 2012; Interview no. 34, January 24, 2013; Interview no. 30, January 4, 2013; Interview no. 22, December 6, 2012; Interview no. 34; Interview no. 11, October 25, 202; Interview no. 33, January 17, 2013.

6. Interview no. 18, December 1, 2012.

7. Author's photo of billboard taken in 2011. Tokatli (2013, 240) calls such strategies "enhancing reality" to refer to the "building of myths by brand-owning firms, not only around their products but also around their products' geographical associations."

8. The last lines of his essay, "The Future in Question: History and Utopia in Latin America (1989–2010)," were quoted in a memorial essay by Gary Wilder. See http://globalization.gc.cuny.edu/2011/08/in-memoriam-fernando-coronil/.

# References

Abrams, Philip. 1988. "Notes on the Difficulty of Studying the State (1977)." *Journal of Historical Sociology* 1 (1): 58–89.

Absalom, Roger, Giacomo Becattini, Gabi Dei Ottati, and Paolo Giovannini. 1997. "Il bruco e la farfalla: Ragionamenti su di un decennio di vita pratese." In *Prato, storia di una città*, 369–461. Prato, Italy: Comune di Prato; Le Monnier.

Agnoletti, Stefonia, Elena Della Schiava, Maria Donata Mazzoni, and Filippo Tattini. 2014. "Il restauro di una scultura contemporanea in bronzo: Il martinaccio, opera di Quinto Martini inserita nel complesso scultoreo dell' omonimo Parco-Museo a Seano (Prato)." *OPD Restauro: Rivista dell'Opificio delle Pietre Dure e Laboratori di Restauro di Firenze* 26: 130–40.

Anderson, Benedict R. 1991. *Imagined Communities: Reflections on the Origin and Spread of Nationalism*. New York: Verso.

Angel-Ajani, Asale. 2000. "Italy's Racial Cauldron: Immigration, Criminalization, and the Cultural Politics of Race." *Cultural Dynamics* 12 (3): 331–52.

Anon. 1967a. "Editorial: The Florentine Flood Disaster." *Burlington Magazine*, April.

Anon. 1967b. "Embattled Heritage." *Newsweek*, May 29.

Appadurai, Arjun. 1986. *The Social Life of Things: Commodities in Cultural Perspective*. Edited by Ethnohistory Workshop. Cambridge: Cambridge University Press.

Arrighetti, Alessandro, and Gilberto Seravalli. 1997. "Istituzioni e dualismo dimensionale nell'industria italiana." In *Storia del capitalismo italiano*, edited by Fabrizio Barca, 335–88. Roma: Donzelli Editore.

Asad, Talal. 1973. *Anthropology & the Colonial Encounter*. New York: Humanities Press.

Bagnasco, Arnaldo. 1992. *Tre Italie: La problematica territoriale dello sviluppo italiano*. Bologna: il Mulino.

Bagnasco, Arnaldo, and Charles F. Sabel. 1995. *Small and Medium-Size Enterprises*. London: Pinter.

Baldassar, Loretta, Graeme Johanson, Narelle McAuliffe, and Massimo Bressan, eds. 2015. *Chinese Migration to Europe: Prato, Italy, and Beyond*. New York: Palgrave Macmillan.

Balibar, Etienne. 1991. "Is There a 'Neo-Racism'?" In *Race, Nation, Class: Ambiguous Identities*, edited by Etienne Balibar and Immanuel Wallerstein, translated by Chris Turner, 17–28. London: Verso.

Bandettini, Pierfrancesco, ed. 1961. *La popolazione della Toscana dal 1810 al 1959*. Florence: Camera di Commercio, Industria e Agricultura.

Banfield, Edward C. 1958. *The Moral Basis of a Backward Society*. Glencoe, IL: Free Press.

Barbagli, Marzio. 1984. *Sotto lo stesso tetto: Mutamenti della famiglia in Italia dal XV al XX secolo*. Bologna: il Mulino.

Bargal, David. 2004. "Structure and Process in Reconciliation-Transformation Workshops." *Small Group Research* 35 (5): 596–616.

Batini, Giorgio. 1967a. *4 November, 1966: The River Arno in the Museums of Florence. Galleries, Monuments, Churches, Libraries, Archives and Masterpieces Damaged by the Flood*. Florence: Bonechi.

———. 1967b. *L'Arno in museo*. Florence: Bonechi.

Becattini, Giacomo. 1986. "Riflessioni sullo sviluppo socio-economico della Toscana in questa dopoguerra." In *Storia d'Italia/Le regioni dall'Unità a oggi. [4], [4]*, edited by Piero Bevilacqua, Valerio Castronovo, and Silvio Lanaro, 901–26. Turin: Einaudi.

———, ed. 1997. *Prato, storia di una città: Il distretto industriale (1943–1993)*. Vol. 4. Prato, Italy: Comune di Prato; Le Monnier.

———. 1998. "The Development of Light Industry in Tuscany: An Interpretation." In *Regional Development in a Modern European Economy: The Case of Tuscany*, edited by Robert Leonardi and Raffaella Nanetti, 77–94. London: Pinter.

———. 2001. *The Caterpillar and the Butterfly: An Exemplary Case of Development in the Italy of the Industrial Districts*. Florence: Felice Le Monnier.

Behar, Ruth. 1999. "Ethnography: Cherishing Our Second-Fiddle Genre." *Journal of Contemporary Ethnography* 28 (5): 472–84.

Belfanti, Carlo Marco. n.d. "Renaissance and Made in Italy: History as an Intangible Asset for the Fashion Business." Department of Social Sciences, University of Brescia.

———. 2008. *Civiltà della moda*. Bologna: il Mulino.

Bell, Emma. 2012. "Introduction." In *No Borders: Immigration and the Politics of Fear*, edited by Groupe européen d'étude sur la déviance et le contrôle social and Emma Bell, 11–24. Chambéry, France: Université de Savoie.

Benigni, Roberto, Massimo Troisi, and Cecchi Gori Home Video. 2007. *Non ci resta che piangere*. Collector's Edition. Italy: Cecchi Gori Home Video.

Berenson, Bernard. 1952. *Rumor and Reflection*. New York: Simon & Schuster.

Bernard, H. Russell, and Gery W. Ryan. 2010. *Analyzing Qualitative Data: Systematic Approaches*. Los Angeles: Sage.

Berti, Fabio, Valentina Pedone, and Andrea Valzania. 2013. *Vendere e comprare: Processi di mobilità sociale dei cinesi a Prato*. Pisa: Pacini.

Biehl, João. 2005. *Vita: Life in a Zone of Social Abandonment*. Berkeley: University of California Press.

Blim, Michael L. 1990. *Made in Italy: Small-Scale Industrialization and Its Consequences*. New York: Praeger.

Boano, Camillo, Giovanna Astolfo, and Paola Pellegrini. 2014. "On Distance and Bernardo Secchi." *Society & Space*. December 16. http://societyandspace.org/2014/12/16/on-21/.

Borneman, John, and Abdellah Hammoudi. 2009. *Being There: The Fieldwork Encounter and the Making of Truth*. Berkeley: University of California Press.

Bourdieu, Pierre. 1984. *Distinction: A Social Critique of the Judgement of Taste*. Cambridge, MA: Harvard University Press.

———. 1993. *The Field of Cultural Production: Essays on Art and Literature*. New York: Columbia University Press.

———. 2000. "Making the Economic Habitus: Algerian Workers Revisited." *Ethnography* 1 (1): 17–41.

Bracci, Fabio. 2012. "The 'Chinese Deviant': Building the Perfect Enemy in a Local Arena." In *No Borders: Immigration and the Politics of Fear*, edited by Emma Bell, 97–116. Chambéry, France: Université de Savoie.

———. 2013. "Donne straniere e servizi consultoriali nel territorio pratese." In *L'immigrazione nella Provincia di Prato: VIII Rapporto*. Prato, Italy: Provincia di Prato. www.pratomigranti.it.

Bradford, Sarah. 2000. *America's Queen: The Life of Jacqueline Kennedy Onassis*. New York: Viking.

Brandi, Enrico, and Sara Iacopini. 2013. "Dal cocomero al Suv: I consumatori cinesi a Prato." In *Vendere e comprare: Processi di mobilità sociale dei cinesi a Prato*, edited by Fabio Berti, Valentina Pedone, and Andrea Valzania, 135–220. Pisa: Pacini Editore.

Brandi, Enrico, and Andrea Sabatini. 2012. "Dossier statistico sociale 2012." Osservatorio Sociale ed Ufficio Statistica della Provincia di Prato. http://www3.provincia.prato .it/w2d3/internet/download/provprato/intranet/utenti/domini/risorse/documenti/ store—20130326120534874/Copertina+e+indice_DSS2012.pdf.

Bressan, Massimo, and Elizabeth L. Krause. 2014. "'Ho un luogo dove lavoro e un luogo dove abito.' Diversità e separazione in un distretto industriale in transizione." *Mondi Migranti* 8 (1): 59–81.

Bressan, Massimo, and Sabrina Tosi Cambini. 2009. "The 'Macrolotto 0' as a Zone of Transition: Cultural Diversity and Public Spaces." In *Living outside the Walls: The Chinese in Prato*, edited by Graeme Johanson, Russell Smyth, and Rebecca French, 149–60. Newcastle upon Tyne, UK: Cambridge Scholars Publishing.

———. 2011. *Zone di transizione: Etnografia urbana nei quartieri e nello spazio pubblico*. Bologna: il Mulino.

Brettell, Caroline. 2014. "Theorizing Migration in Anthropology: The Cultural, Social, and Phenomenological Dimensions of Movement." In *Migration Theory Talking across Disciplines*, edited by Caroline Brettell and James F. Hollifield, 148–97. Hoboken, NJ: Taylor & Francis.

Calamati, Fabio. 2014. "In 79 nei guai per i permessi facili ai cinesi." *Il Tirreno*, June 20.

Cammelli, Riccardo. 2014. *Tra i panni di rosso tinti: Appunti di storia pratese 1970–1992*. Carmignano, Italy: Attucci Editrice.

Cao, Nanlai. 2013. "Renegotiating Locality and Morality in a Chinese Religious Diaspora: Wenzhou Christian Merchants in Paris, France." *The Asia Pacific Journal of Anthropology* 14 (1): 85–101.

Cardarello, Andrea. 2015. "The Right to Have a Family: 'Legal Trafficking of Children,' Adoption and Birth Control in Brazil." In *Reproduction and Biopolitics: Ethnographies of Governance, "Irrationality" and Resistance*, edited by Silvia De Zordo and Milena Marchesi, 89–104. London: Routledge.

Carter, Donald Martin. 1997. *States of Grace: Senegalese in Italy and the New European Immigration*. Minneapolis: University of Minnesota Press.

Carter, Donald, and Heather Merrill. 2007. "Bordering Humanism: Life and Death on the Margins of Europe." *Geopolitics* 12 (2): 248–64.

Caserta, D. 2016. "L'imprenditoria straniera in Provincia di Prato." Prato, Italy: Camera di Commercio di Prato.

Caserta, D., and A. Marsden. 2013. "L'imprenditoria straniera in Provincia di Prato." Prato, Italy: Camera di Commercio di Prato.

———. 2014. "L'imprenditoria straniera in Provincia di Prato." Prato, Italy: Camera di Commercio di Prato.

Caserta, Dario, and Alessio Monticelli. 2010. "L'economia pratese nel 2009 e le prospettive per il 2010." Prato, Italy: Camera di Commercio di Prato.

Castañeda, Heide. 2008. "Paternity for Sale: Anxieties over 'Demographic Theft' and Undocumented Migrant Reproduction in Germany." *Medical Anthropology Quarterly* 22 (4): 340–59.

Castiglione, Baldassarre. 1965. *Il libro del Cortegiano*. Edited by Giulio Preti. Torino: Einaudi.

Cavanaugh, Jillian R., and Shalini Shankar. 2014. "Producing Authenticity in Global Capitalism: Language, Materiality, and Value." *American Anthropologist* 116 (1): 51–64.

Ceccagno, Antonella. 2003. "Le migrazioni dalla Cina verso l'Italia e l'Europa nell'epoca della globalizzazione." In *Migranti a Prato: Il distretto tessile multietnico*, edited by Antonella Ceccagno, 25–68. Milan: FrancoAngeli

———. 2004. *Giovani migranti cinesi: La seconda generazione a Prato*. Milan: Angeli.

———. 2007. "Compressing Personal Time: Ethnicity and Gender within a Chinese Niche in Italy." *Journal of Ethnic and Migration Studies* 33 (4): 635–54.

———. 2009. "Chinese Migrants as Apparel Manufacturers in an Era of Perishable Global Fashion: New Fashion Scenarios in Prato." In *Living outside the Walls: The Chinese in Prato*, edited by Graeme Johanson, Russell Smyth, and Rebecca French, 42–70. Newcastle upon Tyne, UK: Cambridge Scholars Publishing.

Ceccagno, Antonella, Renzo Rastrelli, and Alessandra Salvati. 2008. *Ombre Cinesi?: Dinamiche migratorie della diaspora cinese in Italia*. Rome: Carocci editore.

Celant, Germano, Solomon R. Guggenheim Museum, Kunstmuseum Wolfsburg, and Triennale di Milano. 1994. *The Italian Metamorphosis, 1943–1968*. New York: Guggenheim Museum Publications.

Cento Bull, Anna, and Paul Corner. 1993. *From Peasant to Entrepreneur: The Survival of the Family Economy in Italy*. Oxford: Berg.

Chavez, Leo R. 2008. *The Latino Threat: Constructing Immigrants, Citizens, and the Nation*. Stanford, CA: Stanford University Press.

Chossudovsky, Michel, and Andrew Gavin Marshall, eds. 2010. *The Global Economic Crisis: The Great Depression of the XXI Century*. Pincourt, QC: Global Research, Center for Research on Globalization.

Chu, Julie Y. 2006. "To Be 'Emplaced': Fuzhounese Migration and the Politics of Destination." *Identities: Global Studies in Culture and Power* 13 (3): 395–425.

———. 2010. *Cosmologies of Credit: Transnational Mobility and the Politics of Destination in China*. Durham, NC: Duke University Press.

Ciardi, Eleonora. 2013. "L'immigrazione cinese a Prato (1985–2012): Analisi storica del fenomeno, modelli politici e testimonianze." Florence: Università degli Studi di Firenze Facoltà di Lettere e Filosofia.

Clark, Robert. 2008. *Dark Water: Flood and Redemption in the City of Masterpieces*. New York: Doubleday.

Clean Clothes Campaign. 2014a. "Tailored Wages: Are the Big Brands Paying the People Who Make Our Clothes Enough to Live On?" https://cleanclothes.org/livingwage/tailoredwages.

———. 2014b. "Can You Earn a Living Wage in Fashion in Italy?" https://cleanclothes.org/resources/publications/italian-living-wage-report.

Clifford, James. 1994. "Diasporas." *Cultural Anthropology* 9 (3): 302–38.

Codere, H. 1950. *Fighting with Property: A Study of Kwakiutl Potlatching and Warfare 1792–1930.* Monographs of the American Ethnological Society 18. New York: J. J. Augustin.

Coe, Cati. 2014. *The Scattered Family: Parenting, African Migrants, and Global Inequality.* Chicago: University of Chicago Press.

———. 2016. "Orchestrating Care in Time: Ghanaian Migrant Women, Family, and Reciprocity." *American Anthropologist* 118 (1): 37–48.

Cole, Jeffrey. 2009. *The New Racism in Europe: A Sicilian Ethnography.* Cambridge: Cambridge University Press.

Collins, Jane Lou. 2003. *Threads: Gender, Labor, and Power in the Global Apparel Industry.* Chicago: University of Chicago Press.

Comaroff, John. 2011. "The End of Neoliberalism?: What Is Left of the Left." *The Annals of the American Academy of Political and Social Science* 637 (1): 141–47.

Comune di Prato. n.d. *I censimenti della popolazione: Gli abitanti di Prato dal 1861 al 2011.* http://www.comune.prato.it/prato/htm/cens.htm.

Comune di Prato. 2010. *Ordinanza orari Macrolotto Zero e vie limitrofe.* Vol. Ordinanza N. 2054.

———. 2014. "Impropria e diseducativa l'esaltazione del Macrolotto zero." Comune di Prato.

Contini, Giovanni. 1997. *La memoria divisa.* Milan: Rizzoli.

Corrigan, Philip Richard D., and Derek Sayer. 1985. *The Great Arch: English State Formation as Cultural Revolution.* Oxford: Blackwell.

Counihan, Carole. 2004. *Around the Tuscan Table: Food, Family, and Gender in Twentieth Century Florence.* New York: Routledge.

Crehan, Kate. 2002. *Gramsci, Culture, and Anthropology.* London: Pluto.

———. 2016. *Gramsci's Common Sense: Inequality and Its Narratives.* Durham, NC: Duke University Press.

Crocitti, Stefania. 2012. "Do Immigration Policies Work? The Case of Italy." In *No Borders: Immigration and the Politics of Fear,* edited by Emma Bell, 81–95. Chambéry, France: Université de Savoie.

Cronin, Vincent. 1967. "Fire and Flood on the Arno." *Saturday Review,* December 30.

Dante Alighieri. 2013. *The Divine Comedy.* Translated by Clive James. New York: Liveright.

De Angelis, Massimo. 2007. *The Beginning of History: Value Struggles and Global Capital.* London: Pluto.

De León, Jason. 2015. *The Land of Open Graves: Living and Dying on the Migrant Trail.* Berkeley: University of California Press.

De Martino, Ernesto, and Clara Gallini. 1977. *La fine del mondo: Contributo all'analisi delle apocalissi culturali.* Turin: Einaudi.

Debs, Mira. 2013. "The Suffering of Symbols: Giotto Frescoes and the Cultural Trauma of Objects." *Cultural Sociology* 7 (4): 479–94.

Dei Ottati, Gabi, and Daniele Brigadoi Cotogna. 2015. "The Chinese in Prato and the Current Outlook on the Chinese-Italian Experience." In *Chinese Migration to Europe: Prato, Italy, and Beyond,* edited by Loretta Baldassar, Graeme Johanson, Narelle McAuliffe, and Massimo Bressan, 29–48. New York: Palgrave Macmillan.

Della Sala, Vincent. 2004. "The Italian Model of Capitalism: On the Road between Globalization and Europeanization?" *Journal of European Public Policy* 11 (6): 1041–57.

Denison, Tom, Dharmalingam Arunachalam, Graeme Johanson, and Russell Smyth. 2007. *The Chinese Community in Prato.* Prato, Italy: Centre for Community Networking Research. http://arrow.monash.edu.au/hdl/1959.1/274733.

Dettwyler, Katherine A. 1995. "A Time to Wean: The Hominid Blueprint for the Natural Age of Weaning in Modern Human Populations." In *Breastfeeding: Biocultural Perspectives*, edited by Patricia Stuart-Macadam and Katherine A. Dettwyler, 39–73. New York: Aldine De Gruyter.

Di Castro, Andrea, and M. Vicziany. 2010. "Dragoni cinesi a Prato: rapporti tra la comunità italiana e quella cinese in una piccola città europea." In *Oltre ogni muro. I cinesi di Prato*, edited by Graeme Johanson, Russell Smyth, and Rebecca French, 185–99. Pisa: Pacini Editore.

Du Bois, W. E. B. 1997. *The Souls of Black Folk.* Edited by David W. Blight and Robert Gooding-Williams. Boston: Bedford Books.

Dunford, Michael, Robin Dunford, Mirela Barbu, and Weidong Liu. 2016. "Globalisation, Cost Competitiveness, and International Trade: The Evolution of the Italian Textile and Clothing Industries and the Growth of Trade with China." *European Urban and Regional Studies* 23 (2): 111–35.

Dunn, Elizabeth C. 2004. *Privatizing Poland: Baby Food, Big Business, and the Remaking of Labor.* Ithaca, NY: Cornell University Press.

Economist. 2005. "Structurally Unsound. Addio, Dolce Vita: A Survey of Italy." *Economist*, November 26.

Entwistle, Joanne. 2000. *The Fashioned Body: Fashion, Dress, and Modern Social Theory.* Malden, MA: Blackwell.

Escobar, Arturo. 1991. "Anthropology and the Development Encounter: The Making and Marketing of Development Anthropology." *American Ethnologist* 18 (4): 658–82.

———. 2010. "Latin America at a Crossroads." *Cultural Studies* 24 (1): 1–65.

Fabian, Johannes. 1983. *Time and the Other: How Anthropology Makes Its Object.* New York: Columbia University Press.

Fagioli, Marco, and Quinto Martini. 1997. *Parco-Museo Quinto Martini a Seano: Catalogo Sculture = the Quinto Martini Museum-Park in Seano: Sculpture Catalog.* Carmignano, Italy: Comune di Carmignano.

Fanon, Frantz. 1967. *Black Skin, White Masks.* New York: Grove.

Farnetti, Tobia, and Charles Stewart. 2012. "Translator's Preface: An Introduction to 'Crisis of Presence and Religious Reintegration' by Ernesto de Martino." *HAU: Journal of Ethnographic Theory* 2 (2): 431–33.

Fassin, Didier. 2011. "Policing Borders, Producing Boundaries. The Governmentality of Immigration in Dark Times." *Annual Review of Anthropology* 40 (1): 213–26.

Federighi F. 2007. "Il Capodanno cinese si farà. Niente sfilate, festa al Pecci." *La Nazione* (Prato), Februrary 2.

Feldman-Savelsberg, Pamela. 2016. *Mothers on the Move: Reproducing Belonging between Africa and Europe.* Chicago: University of Chicago Press.

Ferguson, James. 2009. "The Uses of Neoliberalism." *Antipode* 41 (S1): 166–84.

Ferry, Elizabeth Emma. 2013. *Minerals, Collecting, and Value across the U.S.-Mexico Border.* Bloomington: Indiana University Press.

Ferzacca, Steve. 2000. "'Actually, I Don't Feel That Bad': Managing Diabetes and the Clinical Encounter." *Medical Anthropology Quarterly* 14 (1): 28–50.

Folbre, Nancy. 2010. *Valuing Children: Rethinking the Economics of the Family.* Cambridge, MA: Harvard University Press.

Fong, Vanessa L. 2011. *Paradise Redefined: Transnational Chinese Students and the Quest for Flexible Citizenship in the Developed World.* Stanford, CA: Stanford University Press.

Fordham, Signithia. 2011. "Write-Ous Indignation: Black Girls, Dilemmas of Cultural Domination and the Struggle to Speak the Skin We Are In." In *Anthropology off the Shelf: Anthropologists on Writing*, edited by Maria D. Vesperi and Alisse Waterston, 79–92. Oxford: Wiley-Blackwell.

Forgacs, David, ed. 2000. *The Gramsci Reader: Selected Writings, 1916–1935.* New York: New York University Press.

Foucault, Michel. 1980. *Power/Knowledge: Selected Interviews and Other Writings 1972–77.* Edited by Colin Gordon. New York: Harvester Wheatsheaf.

Gaggio, Dario. 2007. *In Gold We Trust: Social Capital and Economic Change in the Italian Jewelry Towns.* Princeton, NJ: Princeton University Press.

———. 2011. "Selling Beauty: Tuscany's Rural Landscape since 1945." In *The Cultural Wealth of Nations*, edited by Nina Bandelj and Frederick F. Wherry, 90–113. Stanford, CA: Stanford University Press.

Geertz, Clifford. 1988. *Works and Lives: The Anthropologist as Author.* Stanford, CA: Stanford University Press.

Giannini, Sabrina. 2014. "Va di Lusso." RAI. http://www.report.rai.it/dl/Report/puntata/ContentItem-86a1bd15–9fae-4c9c-a32e-03ec1e6dd735.html.

Gibson-Graham, J. K. 2006. *A Postcapitalist Politics.* Minneapolis: University of Minnesota Press.

Ginsburg, Faye D., and Rayna Rapp. 1995. *Conceiving the New World Order: The Global Politics of Reproduction.* Berkeley: University of California press.

Giordano, Cristiana. 2011. "Translating Fanon in the Italian Context: Rethinking the Ethics of Treatment in Psychiatry." *Transcultural Psychiatry* 48 (3): 228–56.

———. 2014. *Migrants in Translation: Caring and the Logics of Difference in Contemporary Italy.* Berkeley: University of California Press.

Glick Schiller, Nina. 2012. "Migration and Development without Methodological Nationalism: Towards Global Perspectives on Migration." In *Migration in the 21st Century: Political Economy and Ethnography*, edited by Pauline Gardiner Barber and Winnie Lem, 38–63. New York: Routledge.

Godelier, Maurice. 1999. *The Enigma of the Gift.* Chicago: University of Chicago Press.

Goldberg, David Theo, and John Solomos, eds. 2002. *A Companion to Racial and Ethnic Studies.* Malden, MA: Blackwell.

Good, Byron. 1994. *Medicine, Rationality, and Experience: An Anthropological Perspective.* Cambridge: Cambridge University Press.

Graeber, David. 2001. *Toward an Anthropological Theory of Value: The False Coin of Our Own Dreams.* New York: Palgrave.

Gramsci, Antonio. 1971. *Selections from the Prison Notebooks of Antonio Gramsci.* Edited by Quintin Hoare and Geoffrey Nowell-Smith. New York: International Publishers.

Greenhalgh, Susan. 1994. "De-Orientalizing the Chinese Family Firm." *American Ethnologist* 21 (4): 746–75.

———. 2003. "Planned Births, Unplanned Persons: 'Population' in the Making of Chinese Modernity." *American Ethnologist* 30 (2): 196–215.

———. 2008. *Just One Child: Science and Policy in Deng's China.* Berkeley: University of California Press.

Gubrium, Aline C., Elizabeth L. Krause, and Kasey Jernigan. 2014. "Strategic Authenticity and Voice: New Ways of Seeing and Being Seen as Young Mothers through Digital Storytelling." *Sexuality Research and Social Policy* 11 (4): 337–47.

Gubrium, Aline, and Krista Harper. 2013. *Participatory Visual and Digital Methods.* Walnut Creek, CA: Left Coast Press.

Hall, Stuart. 1996. "Gramsci's Relevance for the Study of Race and Ethnicity." In *Stuart Hall: Critical Dialogues in Cultural Studies*, edited by David Morley and Kuan-Hsing Chen, 411–40. London: Routledge.

Haraway, Donna. 1988. "Situated Knowledges: The Science Question in Feminism and the Privilege of Partial Perspective." *Feminist Studies* 14 (3): 575–99.

Hartog, François. 1988. *The Mirror of Herodotus: The Representation of the Other in the Writing of History*. Berkeley: University of California Press.

Harvey, David. 1989. *The Condition of Postmodernity*. Oxford: Basil Blackwell.

———. 2005. *A Brief History of Neoliberalism*. Oxford: Oxford University Press.

Hemment, Julie. 2015. *Youth Politics in Putin's Russia: Producing Patriots and Entrepreneurs*. Bloomington: Indiana University Press.

Herzfeld, Michael. 2004. *The Body Impolitic: Artisans and Artifice in the Global Hierarchy of Value*. Chicago: University of Chicago Press.

Hill, Jane H. 2008. *The Everyday Language of White Racism*. Malden, MA: Wiley-Blackwell.

Ho, Karen Zouwen. 2009. *Liquidated: An Ethnography of Wall Street*. Durham, NC: Duke University Press.

Hobsbawm, E. J., and T. O Ranger. 1983. *The Invention of Tradition*. Cambridge: Cambridge University Press.

Hochschild, Arlie Russell. 2000. "Global Care Chains and Emotional Surplus Value." In *On the Edge: Living with Global Capitalism*, edited by Anthony Giddens and Will Hutton, 130–46. London: Jonathan Cape.

Hofstadter, Dan. 2013. "Dan Hofstadter on Portraits of Italian Fascism." *Wall Street Journal*, July 27, sec. Books.

Holmes, Douglas R. 1989. *Cultural Disenchantments: Worker Peasantries in Northeast Italy*. Princeton, NJ: Princeton University Press.

———. 2011. *Integral Europe: Fast-Capitalism, Multiculturalism, Neofascism*. Princeton, NJ: Princeton University Press.

Holmes, Seth M. 2013. *Fresh Fruit, Broken Bodies: Migrant Farmworkers in the United States*. Berkeley: University of California Press.

Holmes, Seth M., and Heide Castañeda. 2016. "Representing the European Refugee Crisis: Deservingness and Difference, Life and Death." *American Ethnologist* 43 (1): 1–13.

Hsu, Carolyn L. 2005. "Capitalism without Contracts versus Capitalists without Capitalism: Comparing the Influence of Chinese Guanxi and Russian Blat on Marketization." *Communist and Post-Communist Studies* 38: 309–27.

Il Tirreno. 2014. "Bernardo Secchi: Chinatown è uno dei luoghi più affascinanti di Prato." *Il Tirreno*, February 21.

Ioannidis, John P. A. 2005. *Why Most Published Research Findings Are False*. Public Library of Science. http://www.ncbi.nlm.nih.gov/pmc/articles/PMC1182327.

IRIS (Strumenti e Risorse per lo Sviluppo Locale). 2015. "Percorso per la definizione di interventi prioritari e relative prospettive di finanziabilità in tema di politiche di integrazione." Prato, Italy. http://www2.comune.prato.it/partecipazione-integrazione/analisi/pagina487.htm.

Istat (Istituto Nazionale di Statistica). 2011. "La popolazione straniera residente in Italia: Statistiche report." http://www.istat.it/it/archivio/39726.

———. n.d. "Demografia in cifre—Bilancio demografico 2011 post censimento." http://www.demo.istat.it.

Ito, Karen L. 1999. "Health Culture and the Clinical Encounter: Vietnamese Refugees' Responses to Preventive Drug Treatment of Inactive Tuberculosis." *Medical Anthropology Quarterly* 13 (3): 338–64.

Jeong, J. H. 2014. "Transplanted Wenzhou Model and Transnational Ethnic Economy: Experiences of Zhejiangcun's Wenzhou Migrants and Wangjing's Chaoxianzu (Ethnic Korean Chinese) Migrants in Beijing." *Journal of Contemporary China* 23 (86): 330–50.

Johanson, Graeme, Russell Smyth, and Rebecca French. 2009. *Living outside the Walls: The Chinese in Prato.* Newcastle upon Tyne, UK: Cambridge Scholars Publishing.

Johnson, George. 2014. "New Truths That Only One Can See." *New York Times*, January 20, sec. Science.

Johnson, Kay. 2014. "China's One Child Policy: Not Yet in the Dustbin of History." *DifferenTakes* 83: 1–4.

Johnson-Hanks, Jennifer. 2006. "On the Politics and Practice of Muslim Fertility: Comparative Evidence from West Africa." *Medical Anthropology Quarterly* 20 (1): 12–30.

Jones, Kelly. 2007. *The Lost Madonna.* New York: Berkley Books.

Judge, Joseph. 1967. "Florence Rises from the Flood." *National Geographic* 132 (1): 1–42.

Kertzer, David I. 1993. *Sacrificed for Honor: Italian Infant Abandonment and the Politics of Reproductive Control.* Boston: Beacon.

Kezich, Giovanni. 2013. *Some Peasant Poets: An Odyssey in the Oral Poetry of Latium.* Bern: Peter Lang.

Khandelwal, Meena. 1996. "Walking a Tightrope: Saintliness, Gender, and Power in an Ethnographic Encounter." *Anthropology and Humanism* 21: 111–134.

Knight, Daniel M. 2015. *History, Time, and Economic Crisis in Central Greece.* New York: Palgrave Macmillan.

Knight, Daniel M., and Charles Stewart. 2016. "Ethnographies of Austerity: Temporality, Crisis, and Affect in Southern Europe." *History and Anthropology* 27 (1): 1–18.

Kofman, Eleonore. 2012. "Rethinking Care through Social Reproduction: Articulating Circuits of Migration." *Social Politics* 19 (1): 142–62.

Kramer, Jane. 2015. "The Demolition Man: Can Matteo Renzi Fix Italy?" *New Yorker*, June 25, 36–42.

Krause, Elizabeth L. 2005a. *A Crisis of Births: Population Politics and Family-Making in Italy.* Belmont, CA: Thomson/Wadsworth.

———. 2005b. "Encounters with the 'Peasant': Memory Work, Masculinity, and Low Fertility in Italy." *American Ethnologist* 32 (4): 593–617.

———. 2005c. "'Toys and Perfumes': Imploding Italy's Population Paradox and Motherly Myths." In *Barren States: The Population "Implosion" in Europe,* edited by Carrie B. Douglass, 159–82. Oxford: Berg.

———. 2009. *Unraveled: A Weaver's Tale of Life Gone Modern.* Berkeley: University of California Press.

———. 2012a. "Doing Fieldwork and Writing Anthropology." *Transforming Anthropology* 20 (2): 189–92.

———. 2012b. "'They Just Happened': The Curious Case of the Unplanned Baby, Italian Low Fertility, and the 'End' of Rationality." *Medical Anthropology Quarterly* 26 (3): 361–82.

Krause, Elizabeth L., and Massimo Bressan. 2014. "Slow Rites, Fast Wrongs." *Truthout.* http://truth-out.org/opinion.

Krause, Elizabeth L., and Silvia De Zordo. 2012. "Introduction. Ethnography and Biopolitics:

Tracing 'Rationalities' of Reproduction across the North-South Divide." *Anthropology &*
*Medicine* 19 (2): 137–51.

Krause, Elizabeth L., and Milena Marchesi. 2007. "Fertility Politics as 'Social Viagra': Reproducing Boundaries, Social Cohesion, and Modernity in Italy." *American Anthropologist* 109 (2): 350–62.

Kulchina, Elena. 2016. "A Path to Value Creation for Foreign Entrepreneurs." *Strategic Management Journal* 37 (7): 1240–62.

La Nazione. 2008. "Straniero un neonato su due e il record è ovviamente cinese." July 12, 11.

Lahiri, Jhumpa. 2015. "Teach Yourself Italian: A Writer Embraces Another Language." *New Yorker*, December 7, 30–36.

———. 2016. *In Other Words.* Translated by Ann Goldstein. New York: Knopf.

Lan, Tu. 2015. "Industrial District and the Multiplication of Labour: The Chinese Apparel Industry in Prato, Italy." *Antipode* 47 (1): 158–78.

Lawrence, D. H. 1957. *Etruscan Places.* New York: Viking Press.

Lazzeretti, Luciana. 2003. "City of Art as a High Culture Local System and Cultural Districtualization Processes: The Cluster of Art Restoration in Florence." *International Journal of Urban and Regional Research* 27 (3): 635–48.

Lees-Maffei, Grace, and Kjetil Fallan. 2014. *Made in Italy: Rethinking a Century of Italian Design.* London: Bloomsbury.

Leinaweaver, Jessaca B. 2008. *The Circulation of Children: Kinship, Adoption, and Morality in Andean Peru.* Durham, NC: Duke University Press.

———. 2013. *Adoptive Migration: Raising Latinos in Spain.* Durham, NC: Duke University Press.

Leinaweaver, Jessaca B., and Claudia Fonseca. 2007. "The State and Children's Fate: Reproduction in Traumatic Times." *Childhood: A Global Journal of Child Research* 14 (3): 291–99.

Lem, Winnie. 2010. "Mobilization and Disengagement: Chinese Migrant Entrepreneurs in Urban France." *Ethnic and Racial Studies* 33 (1): 92–107.

Levi, Carlo. 2000. *Christ Stopped at Eboli.* London: Penguin.

Li, Minghuan. 1999a. "'To Get Rich Quickly in Europe!': Reflections on Migration Motivation in Wenzhou." In *Internal and International Migration: Chinese Perspectives*, edited by Frank N. Pieke and Hein Mallee, 181–98. Richmond, UK: Curzon.

———. 1999b. *We Need Two Worlds: Chinese Immigrant Associations in a Western Society.* Amsterdam: Amsterdam University Press.

Liu, Alan P. L. 1992. "The 'Wenzhou Model' of Development and China's Modernization." *Asian Survey* 32 (8): 696–711.

Livi-Bacci, Massimo. 2001. "Too Few Children, Too Much Family." *Daedalus: Proceedings of the American Academy of Arts and Sciences* 130 (3): 139–55.

Lo, Ming-Cheng M., and Eileen M. Otis. 2003. "Guanxi Civility: Processes, Potentials, and Contingencies." *Politics and Society* 31: 131–62.

London, C. R. 2013. "Italy's Productivity Puzzle." *Economist*, October 13. http://www.economist.com/blogs/freeexchange/2013/10/competitiveness.

Ma Mung, Emmanuel. 2004. "Dispersal as a Resource." *Diaspora: A Journal of Transnational Studies* 13 (2): 211–25.

Mahmud, Lilith. 2014. *The Brotherhood of Freemason Sisters: Gender, Secrecy, and Fraternity in Italian Masonic Lodges.* Chicago: University of Chicago Press.

Malaparte, Curzio. 1964. *Those Cursed Tuscans.* Athens: Ohio University Press.

———. 1998. "The Little Hand." Translated by Walter S. Murch. *Grand Street* 64: 224–26.

Malinowski, Bronislaw. 1921. "The Primitive Economics of the Trobriand Islanders." *The Economic Journal* 31 (121): 1–16.

———. 1922. *Argonauts of the Western Pacific: An Account of Native Enterprise and Adventure in the Archipelagoes of Melanesian New Guinea.* London: Routledge.

Malkki, Liisa H. 1995. "Refugees and Exile: From 'Refugee Studies' to the National Order of Things." *Annual Review of Anthropology* 24: 495–523.

Marchesi, Milena. 2013. "Contested Subjects: Biopolitics & the Moral Stakes of Social Cohesion in Post-Welfare Italy." PhD diss, University of Massachusetts, Amherst.

Marcus, George E. 1995. "Ethnography in/of the World System: The Emergence of Multi-Sited Ethnography." *Annual Review of Anthropology* 24: 95–117.

———. 2005. "Family Firms Amidst the Creative Destruction of Capitalism." *American Ethnologist* 32 (4): 618–22.

Martin, Emily. 1987. *The Woman in the Body: A Cultural Analysis of Reproduction.* Boston: Beacon.

Martini, Chiara. 2011. "I bassorilievi della pioggia di Quinto Martini." Florence: Università degli Studi di Firenze Facoltà di Lettere e Filosofia.

Martini, Quinto, Sergej Androsov, and Gosudarstvennÿ Ėrmitazh. 2013. *Quinto Martini: Museo Statale Ermitage, San Pietroburgo, 24 maggio–30 giugno, 2013 = Gospodarstvenij Muzei Ermitaz, Sankt-Peterburg, 24 Maj–30 Juni, 2013.* Florence: Mandragora.

Marx, Karl. 1993. "The Values of Commodities, and the Fetishism of Commodities." In *Social Theory: The Multicultural and Classic Readings*, edited by Charles C. Lemert, 58–67. Boulder, CO: Westview.

Mattingly, Cheryl. 2008. "Reading Minds and Telling Tales in a Cultural Borderland." *Ethos* 36 (1): 136–54.

Maurer, Bill. 2006. "The Anthropology of Money." *Annual Review of Anthropology* 35: 15–36.

———. 2016. "Foreword: Puzzles and Pathways." In *The Gift: Expanded Edition. Marcel Mauss*, edited by Jane I. Guyer, ix–xvii. Chicago: Hau Books.

Maurus, Véronique. 1980. "Hongkong à l'italienne." *Le Monde*, September 1.

Mauss, Marcel. 1979. *Sociology and Psychology: Essays.* Translated by Ben Brewster. London: Routledge & Kegan Paul.

———. 1990. *The Gift: The Form and Reason for Exchange in Archaic Societies.* Translated by W. D. Halls. New York: Norton.

Merlo, Elisabetta, and Francesca Polese. 2006. "Turning Fashion into Business: The Emergence of Milan as an International Fashion Hub." *Business History Review* 80 (3): 415–47.

Metcalf, Peter. 2002. *They Lie, We Lie: Getting on with Anthropology.* New York: Routledge.

Mezzadra, Sandro, and Brett Neilson. 2013. *Border as Method, or, the Multiplication of Labor.* Durham, NC: Duke University Press.

Millard, Ann V. 1990. "The Place of the Clock in Pediatric Advice: Rationales, Cultural Themes, and Impediments to Breastfeeding." *Social Science & Medicine* 31 (2): 211–21.

Ministry of Interior. 2007. *Charter of Values of Citizenship and Integration. Scientific Council. Official Translation.* Rome: Ministry of Interior. http://www.interno.gov.it/mininterno/export/sites/default/it/assets/files/14/0919_charter_of_values_of_citizenship_and_integration.pdf.

Molé, Noelle J. 2012. *Labor Disorders in Neoliberal Italy: Mobbing, Well-Being, and the Workplace.* Bloomington: Indiana University Press.

Muehlebach, Andrea Karin. 2012. *The Moral Neoliberal: Welfare and Citizenship in Italy.* Chicago: University of Chicago Press.

Nadar, Laura. 2011. "Ethnography as Theory." *HAU: Journal of Ethnographic Theory* 1 (1): 211–19.

Narotzky, Susana. 2016. "Between Inequality and Injustice: Dignity as a Motive for Mobilization during the Crisis." *History and Anthropology* 27 (1): 74–92.

Nelis, Jan. 2007. "Constructing Fascist Identity: Benito Mussolini and the Myth of Romanità." *Classical World* 100 (4): 391–415.

Nencioni, Paolo. 2014. "La strage del Macrolotto: L'ombra dei risarcimenti sui funerali." *Il Tirreno,* June 20.

Nesi, Edoardo. 2012. *Story of My People.* Translated by Antony Shugaar. New York: Other Press.

Ni Laoire, Caitriona, Allen White, Naomi Tyrrell, and Fina Carpena-Méndez. 2012. "Children and Young People on the Move: Geographies of Child and Youth Migration." *Geography* 97 (3): 129–34.

Nonini, Donald M., and Aihwa Ong. 1997. "Introduction: Chinese Transnationalism as an Alternative Modernity." In *Ungrounded Empires: The Cultural Politics of Modern Chinese Transnationalism,* 3–33. New York: Routledge.

Office of Statistics, Commune of Prato, ed. 2013. "Prato conta: Stranieri per cittadinanza dal 2008 al 2012 (dati al 31/12), Tabella 3.2." http://statistica.comune.prato.it/annuario/?act=f&fid=5992.

O'Neil, John D. 1989. "The Cultural and Political Context of Patient Dissatisfaction in Cross-Cultural Clinical Encounters: A Canadian Inuit Study." *Medical Anthropology Quarterly* 3 (4): 325–44.

Ong, Aihwa. 1999. *Flexible Citizenship: The Cultural Logics of Transnationality.* Durham, NC: Duke University Press.

———. 2006. *Neoliberalism as Exception: Mutations in Citizenship and Sovereignty.* Durham, NC: Duke University Press.

Origo, Iris. 1984. *The Merchant of Prato.* London: Folio Society.

Osnos, Evan. 2014. "Confucius Comes Home." *New Yorker,* January 13, 30–35.

Padgett, John Frederick, and Walter W. Powell. 2012. *The Emergence of Organizations and Markets.* Princeton, NJ: Princeton University Press.

Palevsky, Mary. 2000. *Atomic Fragments: A Daughter's Questions.* Berkeley: University of California Press.

Paris, Ivan. 2010. "Orígenes del Made in Italy. Moda italiana y mercado internacional en la segunda posguerra (1951–1969)." *Revista de Historia Industrial* 42: 121–55.

Passerini, Luisa. 1987. *Fascism in Popular Memory: The Cultural Experience of the Turin Working Class.* Cambridge: Cambridge University Press.

Paulicelli, Eugenia. 2001. "Reconstructing Italian Fashion: America and the Development of the Italian Fashion Industry, by Nicola White." *Fashion Theory* 5: 453–56.

———. 2004. *Fashion under Fascism: Beyond the Black Shirt.* New York: Berg.

Pedone, Valentina. 2013. "Chuguo, uscire dal Paese: Breve quadro dei flussi migratori dalla Cina verso l'estero." In *Vendere e comprare: Processi di mobilità sociale dei cinesi a Prato,* edited by Fabio Berti, Valentina Pedone, and Andrea Valzania, 59–84. Pisa: Pacini.

Pescarolo, Alessandra. 1988. "Modelli di industrializzazione, ruoli sociali, immagini del lavoro." In *Prato: Storia di una città, Il tempo dell'industria (1815–1943),* edited by Giorgio Mori, 51–114. Comune di Prato: Le Monnier.

Petro, Greg. 2015. "The Future of Fashion Retailing, Revisited: Part 2—Zara." *Forbes,* July 23.

http://www.forbes.com/sites/gregpetro/2015/07/23/the-future-of-fashion-retailing
-revisited-part-2-zara/#1484e97d13cc.

Pieke, Frank N., Pál Nyíri, Mette Thunø, and Antonella Ceccagno. 2004. *Transnational Chinese: Fujianese Migrants in Europe.* Stanford, CA: Stanford University Press.

Pieraccini, Silvia. 2010. *L'assedio cinese: Il distretto senza regole degli abiti low cost di Prato.* Milan: Gruppo 24 Ore.

Piketty, Thomas, and Arthur Goldhammer. 2014. *Capital in the Twenty-First Century.* Cambridge, MA: Belknap Press of Harvard University Press.

Piore, Michael J., and Charles F. Sabel. 1984. *The Second Industrial Divide: Possibilities for Prosperity.* New York: Basic Books.

Plattner, Stuart. 1996. *High Art down Home: An Economic Ethnography of a Local Art Market.* Chicago: University of Chicago Press.

Poggioli, Silvia. 2011. "'Fast Fashion': Italians Wary of Chinese on Their Turf." June 15. http://www.npr.org/2011/06/15/137107361/fast-fashion-italians-wary-of-chinese-on-their-turf.

Pomeranz, Kenneth. 2000. *The Great Divergence: China, Europe, and the Making of the Modern World Economy.* Princeton, NJ: Princeton University Press.

Povoledo, Elisabetta. 2013. "Deadly Factory Fire Bares Racial Tensions in Italy." *New York Times,* December 6. http://www.nytimes.com/2013/12/08/world/europe/deadly-factory-fire
-bares-racial-tensions-in-italy.html?pagewanted=all&_r=0.

Raffaetà, Roberta, and Loretta Baldassar. 2015. "Spaces Speak Louder Than Words: Contesting Social Inclusion through Conflicting Rhetoric about Prato's Chinatown." In *Chinese Migration to Europe: Prato, Italy and Beyond,* edited by Loretta Baldassar, Graeme Johanson, Narelle McAuliffe, and Massimo Bressan, 119–37. New York: Palgrave Macmillan.

Raikhel, Eugene. 2009. "Institutional Encounters: Identification and Anonymity in Russia's Addiction Treatment (and Ethnography)." In *Being There: The Fieldwork Encounter and the Making of Truth,* edited by John Borneman and Abdellah Hammoudi, 201–36. Berkeley: University of California Press.

Rapp, Rayna. 1999. *Testing Women, Testing the Fetus: The Social Impact of Amniocentesis in America.* New York: Routledge.

Razsa, Maple. 2015. *Bastards of Utopia: Living Radical Politics after Socialism.* Bloomington: Indiana University Press.

Reddy, John. 1967. "Up from the Mud: A Second Renaissance for Florence." *Reader's Digest,* October.

Reinach, Simona Segre. 2005. "China and Italy: Fast Fashion versus Prêt à Porter. Towards a New Culture of Fashion." *Fashion Theory: The Journal of Dress, Body & Culture* 9 (1): 43–56.

Reitter, Paul. 2002. "'Racism: Coded as Culture?'" *Nation,* October 28. http://www.thenation
.com/doc/2002 s1028/reitter.

Richards, Chris. 2005. "Translations: Encounters with Popular Film and Academic Discourse." *European Journal of Cultural Studies* 8 (1): 23–43.

Rofel, Lisa. 2007. *Desiring China: Experiments in Neoliberalism, Sexuality, and Public Culture.* Durham, NC: Duke University Press.

Ryan, Gery W., and H. Russell Bernard. 2003. "Techniques to Identify Themes." *Field Methods* 15 (1): 85–109.

Ryoo, Hye-Kyung. 2005. "Achieving Friendly Interactions: A Study of Service Encounters between Korean Shopkeepers and African-American Customers." *Discourse & Society* 16 (1): 79–105.

Saada, Emmanuelle. 2000. "Abdelmalek Sayad and the Double Absence: Toward a Total Sociology of Immigration." *French Politics, Culture, and Society* 18: 28–49.

Safri, Maliha, and Julie Graham. 2010. "The Global Household: Toward a Feminist Postcapitalist International Political Economy." *Signs* 36 (1): 99–126.

Sahlins, Marshall. 1972. *Stone Age Economies.* Chicago: Adine-Atherton.

———. 2000. "Cosmologies of Capitalism: The Trans-Pacific Sector of 'the World System.'" In *Culture in Practice: Selected Essays,* 415–69. New York: Zone Books.

———. 2013. *What Kinship Is—and Is Not.* Chicago: University of Chicago Press.

Sambo, Paolo. 2013a. "Gli immigrati cinesi a Prato: Fotografia di una realtà in movimento." In *Vendere e comprare: processi di mobilità sociale dei cinesi a Prato,* edited by Fabio Berti, Valentina Pedone, and Andrea Valzania, 105–34. Pisa: Pacini.

———. 2013b. "La presenza straniera nella Provincia di Prato." In *L'immigrazione nella Provincia di Prato: VIII rapporto,* 7–40. Prato, Italy: Provincia di Prato.

Saraceno, Chiara. 2017. *L'equivoco della famiglia.* Bari: GLF Editori Laterza.

Sargent, Carolyn F. 2006. "Reproductive Strategies and Islamic Discourse: Malian Migrants Negotiate Everyday Life in Paris, France." *Medical Anthropology Quarterly* 20 (1): 31–49.

Saunders, George R. 1993. "'Critical Ethnocentrism' and the Ethnology of Ernesto De Martino." *American Anthropologist* 95 (4): 875–93.

Scheper-Hughes, Nancy. 1992. *Death without Weeping: The Violence of Everyday Life in Brazil.* Berkeley: University of California Press.

Schneider, Jane. 1998. *Italy's "Southern Question": Orientalism in One Country.* Oxford: Berg.

———. 2009. "From Potlatch to Wal-Mart: Courtly and Capitalist Hierarchies through Dress." In *The Fabric of Cultures: Fashion, Identity, and Globalization,* edited by Eugenia Paulicelli and Hazel Clark, 13–27. London: Routledge.

Schneider, Jane, and Peter T. Schneider. 1996. *Festival of the Poor: Fertility Decline & the Ideology of Class in Sicily, 1860–1980.* Tucson: University of Arizona Press.

Secchi, Bernardo. 1996a. *Laboratorio Prato PRG.* Florence: Alinea.

———, ed. 1996b. *Un progetto per Prato: Il nuovo piano regolatore.* Florence: Alinea.

Segre, Simona. 1999. *Mode in Italy: Una lettura antropologica.* Milan: Guerini scientifica.

Senders, Stefan. 2009. "Encounters with the Mother Tongue: Speech, Translation, and Interlocution in Post–Cold War German Repatriation." In *Being There: The Fieldwork Encounter and the Making of Truth,* edited by John Borneman and Abdellah Hammoudi, 183–200. Berkeley: University of California Press.

Settembrini, Luigi. 1994. "From Haute Couture to Prêt-à-Porter." In *The Italian Metamorphosis, 1943–1968,* edited by Germano Celant, 484–94. New York: Guggenheim Museum Publications.

Sharma, Anurag. 2016. *Book of Value: The Fine Art of Investing Wisely.* New York: Columbia University Press.

Sheckley, Robert. 1966. *Mindswap.* New York: Orb.

Signorelli, Amalia. 1996. *Antropologia urbana: Introduzione alla ricerca in Italia.* Milan: Guerini studio.

Silverman, Sydel. 1968. "Agricultural Organization, Social Structure, and Values in Italy: Amoral Familism Reconsidered." *American Anthropologist* 70 (1): 1–20.

Simmel, Georg. 1978. *The Philosophy of Money.* London: Routledge & Kegan Paul.

Small, Meredith F. 1998. *Our Babies, Ourselves: How Biology and Culture Shape the Way We Parent.* New York: Anchor.

Snodgrass, R. E. 1961. *The Caterpillar and the Butterfly.* Washington, DC: Smithsonian Institution.

Steele, Valerie. 1994. "Italian Fashion and America." In *The Italian Metamorphosis, 1943–1968*, edited by Germano Celant, 494–505. New York: Guggenheim Museum Publications.

Stevenson, Lisa. 2009. "The Suicidal Wound and Fieldwork among Canadian Inuit." In *Being There: The Fieldwork Encounter and the Making of Truth*, edited by John Borneman and Abdellah Hammoudi, 55–76. Berkeley: University of California Press.

Strathern, Marilyn. 1988. *The Gender of the Gift: Problems with Women and Problems with Society in Melanesia*. Berkeley: University of California Press.

Suárez-Orozco, Carola, and Irina L. G Todorova. 2002. "Making Up for Lost Time: The Experience of Separation and Reunification among Immigrant Families." *Family Process* 41 (4): 625–43.

Sykes, Karen Margaret. 2005. *Arguing with Anthropology: An Introduction to Critical Theories of the Gift*. London: Routledge.

Talen, Emily. 2008. *Design for Diversity: Exploring Socially Mixed Neighborhoods*. Oxford: Architectural Press.

Tan, Kok C. 1991. "Small Towns and Regional Development in Wenzhou." In *The Uneven Landscape: Geographic Studies in Post-Reform China*, edited by Gregory Veeck, 207–234. Baton Rouge: Geoscience Publications, Department of Geography and Anthropology, Louisiana State University.

Taplin, Ian M. 1989. "Segmentation and the Organisation of Work in the Italian Apparel Industry." *Social Science Quarterly* 70 (2): 408–24.

———. 2014. "Global Commodity Chains and Fast Fashion: How the Apparel Industry Continues to Re-Invent Itself." *Competition & Change* 18 (3): 246–64.

Taylor, Kathrine Kressmann. 1967. *Diary of Florence in Flood*. New York: Simon & Schuster.

Thomas, Dana. 2007. *Deluxe: How Luxury Lost Its Luster*. New York: Penguin.

Thompson, E. P. 1967. "Time, Work-Discipline, and Industrial Capitalism." *Past and Present* 38: 56–97.

Ticktin, Miriam. 2011. *Casualties of Care: Immigration and the Politics of Humanitarianism in France*. Berkeley: University of California Press.

Timmerman, Kelsey. 2012. *Where Am I Wearing? A Global Tour to the Countries, Factories, and People That Make Our Clothes*. Hoboken, NJ: Wiley.

Tokatli, Nebahat. 2013. "Doing a Gucci: The Transformation of an Italian Fashion Firm into a Global Powerhouse in a 'Los Angel-Izing' World." *Journal of Economic Geography* 13: 239–55.

Tomba, Luigi. 1999. "Exporting the 'Wenzhou Model' to Beijing and Florence: Suggestions for a Comparative Perspective on Labour and Economic Organization in Two Migrant Communities." In *Internal and International Migration: Chinese Perspectives*, edited by Frank N. Pieke and Hein Mallee, 280–94. Richmond, UK: Curzon.

Tsing, Anna. 2005. *Friction: An Ethnography of Global Connection*. Princeton, NJ: Princeton University Press.

———. 2013. "Sorting Out Commodities: How Capitalist Value Is Made through Gifts." *HAU: Journal of Ethnographic Theory* 3 (1): 21–43.

———. 2014. "How Do Supply Chains Make Value?" In *Cash on the Table: Markets, Values, and Moral Economies*, edited by Edward F. Fischer and Jonathan A. Shayne, 39–44. Santa Fe, NM: School for Advanced Research Press.

———. 2015. *The Mushroom at the End of the World: On the Possibility of Life in Capitalist Ruins*. Princeton, NJ: Princeton University Press.

Veblen, Thorstein, and Stuart Chase. 1934. *The Theory of the Leisure Class: An Economic Study of Institutions*. New York: Modern Library.

Velen, Victor, and Elizabeth Velen. 1966. "Florence: After the Flood." *Saturday Review*, December 24.

Vertovec, Steven. 2011. "The Cultural Politics of Nation and Migration." *Annual Review of Anthropology* 40 (1): 241–56.

Waterston, Alisse, and Maria D. Vesperi. 2009. *Anthropology off the Shelf: Anthropologists on Writing*. Malden, MA: Blackwell.

Watson, James L. 1975. *Emigration and the Chinese Lineage: The Mans in Hong Kong and London*. Berkeley: University of California Press.

Wei, Y. H. Dennis. 2011. "Beyond the GPN-New Regionalism Divide in China: Restructuring the Clothing Industry, Remaking the Wenzhou Model." *Geografiska Annaler. Series B, Human Geography* 93: 237–51.

Weiner, Annette B. 1976. *Women of Value, Men of Renown: New Perspectives in Trobriand Exchange*. Austin: University of Texas Press.

Whitaker, Elizabeth Dixon. 2000. *Measuring Mamma's Milk: Fascism and the Medicalization of Maternity in Italy*. Ann Arbor: University of Michigan Press.

White, Nicola. 2000. *Reconstructing Italian Fashion: America and the Development of the Italian Fashion Industry*. Oxford: Berg.

Wilder, Gary. 2015. *Freedom Time: Negritude, Decolonization, and the Future of the World*. Durham, NC: Duke University Press.

Wilkinson, Tracy. 2008. "Slaving in the Lap of Luxury." *Los Angeles Times*, February 20. http://articles.latimes.com/2008/feb/20/world/fg-madeinitaly20.

Williams, Raymond. 1977. *Marxism and Literature*. Oxford: Oxford University Press.

Williams, Brackette F. 1989. "A Class Act: Anthropology and the Race to Nation Across Ethnic Terrain." *Annual Review of Anthropology* 18: 401–44.

Willis, Paul, and Mats Trondman. 2000. "Manifesto for Ethnography." *Ethnography* 1 (1): 5–16.

Wolf, Eric R. 1982. *Europe and the People without History*. Berkeley: University of California Press.

———. 1999. *Envisioning Power: Ideologies of Dominance and Crisis*. Berkeley: University of California Press.

Wong, Cindy Hing-Yuk, and Gary W. McDonogh. 2013. "Negotiating Global Chinatowns: Difference, Diversity, and Connection." *Cambio* 3 (6): 41–54.

Wong, Winnie Won Yin. 2013. *Van Gogh on Demand: China and the Readymade*. Chicago: University of Chicago Press.

Wutich, Amber, and Melissa Beresford. 2015. "Community Development in 'Post-Neoliberal Bolivia': Decolonization or Alternative Modernizations?" *Community Development Journal*. https://doi.org/10.1093/cdj/bsv049.

Yanagisako, Sylvia J. 2002. *Producing Culture and Capital: Family Firms in Italy*. Princeton, NJ: Princeton University Press.

———. 2013. "Transnational Family Capitalism: Producing 'Made in Italy' in China." In *Vital Relations: Modernity and the Persistent Life of Kinship*, edited by Susan McKinnon and Fenella Cannell, 63–84. Santa Fe, NM: School for Advanced Research Press.

Yang, Lihui, and Deming An. 2005. *Handbook of Chinese Mythology*. Santa Barbara, CA: ABC-CLIO.

Yang, Mayfair Mei-hui. 2000. "Putting Global Capitalism in Its Place: Economic Hybridity, Bataille, and Ritual Expenditure." *Current Anthropology* 41 (4): 477–509.

———. 2002. "The Resilience of Guanxi and Its New Deployment: A Critique of Some New Guanxi Scholarship." *The China Quarterly* 170: 459–76.

Zachert, Martha Jane K. 1970. "Sources: Oral History Interviews." *Journal of Library History* 5 (1): 80–87.

Zamagni, Vera. 1995. "American Influence on the Italian Economy (1948–58)." In *Italy in the Cold War: Politics, Culture, and Society, 1948–58,* edited by Christopher Duggan and Christopher Wagstaff, 77–87. Oxford: Berg.

Zelizer, Viviana A. Rotman. 1994. *The Social Meaning of Money.* New York: BasicBooks.

Zhan, Mei. 2009. *Other Worldly: Relocating Traditional Chinese Medicine through Encounters.* Durham, NC: Duke University Press.

Zhang, Li. 2001a. "Migration and Privatization of Space and Power in Late Socialist China." *American Ethnologist* 28 (1): 179–205.

———. 2001b. *Strangers in the City: Reconfigurations of Space, Power, and Social Networks within China's Floating Population.* Stanford, CA: Stanford University Press.

Zhao, Jianhua. 2013. *The Chinese Fashion Industry: An Ethnographic Approach.* London: Bloomsbury Academic.

# Index